Created and Directed by Hans Höfer

INSIGHT GUIDES

CZECH & SLOVAK

REPUBLICS

Edited by Alfred Horn

Managing Editor: Tony Halliday

Editorial Director: Brian Bell

HOUGHTON MIFFLIN COMPANY

APA PUBLICATIONS

CZECH & SLOVAK
R E P U B L I C S

First Edition
© **1993 APA PUBLICATIONS (HK) LTD**
All Rights Reserved
Printed in Singapore by Höfer Press Pte. Ltd

Distributed in the United States by:
Houghton Mifflin Company
2 Park Street
Boston, Massachusetts 02108
ISBN: 0-395-65987-6

Distributed in Canada by:
Thomas Allen & Son
390 Steelcase Road East
Markham, Ontario L3R 1G2
ISBN: 0-395-65987-6

Distributed in the UK & Ireland by:
GeoCenter International UK Ltd
The Viables Center, Harrow Way
Basingstoke, Hampshire RG22 4BJ
ISBN: 9-62421-163-9

Worldwide distribution enquiries:
Höfer Communications Pte Ltd
38 Joo Koon Road
Singapore 2262
ISBN: 9-62421-163-9

ABOUT THIS BOOK

When Communism crumbled in 1989, so too did many of the states on which it had been founded – including, ultimately, the former Czechoslovakia. The forces of separatism that split Czechoslovakia in two were as predictable as they were inevitable. Through most of their history, the Czechs and the Slovaks had not lived together; Czechoslovakia became their common country only after the collapse of the Habsburg empire in 1918. But being "Czechoslovak" never had much appeal for either group and, since 1 January 1993, the Czechs and Slovaks have been citizens of their own independent states: the Czech Republic and Slovakia.

Apa Publications, whose award-winning mixture of hard-hitting text and stunning photojournalism lends itself perfectly to destinations in a state of flux, began planning this book as the tumultuous events of the early 1990s took place and now presents *Insight Guide: The Czech and Slovak Republics*, thus plugging a gap in the series' coverage of Central European destinations.

An Expert Team

As project editor of this book, **Alfred Horn** assembled an expert team of writers and photographers. Horn, who lives in Cologne, first visited Czechoslovakia in 1965 with his school class and has since been back countless times. He has a particularly intimate knowledge of Bohemia, so in addition to his editorial duties was well placed to write the chapters on the "Golden City" of Prague and the famous spa towns of Western Bohemia.

To provide an authoritative account of the region's past and present, he chose predominantly native authors and photographers to work on the book, and hired a leading Prague journalist, **Jan Jelínek**, as adviser to the project. Jelínek, managing editor of the Prague newspaper *mladá fronta dnesn*, liaised between Horn and the local authors and helped to ensure that this book benefited from friendly cross-border cooperation.

Jelínek engaged specialists for the feature essays as well as the cities and regions. **Petr Volf** researched the complex but fascinating history of the area. While the Czech Republic and Slovakia have their own individual histories, many developments were common to both countries. The chapters tell you where their destinies merged, and where and why they split.

Boris Dočekal lives and works in Moravian Jihlava and is well acquainted with life in the small towns and villages. He wrote the revealing article on rural life.

Josef Tuček, a top environmental journalist in the former Czechoslovakia, highlighted in his chapter the especially tense relationship between ecology and economy in two countries in the midst of such dramatic change.

Jan Plachetka supplied the articles on theatre, literature and music, all of which have an illustrious and venerable tradition, particularly in the Czech Republic.

Bronislav Pavlík covers Central Bohemia; his expertise on the area enabled him to give a vivid account of some of the magnificent destinations within easy reach of Prague.

Jan Čech, who lives in Plzeň, highlights in his article on Western Bohemia some of the common historical ties between his homeland and Germany.

Hana Vojtová, from Ústi nad Labem in Northern Bohemia, describes her fascinating

Horn

Jelinek

Volf

Plachetka

homeland, not omitting to point out some of its serious environmental problems.

Irena Jirků outlines a tour of Eastern Bohemia, where she lives and works in Hradec Králové, a town steeped in history.

Joroslav Haid, a wine connoisseur from Brno, describes his personal experiences from the wine cellars of the delightful little towns of Southern Moravia.

Petr Žižka, from the industrial town of Ostrava in Northern Moravia, brings alive the multicultural traditions in this region bordering Silesia in Poland.

Ondrej Neff, one of Bohemia's best-known science-fiction writers, is also a specialist in Czech and Slovakian internal affairs. For this book, he provided material for the article "Czechs and Slovaks", describing the sometimes uneasy relationship between the two peoples.

Rudolf Procházka is press secretary of the prime minister of Slovakia. A trained journalist, he lives in the capital Bratislava, but knows his homeland not only from the perspective of a political commentator but also as a person who really appreciates the outstanding natural beauty of the region.

A number of German authors were also assigned to assist with the project. **Kerstin Rose**, a travel writer from Frankfurt, relates her experiences on an evening stroll around Prague and in addition provides a host of useful information for the concluding Travel Tips section.

As a student in Prague, the theologian **Werner Jakobsmeier** from Munich witnessed the dramatic events of 1968–69 at first hand. He contributed his expertise to the articles dealing with life today in the Czech and Slovak republics, with religion, theatre and architecture, and wrote the features on Jaroslav Hašek and Smetana. He also edited the Travel Tips section and undertook the intricate task of inserting into the text a baffling variety of Czech accents.

Wieland Giebel, a former Insight Guides editor now based in Berlin, examines the situations of the various minorities living in both the Czech Republic and Slovakia.

Annette Tohak, from Bonn, guides readers through the romantic nooks of the beautiful Southern Bohemia.

Chris Pommery in Prague provided valuable information concerning the momentous developments that led to the emergence of the two independent states, and **Peter Cargin** of FIPRESCI gave helpful hints concerning the future of the Karlovy Vary Film Festival.

The Photographers

In the established tradition of the Insight Guides series, this book mesmerises with its superb photography. Together with their Munich colleague **Werner Neumeister**, the internationally recognised Prague photojournalists **Mirek Frank**, **Oldrich Karásek** and **Jan Ságl** offered the publisher a dazzling selection of shots for the final selection.

The book was translated into English by Jane Michael-Rushmer, and production was masterminded in Insight Guides' London office by **Tony Halliday** and **Dorothy Stannard**. Proof-reading and indexing was completed by **Mary Morton**.

Pavlik

Jirku

Rose

Jakobsmeier

History

—by Alfred Horn and Petr Volf

People & Features

Maps

TRAVEL TIPS

**For detailed information
see page 321**

WELCOME

While breaking up is always hard to do, the final parting of the Czech and Slovak republics was a remarkably amicable affair. The formalities of separation were completed with relative ease and in January 1993 the two states went their own separate ways. They had actually been married before, over 1,000 years ago in a kingdom called Great Moravia. Although that didn't last very long either, it does at least show that despite their cultural and linguistic differences, the Czechs and Slovaks have common links that go back a long way. Their destinies have also been closely bound with the rest of Europe, by a complex network of historical and cultural ties.

For centuries Bohemia played a central role in the Holy Roman Empire; under Charles IV, Prague even became one of the greatest capitals of Europe. The Czech religious reformer Jan Hus should be mentioned in the same breath as Wycliffe, Calvin and Luther; the compositions of Smetana and Dvořák form part of the world repertoire of classical music. In "Golden Prague" the European tradition has not been relegated to dusty history books, but has remained full of life and atmosphere to this day. The town is no lacklustre museum of medieval urban architecture, but rather an international arena throbbing with vitality which still manages to retain its charm and flair under the assault of millions of tourists.

Prague has long occupied a prominent position on the tourist trail; as far as the rest of the Czech Republic is concerned, however, the boom is still to come. Karlovy Vary – the elegant Carlsbad of days gone by – and Marienbad, where emperors, tsars, Goethe and Chopin took the waters, are refurbishing their manicured promenades and nostalgic spa hotels. Embracing the effusive townscapes lie the forbidding castles and romantic river valleys of Bohemia and Moravia. All are just waiting to be explored.

Slovakia has yet to be discovered. As far as history and culture are concerned, until 1918 the country's destiny was always more closely wound up with events in Hungary than with the course of mainstream developments further west. After the Turks invaded the Hungarian heartlands, Bratislava even became Hungary's *de facto* capital. During the Austro-Hungarian monarchy, when the Czech lands of Bohemia and Moravia were politically and economically so powerful, Slovakia was relegated to the position of impoverished neighbour. Despite subsequent industrialisation under the Communists, the country remains essentially rural in character, and is proud of its enduring traditions and folklore. It also possesses some splendid scenery, including the High Tatras, which are among the most spectacular mountains in Europe.

Preceding pages: panel paintings in the Chapel of the Holy Cross in Karlstejn Castle; wintertime in the Krkonoše (Giant Mountains); first snows in the High Tatra; the ruins of Strecno Castle stand sentinel above the Váh (Slovakia); facades on the Old Town Square in Prague. Left, generations of tradition in Slovakia.

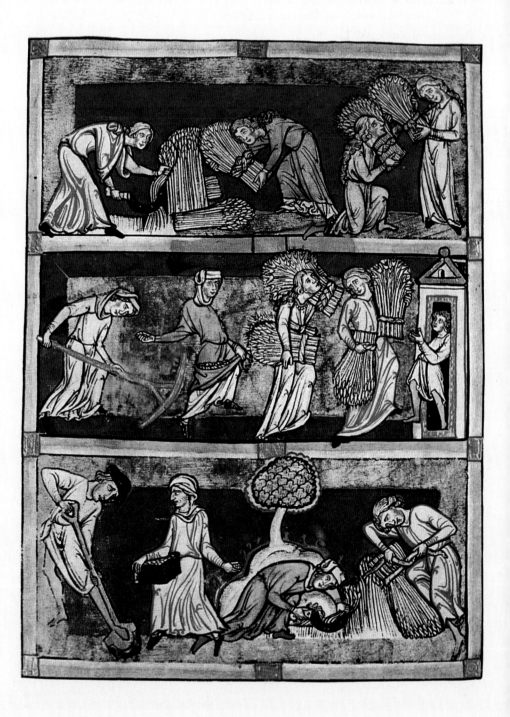

The frontiers of the Czech Lands and Slovakia did not assume their present boundaries until this century, and yet the region can claim a long history as one of the focal points of Central European civilisation and as a bridge – or sometimes a watershed – between the cultures of Eastern and Western Europe. Furthermore, the Czech Lands of Bohemia and Moravia lay at the crossroads of the traditional trade routes from the Atlantic coast to the Black Sea and from the Mediterranean to the Baltic. This valuable strategic position gave the entire continent a vested interest in the region's history.

Archaeological excavations have produced fine examples of pottery, testifying to the fact that Moravia and Slovakia were the home of settled communities as long as 25,000 years ago. During the fifth millennium BC the members of the Danube civilisation practised extensive agriculture. The potter's wheel was discovered in about 3,000 BC; by between 2,000 and 1,500 BC the members of the Únětice Culture near Prague had discovered how to smelt bronze and hence how to produce tools and weapons as well as religious cult figures and intricate jewellery.

The first Slavs – the earliest ancestors of the present-day Czechs and Slovaks – settled in the region from the 6th century AD onwards. Their migration route across Europe from the East brought them through the Carpathian Pass, the Moravian Gate and the Tisa valley, until they reached the area which was subsequently to become their new home. Here they encountered the Celts, who had been in the area for many years, as well as groups of Germanii who had also gained a foothold in the region.

The gradual assimilation of the original inhabitants marked the beginning of the political history of the Western Slavs. To protect themselves against the warlike incur-

sions of the nomadic Avars they first formed a tribal association. They chose as their leader the Frankish merchant Samo, who had built up a powerful private army to protect his trading caravans. But no sooner had they beaten off the Avars, than they were attacked on their western flank by the King of the Franks, in 637. In the subsequent Battle of the Vogastisburg, the Slavic army won the day, and the Western Slavs proceeded to establish an extensive kingdom, though this quickly disintegrated after the death of Samo.

Christianity spreads: More clearly defined and better organised was the state of Great Moravia, which grew up after 833 in the regions of modern Moravia and Western Slovakia and expanded to include all of Bohemia, the southern part of modern Poland and the western part of modern Hungary. Thanks to his good relations with Byzantium, Prince Ratislav was able to arrange for Christian missionaries to be sent by the rulers of the Byzantine Empire. The arrival in 863 of two learned brothers, Cyril and Methodius, the apostles of the Slavs, was a key event in the subsequent political, religious and cultural development of the re-

<u>Preceding pages</u>: an old engraving of Carlsbad. <u>Left</u>, loose tribes from the regions of present-day Moravia and Bohemia formed a feudal state around AD 1000: a depiction of the harvest at that time. <u>Right</u>, a figure from the Libuše legend of the founding of Prague at Vyšehrad.

gion. They not only converted large numbers of the population to the new state religion, but also developed the Slavonic Glagolitic script. Once the Pope had given his official blessing to their accomplishments, permission was granted for sermons to be given in Slavic after the lesson had been read in Latin. This concession was crucial to the rapid spread of Christianity.

But Prince Svatopluk, the most notable ruler of this early state, was soon forced to recognise the superior strength of his neighbours, the Franks, and to grant additional rights to the Western Church. A Swabian bishop was installed in his capital, Nitra, and the followers of the Slavic apostles were

dination to the Empire and an alliance with Saxony lost him the support of the Bohemian ruling classes. Their resistance became more determined when Henry I started to enslave the Slavs east of the frontier with Saxony.

The king's own brother, Boleslav, led the conspiracy against him. He was personally responsible for Wenceslas' murder in 935. Boleslav then succeeded in creating one of the most powerful states in Central Europe. He ruled over Bohemia, Moravia and parts of Slovakia as well as Silesia and Southern Poland. But he had to defend his kingdom against repeated attack by the Holy Roman Emperor, Otto I. After the death of Boleslav I (c. 967) and with the support of the Pope,

expelled. At the turn of the 10th century the state came under increasing threat from the Magyars, and finally collapsed following a crushing defeat at their hands near Bratislava in 907.

German dominance in Bohemia: The princes of Bohemia had already asserted their independence. Under their rule, the Czech Přemyslid dynasty gradually emerged as the supreme power in the whole of Bohemia. Although the first of the Přemyslid monarchs, Prince Wenceslas (Václav) I, was able to assert himself as sole ruler over Bohemia, he was forced to swear allegiance to the German emperor Henry I in 929. This subor-

Boleslav II succeeded in stabilising the kingdom. He was also responsible for the founding of the Bishopric of Prague.

Boleslav's successor, Břetislav (1035–1055), tried to defend the borders and even to extend his realm. His principal achievement was the permanent union of Moravia and Bohemia in about 1029. But for King Henry III the united kingdom represented an unacceptable threat; in 1041 he forced Břetislav to recognise Bohemia's dependence on the German Empire.

The German rulers endeavoured to maintain the Czechs' position as vassals in a state of subordination to the Empire. In this they were frequently assisted by local noblemen. Even the Přemyslids approached them for support in quarrels concerning the princely throne. This provided the German rulers with a welcome excuse to play an active role in Czech affairs. However, the Přemyslids were able to maintain their autonomy even in the most difficult situations. They were also experts at turning the repeated problems of the Germans to their own advantage and offered their services as reliable allies.

The 13th century saw a fundamental change in the status quo. In 1198 Otakar was crowned the first king of the Czechs; in 1204 Pope Innocent III also recognised the title. A further milestone was reached in 1212, when Emperor Frederick II ratified the Sicilian Golden Bull. This confirmed all the privileges which the Přemyslids had achieved to date and emphasised the unity of the land inhabited by the Czechs, which meant that the nation was finally granted official recognition by its rulers at the international level.

Pushing out the frontiers: The second half of the 13th century was dominated by the political and military successes of King Přemysl Otakar II (1253–78). His power, which rested securely on the vast wealth derived from the silver mines of Bohemia, rose steadily until he reached a position of hegemony in Central Europe. After his victory at the battle of Kressenbrunn in 1260 he succeeded in advancing into Hungary, occupying Bratislava and pushing the frontiers of Bohemia as far as the Adriatic.

The compliant attitudes of both the Pope and the Emperor show the extent of Otakar II's authority; not without reason do the chroniclers of the period call him the Golden King. He died in 1278 in the midst of the Battle of Dürnkrut, fighting against Rudolf of Habsburg, who considered the Czech king his greatest rival. His death unleashed a crisis concerning the succession, but the situation became more stable when the claims of King Wenceslas (Václav) II to the Polish throne were recognised. His young son Wenceslas III tried to continue the expansionist policies of his forbears, but he was assassinated during his Polish campaign in the year 1306.

Left, replica of St Wenceslas' crown in the National Museum in Prague. Above, St Cyril and Methodius as depicted by the Slovak artist Fulla.

The Přemyslid dynasty died out following his death, since he was the last male heir of the line. The following years were characterised by bitter fighting for the throne of Bohemia, which had become the most lucrative sinecure in Europe. Forming an alliance with the Czech aristocracy, Duke John of Luxembourg was in a position to swing the balance of power in his favour. His marriage to the heiress of Bohemia Elizabeth, the younger daughter of Wenceslas II, added a note of legitimacy to his claims; when he stood with his armies before the walls of Prague on 3 December 1310, the citizens offered no resistance. He was crowned king of Bohemia the following year.

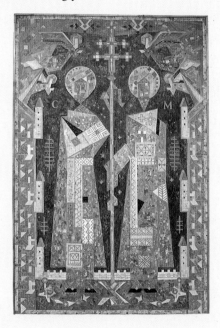

John's character was full of contradictions; he was a swashbuckling soldier who devoted more energy to waging war than to ruling his kingdom. This resulted in a perpetual drain on the national finances, but also led to a weakening of his own position within Bohemia, where the aristocracy was becoming progressively more discontented. The loss of confidence in the crown and the internal crisis within the Czech provinces soon reached major proportions. The hopes of the aristocracy and bourgeoisie alike were concentrated in the person of the crown prince Charles, John's son. They were not disappointed.

Charles IV was born in Prague in 1316 and spent much of his early childhood playing on the banks of the Vltava. As a small boy he was sent to Paris to the court of his uncle, the King of France. His tutor during these years was the future Pope Clement VI. Although he was christened Wenceslas, Charles abandoned his baptismal name and adopted that of his role model, Charlemagne. He studied at the university of Paris and travelled extensively in Europe, learning at first hand the languages and cultures of the different na-

tions. His first wife, Blanche of Valois, was an equally worldly and influential woman.

Charles's early years were marked by a tempestuous relationship with his father. At one point he even took refuge in Italy, entering the service of the Doge of Venice as the leader of an army of mercenaries. Following a reconciliation, his father proclaimed him governor of Bohemia and Moravia. Although only 17 at the time, Charles already had considerable experience of life. From now on he dedicated himself to the task of bringing new prosperity to the country.

Charles's first real success was the elevation of the bishopric of Prague to the rank of archbishopric in 1344. The support of the Pope was also instrumental in securing his nomination as king of Germany in place of the excommunicated Louis IV, on 11 July 1346. His father, now blind, died in the saddle at Crécy only six weeks later, and Charles became king of Bohemia in 1347.

The Golden Bull: It was now understood that the German imperial crown was based on the crown of Bohemia, and in 1355 Charles travelled to Rome, where he was duly crowned Emperor. Although throughout his reign he was mainly concerned with his native Bohemian lands, as these provided his greatest source of strength, Charles did not neglect his imperial duties. In 1356 he proclaimed the Golden Bull, a kind of imperial constitution. It confirmed the right of the seven electors to choose the German king; in return, the Emperor acknowledged their absolute jurisdiction within their own territories, and decreed that the rule of primogeniture was henceforth to govern the laws of inheritance and succession. These statutes eliminated a potential source of strife for the emperor and ensured the loyalty of his most powerful vassals.

Whilst the rest of Europe seemed in danger of sinking into chaos, with England and France engaged in the mutually destructive Hundred Years' War and Italy shattered by petty intrigues and civil wars between its minor princes and city states, Charles cleared the way for making his native country the hub of his newly acquired empire. The conquest and purchase of further territories and his four marriages, each of which brought him increased power and additional land, as well as the skilful negotiation of the marriage of his son, Sigismund, to the daughter of the King of Poland and Hungary, strengthened his sphere of influence and gradually shifted the centre of political power within his empire in an easterly direction.

Charles actively encouraged the cult of St Wenceslas, the national patron saint. The "Lands of the Crown of St Wenceslas", which apart from Bohemia and Moravia also included Silesia, Lusatia and for a short while even Brandenburg, acquired increasing relevance in the empire.

A booming economy: Bohemia was located on the crossroads of the trading routes between Venice and the Baltic countries as well as those between Flanders and Kiev and the Byzantine Empire. Under Charles the standard of the existing roads was greatly improved. The Vltava and the Labe (Elbe) provided access to the North Sea and the additional markets of the Free Imperial Cities and the towns of the Hanseatic League.

New settlers were persuaded to make their homes in the country, thereby encouraging

sentative European metropolis. He summoned the best architects of the time to his capital on the banks of the Vltava for the construction of the Cathedral of St Vitus. In 1348 he founded in Prague the first university in central Europe. Also during his reign, Prague's area was greatly enlarged by the establishment of the New Town.

The king was generous in his support of the Church. No fewer than 35 new monasteries were established throughout Bohemia and Moravia, and many old churches were

the renewed use of agricultural land which had been allowed to lie fallow and increasing the manufacturing potential. Charles spoke German as well as Czech; despite large numbers of German immigrants, he managed to prevent the outbreak of ethnic and nationalist conflict.

Prague becomes capital: Charles raised Prague to the position of capital of the Holy Roman Empire, gradually transforming the city where he had been born into a repre-

Left, Emperor Charles IV made Prague into the capital of the Holy Roman Empire. Above, the Emperor with the imperial insignia.

rebuilt. All this feverish activity was not without its disadvantages, however; the underdeveloped taxation system placed a disproportionate burden on the poorer classes, heightening the social tensions between the masses on the one hand and the aristocracy and the Church on the other. This growing problem was to lead ultimately to the Hussite rebellion during the 15th century.

But in spite of these difficulties Charles IV was one of the outstanding figures of Czech and European history. During his reign Bohemia and Moravia flourished as never before, so that the era was described even by contemporaries as the "Golden Age".

55

Alez yz biſkupem ſe nazmali a od prme w gimiti Swęty Ambroz
O pane gezi ſſi tworm paſterzi zmiani ſuſ y wlk. Harzi wbin
ge knize w ſwodze ſprelati wpilati giſa w ſmilne S. Bernath

Charles was succeeded as German emperor and king of Bohemia by his eldest son, Wenceslas IV (1378–1419). The latter unfortunately lacked his father's talent and energy; he allowed Germany to slide into anarchy and was ultimately deposed as emperor by the electors in 1400.

At home in Bohemia, his main problem was the Church, which during the reign of his father had still been a reliable pillar of support for the ruling house. The English reformer, John Wycliffe, had already openly challenged the authority of the Church as a secular power. By virtue of the marriage of Wenceslas's sister Anne to King Richard II of England and the ensuing close contact between the two countries, Wycliffe's theories spread rapidly throughout Bohemia.

The blatant self-enrichment and extravagance of the senior clergy, the bigoted attitude of the priests and the prevailing situation in the abbeys and convents, where monastic rules were openly defied, now called for decisive action on the part of the monarch. But Wenceslas IV was not a decisive man and entrenched himself in a diehard conservative position.

In Prague, the centre of critical theologians was not the university but the Bethlehem Chapel in the Old Town, erected in 1391 to accommodate up to 3,000 faithful. The sermons were often held in Czech – an almost unprecedented act of boldness for the time, but one which greatly increased their appeal to the ordinary people. A new generation of Czech and German-speaking preachers arose, amongst whom Jan Hus was to become the most famous.

Fuel to the fire: Hus's death at the stake in 1415 (*see page 33*) gave rise to a storm of indignation and protest throughout Bohemia. In Prague, a defensive league of aristocratic supporters of the Hussites from Bohemia, Moravia and Silesia was formed. They asserted their belief in the freedom of the Word of God and protested against the violent death of Jan Hus.

Left, the Pope as depicted by the Hussites (around 1500). **Above**, Jan Žižka (died 1424), the commander of the Hussite army.

Their petition, addressed to the Council, was signed by 450 noblemen. The Hussite movement also found widespread support amongst the working classes, both within the towns and in rural areas. What had initially begun as an internal reform movement within the Church developed into a broadly-based protest movement against the monarchy, the Catholic Church and the supremacy of the Germans throughout Bohemia.

The first Defenestration of Prague: The violent overture to what was to turn into 20 years

STRENUUS CASTIGATOR ECCLESIASTICÆ SUAVITATIS JOANNES ZIZKA DE TROCNOVA ET MACHOVIC QUI NON ENSE SED PESTE OBIIT ANNO 1424 DIE 8VA SEPTEMBRIS ERAT EQUES BOHEMUS ET INVICTISSIMUS HEROS IN OPPUGNATIONE CASTRI PRZIBISLAVIENSI

of conflict was an event that took place even before the death of Wenceslas. At the end of June 1419, the enraged citizens of Prague threw the jurors from the window of the New Town Hall because the Town Council refused to release of a number of Hussite prisoners. Wenceslas died in 1419; the Bohemian throne was then claimed by his half brother Sigismund, the German king responsible for Hus's death. The citizens of Prague reacted by forming a defensive alliance linking all the towns in the land. They even took over the government of the country.

For Sigismund the mob's action was sufficient justification to start a crusade against the heretics. During the following year, at the head of an army, he laid siege to the city. By employing guerilla tactics, however, the Hussite "soldiers of God", under the command of their heroic leader Jan Žižka, were able to put the attackers to flight. Žižka, whose military experience included fighting for the British at Agincourt in 1415, had been chosen leader of the popular party in 1419. Having conquered Emperor Sigismund's army and captured Prague after the Battle of Vítkov Hill in 1421, he proceeded to erect a fortress at Tábor, which became the centre of the Hussites' utopian religious state. The Hussites overran and plundered not only Bohemia, Moravia and Slovakia, but also

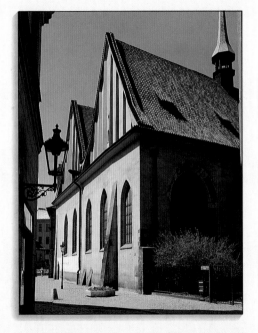

Austria, Bavaria, Saxony and Brandenburg. The Imperial army, hurriedly called up, was defeated by Žižka and his forces in a succession of decisive battles.

The Council of Basle finally took up negotiations with the Hussite leaders, at which point a schism developed within the movement. The moderate Utraquists, supported by the nobles, agreed to a compromise in the Four Articles of Prague in 1433, which contained acceptance of their principal requirement: the administration of the Communion to the laity in both kinds during the Mass. The radical Taborites, on the other hand, fought on under their general Andrew Procop

until, in 1434, they were defeated in a battle at Lipany by the combined forces of the Catholics and the Utraquists.

And so, after almost 20 years of Hussite wars, the moderate Czech Utraquists were the clear victors. For the next 200 years the power of the Catholic Church was to remain at a low ebb, despite the fact that the majority of the population was still Catholic – or professed to be. The Germans, who had hitherto enjoyed political and economic superiority, lost both power and possessions; furthermore, they were forced to settle in the frontier regions of the country. Their dominant position was taken over by the Czech nobility and upper middle classes; the poorer people still had no say in the government of the country. The devastation of war drove farmers and peasants even deeper into debt and subservience.

And yet, the religious and social revolution represented by the Hussite movement remains the first reform movement to have a broadly based political impact on Europe as a whole. Its influence on the development of Bohemia's neighbours was to be long-lasting. This was one of the key episodes in Czech history, in particular because it represented the first time – albeit without success – when there was support for the foundation of a separate Czech state.

The new order arising from the aftermath of war was personified by George of Poděbrady and Kunštát, who as leader of the aristocratic Utraquists was to rule the country from 1439 as Imperial administrator, and from 1458–71 as King.

Even he, however, was to prove incapable of bringing a lasting peace to Bohemia and reviving the country's former prosperity. After his death the Bohemian estates elected a son of the King of Poland as their new monarch. In 1491, in the Testament of Bratislava, the succession to the throne of Bohemia and Moravia was granted to the House of Habsburg. When the king's son Ludwig died without issue fighting against the Turks in 1526, the country passed into Habsburg hands. Together with Austria it was to remain under their rule until 1918.

Above, the Bethlehem Chapel in Prague was where Jan Hus preached his damming sermons in the Czech language. Right, a portrait of the great reformer.

JAN HUS

Master Jan Hus, the preacher and philosopher whose teachings formed the foundation of the revolutionary Hussite Movement, is one of the legendary characters of Czech history. More than any other national hero, he was an inspiration to the common people. His name crops up in folk songs, he is the hero of several plays and in recent years he has even been the subject of films. The anniversary of his death, on 6 July 1415, is still celebrated as a national festival of remembrance.

Jan Hus was born in 1371 in the village of Husinec in Southern Bohemia. He studied at the local school and went on to Charles University, from which he graduated in 1396 with a Master of Liberal Arts degree. Two years later he was appointed as an ordinarius professor. In 1400 he was ordained priest and became the first Czech rector of the Charles University in 1409.

During his youth he began to devote his attention to the works of the English theologian and reformer John Wycliffe, who attacked the secularisation of the Church and demanded a return to the doctrine and practices of the early Christian communities. Wycliffe considered that the only real sign of membership of the Church was an exemplary lifestyle; he acknowledged the Bible as the one true foundation of faith. Hus developed Wycliffe's thesis further, emphasising the social aspects.

The unadorned Bethlehem Chapel in Prague, to which Hus was summoned as preacher in 1402, proved an ideal forum for disseminating his message to the widest possible audience. In order to get his points across Hus, who was a brilliant rhetorical speaker, developed his own, often unconventional methods. He delivered most of his sermons and commentaries in Czech, even going so far as to write a number of texts on the walls of the chapel. He translated hymns and religious songs, thereby enabling a wide spectrum of churchgoers to take an active part in the service. One by-product of this approach was that Hus modernised spoken Czech, elevating it to the level of the written language. Hus found widespread support amongst many German-speaking theologians of the time; they even endorsed his demands for equal rights for the Czechs in Bohemia, seeing it as a justifiable pastoral and social affair.

But what had begun as brotherly criticism of the Catholic Church soon developed into a vitriolic attack upon the institution as he saw it. Hus's passionate demands for a return to the traditional poverty of the clergy and a general improvement in the moral standards of public life aroused the enmity of the upper echelons of the priesthood as well as causing animosity on the part of those members of the aristocracy who saw their privileged lifestyle about to disappear.

The conflict reached a head in 1411, when Hus castigated the sale of indulgences as amoral charlatanism. There were public demonstrations for and against his theories; the Church excommunicated Hus and forbade him from exercising his priestly office, although he continued to preach at the Bethlehem Chapel and to teach at the university. But when he lost the support of

King Wenceslas IV, who shared in the proceeds of the sale of indulgences, Hus left Prague and began to preach in rural areas; here he found time to examine his doctrines in greater depth and to publish them under the title *De ecclesia*, in 1413.

During the spring of 1414 Sigismund, the King of the Germans, challenged Hus to declare his position before the Council of Constance. He was promised a safe passage and so, against the advice of his friends, Hus set out to attend. His hearing before the Council developed into a fierçe theological dispute; in the end, the conservatives won the day and Hus was found guilty of heresy. When he refused to recant his beliefs he was burned at the stake. ∎

After the Hussite wars Bohemia's frontiers remained inviolate, but within the country itself unrest continued to ferment. An uneasy peace ensued when George of Poděbrady, the leader of the Utraquist aristocracy, came to the throne in 1458. He earned a place in the annals of European history with his proposals for a general treaty of non-aggression involving all the countries of Europe including Turkey. The plan was never realised because of the rivalries between the various rulers, but it was the first attempt of its kind and served as a model for future alliances.

George of Poděbrady was the last Czech king. Between 1470 and 1526 he was succeeded by the Jagiellon dynasty from Poland. Under their rule the power of the upper aristocracy resumed its former strength. With the coronation of Vladyislav II Jagiello as King of Hungary in 1490, Slovakia, which had been part of the Hungarian kingdom ever since the destruction of Great Moravia in the 11th century, was once more included in the union with Bohemia and Moravia.

In 1526, following the death of the young Jagiellon King Ludwig while fighting the Turks in the Battle of Mohacs in Southern Hungary, the throne of Bohemia and Hungary passed to Ferdinand von Habsburg, thus marking the start of a period of almost four centuries of Habsburg rule over Bohemia, Moravia and Slovakia. The Habsburgs concentrated political power in the hands of the king, supported by the Catholic Church and a handful of powerful magnates.

Ferdinand, who was also crowned Holy Roman Emperor in 1556 following the abdication of his elder brother Charles V, attempted to strike a balance throughout his vast empire between Catholics and Protestants. At the same time, however, he actively supported the Counter-Reformation in the lands of the Bohemian crown by summoning the Jesuits to Prague. With the Collegium Clementinum the king founded an additional Catholic university in the Bohemian capital; its reputation soon outstripped that of the venerable Carolinum.

From Vienna to Hradčany: However, even this could not prevent the Catholics sinking progressively into the minority within the lands of the Bohemian crown; by the end of the 16th century at least 80 percent of the population claimed to be Protestant. Ferdinand's son, Maximilian II, found himself faced with almost insurmountable problems in the face of the increasingly violent

confessional quarrels within his kingdom. His successor, Rudolf II, was more interested in the arts than in affairs of state – his collection of the visual arts included a fascinating assemblage of curiosities from all over the world. Although he was born in Vienna, he moved his official residence to Hradčany Castle in 1583, thereby initiating unexpected economic prosperity in Prague.

In 1593 the Turks attacked again following a long period of truce and the Habsburgs had difficulty keeping them at bay. Matthias, Rudolf's younger brother, eventually took over command of the army and managed to conclude a new peace with the Turks in

Preceding pages: The Battle of Austerlitz, in which Napoleon defeated the Habsburgs on 2 December 1805, is reenacted every year. **Left**, George of Poděbrady, the last Bohemian king (1458–71). **Above**, Rudolf II of Habsburg.

1606. The Emperor, now mentally deranged, died in 1612, one year after he had been forced to abdicate the Bohemian throne in favour of his power-hungry brother.

The Bohemian estates could only make temporary capital out of the family quarrel; in 1609 Rudolf had granted them complete freedom of confession and various other privileges in a *Letter of Majesty* – advantages which they had to defend against Matthias. The conflict intensified as both sides attempted to secure their positions by means of alliances: the Catholic princes formed the League, the Protestants the Union.

The second Defenestration of Prague: The religious time bomb finally exploded on 23 chy, deposed Ferdinand and in August 1619 chose Friedrich of the Palatinate as their new king. The insult hit deep, for with the election of the leader of the Union it seemed as if the empire would not only lose Bohemia itself, one of the central countries of Europe, but also that the balance of power on the continent would be tipped in favour of the Protestants. The Emperor and the Catholic League reacted immediately by sending in a powerful army under General Tilly.

The Thirty Years' War: The Battle of the White Mountain, before the gates of Prague, took place on 8 November 1620. It was decided within the space of a few hours. Friedrich, the "Winter King" – so called

May 1618. In accordance with an old Bohemian custom, the rebellious representatives of the Prague estates threw the Emperor's two stadholders and their secretary from the window of the Bohemian chancellery in Hradčany Castle. This second Defenestration of Prague unleashed the Bohemian War, which was soon to develop into the Thirty Years' War involving all of Europe.

Occupying the throne of Bohemia at the time was Ferdinand II, who became King of Hungary in 1618 and Holy Roman Emperor a year later. This fact no longer interested the self-confident Protestant Bohemian estates; they declared Bohemia an electoral monar-

because his reign had lasted for less than one year – was forced to flee, losing all his electoral privileges within the Empire. The enemy troops had little difficulty overcoming the hastily erected barricades; for weeks they plundered and destroyed everything they could lay their hands on. Hundreds of people were indiscriminately condemned to death or driven into exile, from ringleaders to people who hadn't even been involved.

Ferdinand tore up Rudolf's *Letter of Majesty* with his own hands, expelling all non-Catholic priests from the city and forcing the aristocracy and citizens alike to return to the Catholic fold. During the following years the

Catholic Church soared to new heights of power, achieving an authority it had failed to enjoy since the Hussite Revolution. Protestant intellectuals, such as the famous philosopher and teacher Jan Amos Comenius, the bishop of the Bohemian Brethren, were forced to leave their native land.

Even after this fearful blood-letting there was no peace within the country. Merciless persecution and local uprisings continued to shatter Bohemia and Moravia and, following the intervention of Sweden, the war entered a second violent phase. This was the hour of Albrecht von Wallenstein, a Bohemian nobleman who had converted from Protestantism to Catholicism in 1606 and had earned him, the imperial army won a decisive victory over the Swedish forces near Nördlingen; with the Treaty of Westphalia of 30 May 1635, the stifling peace of the Habsburgs descended on this part of Europe.

Under the Habsburg yoke: The failure of the rebellion had catastrophic consequences. The Habsburgs could now expand their absolute power without fearing any resistance; they moved the centre of political power once and for all to Vienna. Although nominally retaining their independence, the lands of the Bohemian crown became a provincial backwater, a situation which had disastrous effects on what had once been a buoyant independent culture. This was most obvious in the

his military spurs as an officer under General Tilly. Having been awarded supreme power over all imperial armies, Wallenstein reached the zenith of his power when his opponent, Gustav Adolf, was killed in the battle of Lützen, near Leipzig, in 1632. But wary of his ambitions for power, his enemies soon closed rank and persuaded the Emperor to denounce him; Wallenstein was ultimately assassinated in 1634 in Cheb. Even without

Left, the Defenestration of 1618. **Above left**, the Vladislav Hall in Hradčany at the time of Rudolf II (detail of an engraving by Aegidius Sadeler, 1607); Albrecht von Wallenstein.

field of literature; Czech came to be regarded as no more than the language of lower-class country yokels while German came to dominate lawyers' offices and literary salons alike. From 1763, even university lectures were mostly held in German; it was not until 1791 that a chair of Czech language and literature was established at Prague University.

The economy, also largely controlled by the Germans, suffered badly from the devastation of towns that had prospered on their flourishing trade and skilled craftsmen. The tightening of serfdom in the country slowed down productivity and prevented a rapid revival. Peasants whose farmsteads had survived the war were now faced with the burden of paying feudal dues and socage to the nobility so exorbitant that their very existence was threatened. The personal freedom of the individual was severely restricted: not only every marriage, but also the practice of a trade or the attendance at a place of further education had to be given the official seal of approval.

An era of tolerance: The status quo remained unchanged until the reign of the Empress Maria Theresa, who was crowned Queen of Bohemia in 1743 in Prague. Her son, Joseph II, who from 1765 ruled Bohemia jointly with his mother, was responsible for a new tolerance which permitted the existence of

region within the Habsburg empire. The manufacture of textiles provided the basis for an accelerated exploitation of industrial resources. Before the turn of the century an English spinning machine was inaugurated in Northern Bohemia. A few years later, steam-driven machinery conquered Brno and Prague. The attractive products of the glass-blowing and porcelain manufacturing industries conquered the European market; heavy industry followed in 1821 with the first iron blast furnace.

The national revival and revolution: The rapid economic expansion failed, however, to remove social and national tensions. Above all, the language dispute continued to seethe,

faiths other than Catholicism and allowed Jews to leave the ghettos.

Of more far-reaching importance for the subsequent development of the country was the edict proclaiming the abolition of serfdom in 1781, a move which paved the way for a liberalisation of the economy and society as a whole. The release of workers to satisfy the rapidly growing requirements of firms and businesses was as much a prerequisite for the industrial revolution as the improvement and expansion of educational opportunities.

Bohemia and Moravia rapidly expanded to become the most profitable economic

for Czechs and Slovaks alike demanded official recognition for their languages, and parity with German. The dispute provided a continual source of strife: for example, when the Czech aristocracy was gathered in Prague for the coronation of King Leopold II, they refused to speak anything but Czech in protest at the language policy of the Habsburgs. The resulting discord shattered the hopes for harmony of the new monarch, who had travelled to Prague specially for the occasion.

In spite of a number of concessions the Czechs and Slovaks were unable to reach agreement; indeed, they believed that the discrimination against their language was a symptom of the lack of respect for their nationality and an attempt to wipe out once and for all their cultural identity. The National Question became the dominant theme of the revolutionary years 1848–49. But although all the movements were directed against absolutism and centralism, there was a conflict of national interests and goals.

It was the main goal of the German Nationalist Movement that it should create a united Germany. Even those Germans who lived in Czechoslovakia aspired to this goal. They automatically assumed that Czech territories were part of the united Germany. This idea met with violent opposition on the part of the Czechs themselves, who in their turn sought

He demanded the transformation of the Austrian monarchy into a national federation, in which the united Slavs were to have decisive influence. But the Slavic rulers were uncoordinated. When unrest broke out in Prague and barricades were erected in Vienna, the imperial troops were soon able to regain the upper hand.

During the spring of 1848, Slovakian society supported the results of the Hungarian revolution. Their representatives voted for Slovakia to assume an autonomous position within the framework of a federal Hungarian state. Although encouraged by the Habsburgs's centralised administration, these Slovakian nationalist demands met with op-

allies amongst the other oppressed Slavic peoples and who – like the Czech delegation from Bohemia – turned down the invitation to attend the German National Assembly in St Paul's Church in Frankfurt on the grounds that they were not Germans. This attitude found expression in the doctrine of so-called Austroslavism.

The historian František Palacký had himself elected speaker of the movement at the First Slavic Congress in June 1848 in Prague.

Left, life in the Jewish quarter around 1900. **Above**, a Czech farmer and his wife around the turn of the century.

position on the part of the Hungarian revolutionary government, which instead used all its influence to assert a Hungarian Nationalist policy. After the creation of the dual monarchy of Austro-Hungary in 1867, the Hungarian government resumed control over Slovakia, and its policy of Magyarisation stimulated many Slovaks to emigrate, particularly to the United States. Slovakia remained a province of Upper Hungary right up to 1918.

A president from Moravia: After 1848 Czech political representatives supported the federalisation of the monarchy. When Austria rejected such demands out of hand, more radical suggestions gradually gained support. Towards the end of the 19th century a generation of self-confident professional politicians emerged and the various sections of Czech society, increasingly aware of their group and class interests, formed independent political organisations.

By the turn of the century, German national groups began to demand the unification of areas settled predominantly by Germans with the German empire; the radical Young Czechs, on the other hand, demanded a Czech state within a federation with Hungary and Austria as well as unity with the Slovaks. The new trend was known as Political Realism; its most famous representative

was Tomáš Garrigue Masaryk, who was to become the first Czech president.

Masaryk (1850–1937) was born in Hodonin in Southern Moravia, the son of a Slovak father and a German mother. He attended the German grammar school in Brno (Brünn), later studying philosophy and philology in Vienna and Leipzig. He was an academic educated in the best German cultural tradition. At the age of 32 he was summoned to the newly founded Czech University of Prague, created by the division of the venerable Charles University.

In 1891 he was elected by the Young Czechs and in 1907 as leader of the People's Party in the Austrian Imperial Parliament. He established a reputation as a moderate politician devoted to a humanistic ideal of statehood. When war broke out, he emigrated in turn to Rome, Geneva and Paris, convinced that he could only fight successfully for an independent Czechoslovakia from abroad. Together with Eduard Beneš, he founded from his Paris exile a Czechoslovak National Council, from which a provisional government was created in 1918. In 1917 he organised the "Czech Legion", comprising deserters, which earned a fine reputation among the Allies for their fighting during the anti-Soviet intervention.

Whilst the Allies initially saw Masaryk as no more than a useful instrument in their anti-Habsburg propaganda machine, Masaryk gradually succeeded in convincing the leaders of the Entente powers – the United Kingdom, France and the United States – of the viability of a united Czech and Slovak state, which he saw as the best antidote to Habsburg arrogance and German lust for power. It was Masaryk's greatest achievement that he succeeded in bringing to the conference table the scattered Czechs and Slovaks, an achievement which culminated in the Pittsburgh Convention of May 1918 containing the joint statement of the Czech and Slovak leaders in support of the foundation of a common federal state.

At the eleventh hour, Emperor Charles I of Austria attempted to save what was beyond repair: on 16 October he announced the transformation of his empire into an alliance of sovereign nations. Only a few years previously the Slavic nations would have greeted such a move with boisterous enthusiasm – but now it was too late. On 28 October the Czechoslovak Republic was proclaimed in Prague; on 14 November, three days after the Emperor's abdication, the National Assembly elected Masaryk as the president of the new nation. Over 14 million people – 5.5 million Czechs and 3.1 million Germans, 3.5 million Slovaks and 750,000 Hungarians, 460,000 Carpathian Ukrainians and 70,000 Poles in areas with unclearly defined boundaries, not to mention 200,000 Jews and other minority groups – unexpectedly found themselves in possession of a new country.

Above, Bohemia grew famous for its fine cutglass. **Right**, a tram in Prague (1913).

The section of society which set the tone in the new independent state of Czechoslovakia was the Czech bourgeoisie. During those first years, it devoted its energies to transforming Prague into the capital of a modern European industrial country.

But it soon became evident that the country had inherited a number of basic structural problems stemming from the centuries of non-autonomous development: whilst a well-developed consumer goods industry found its market reduced in the first instance from the vast area occupied by the former Habsburg Empire to the much smaller internal market of Czechoslovkia, the country's heavy industry suffered from the lack of previous development and proved inadequate to supply the demands of the internal market. Even during the boom years of the 1920s the planners were unable to make any fundamental changes to this imbalance; after the advent of the Great Depression, there was neither the time nor the money for far-reaching reform. Agricultural development suffered a similar fate. The potential of the comparatively intensive farming industry was squandered by the inadequate attempts at land reform; the victims of the spreading crisis were above all the small and medium-sized farmers, especially those living in the ethnically mixed border regions.

The Great Depression exacerbated the ethnic conflicts, which had remained a perpetual problem within the new republic. On the one hand, Czechoslovakia was a state with a democratic constitution, offering religious and ethnic minorities a high degree of protection and therefore providing asylum to growing numbers of political refugees from the increasingly authoritarian countries whose borders it shared: Germany, Poland and Hungary. On the other hand, the ruling Czech elite was not prepared to keep the rash promises it had made to other minority groups within the country.

Preceding pages: mine workers start their shift in Jáchymov. **Left**, Tomáš Masaryk, the founder and first president of the Republic. **Above**, the double-eagle of the Austro-Hungarian monarchy was thrown out of the castle's window in 1918.

The Slovaks and the Carpatho-Ukrainians, who had been bold enough to join in the common adventure of Czechoslovakia in 1918, felt they had been cheated of their promised autonomy. And instead of cultural autonomy the German-speaking population found itself faced with wide-ranging discrimination in public life, culminating in the closure of the German university in Prague in 1934. There were already signs that a storm was brewing within the country when the new republic came face to face with

dramatically deteriorating conditions on the international scene.

Collapse and German rule: From the beginning the state's founders and first two presidents, Tomáš G. Masaryk from 1918–35, and Eduard Beneš from 1935–38, had seen the hegemony of France's position within the continent of Europe and the cooperation with the victorious Entente powers as a guarantee of Czechoslovakia's survival. But the Treaties of Versailles, St Germain and Trianon (1918/19/20), which dtermined Czechoslovakia's international frontiers, soon proved to be a very shaky barrier in the face of new territorial demands on the part of neighbouring countries. The Little Entente, the alliance formed in 1922 by the Czech foreign minister Eduard Beneš with Yugoslavia and Romania, both equally threatened by Hungary's quest for land, provided some temporary stability on the southeast flank. Nonetheless, everyone was aware that the biggest danger threatening Czechoslovakia lay to the west and north, where not only the Germans but also the Poles were demanding more land. Furthermore, both countries were in a position to exert considerable pressure on account of the minority groups actually living on Czech territory.

As early as November 1918, the German-speaking areas of Bohemia and Moravia

creased his demands in the "Carlsbad Programme" of 24 April 1938. The basic tenets were self-administration, equal rights and reparation; during the local authority elections in May of that year the party won 92 percent of all German votes. When, under pressure from the Western powers, the Prague government intervened, Henlein demanded the Anschluss with the German Reich.

The Munich Agreement: During the late summer, Britain's special envoy, Viscount Runciman, tried to act as arbitrator in Prague. He recommended the relinquishment of the German-speaking areas. During the discussions with Neville Chamberlain which followed, Hitler agreed to making 1 October

declared themselves part of "German-Austria", upon which Czech troops had used force to break up the local and provincial government apparatus. In 1933 Konrad Henlein founded the Sudeten German Home Front as an umbrella organisation for all German nationalist organisations in Czechoslovakia. In the 1935 elections, as the leader of the "Sudeten German Party", he won 68 percent of all German votes, thereby becoming the head of the strongest group within the parliament in Prague. Henlein now demanded autonomy for the regions inhabited by German settlers in Bohemia and Moravia. After discussions with Hitler, he clarified and in-

1938 the date for the transfer. Under the chairmanship of Mussolini, the Munich Agreement was signed by France, the United Kingdom and the German Reich on 29 September 1938.

Chamberlain and Daladier were convinced that they had thus ensured peace within Europe; the Soviet Union criticised the treaty but was neither able nor willing to risk war. Czechoslovakia was not consulted, and was forced to look on passively when, on 1 October, German troops in official support of human rights marched into the so-called Sudeten German Gau, to the jubilant cheers of the German populace. Poland and Hungary also took advantage of the favourable conditions to annex border areas. The Little Entente collapsed. On 5 October Beneš resigned and fled into exile in England.

The Protectorate of Bohemia and Moravia:

Not content with this triumph, Hitler was anxious to "deal with the rest of Czechoslovakia", as a secret order of 21 October 1938 reveals. He encouraged the continued territorial demands of Poland and Hungary, incited the Slovaks to proclaim their own independence and, by means of undisguised military threats, forced the national president of Czechoslovakia, Emil Hacha, to sign in Berlin on 15 March an agreement confirming the creation of the National Protectorate of Bohemia and Moravia. Only hours later, German troops marched into Prague.

Formally speaking the Protectorate remained a state under the protection of the German Reich; it had, however, no independent policies in the realms of foreign affairs, economics and defence. It retained its own head of state and a puppet government for home affairs, justice and culture. This secured the cooperation of some of the 7.3 million inhabitants.

The true power lay in the hands of the German protector, whose seat of administration was in Prague. The governing body organised not only the arrest and deportation of Jews but also devoted considerable efforts to silencing the Czech intelligentsia. The closure of schools and universities, institutes of culture and newspapers, the ban placed upon the choice of some professions and the enforced deportation took a heavy toll amongst teachers, academics, artists and journalists. The world-famous Barrandov studios were forced to devote themselves to making propaganda films, such as the shallow comedies about the passionate Matjuschka and her handsome young lieutenant, designed to keep the troops at the front entertained and happy.

The Nazis employed the same thorough approach in their efforts to turn the Protectorate into an impregnable centre of armaments production and industry. Weapons could continue to be manufactured here right up to the end of the war, owing to the limited range of the Allied bombers.

Massacre at Lidice:

The workforce allowed itself to be deceived by high wages and comparatively favourable working conditions. Since repression within Czechoslovakia was almost complete, resistance efforts had to be steered from abroad. The attempt on the life of the deputy Reichsprotector Reinhard "the hangman" Heydrich on 27 May 1942 was the work of a group of émigrés. Upon instructions from the government in exile in London, they parachuted into Prague and threw a bomb at Heydrich's convertible car. They were finally shot in their hiding place in the church of SS Cyril and Methodius.

Not content with a wave of executions and arrests, as a warning the Gestapo shot all 184 adult male inhabitants of the mining village of Lidice on 10 June 1942 and carried off the women and children.

On 5 May 1945 the citizens of Prague rose in united rebellion against the Germans. Three days before the end of the war they directed their pent-up anger against the Sudeten Germans too; most of the Sudeten Germans were forced to leave their homes; of a total of some 3 million, only 200,000 stayed. The victorious Red Army was rapturously greeted by the populace, who believed the moment of freedom had come at last.

<u>Left</u>, Tomáš G. Masaryk promulgated the independent Czechoslovak Republic in Philadelphia, on 18 October 1918. <u>Above</u>, the staircase in the National Museum in Prague.

The Protectorate of Slovakia: The majority of Slovaks, deeply disappointed at the policy of the Prague government in the nationalities question, had watched more or less passively the threatened dismemberment of Czechoslovakia. The strongest voice was the fiercely nationalist Slovakian People's Party under the leadership of the Catholic priest Jozef Tiso. Slovakian politicians who spoke out in favour of cooperation with the Czechs quickly lost the support of the people.

On 6 October 1938, as a consequence of the Munich Agreement, Slovakia proclaimed itself an autonomous unit within the federal Czecho-Slovak state. Tiso was appointed Prime Minister. Early during the following

Hungary, which had entered into an alliance with Germany.

The most tragic chapter in the story of the German-Slovakian protective alliance was the active cooperation of the Slovakian government in the persecution and extermination of the Jews. Some 110,000 Slovakian Jews were mercilessly "handed over" to the Germans and sent to concentration camps. Only when the Vatican's protests became unequivocal did Tiso abandon the practice. In 1944 the approaching Red Army incited the populace to resist actively the Fascist regime; in August, even Čatloš, the Minister of War, defected to the resistance with some sections of the army. But assisted by German

year, however, he demanded complete sovereignty for Slovakia. Hitler announced his support for this move on 13 March 1939 in Berlin; the following day Tiso declared the state to be fully independent.

Hitler made the Slovaks pay dearly for this favour; on 23 March 1939 the state was forced to place itself under the protection of the German Reich, relinquishing all claims to independent foreign, economic and defence policies. Further humiliations followed in the form of the construction of German defences in Western Slovakia, complete cultural autonomy for the German minority population and territorial concessions to

troops, the regime was able to remain in power for some months longer. On 4 April 1945 the Red Army entered Bratislava; in the Košice Programme of 5 April the resistance leaders under Communist leadership proclaimed the fraternal unity of the Czech and Slovak peoples and demanded the nationalisation of key industries and financial institutions. Tiso was executed on 18 April 1947 in Bratislava.

Above, to the indignation of the populace, German troops marched into Prague on 15 March 1939. **Right,** a tour of the concentration camp in Terezín (Theresienstadt).

THE GHETTO OF TEREZÍN

The little town of Terezín (Theresienstadt) nestles idyllically in the valley of the Labe (Elbe) at the foot of fertile volcanic hills. The pretty surroundings are deceptive, however; today, for most citizens of the Czech Republic, Terezín is a symbol of man's inhumanity to man.

The *malá pevnost*, the little fortress overlooking the town, was built by Emperor Joseph II at the end of the 18th century as part of the line of defences protecting Austria against Prussian aggression. Because of the alleged military urgency of the project, the entire complex was completed within only 10 years. Paradoxically, however, it never proved necessary for the castle to serve its true purpose. During World War I it was used as a prison; when the Nazis invaded Bohemia, they used it for the same purpose – but this time for the imprisonment of Jews.

During World War II the German occupying forces created in Theresienstadt a notorious walled ghetto for Jews. Shipment of Jewish captives into Theresienstadt began in November 1941. Accordingly, the entire non-Jewish population of the town, numbering some 3,700, was hurriedly resettled elsewhere in order to make room for the new arrivals.

The Nazis claimed that the camp they were building here was a Jewish settlement with its own administration. When the International Red Cross insisted on visiting a concentration camp, the delegation was sent to Theresienstadt where it was treated to a week of cultural entertainment. It was, of course, a propaganda lie designed to deceive the rest of the world; for a long time, however, many Jews also believed in it and failed to flee to safety.

Theresienstadt occupied a special position in Hitler's plans for the extermination of the Jewish race. It served as a distribution centre for the transport of Jews (its location at the heart of Europe prevented the construction of a proper extermination camp of the kind to be found in the remotest corners of Eastern Poland). The Gestapo sent prisoners not only from Prague but also from the entire Protectorate of Bohemia and Moravia.

Deportation trains from other countries also deposited their human cargo here. Through the gate surmounted by the cynical motto ARBEIT MACHT FREI (Work Liberates) passed thousands of Jewish prisoners from Poland, Austria, Belgium, the Netherlands, Italy, Russia, Latvia, Lithuania, Greece, Spain, Yugoslavia, France. Towards the end of the war, as the battle front closed in on Germany and camps such as Treblinka had to be dissolved in order to hide the traces of the brutal mass murders, internees of other concentration camps were brought to Theresien–stadt. During the five years of its existence some 140,000 prisoners passed through the camp; over 30,000 died in the dense overcrowding of the ghetto itself and 88,000 were shipped on to the extermination camps, especially Auschwitz.

Transport convoys bringing new inhabitants arrived continuously in the camp. No fewer than 500 trains – in other words, an average of one every three days – came to a halt here between November 1941 and April 1945. Amongst the

largest contingents were the 40,000 Jews brought from Prague, 9,000 from Brno, 13,500 from Berlin, and 4,000 from Frankfurt.

When liberation finally came in May 1945, the Allies encountered thousands of emaciated, terrified prisoners. This statement of bald facts cannot convey the agonies they endured in their perpetual state of uncertainty and fear that the following day they, too, might also be taken away. Today, their most poignant memorial lies not in words but in the national place of remembrance.

After World War II, Theresienstadt was resurrected as a Czech town, under its Czech name Terezín. It became a notable centre for the manufacture of furniture and knitwear. ∎

In the autumn of 1939, from his London exile, Beneš had established a Czechoslovak National Committee which was recognised by the Allies as a provisional government. Despite their support from Moscow, even the Czech Communists under the leadership of Klement Gottwald recognised the legitimacy of this government in exile; in 1943 the Soviet Union concluded a treaty of friendship and assistance. They agreed on the rejection of the Munich Agreement and the expulsion of the Sudeten Germans.

The role of the Soviet Union was in any case crucial as the Western Allies had already agreed at the Yalta Conference that the rearrangement of political relationships within Czechoslovakia should take place under the aegis of Stalin, and that the country should be liberated by the Red Army. Accordingly, in 1945 the American troops who had liberated Plzeň and Western Bohemia retreated once more in the face of the advancing Russian forces.

The National President, Beneš, and the Prime Minister, Zdeněk Fierlinger, who had taken up office in Prague in May 1945, saw no reason for alarm. During the turmoil and tragedy of the previous years the Soviet Union had shown itself to be a loyal ally, and in any case the Russians were fellow Slavs. The population at large demonstrated their confidence in the Communists by awarding them almost 38 percent of the votes during the last free elections in 1946. The Communist Klement Gottwald was appointed leader of a coalition government. President Beneš defined the role of the new Czechoslovakia as a bridge between East and West.

The peace was deceptive: in February 1948 the Communists seized power by means of an arranged putsch with staged demonstrations and strikes. The move was non-violent but effective. The non-Communist ministers resigned from the government; Beneš also stepped down. Jan Masaryk, the son of the founder of the Czech state, had been Foreign Minister since 1945. On 10 March 1948 his body was found beneath the open window of the foreign ministry in Prague, and it was assumed he had killed himself in protest at the Stalinisation of his homeland.

Collapse of a utopia: During each year of its existence (from 9 May 1948 as a People's Democratic Republic, and from 1960 as the Socialist Republic), the inevitable failure of the utopian vision became increasingly evident. The country, once one of Central Europe's most prosperous bastions of tolerance, was transformed into a prison. The political climate was dominated by elaborate mock trials. All Western influence was designated as evil by the Communist ideologists. The Soviet Union was upheld as the

only logical model for development; Marxist-Leninist doctrines were glorified as the all-embracing ultimate philosophy.

The country became the victim of intransigent socialist policies. Whilst thousands of citizens, especially the intellectuals, fled from the country once more – leading to an acute shortage of qualified doctors, teachers and scientists – the government embarked upon the enforced collectivisation of agriculture and the development of heavy industry without any proper regard for mankind or the environment.

The economy was subject to long-term planning policies, known as the Five-Year

Plans, and was under the direct guidance of the Central Committee. External trade became increasingly dependent upon the Soviet Union. In 1949 Czechoslovakia became a member of the Council for Mutual Economic Aid (COMECON); in 1955 it joined the Warsaw Pact.

Even after Stalin's death and the XX Communist Party Conference in 1956, the situation within Czechoslovakia remained unchanged. The reign of terror inflicted by the leaders in Hradčany Castle was surpassed

only on occasion by that of the rulers of the German Democratic Republic.

The Prague Spring: From the early 1960s it was public knowledge that the system was bankrupt; even within the Party, voices of criticism could be heard, supported by writers, film makers and journalists, who ventured out of hiding despite threats of banishment and their repeated arrest. The IV Congress of the Czechoslovakian Writers' Un-

Left, falling into line at the Spartacus Games. Above, Alexander Dubček (died 1992), pioneer of the Prague Spring and back on the scene in 1990 as President of the Parliament.

ion in June 1967 marked a milestone along the road to the Prague Spring of 1968; for the first time a number of young writers dared to speak out openly in vehement protest. The lecture given by the dramatist Václav Havel, who was only 31 at the time, was greeted with wild enthusiasm.

In January 1968 the reform movement asserted itself. Alexander Dubček became the Party leader and announced the new era of "socialism with a human face", respect for civic rights, protection for minorities and the urgently needed settlement of the Slovak problem. Oldřich Černík, a qualified economist, began a comprehensive reform of the economy. The Prague Spring was seen by millions of Czechs as well as by citizens of other countries within Eastern and Western Europe as the last chance to put into political practice the true ideals of socialism.

The leaders of the Soviet Union and their puppets in Eastern Europe were alarmed; they feared the collapse of the Soviet national system and the loss of their own power. Brezhnev developed the concept that the Soviet path was the only path to real socialism. The Brezhnev Doctrine justified the invasion of Czechoslovakia by Warsaw Pact troops on 20 August 1968. The citizens struggled desperately; photos of old women and young students attempting to hold back the tanks with banners and slogans on Wenceslas Square were wired around the world. All to no avail – the hopes of an entire generation were crushed. Dubček was forced to retract his reform doctrines in Moscow; he returned to Prague a broken man and was replaced by the political hard-liner Gustav Husák.

The agony of Czech society was to continue for two more decades. In spite of the widespread resignation, many refused to give up; however, they now no longer demanded a reform of socialism, but rather a complete and unconditional democratisation of their country. With no organised support from the people, Czech civic rights campaigners such as Jiří Hájek, Jan Potočka and Václav Havel formed in 1977 the "Charter 77", demonstrating that even under a system which denied basic human rights it was still possible to hold up one's head.

The year 1989 is without doubt one of the historic milestones of the 20th century, since within an incredibly short space of time a system which embraced the whole of Eastern Europe collapsed like a pack of cards. The conscious refusal of the Soviet government under Mikhail Gorbachev to use force to interfere in events permitted the countries of the Warsaw Pact to take their fate into their own hands again. Poland was the first to take advantage; in Hungary, too, the democratic process advanced at a rapid pace, and in East Germany the citizens rose in protest until the Berlin Wall – the most tangible symbol of the Iron Curtain – also fell.

The Communist leaders of Czechoslovakia saw the disintegration happen before their very eyes, but they observed the tempestuous changes with indifference, as if paralysed. The team was the same one which had been carried to power by Brezhnev's tanks. A peaceful demonstration began on 15 January 1989 on Wenceslas Square in memory of the self-immolation of the student Jan Palach in 1969. Police and army troops brutally separated the crowd. They returned at double and triple strength, and the demonstration continued until 19 January. Blows and arrests no longer frightened the citizens.

In June a petition entitled "A Few Sentences" was put into circulation, and thousands clamoured to add their names. Even now, however, the Communists were not prepared to enter into discussions with the opposition, but preferred to maintain their approach in an attitude of unreal invincibility. The rejection of the last offer of talks was, it transpired, the final and crucial mistake of the ruling committee.

The peaceful student demonstration on 17 November 1989, in memory of the student Jan Opletal, who had been shot by the Nazis 50 years previously, triggered the course of events. Some 50,000 people took part; it was the largest mass demonstration since 1969. Although the protest march through Prague took place without incident, the police tried to prevent it by parking lorries across the route and by driving cars in a threatening manner. The hated Red Beret units attacked the demonstrators with batons. After this first example of brutality against the younger generation, events got out of hand more rapidly than in any other Eastern European country. The Opposition took matters seriously. Two days later it founded the Civic Forum Movement (Občanské fórum – OF), demanding the resignation of all members of the inner circle of the Central Committee of the Communist Party who had been involved in the intervention of 1968, and calling simultaneously for the immediate release of all political prisoners as well as a general strike. One day later the movement Public against Violence (Verejnost proti násilu – VPN) was founded in Bratislava.

Non-aggression wins through: In spite of much provocation, the democratic opposition honoured this rule of non-aggression. The resistance demonstrated during those November days in 1989 went down in history as the "velvet" revolution. For a whole week – 20–27 November – hundreds of thousands of citizens demonstrated on Wenceslas Square, demanding the resignation of the government. The Secretary General of the Central Committee, Milos Jakeš, was forced to resign on 24 November. Nonetheless a general strike throughout the country began on 27 November. Students were followed by actors, writers, artists and musicians.

On 29 November the general assembly of both chambers of the Federal Parliament passed a series of radical changes to the constitution. The lifting of the dictate of a party – which had originally been officially passed by the highest legal authority – was greeted with delight within the country and with respect abroad. It was a decisive moment for the continued progress of the peaceful revolution, for it paved the way for the necessary dialogue which was subsequently to develop over the following days and weeks in a climate of free speech and growing openness.

On 10 December the Prime Minister Marián Calfa, a Slovakian Communist, formed a new "Government of National Understand-

Left, many revolutionary changes in the history of the country started out from Wenceslas Square.

ing". Gustav Husák resigned from his post as President and on 28 December the Federal Assembly elected Alexander Dubček as his successor. It was an office he had already filled during the Prague Spring, and for which he possessed not only the necessary moral authority but also the best qualifications as a representative of Slovakia, in accordance with the conditions of the federal constitution.

On 29 December the parliament met in an historic session in Hradčany Castle. After 41 years of Communist rule, Václav Havel, until then a persecuted playwright and dissident, was elected by a predominantly Communist parliament as the new representative of a democratically reformed Czechoslova-

kia. In June 1990 he led Czechoslovakia into the first truly free elections since 1946.

The Civic Forum and the movement Public Against Violence in Slovakia received the endorsement of most of the electorate. But its leaders gradually drifted apart as the common enemy disappeared. The differences of opinion surfaced during debates on lustration, the "outing" of those who had held high office in the Communist Party or who had any connection with the secret police. It was meant not only to be an atonement by a handful for the rest of society, but also a practical measure to bar tainted officials from public office for five years.

Goodbye Czechoslovakia: The key question was how to achieve the economic reforms that would lead to a free market. Throughout 1990 and early 1991, the great hope was foreign investment. When this failed to materialise on the scale required, an ambitious coupon scheme was introduced, giving every adult the chance to buy shares in the state firms being privatised.

The enormous success of the scheme boosted support for Václav Klaus, the country's Finance Minister and champion of the free market. After the election of June1992, this sharp-witted speaker became the most important political figure in Czechoslovakia, eclipsing even Havel. It was Klaus who set about engineering the split between the Czechs and the Slovaks, a situation which Havel had spent two years in office trying desperately to prevent.

When the economy began its shift away from socialist planning after the revolution, the Slovaks were on the receiving end, suffering disproportionately from the pain of transition to a market economy. The 1992 elections produced a clearer result than expected. Around 34 percent voted for Klaus's right-wing ODS (Civic Democratic Party) and Meciar's HZDS (Movement for Democratic Slovakia). The people had chosen two strong leaders with two different higher ideals, fast economic reform versus a sovereign Slovakia able to dictate a slower pace.

At the beginning of December 1992, parliament finally passed the law providing for the dissolution of the country. But there are many, both Czechs and Slovaks, who feel that in brokering the divorce so quickly, their respective leaders betrayed the very same democratic principles that the opposition movements had fought to establish barely three years earlier. Neither party had been elected on the mandate of dividing the country. The Slovak Prime Minister, Vladimir Meciar, is a Moscow-trained lawyer. The growth of his power is seen by many in Prague not as proof that democracy works but a threat to its very existence. By the same token, many who originally supported the Czech Republic's Václav Klaus now feel that his market-driven ambition risks leading the country up a blind alley.

<u>Left</u>, prisoners cast their vote in the first free elections of 1990. <u>Right</u>, their candidate.

VÁCLAV HAVEL

> **"I** shall be one of many, and no one will expect more of me or pay particular attention to me."
>
> –Václav Havel, Letters to Olga from Prison (1979)

How is it possible that a man who is a writer, a self-confessed non-political man who was persecuted and humiliated for decades by the Communist authorities, was unanimously elected as the president of Czechoslovakia by the national parliament in December 1989?

It happened in Prague: "Havel na Hrad!" – Havel for the Castle! – chanted the crowds. Posters and leaflets all supported Havel. The outcome had long been decided in accordance with the most ancient of democratic traditions by the time the parliament, still largely made up of Communist supporters, went to the vote. The Velvet Revolution elected an honest, modest man to lead the country. Overnight, Czechoslovakia became a state with a human face, one of the most popular tourist destinations. The transformation looked at the time like a modern fairy tale.

Václav Havel was born in Prague in 1936. His father was an architect, his mother the daughter of a famous Czech publicist. Havel's privileged background blocked his chances of profiting from further education. He wrote his first dramas and essays at the end of the 1950s; his plays were first performed in 1963. In 1968 he became involved in the Prague Spring, as the president of the "Club of Independent Writers".

As a result of a worldwide outcry at Havel's arrest for participation in a memorial service for Jan Palach, the student who set fire to himself in protest at the Soviet invasion, the Prague leadership was forced to release him in October 1989. But he was refused an exit visa to travel to Frankfurt where he was to receive the Peace Prize of the German Book Trade.

In November 1989, the Civic Forum was founded as an amalgamation of the old and new opposition. One of the spokesmen and subsequent speakers at the countless demonstrations was Václav Havel. On 29 December 1989 he was elected president of the new state. His New Year's address to the nation on 1 January 1990 included the following remarks:

"No doubt you will ask me what it will be like, the republic of which I dream. Well, it is a republic which is independent, free and democratic – a republic with a flourishing economy which is at the same time socially just. In short, it is a republic which serves its citizens and which can therefore hope that its citizens will be prepared to serve it too. Its policies are decided by citizens who are well educated and politically mature, for without them we shall not be able to solve any of our problems."

But the dream of being president of a united, prosperous Czechoslovakia did not last for long. Even before the elections of 1992, forces were at work engineering the division of the country. Days before the election, he gave a veiled warning against Meciar's style of politics. When elected, Meciar did not forgive him and his party did not

vote him back into office. When the Slovak parliament passed its own constitution in August, Havel resigned.

But that was not the end. Soon after his resignation, Havel indicated that he would like to make a comeback as President of the Czech Republic. While admitting that if elected he would never have such an influence as in 1989, he nonetheless continues to enjoy the love and admiration of his countrymen. Most Czechs see him as the one person of stature who can endow the new republic with that "human dimension" it so sorely needs. In January 1993, elections had not yet taken place, but most people were putting their money on a Havel victory. ∎

The final division of Czechoslovakia into two completely separate republics was completed in January 1993. The divorce proceedings went smoothly and, unlike elsewhere in Eastern Europe, it was a relatively amicable separation. While many feel that the marriage could and should have been made to work, neither the Czechs nor the Slovaks had even considered living together in one state until the end of World War I. They subsequently failed to develop a common national identity, despite common goals and common achievements.

From the very outset, Czechoslovakia suffered from the fact that it was an artificial political unit welded together from fragments of the disintegrated Habsburg Empire. The last attempt of Czechs and Slovaks at forming a common state had been with the Kingdom of Great Moravia more than 1,000 years ago. After its collapse, the Czech Lands and Slovakia essentially went their own separate ways, and their paths did not converge again until 1918. During all that time, the destiny of Slovakia was controlled by the Hungarians; even under the Habsburgs, Slovakia was counted as being part of Hungary. The industrial backbone of the Habsburg monarchy was formed by the twin Czech lands of Bohemia and Moravia; Slovakia was the poor neighbour.

The founding of the new nation in 1918 was a rushed affair; its leading lights – Masaryk, Beneš and General Štefánik – were all academics. Their political approach has been described, not unjustly, as the Professors' Revolution; something of this historic legacy no doubt played a role in the country's latest "velvet" revolution in 1989.

At the Writers' Congress in 1967, Milan Kundera asserted the responsibilities of the Czech intellectuals when he claimed that "Czech writers bear the burden of being for the entire nation" – a responsibility that Václav Havel accepted quite literally. Even the national revival during the 19th century was in the first instance a purely Czech, academic affair. The national tongue, Czech, had to be transformed from a despised rural dialect into a written language capable of doing justice to literary aspirations. Slovakia,

however, had been subjected to Hungarianisation for so long that by the beginning of the 18th century the Slovak language had altogether ceased to exist. It was only under the influence of the Czech national revival that the Slovaks rediscovered their language; the awareness of an independent written culture started some 50 years later than in Bohemia and Moravia.

The Czech historian František Palacký, the "Father of the Fatherland", began his lengthy account of the country's history in 1836. The first volumes appeared under the title *The History of Bohemia*, and were written in German. The Czech edition followed in 1848, by which time the title had become *The History of the Czech People in Bohemia and Moravia*. Palacký exerted a considerable influence over the development of the Czech people during the 19th century, but he did not pay any attention at all to the Slovaks. To date, a Slovak version of Palacký has yet to appear on the scene.

A further example of Slovakia playing second fiddle can be seen in the National Theatre. The theatre in Prague was constructed between 1868 and 1881 with funds raised by the Czech populace: it was even reopened less than two years after being destroyed by fire. By contrast, until 1920 only German and Hungarian ensembles appeared in the National Theatre in Bratislava.

Breaking up is hard to do: Disparities continued during and after the formation of Czechoslovakia. The Czechoslovak National Council was formed in 1916 by Czech and Slovak exiles in the US, but not until the Habsburg monarchy was collapsing did the Slovaks in America accept the ideas of Masaryk, and join in signing the so-called Pittsburgh Convention on 31 May 1918. In the future republic of Czechoslovakia, Czechs and Slovaks were to be accorded equal individual rights.

After 1918, the Czechs and the Prague government tried hard to build up the Slovak education system and to help the Slovaks build up their own intelligentsia. There were Czechs working in Slovak schools and colleges, in administration, in the judicial system and in other departments. Of course, this led to misunderstandings – the Slovaks felt patronised and later even oppressed by the Czechs. However, the Czechs also contributed to this misunderstanding. The Pittsburgh Convention stated that the Slovak people were to be an equal partner in the new republic, but this was soon forgotten in Prague, and many Czechs came to look upon Slovakia as their colony.

Discontent in Slovakia found its expression in the programme of the Slovak separatists, the Slovak Populist Party. In March 1939, when the rest of Czechoslovakia was

rights with the Czech Lands, and after 1969 the Slovak Socialist Republic had equal representation with its Czech counterpart in the Federal Assembly.

Spirit of free enterprise: It is easy to understand ordinary Czech and Slovak citizens who may feel rather bemused by all the dramatic changes that have taken place in their name. Despite the intrinsic differences between the two countries, many people, particularly Slovaks, fail to see any advantage to be gained from splitting up in a

occupied by Hitler, the Slovak separatists felt that their moment in history had come. Under Monsignor Tiso, they split off from the republic and, under Hitler's "protection", formed an "independent" fascist Slovak state, allied to Nazi Germany.

After the Communists came to power in February 1948, Slovakia was subjected to a strictly centralised, Czech-dominated government. The constitution promulgated in July 1960 theoretically gave Slovakia equal

Preceding pages: lovers in arms on the Charles Bridge. Above, Northern Bohemian miners at the coal face.

Europe that is supposed to be edging closer together. Many look back to the days of the First Republic, when Czechoslovakia possessed one of the most flourishing economies of Europe, with a well-qualified workforce, a solid foundation of medium-sized companies and a highly developed industrial production in a variety of fields. One need only think of the Bat'a (pronounced: Batya) shoe manufacturing company. During the long years of state control, the name remained for Czechs and Slovaks alike a living memory of the golden years of free enterprise. Even today the many young people who are embracing free enterprise look for inspiration towards the shining example set by Bat'a. Although in 1949 the company's home town was renamed Gottwaldov by the Communists, it is now once again known by its original name of Zlín.

Upholding traditions: Although the first empire founded within their borders was much older than, for example, the Holy Roman Empire of German Nations, the periods when Czechs and Slovaks lived under the rule of a king of their own are negligible compared with the many centuries of foreign domination. It was correspondingly difficult for the young republic to build up an awareness of its own historic traditions. The memories of the Hussite tradition had to be resuscitated during the 19th century. But this identification was only partly successful, for despite massive criticism of the Church of Rome, Catholicism has remained a determining factor, particularly in Slovakia.

The Socialist government became aware of a national vacuum and tried to fill it with patriotic traditions and folklore. National costumes suddenly reappeared in towns and rural areas where they had long since been forgotten. In his novel *The Joke,* Milan Kundera describes the ideological intentions behind this "Revival":

"Nobody had ever done more for folklore than the Communist government. It made vast sums of money available for the foundation of new ensembles. Violin and dulcimer were to be heard every day on the radio. Moravian and Slovakian folk songs flooded the colleges, May Day parades, youth rallies and open-air concerts. Not only did jazz disappear completely from our country; it came to be seen as a symbol of Western capitalism and decadence. The young people no longer danced the tango or the boogie-woogie at parties; instead, they grasped each other by the shoulder and circled the floor in a round dance. The Communist Party was at pains to create a new lifestyle. It took as its credo Stalin's definition of the New Art: Socialist doctrine in national form. Only

folklore was able to give this national form to our music, our dancing and our poetry."

The folkloric tradition was employed to serve the interests of Socialism. Folklore festivals mushroomed, open-air museums were opened and new life was breathed into many an ancient village tradition. Writers laboured under the collective duty of creating a folk literature. An endless succession of folk song competitions was announced. Much of what was written during this period was later condemned as kitsch, but some of it had a lasting value.

Many artists who were later critical of the regime found their first arena in the folklore movement. In the guise of a folk song or fairy tale they could give expression to many opinions which ran counter to the idealised Communist world. During the times when public lies were on every tongue, this critical strain within the folklore movement became one of the pillars of national identity. These artists have lost none of their popularity.

The cultivation of national customs survived even without Socialist subsidies. Eastern Moravia, with its big folklore festival in Stráznice, is one important centre in this respect; the region around Vychodna in Slovakia is another area where the traditional folk culture has been retained. In July Slovakian ensembles gather with their tradi-

Messing about on the water: Despite – or perhaps because of – the fact that they live so far from the sea, both Czechs and Slovaks have always had a special affiliation with water. Smetana's best-loved composition was dedicated to the River Vltava, and in summer the republic's rivers and lakes are abuzz with amateur sailors. The relatively unpolluted tributaries of the Vltava, Lužnice and Sázava rivers become the domain of canoeists and families in rubber dinghies, who coast along from landing stage to landing stage, gathering as dusk falls by the obligatory camp fire to toast *spekáček* (the traditional sausages).

Touring by boat is still one of the least expensive forms of holiday, particularly rec-

tional instruments – the bagpipes (*gajdy*), the native fiddle and the dulcimer, pipe (*píšťala*) and the powerful shepherd's shawm (*fujara*). The dance groups perform old dances such as the *Chorodový*, a communal dance for women, the *Kolo, Hajduch, Verbunk* and *Čardaš*, the polka and the *Odzemok*, the traditional shepherds' dance. A highlight of the festival is the Janošík songs, which relate the exploits of the eponymous robber and folk hero from the time of the Turkish invasions.

Left, a serenade from the tower of the Old Town Hall in Prague. **Above**, learning ballet.

ommended to those who prefer the countryside to visiting historical and architectural sites. More ambitious canoeists will find that since the opening up of former military areas (e.g. in the Bohemian Forest), a number of more challenging watercourses have become available.

Although the major watercourses swell beyond the national borders into mighty rivers, within the Czech and Slovak republics they retain more modest proportions. Over the years the inhabitants have devoted considerable energies to the art of keeping their water within the country for as long as possible. For this reason, artificial lakes account for a large proportion of the water surface area. They serve a variety of purposes: some are used for fish farming, whilst others are reservoirs designed for flood protection or power generation.

Most impressive are the carp lakes of Southern Bohemia; these were excavated during the Middle Ages by engineers whose fame spread far and wide throughout Europe. Further important carp lakes are found in the lowlands of the Labe (Elbe) and in Southern Moravia. In late autumn they are fished with heavy-duty nets to provide the carp for the national Christmas dish. As Christmas Day approaches you will often see long queues waiting in front of barrels of fish placed at

Another reservoir on the Vltava, the picturesque Slapy Reservoir to the south of Prague, has become a favourite recreation area for the residents. Moored along its banks are houseboats, sailing yachts and simple rowing boats for fishing. Any visitor who has witnessed the bustling activity here on a hot summer weekend will immediately realise why the city centre seems populated only by tourists.

By the water, in the water, on the water – Czechs and Slovaks alike are in their element. That may at least partially explain why the joint Slovakian-Hungarian section of the vast Danube canalisation scheme, the controversial Gabčíkovo-Nagymaros project, has

street corners. For many people, Christmas Eve would be unthinkable without a baked carp (smaženy kapr).

The construction of reservoirs and dams for industrial purposes began during the First Republic. After World War II, increased energy demands led to the building of many more. The most important are the Lipno Dam on the upper reaches of the Vltava, the Orava Reservoir and the dam below Orlík Castle. The latter, which once stood sentinel on a rock – hence the name ("Eagle's eyrie") – is now a moated castle. The foundations were reinforced with a thick layer of concrete against the waters.

met with far less opposition here than in Hungary or Austria.

Acid rain: The Czech national anthem waxes lyrical about the forests, which "tumble across the rocks". But despite the fact that one-third of the land is covered with woodland, any talk of the harmony between man and nature in this part of the world must be hedged with reservations. Acid rain, partly blown in from abroad and partly caused by the high sulphur levels in the brown coal reserves, has been responsible for appalling environmental damage, especially in Northern Bohemia. On many days of the year there is a smog warning in Teplice – once one of the most famous spas in Bohemia, where Goethe, Beethoven and Wagner took the waters. To the east of Chomutov the vast brown coal excavators have eradicated more than 100 villages. The historic town of Most, where coal mining began in 1613, was simply moved and re-built on another site: the venerable Deaconry church had to be moved half a mile.

Refuge in the forests: However, if you ap-proach from another direction, you may well gain very different first impressions. Enter-ing the Czech Republic via the Bohemian Forest or Slovakia via the High Tatra, you can wander through immaculate woodland which casts into doubt the accuracy of a UN study claiming that over 70 percent of the total forested regions of the Czech and Slovak republics are severely damaged. You will frequently encounter areas of untouched pri-meval forest – the best-known is the Boubín in the Bohemian Forest – in which time seems to have made little progress since the Middle Ages.

The nearer you are to the cities, the busier the forests seem. For city dwellers they pro-vide a refuge from the stresses of everyday life. The desire to seek solace in nature is not just a modern phenomenon. The straitjacket of Socialism and the steadily increasing hous-ing shortage have only increased a trend which started between the wars. In those days young anarchists disenchanted with conventional living formed groups and, equipped with little more than guitars and rucksacks, set off to pursue an alternative lifestyle in the countryside. Most of them came from the less prosperous walks of society; many of them were jobless. They built shacks in the forest which soon devel-oped into little colonies. They saw them-selves as the pioneers of a new, anti-bour-geois lifestyle, and their ideals, based on a return to nature and brotherly love, were popularised in songs, many of which are still sung today. They built up a sort of campfire romanticism which was the antithesis of the aggressive environment of the city.

Houses in the country: You will, however, find few traces of anarchy in the weekend colonies of today, for they have long since succumbed to the comforts of bourgeois

living. In the years immediately following World War II, the houses of the expelled Germans were appropriated; soon after that, the flight from the cities became a mass exodus, with the result that the government found itself obliged to intervene in the wild-cat development of the *chalupy* (farmhouses) and *chaty* (cottages) and to allocate specific areas for such settlements. The new owners erected prefabricated houses, so recent colo-nies tend to have a uniform appearance. Many areas have become so built up that planning policy for building weekend cot-tages has been severely restricted.

For many Czechs, their weekend *chata* forms the real centre of family life. Over the

years many families have transformed what was once their simple cottage into quite a comfortable dwelling, which they plan to retire to in due course. Mushrooms and black-berries grow in profusion in the nearby woods, meat and potatoes are brought from town, and beer is fetched in a tankard from the village tavern. Behind each house stands a large wooden barrel in which the owners collect the fruit to make their *slivovice* (Slivovitz), an eau-de-vie, which is drunk during the cold days of winter. The produce of such private stills is strictly illegal – but what would life be like without a little bit of anarchy here and there?

Left, a Slovakian knees-up. Above, a souvenir from the past: punks show of their Socialist Youth Organisation passes.

Following the collapse of the Habsburg Empire in 1918, the Treaty of Versailles allotted generous territories to the newly formed state of Czechoslovakia. It seemed as if the Czech and Slovak patriots' dream of independent nationhood had finally been fulfilled. But the very existence of the multinational state was threatened from the outset by the tensions between the politically dominant Czech majority and the sizeable ethnic minority groups. Out of a total population of 13.6 million, barely half were actually Czech; in addition there were over 2 million Slovaks, 750,000 Hungarians living in Slovakia, some 100,000 Poles in the region bordering on Silesia and 500,000 Ukrainians and Carpatho-Ukrainians. The largest minority group comprised 3.2 million Germans living in Western and Northern Bohemia, Southern Moravia and the Carpathian mountains. To complicate matters still further, the racial melting pot was enriched by the presence of more than 100,000 Jews who had been living in the region for centuries.

The Czechs took advantage of their numerical superiority, whilst the minority groups, especially the so-called "Sudeten Germans", made increasingly aggressive demands, which resulted in the collapse of the First Republic and the subsequent German invasion. Later, under the Communists, the red flag of international brotherhood fluttering in the breeze served only to distract attention from the conflicts. In the 1990s both the Czech and Slovak republics are facing yet another crisis riddled with ethnic tensions and deep-rooted prejudice.

The Germans: Germans began settling in the region as long ago as the Middle Ages. The town of Olomouc (Olmütz), for example, grew up on the site of a colony of German merchants; in 1253 it was awarded a German municipal charter by King Otakar II. České Budějovice (Budweis) became world famous as a result of the beer (*Budvar*) produced by the Municipal Brewery founded

in 1794. The chequerboard layout of the Old Town displays the typical characteristics of a German town of the time. Bruntál (Freudenthal) was founded by settlers from Bavaria and Franconia; they came as farmers, summoned by the kings of Bohemia to improve the fertility of the barren soil. The free cities of Engelsberg, Herlitz and Würbenthal developed from German mining communities.

Traditionally, the Bavarian–Bohemian border region was an area of cultural interac-

tion rather than division. For example, the Bavarian-born master builders, the Dientzenhofer brothers, were apprenticed in Bohemia. During the 17th century, important South German baroque buildings were designed along the lines of the Jesuit church of St Ignatius in Prague. Today, many Czechs work in Franconia, and German shops have engaged Czech-speaking staff to cope with the influx of customers from the other side of the border.

But when it comes to a darker period in 20th-century history the Sudeten Germans are notoriously reluctant to enter into discussion. Instead, they prefer to idealise the "good

Left, German costume from Vyškov (Wischau) in Moravia. **Above**, S. J. Rapport, the Prague Chief Rabbi and scholar, around 1840 (Antonín Machek).

old days" and are happiest when they can present themselves as a cheerful community who enjoy their brass bands, singing and dancing. It is therefore essential to consider the events which preceded their exile. During the 1930s the Sudeten Germans fixed their hopes firmly upon the German Reich; they spread the message of the "Breakthrough to Nationhood" and saw National Socialism as their salvation, for the Czechoslovak government had denied them any right of self-determination.

Following the Munich Agreement of September 1938, Czechoslovakia lost a considerable proportion of its industry and defensive power. Only six months later, Prague

their houses with only a minimum of personal possessions. According to reliable sources, over 200,000 died as a result of massacre, hunger, exhaustion or suicide.

Early in 1990, President Václav Havel of Czechoslovakia issued an official apology for his country's expulsion of the Germans. The Speaker of the Sudeten German Welfare and Cultural Association, Franz Neubauer, accepted the olive branch, although his stand was not shared by all Sudeten Germans. Now, at both national and regional level, cooperation is making rapid progress. Within the three-country triangle where the frontiers of Poland, the Czech Republic and Germany meet, the three towns of Jelenia

was occupied by the German army. Within the German Protectorate of Bohemia and Moravia, the former status of the ethnic groups was reversed. In line with the doctrines of the National Socialists, the Czech working class was to be Germanised, whilst the intelligentsia was to be repressed. From 1939 until the end of the war, all Czech universities, places of higher education and teacher training colleges were closed; as early as March 1939, over 5,000 individuals suspected of opposition were arrested.

The expulsion of 3 million Sudeten Germans began in 1945, shortly after the war ended. Overnight they were driven from

Gora on the northern Polish side of the Krkonoše, Liberec (Reichenberg) in Northern Bohemia, and Zittau, in Upper Lusatia in Germany have formed a close bond. They have signed twinning agreements and organised an international conference on the "Three-Country European Project". The will to cooperate is in evidence on a human, practical and political level.

The Hungarians: At the other side of former Czechoslovakia, there appears to be rather less harmony. The 600,000 strong Hungarian minority in Slovakia, which makes up 11 percent of the new state's population, is fearful that the rights of non-Slovaks will be overlooked in the wake of the resurgence of Slovak national conciousness. Now that the Czechs can no longer be blamed for Slovakia's ills, some feel the Hungarians will be the next scapegoats. For their part, Slovaks are afraid of demands for autonomy by ethnic Hungarians: a Hungarian enclave in the south of the country would be humiliating, particularly if it voted to join Hungary. Tensions have been heightened by the argument over the completion of the controversial Gabčíkovo dam project by the Slovaks, resulting in the displacement of ethnic Hungarians living along the effected stretch of the Danube.

The Gypsies: But at least the Hungarians, as well as the ethnic Ukrainians and Poles, can

Bohemian towns of Teplice and Most, and even in the Prague suburb of Zizkov, the *cikani*, as they are derogatorily referred to, are daily confronted with hate.

After the creation of the First Republic, President Masaryk encouraged many Gypsies to move from Eastern Slovakia and settle in the industrial centres that were emerging at that time. Following the expulsion of the Sudeten Germans in 1945, a similar migration of Gypsies occurred into that area, where labour was in great demand. Large communities of Gypsies still live there today. Life is hard; many have no work and are forced to live in extremely basic conditions. Both Czechs and Slovaks claim that in areas

rely on the support of their respective mother countries. Not so the Gypsies. They are a people without a state; for better or for worse their fortunes are totally dependent on the prevailing attitudes in the country in which they live. Since the revolution in 1989, life has become less tolerable for the approximate 1 million Gypsies living within the boundaries of former Czechoslovakia. In their settlement areas in Eastern Slovakia, as well as in Ostrava in Moravia, the Northern

Left, Salzmanns Beer Hall in Liberec (Reichenberg) before World War II. **Above**, a Gypsy family having a picnic.

inhabited by Gypsies the crime rate is much higher than in the rest of the country. The authorities are attempting to counter this racial discrimination, although there is little evidence that any practical measures are being taken. Only a handful of social workers have been assigned to look after the fate of the thousands of Gypsies who have sought refuge in the city of Prague.

The Jews: A modest plaque in the little village of Bánovce in Slovakia was the cause of a minor uproar during the autumn of 1990. Two weeks after its unveiling Marian Čalfa, the local Prime Minister, had it removed because he was concerned about its effect on the reputation of Slovakia abroad. The plaque was in memory of the Slovakian Fascist Josef Tiso, who in 1939 declared the independence of Slovakia as a "Protectorate" of the German Reich. Tiso had been involved in the extermination of the Jews, and by the autumn of 1942 had sent 58,000 Slovakian Jews to certain death. Of an original total of 135,000 Jews living in Slovakia, only one-third survived.

The removal of the memorial plaque in Bánovce nad Bravou was not the end of the story, however. Nationalistic attitudes to life and anti-Semitism are both deep-seated. During March 1991, 7,000 supporters of Tiso demonstrated for an independent Slovakia. Not only did they voice their demands for independence; in the presence of President Havel and Slovakian leaders, a crowd of thousands also chanted "We want no Jews!"

Gangs of nationalist skinheads continue to stalk the streets of cities like Bratislava, waving the Slovak flag and chanting their anti-Semitic and pro-Tiso slogans. For the few Jews, such actions revive fearful memories, for, apart from brief periods of harmony, they can look back on over 1,000 years of persecution. They have been forced repeatedly to be on the defensive against both rulers and mob. In 1096, Crusaders en route for the Holy Land massacred large numbers of Jews living in Prague and plundered their property. During the 11th century they were deprived of their civil rights and forced to earn their living as money-lenders. This represented a loss of social status for all of them, although for some it meant an improvement in their economic position. The city's oldest synagogue was burned down on the first occasion in 1142, and the Jews were permitted to make their homes only on the right bank of the Vltava.

Things eased under King Otakar II, who used his royal privileges to encourage Jews from Germany to settle in Prague. Nonetheless the position remained unstable for many centuries. Depending on the policies of the various kings – or, more precisely, upon their financial position – the Jews were the victims of stick-and-carrot tactics. In 1648 they were praised for their distinguished service in the defence of the country against Sweden; a few years later, under Maria Theresa, they were exiled from Prague and subjected to unfair taxes. Emperor Joseph II, on the other hand, needed money and passed a decree of religious tolerance, allowing the Jews to build secular schools and requiring them to do military service.

Equality before the law was not achieved until after 1848. This finally led to closer links on a cultural level, and to the widespread adoption by Jews of the German language, traditions and way of life. Until the mid-20th century Jews formed the heart of the capital's liberal élite: writers, musicians and those connected with the theatre. A unique spirit of peaceful assimilation between the two cultures finally evolved.

Annihilation: When the German army invaded in March 1939, 56,000 Jews were living in the city. The "butcher" Adolf Eichmann took over the direction of the "Central Office for Jewish Emigration". By the end of 1939, a total of 19,000 Jews had succeeded in escaping to Palestine, but the rest were transported to the concentration camp at Terezín (see page 51), and from there sent to the extermination camps.

The German authorities created a so-called "Trustee's Office", which collected the property of Jews in 54 warehouses and then sold it. At the suggestion of Jewish historians, valuable items were retained for a proposed "Museum of the Former Jewish Race". It was the most extensive collection of Jewish items in the world; the historians, who were entrusted with the work of catalogueing the items, were executed before the end of the war and the collection was dispersed, in order to erase all traces of the undertaking. Thus much of the history of the cultural achievements of the Jews, their central contribution to the blossoming of civilisation in Bohemia and Moravia and in Slovakia, was lost. The plaque in the Pinkas Synagogue in Prague records the murder of 77,812 Jews within the space of half a decade.

During the short interval before the Communists assumed power in 1948, the Jewish population increased rapidly. In Prague alone there were 11,000 Jews. But during the two decades which followed, half of them emigrated; anti-Semitism, actively encouraged by the authorities, continued. Now it is to be hoped that the Jews can resume their role in society without fear of discrimination.

Right, in the cities, Gypsies find it hard to procure accommodation and employment.

The fact that Czechoslovakia is no longer a single state will undoubtedly have an effect on the tourism trends in this part of central Europe. While the majority of visitors will continue to go to Prague and perhaps take the time to admire some of the magnificent castles and palaces within easy reach of the city, the fact that Slovakia has become a tourist destination in its own right will also make its capital, Bratislava, an increasingly popular centre. But whether travelling to the Czech Republic or Slovakia, the visitor should not forget that the countryside also has its appeal. The country folk themselves have remained friendly and hospitable, despite the vicissitudes of history.

Up until 1950, rural life was based on the traditional pattern, whereby local affairs were run by three people: the chairman of the parish council, the parish priest and the headteacher of the local school. The Communists soon put an end to all that. Small communities came under the control of a central village. The bulk of investment was concentrated here, leaving the established structures of the outlying communities to decay. The top posts in the local authorities were no longer occupied by respected local citizens, but by unknown officials with good Party connections.

Only in a few regions were the priests able to maintain their influence on the population at large; notably in Slovakia and Southern Moravia. Religious education was, in any case, banned everywhere. Evidence of the declining influence of the Church in rural areas can be found in the depressing state of repair of so many of the country's magnificent religious buildings. One seldom sees young people in the congregation.

The influence of the village teacher has also disappeared. Under the Communists school timetables were completely changed and acquired a new bias towards the technical professions. Hundreds of small schools were closed, with the result that many children in rural areas have a long journey each day to the central community school in the larger villages or towns.

Paradise lost: Under the Communists, Czechoslovak agriculture was amongst the most advanced in Eastern Europe, with better than average yields. But the environmental costs of this achievement have been immense. Forty years ago the countryside of Czechoslovakia resembled a multi-coloured patchwork quilt. Narrow strips of tilled land were sown with golden corn, potatoes, hops,

flax or yellow flowering mustard. There were grassy hedgerows and meadows of wild flowers. Today, little remains of this agricultural pattern; valleys and hills are characterised by a dreary monoculture. In the First Republic the estates owned by the aristocracy and big landowners were redistributed in accordance with the new land reforms; the Communists, however, combined existing parcels of land to form large fields, ploughing up the hedgerows as they went along.

Unlike in Poland, virtually all agriculture in Czechoslovakia was collectivised. One-third of the available land was farmed by national collectives; the rest was handed

Preceding pages: a Wallachian village in the Moravian-Silesian Beskids. **Left**, prize specimens from Southern Slovakia. **Right**, Slovakian farmer making hay.

over to the agricultural production cooperatives. The Communists realised that it was essential to destroy all inherited ties with the land if they were to put an end to the dominant conservative ethic in rural areas. In accordance with Soviet practice, medium and large-sized farmers were designated as *kulaks* and evicted by force. The minority of small farmers who resisted this brutal expropriation were quickly made to see reason.

Although land is now supposed to be restored to the individuals from whom it was confiscated, most members of the various cooperatives show little interest in recovering their former farms. They receive a fixed wage and are able to supplement their in-

In search of rural idyll: Despite the gloomy state of agriculture, the rural regions, with their pretty villages linked by tree-lined avenues, still enchant travellers. The country scenes recall paintings by Old Masters: ducks waddle across the road, dogs stretch out contentedly on warm cobblestones and hens scratch around in the ditches. To find the unspoilt backwaters you need to turn off the main road and drive slowly – not least because of the bad roads with their numerous bends, potholes and puddles.

Unfortunately many of the facades of the once splendid houses have decayed and the addition of ugly new houses does sometimes spoil the idyll. Traditional country houses

comes handsomely by means of their smallholdings. In any case, they have good cause to fear the dissolution of the cooperatives: the soil, exhausted by 40 years of irresponsible farming, is no longer capable of yielding a satisfactory harvest. Environment-friendly farming is still in its infancy, and despite a concerted effort it will be many years before the land becomes fertile once again. There is also a shortage of appropriate technology; the antiquated but cumbersome farm machinery – heavy tractors and combine harvesters from the former Soviet Union and East Germany – are unsuitable for use on smaller farms.

are now built only in the foothills of the mountains, above all in Slovakia. In the less well-developed regions such as Southern Bohemia, famous for its baroque buildings, an individual style of rural architecture has developed. Paradoxically, the owners of weekend homes were the first to recognise the value of preserving the fine carpentry of many cottages and farmhouses; the villagers themselves have demolished many of the finest examples of domestic architecture, or ruined them with inappropriate extensions.

Travellers who want to discover the joys of country life, to explore myriad nooks and crannies, must be prepared to tolerate more than just bad roads. In former times every village boasted an array of restaurants and pubs; today there may well be only one – and that may be unable to serve a hot meal. One is lucky to be offered pork, cabbage and the typical Bohemian dumplings; in many cases the landlord can provide nothing more than sausages, cold meats or tinned goulash. Drinking is another matter, although this remains emphatically a masculine preserve. To this day, the presence of women within arm's length of the bar is frowned upon. There are surprisingly few small-scale family hotels and guest houses; the establishments which do exist mostly belong to the so-called consumer cooperatives. With the

costumes – cheered the Red Flag and the local bigwigs to the sound of dulcimer and brass bands. This cynical exploitation of local culture is the principal reason for the younger generation's rejection of their traditions. In some regions folklore is almost extinct, upheld only by semi-professional ensembles – not least because membership of these ensembles used to be one of the few ways of securing a trip to the West.

In the wine-growing areas of Moravia, in the Bohemian Forest, in the Tatra Mountains and along the Danube, an independent tradition has survived the deadly embrace of Socialism; and in some other regions a renaissance of old traditions is gaining impetus.

spread of privatisation it is hoped that the level of service will improve.

Villages and culture: The folklore of Bohemia, Moravia and Slovakia is equally fascinating, though, alas, not as prevalent as it used to be. From the 1950s folklore, "the people's culture", was unscrupulously used by the Socialist State (*see page 62*) as a bulwark against the decadence of Western society. During the annual May Day processions, the villagers – dressed in traditional

Left, a farmer's wife sells fruit and vegetables. **Above**, a pleasant Sunday stroll at the foot of the High Tatra.

Here and there you will see the masques traditionally worn by villagers as they celebrate with due ceremony the arrival of spring or the beginning of the grape harvest.

One of the populist solutions of the Communists was to turn many villages into towns. Many a village thus acquired an ostentatious "House of Culture". During winter these became the venue for balls, dances and cultural evenings in which "famous musicians from Prague" occasionally performed. It is hardly surprising that today district finance officers tear out their hair in despair at the high running costs of these sterile barracks; for some years now the rural population has tended to prefer an evening at home in front of the television to a dose of culture.

Family life: Just as was always the case, the kitchen incorporates the heart and soul of everyday life in the home. However, it has changed considerably in recent years. The old dressers have been replaced by a fitted kitchen and the porcelain-tiled stove has been abandoned in favour of a gas cooker; plastic is the material of choice when it comes to everyday utensils, and the most important item of equipment is a large deep-freezer. Every summer it is filled with fruit, poultry, rabbits and pork.

Only in the evening does the family migrate to the living room, where a three-piece

suite, built-in shelving, a few pictures and sometimes a crucifix or a portrait of the Virgin Mary dominate the scene. Pride of place is occupied by the embodiment of prosperity, a colour television set.

Once upon a time, several generations would live together in the farmhouse; today, this is the exception rather than the rule. Young couples invariably try to escape as quickly as possible from the strict control of their parents by building their own house or moving into the nearby town. Once the children have left the house a whole storey often stands completely empty; only when they and other relatives descend for holidays and

family celebrations will the former family home recover its old vitality, radiating warmth and comfort in spite of the characterless Socialist furnishings.

If you would like to see a house which is still furnished as it would have been in times gone by, you should best try to see the inside of a cottage whose owners are town-dwellers. They are the ones who cherish and repair the old porcelain-tiled stove, rescue hand-painted chests and cupboards, and spend good money on old cups, jugs, pots, butter churns and spinning wheels. Their yard is likely to be lovingly adorned with old cart-wheels and even hand-made replicas of pre-war ploughs. It's all a bit contrived – a weekend refuge from the stress of everyday urban life and an attempt to recover an idealised golden past.

Town and country: Many children who grew up in villages moved to the city as soon as they were independent. A few of them joined the professional classes, becoming teachers, doctors and engineers. The majority, however, ended up in factories. Even today, the town exerts a magnetic pull on many country-dwellers, though most like to maintain some contact with their rural roots. Country life has its advantages: relatives supply them with fresh eggs, meat, vegetables and fruit, and the money thus saved can be spent on furnishings for the flat, cars or holidays. In many cases the parental home is regarded as a comfortable weekend *chata*.

The town-dwellers have quickly adapted to urban conditions. Most of the young people who have migrated to the city argue that nothing ever happened at home in the country, and that the town has more to offer. In recent years, however, the trend has been reversed. Increasing numbers of people are discovering the attractions of living in countryside within commuting distance of a town. They cite the clear air, the forests, the peace and quiet and the close-knit community as their reasons for preferring the country. Of course, the reality of country life isn't always so perfect, but anyone visiting the rural Czech and Slovak Republics can be sure that the old adage still holds true: "Every guest brings blessings upon the house".

Above, the belfry in Hrousek. **Right**, throughout the Czech Republic, pork is commonly served with cabbage and dumplings.

It was not until after the bloodless revolution of November 1989 that the population of the then Czechoslovakia was confronted with black-and-white evidence of what many of them had suspected for a long time: that they were living in what was, ecologically speaking, one of the most severely threatened countries in Europe. The Danube canalisation scheme for the power station at Gabčíkovo in Southern Slovakia, which has caused a major international outcry, is but one of the environmental catastrophes bequeathed by the Communists. The decision

school. For many years the black smoke belching from the factory chimneys was seen as a symbol of progress. If past trends continue, it is estimated that by the year 2000, air pollution will have destroyed or seriously damaged 70 percent of the forests in the Czech republic and 40 percent of those in Slovakia.

The main cause of air pollution lies in heat and power generation, which are heavily dependent upon fossil fuels and the associated release of oxides of sulphur, carbon and

queathed by the Communists. The decision of the Slovaks to see the project through to completion demonstrates just how difficult it is to halt the trends of the past.

It could be pointed out that rivers have been harnessed in this part of the world ever since the Middle Ages. But such arguments cannot be used to justify the biggest environmental problem faced by the Czech and Slovak republics, namely air pollution. "The chimneys are smoking and a band of children is playing on a heap of sand. Life blossoms forth in a thousand things and grows in our hearts…" Thus ran one of the songs which Czechoslovakian children used to learn at

nitrogen as well as heavy metals. A particularly threatened area is northwest Bohemia, where pollution levels exceed all safety limits. Environmental experts describe the situation here as catastrophic. The region is the country's brown coal (lignite) mining centre; almost 70 percent of the total Czech production of this natural resource comes from local opencast seams. Most of the coal, which has a high sulphur content, is burned in the thermal power stations in the area. One-third of the total electricity generated in the Czech and Slovak republics comes from here. The industry has turned the district surrounding the town of Most into a barren lunar landscape and rehabilitation of the fields will take many years. The power stations lack adequate filters for the removal of excess sulphur, which means that local inhabitants constantly breathe in foul-smelling, poisonous fumes.

The sulphur emissions are also responsible for destroying forests on the mountain slopes of the Ore Mountains and the Krkonoše (Giant Mountains). Experts have estimated that the average life expectancy in the region is five years less than that of other areas within the Czech and Slovak republics. In some particularly endangered towns in northern Bohemia the authorities have distributed gas masks to children in the hope that at least some of the pollutants will be filtered out.

Northern Moravia occupies second place in the league of provinces severely at risk. Worst hit are the areas around Ostrava and Karviná. The Ostrava region is predominantly a manufacturing area, with heavy industry and hard coal mining. The worst air pollution comes from the iron foundries and the coke furnaces.

The third most polluted region in the Czech Republic is Prague. The concentration of industrial plant and exhaust fumes from the many antiquated vehicles has resulted in a pall of smog that hangs above the rooftops. Catalytic converters will be compulsory on newly registered cars in 1993, but in the opinion of many environmentalists this is not enough. Another serious problem is the pollution of the lakes and waterways. It is no coincidence that the River Labe (Elbe) is the dirtiest river in Europe. The towns and villages along its course are the main cause, for many do not process their effluent.

Similar problems are faced by the Slovaks. The drive to transform what was traditionally an agricultural and deeply Catholic land into a modern industrial Socialist state has also left its poisoned legacy. From the iron-ore works of Košice to the arms factories of Dubnica and Martin, the pall of pollution hangs in the air. As Slovakia confronts the reality of independence and the leadership

struggles to maintain employment, there seems little chance that such carbuncles will soon disappear from the landscape.

While the modernisation of industrial complexes will depend on the ultimate success of economic reforms, there is no way that the republics will be able to meet the cost of the big clean-up on their own. The European Community will finance some environmental rescue programmes, and the United States and Switzerland have also promised assistance. A number of loans from the World

Bank and Scandinavian banks have been allocated for projects of this nature.

It is also hoped that money generated by the newly booming tourist industry will also help finance environmental projects. With around 50 million visitors to both republics in 1992 alone, tourism has become a major resource. And it would be misleading to give visitors the impression that the region is permanently veiled in smog and its countryside is crossed by polluted, dying rivers. This is far from the case; there remain vast areas of countryside, including broad expanses of virgin forests and pristine mountains, where nature can still be enjoyed.

Left, a tarnished idyll. **Above**, lignite mining near Most.

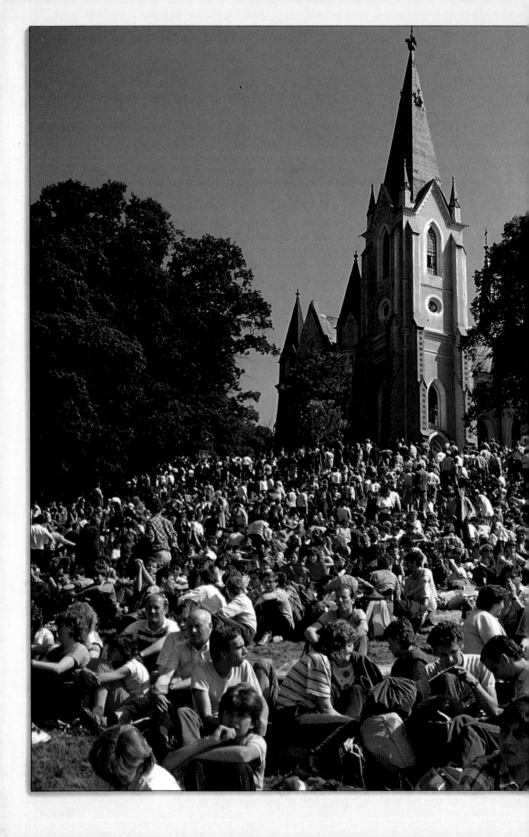

THE RELIGIOUS SPECTRUM

Pravda vítězí! – "Truth prevails!" In 1918, at the request of Czechoslovakia's founder President, Tomaš Masaryk, this old Hussite motto was incorporated into the emblem of the new republic. During the Prague Spring of 1968, it was written in bold on the banners hanging from the windows, demanding the end of Stalinism. The former president of Czechoslovakia, Václav Havel, had the same words emblazoned on his standard, and while in prison had even written a piece entitled: "Try to live in truth". Now that the dreams of Masaryk and Havel are over, the search for the truth goes on.

575 years after Jan Hus was burned at the stake as a heretic in Constance, the head of the Catholic Church visited the native country of the Bohemian religious reformer. On 21 April 1990 in Prague, Pope John Paul II celebrated Mass before a congregation of more than half a million. The Pope, however, only agreed in principle to a rehabilitation by the Church of the Czech national patron. Although he praised his "spotless life" and his "endeavours for the education and moral improvement of the people", the Pope indicated in the same breath that it would be the task of experts to determine Hus's true importance in the history of the Church.

The Catholics: The Pope's journey through the newly democratic country was like a triumphal procession: in Velehrad, the place of pilgrimage in Moravia and the site of the grave of the Slavic apostle Methodius, he was rapturously received by 700,000 faithful followers. The church bells throughout the whole of Slovakia rang out when the papal jet landed at Bratislava airport.

As in the case of Poland, an appreciable proportion of the opposition to the Communist regime was to be found concentrated in the ranks of the Catholic Church and its elderly but imperturbable representative, the then Archbishop of Prague, Cardinal Tomášek. But the Catholic Church sees itself faced with as many problems now as it did in the former Socialist Republic. The consequences of policies towards religion

Left, Levoča (Leutschau) in the High Tatra is the destination of a Holy Virgin pilgrimage.

during the Socialist era are still much in evidence. The Socialist State dissolved religious orders (with a few exceptions), sentencing large numbers of clergy to imprisonment in a series of mock trials. Access to theological college was strictly controlled; national salaries for priests were restricted to the bare minimum. Since the Church of today is faced with a new range of important social tasks, the shortage of newly qualified young priests is especially problematic.

From 1977, an "underground Church" developed alongside the official religious bodies. Lying outside the sphere of influence of the State and maintaining close contact with the activists of the opposition Charter

Many of the monastery buildings are not only in a desolate state of repair, but also house public facilities such as libraries and archives. Only a part of the ancient Czech Premonstratensian monastery of Želiv, for example, could be handed back: converted into a prison during the 1950s, the main abbey now houses a psychiatric clinic.

At least until it became clear that Czechoslovakia was going to split into two separate countries, the Church was also confronted with the problems posed by the attitude of the Catholic clergy in Slovakia. While the Catholic bishops of Bohemia and Moravia – together with the Ecumenical Council of the Churches of Czechoslovakia – warned of the

77 group, it developed a range of spiritual and social welfare activities. Its members formed a congregation around a secretly ordained priest, it celebrated Mass during "mountain walks" and similar events, and illegal publications were distributed and theological courses organised. Today, the number of illegal priests is estimated at 260. The priests are considered to have been officially ordained, even though many of them are married. Their future position within the Church has not yet been resolved.

A further problem is the return of confiscated church property, which is proving more difficult to realise than originally expected.

impending disintegration of the state, the Slovakian Bishops' Conference considered that the Slovaks had a perfectly legitimate right to self-determination. In contrast to Bohemia and Moravia, the proportion of practising Catholics in Slovakia is very high. At the time of writing, it is difficult to say whether the divorce from Slovakia will have any profound effect on the Catholic Church in the Czech Republic.

The Hussites in history: Following the death of Jan Hus, revolution broke out in 1419 in Bohemia. The armies of Hussite zealots penetrated deep into the neighbouring countries, shattering the faith of the Christian Middle

Ages. Their theological negotiators attained a degree of religious recognition during the Council of Basle in 1433, in that they were granted the lay chalice – in other words, the right to receive the Eucharist under the forms of both bread and wine. They acquired their name Utraquists from the Latin *utraque*, meaning "each of two".

But the Hussites failed to gain any political advantages from their military superiority. The moderate Utraquists, who had maintained amicable relations with the Roman Catholic Church, ultimately joined forces with the Czech Catholics and defeated the radical Taborites at the Battle of Lipany in 1434. For almost a century their modified

The present-day Czech and Slovakian Hussite Church has only indirect links with the old Hussite tradition, in that it claims to have created the idea of an independent national church. It was formed in 1920 as the natural result of the movement seeking independence from Rome under Masaryk's inspiration. During the First Republic it claimed some 750,000 members. Under the Socialist regime it conformed largely to the orthodox party line and is consequently still seeking its own identity today.

On the occasion of his assuming office, The Hussites' new Patriarch, Vratislav Štěpánek, spoke of the "many sins" that had scarred the past and stated that the primary

form of Catholicism was to form the basis of an independent Bohemian church. Under the influence of the German Reformation, the majority of Utraquists subsequently allied themselves with the Protestants. Following the defeat of the Protestant forces in the Battle of the White Mountain in 1620, the Utraquists were outlawed in Bohemia and Catholicism became the only established State religion for almost 200 years.

Left, St Vitus is flanked by Charles IV and Wenceslas IV on the Bridge Tower in Prague. **Above**, Cardinal Tomášek on his way to mass in St Vitus' Cathedral, 1989.

task for the future was the search for common ground with the Catholic Church. The most important theological elements of the Hussite church remain the Eucharist in both forms, the Apostolic Succession, as well as the right of a priest to marry and the ordination of women.

The Bohemian Brethren: The Unity of the Bohemian-Moravian Brethren (Unitas Fratrum) was founded in 1457 by Waldensians and a handful of Taborites. They aspired to a religious community based on the stories of the apostles; its pacifist and escapist tendencies originated from writings of Petz Chelčický (1380–1460). Until the expulsion of their last bishop, the educationalist Jan Amos Comenius (1592–1670) in 1628, the Unity was subject to repeated persecution by the Catholic authorities. Some respite was gained by the establishment of links with the German Reformation; Lutherans, Calvinists and Brethren agreed on a common doctrine, the "Bohemian Confession" of 1557. This formed the basis for the Letter of Majesty of 1609, in which Rudolf II granted freedom of religious practice to non-Catholic sects within Bohemian territory.

But after the Catholics' victory in 1620, dissidents were faced with a choice between emigration or conversion to the state religion and Reformed communities in Bohemia and Moravia were amalgamated to form the (unified) Evangelical Church of the Bohemian Brethren.

In Slovakia the two denominations have remained separate to this day. In general, members of the Lutheran church tend to be Slovakians whilst Reformists are mostly Hungarian. During the Communist era all attempts to forge links between Czech and Slovak Protestants were forbidden; today, however, the two communities emphasise their common historical links, particularly in the doctrines of Hus, Comenius and Luther.

Nowadays the "Evangelical Church of the Bohemian Brethren" is a popular church

gion. Many paid only lip service to Catholicism and secretly remained faithful to their old beliefs. At the beginning of the 18th century, a small number of Brethren moved to nearby Lusatia, where they founded a new community in Herrnhut and embarked upon missionary campaigns throughout the world.

Joseph II's Edict of Tolerance in 1781 granted both Lutherans and Calvinists certain freedoms within Habsburg territory. The Unitas Fratrum, however, remained excluded from the new conditions. Freedom of worship was not granted to all confessions until 1918, the year in which the Czechoslovak Republic was founded. In this year the Lutheran with a Presbyterian constitution. Men and women have equal rights and privileges. The highest authority within the Church is the General Synod. In the first democratic government after the fall of the Communist regime the Chief Elder of the synod of the time, Josef Hromádka, was appointed the first Minister of Religion as well as deputy Prime Minister of Czechoslovakia.

The Orthodox Church: For as long as anyone can remember a dispute has raged in eastern Slovakia concerning Church ownership. The protagonists are the Orthodox Church and the Greek Catholic Church (also known as the Uniate Church, since it was a product of the union with Rome in 1646). After World War II, the Orthodox and the Uniate Churches were forced to amalgamate here as in the Soviet Union and in Romania. Although it was considerably more extensive, in 1952 the entire property of the Uniate Church fell to the Orthodox community. In the aftermath of the Prague Spring the Greek Catholic doctrines were permitted once more, but it was not until 1990 that the Uniate Church was finally able to enjoy full reinstatement of its original privileges.

These historical developments have resulted in the Orthodox Church losing much of its original importance in Slovakia. The Church, whose doctrines are based on the

teachings of the Slavic apostles Cyril and Methodius, suffers in particular from its failure to build its own churches and colleges. Today they are faced with the loss not only of their bishoprics but also their seminaries. In country areas, services are not infrequently held in the open air because church buildings were appropriated by the Uniates.

Religion in everyday life: As already indicated, there is a marked religious watershed

Left, Tábor, the town of the Hussites, named after the New Testament mountain of Christ's Transfiguration (Julius Marak). **Above**, Broumov Monastery.

separating the East from the West. In the Czech Republic religious or Church-oriented social patterns are adopted by only a minority. In 1980, only 4 percent of couples in this region were married in church. Church baptisms represented only 13 percent and burials only 30 percent of the respective totals. In Eastern Slovakia, during the same period, 86 percent of all babies were baptised, 84 percent of all couples were married in church and 92 percent of those who died were buried according to the rites of the Church. Today only 10 percent of the population of Bohemia claims membership of the Catholic Church; in Moravia the figure is 35 percent and in Slovakia over 50 percent.

One can only speculate as to the role which the Church – or rather, the various churches – will play in future. Religious communities, like all other sections of society, must rearrange their priorities. It is one thing to overturn a system which has lost its credibility; it is another to develop a new, robust system which finds a consensus in society.

Mild atheism: Bearing in mind the wide media coverage of the Catholic Church during the first weeks following the Velvet Revolution, a number of voices were raised in warning against a new clericalism. As far as Bohemia is concerned, there seems to be no immediate danger of this. The citizens may well have a religious faith, but they are by no means zealots. You will find none of the arch-conservative Catholicism typical of Poland or even some areas of Slovakia. Bohemia is traditionally secular; perhaps it is here that the true legacy of the Hussites is found – in the sceptical approach to all doctrinal philosophies. On every street corner you will hear opinions such as "Anybody who supports a system as authoritarian as that of the Catholic Church cannot be a good democrat." One Prague theologian has recently spoken of a mood of "mild" atheism which has replaced the totalitarianism of the past years.

Demonstrating a deep understanding of popular feelings, Cardinal Vlk has been noticeably mild in his demands for the return of confiscated Church property, for example church buildings being used as schools. In a region which has always presented pastoral difficulties for its clergy, a mood of premature rejoicing on the part of the Church is the last thing required.

Smetana – Dvořák – Janáček: whenever any-one mentions Czech music, the names of the Big Three are uttered in a single breath. Smetana gave the world the most frequently performed Czech opera, *The Bartered Bride*, as well as celebrating the countryside and history of his native land in his programme music cycle *My Fatherland*. Dvořák, on the other hand, was a master of the symphony, chamber music and oratorio; his composi-tions were rapturously received at home and abroad. Janáček took up the aims of Smetana and Dvořák and developed his own theory of the "speech melody", according to which the melodic form followed the tone patterns of speech. Janáček elevated this stylisation of speech melodies to one of the fundamentals of composition in his operas.

Compared with that of its neighbours, music in the Czech Lands developed rela-tively late, although the beginnings of an independent musical tradition reach back to the Middle Ages. During the period of the Greater Moravian Kingdom, Mass was cel-ebrated in Slavic, not in Latin, and the Hussite Chorale influenced considerably the hymns of the German Reformation. During the ba-roque era the attempts at national assertion were nipped in the bud, and many musicians found themselves with no alternative but to emigrate. Among them was Johann Wenzel Stamitz, who composed at the court of the Elector Karl Theodor in Mannheim. He is regarded as one of the leading exponents of musical classicism, especially the sonata.

Vienna, a city long favoured by the muses, attracted numerous Czech composers. The virtuoso violinist and conductor Pavel Vranický settled here – he was chosen by Beethoven to conduct the premiere of his First Symphony – as did Jan Leopold Koželuh, who for many years enjoyed a popularity equal to that of Mozart, and Jan Václav Hugo Voříček, the leading repre-sentative of Czech classicism in Vienna.

Preceding pages: a brass band in Mariánské Lázně (Marienbad). Left, music school for children with impaired sight in Prague. Above, Mozart loved Prague; here is his bust in the Villa Betramka.

Georg Benda composed at the Prussian court; Josef Mysliveček made his home in music-loving Italy, where the Italians chris-tened him the "Divine Bohemian", and Jan Václav Stich and Antonín Rejcha settled in Paris. The works of Rejcha paved the way for Romanticism in music; he developed the programme symphony as a musical form.

Despite this exodus, musical life in Bohe-mia remained rich: on his journey through the country the English traveller Charles Burney christened it the "Conservatoire of

Europe". This wealth of musical talent was largely because of the striving of many mi-nor musicians, mostly church cantors, who found inspiration in the simple folk songs of their land as well as the virtuoso composi-tions of the Italian masters. The most impor-tant amongst them was Jan Jakub Ryba (un-fortunately relatively few of whose works have survived). Perennially popular is his pastorale *Hej mistře!* (The Bohemian Christ-mas), one of the most frequently performed compositions during the festive season.

National consciousness was aroused dur-ing the Romantic era. Johann Gottfried Herder spoke of the "gentle Slavs". In 1823 the first

Czech lyrical drama, the *Swiss Family* of Joseph Weigl, was performed, but over half a century was to pass before the premiere of Smetana's *The Brandenburgs in Bohemia*, the first national opera.

Bedřich Smetana (1824–84) is the favourite composer of the Czech nation, although the works of his somewhat younger contemporary Dvořák are more frequently performed in international concert halls.

The careers of the two men were strangely linked. When Dvořák first arrived in Prague, Smetana left the city to try his luck in Gothenburg for five years. By the time he returned, Dvořák had already completed his first compositions. And when Dvořák re-

turned to the Bohemian capital at the peak of his popularity after a triumphant visit to England, Smetana had just been committed to the city's mental asylum, where he died shortly afterwards.

One of Smetana's biggest preoccupations was the nature of an independent Czech Popular Opera. It was a matter which aroused the entire nation. Whilst the Czech old guard imagined such an institution as a pot-pourri of traditional melodies, the avant-garde Smetana demanded a fully developed dramatic style which would do musical justice to the newly discovered melodic patterns of the Czech language. He was accordingly

scorned by his opponents as a "Wagnerian" or a "Germaniser", almost the equivalent of being charged with high treason.

And yet, Smetana was also granted a few happy hours in his musical life. In 1868, as the representative of all Czech artists, he laid the foundation stone of the National Theatre and conducted that same evening the premiere of his dramatic opera *Dalibor*. Though initially well received, the new work was performed only a few times and was not rediscovered until after the composer's death.

After a catastrophic first performance in 1866, *The Bartered Bride* soon won the hearts of the Czech populace. The opera did not achieve its international breakthrough until after the composer's death, following a brilliant guest performance by the newly-formed Czech National Theatre in Vienna in 1892. Smetana himself had a far higher opinion of *Dalibor* than of his infinitely more successful comic opera. On the occasion of the 100th performance of *The Bartered Bride* in May 1882, he said: "Actually, gentlemen, *The Bartered Bride* is really only a piece of nonsense which I allowed myself at the time. I composed it not out of ambition but in a spirit of contrariness, because after my *Brandenburgs* they all accused me of being a Wagnerian incapable of composing anything in the lighter national idiom."

Antonín Dvorák (1841–1904), the butcher's apprentice and self-styled "simple Czech musician", earned his living initially by playing second viola in Smetana's orchestra in Prague. He revered the older composer; the latter in his turn tried to support Dvořák's work as a composer. All the more incomprehensible to outsiders, therefore, was the conflict between the supporters of Smetana and Dvořák, which reached its climax in 1912 and left traces which are still evident today. Writing about the premiere of Dvořák's opera *Rusalka*, the ardent Smetana fan Zdeněk Nejedlý said: "Since we allow no other form of lyrical drama than musical drama, we must judge *Rusalka* to be flawed in its very inception, a failure." Nejedly later became Minister of Culture and was largely responsible for the reaction against Dvořák's work in the 1950s.

Above, Antonín Dvořák composed the Symphony "From The New World". **Right**, Bedřich Smetana is considered the Czech national composer.

SMETANA'S MOLDAU

From the Smetana Promenade on the right bank of the Vltava (Moldau), Prague presents itself to the visitor from its most attractive angle: the graceful masonry of the Charles Bridge spans the gleaming silver ribbon of water in front of the picturesque panorama of the churches and palaces of the Lesser Quarter, above which tower the massive bulk of the Castle and the Cathedral of St Vitus.

Today the Smetana Museum is housed in what used to be the municipal waterworks, near the former mills of the Old Town, a building complex which extends into the river itself. It is maintained by the Smetana Society, founded in Prague in 1931, and contains the composer's manuscripts and sponsors the publication and performance of his works.

Smetana loved to walk along the banks of the Vltava. He repeatedly found new ideas and inspiration for his compositions. A friend of his, Josef Srb-Debrnov, remembers:

"Most of the enchantingly emotional melodies in *The Bartered Bride* owe their creation to the evening moods on the Moldau Promenade opposite Hradčany Castle and the Lesser Quarter. The maestro would take a walk by the river here at dusk virtually every day, reading as he did the text sent to him piece by piece by Sabina, his librettist. The melodies flowed through his brain like a torrent. Returning to his apartment in the Palais Lazansky, he would sit down at his desk and make rough notes on manuscript paper of the ideas he had already worked out in his mind."

By the time he started to compose a grandiose musical monument to his beloved Vltava, Smetana was no longer able to enjoy his nightly walks along its banks. A rapidly worsening affliction of the hearing tract prevented him from listening to the river's song. Impoverished and derided by resentful critics he was ultimately forced to seek refuge in the country, in the hunting lodge of his son-in-law.

When *The Moldau* was given its concert premiere on 4 April 1875, the audience was ecstatic, but the composer himself was unable to hear a single tone. He had become completely deaf whilst working on the score.

The Moldau is the best-known and most frequently performed movement of the orchestral cycle *My Country* (*Má Vlast*), in which Smetana's love of his Bohemian homeland and its people finds its most eloquent expression. The inspiration for the entire cycle, which Smetana wrote between 1874 and 1879, actually grew gradually over a period of many years. It is maintained that Smetana's first ideas on the subject started to crystalise some 20 years before the work was first performed.

The programme of the six cycles was sketched by Smetana himself: *Vyšehrad* tells of the heroic fights of the knights of old; in *The Moldau* the listener follows the river along its course from its source to the Vyšehrad Castle in Prague (the main theme is played by two oboes, symbolising the mountain springs, and repeated in rondo form in ever-changing variations before ending in a hymn-like E major passage). *Šárka* conjures up a

Bohemian myth with an Amazonian love story dominated by a stormy orchestral symphonic section; *From Bohemia's Meadows and Forests* is a succession of folkloric portraits, with peasants dancing the polka in the clearings and airs played on the horn recalling traditional melodies. *Tábor* recalls the tragic-heroic fate of the Hussites, whilst *Blaník* provides an optimistic final note to the entire cycle, echoing the hope that the warriors of the Lord will return victorious when the people's need is greatest.

Non-Czechs have difficulties with the patriotic symbolism of the two last cycles, but few resist the desire to succumb to the powerful emotions aroused by *The Moldau*. ■

Dvořák's success abroad was all the more controversial. He attracted musical fame beyond the boundaries of his native land, something Smetana was denied throughout his life. Dvořák's first triumph was in London, where his *Stabat Mater* was rapturously received, followed by New York, Berlin, Vienna and Budapest. He was helped in this by his older friend and patron Johannes Brahms, who not only invited Dvořák and his entire family to Vienna at his own expense, but also established his first contact with the Leipzig publisher Simrock and added a number of necessary corrections to the scores.

It was Dvořák's international reputation that brought him in 1891 the offer of directorship of the New York Conservatory. The three years which he spent in America resulted in his most popular orchestral score, *Symphony No. 9 From the New World*, the one most widely played on a worldwide basis. Its premiere in the Carnegie Hall in New York in 1893 was a runaway success. Dvořák wrote home: "The success of my symphony on 15 and 16 December was magnificent: the newspapers maintain that no other composer had ever enjoyed such a moment of triumph. I was in the box; the auditorium was filled with the cream of New York, and the people applauded with such gusto that I had to stand up to acknowledge their clapping like a king – just like Mascagni in Vienna (don't laugh!). You know I like to avoid ovations of this nature if I can, but I simply had to show myself on this occasion."

Critics emphasised the "American accent" of the themes. In this new work the Czech composer set an important trend for the development of an independent American national musical tradition. At the same time he helped the new music of his own country achieve world recognition.

Like Smetana, Dvořák rejected a direct transcription of folk melodies in his works. His adaptation of collections of folk songs always resulted in a completely new setting of the words. His cycle *Music from Moravia* (1875), which paved the way for the composer's international recognition, demonstrates a sensitivity bordering on genius in his interpretation of Moravian folklore. The piano accompaniment is simple but often contains surprisingly sophisticated harmonic progressions which provide a perfect translation of the poetry of the lyrics.

Unlike the city-dweller Smetana, who was only driven to the country by the poverty of old age, Dvořák was a country-dweller who never felt quite at home in the city. While working in New York he remained, like his peasant forebears, an early riser. He did not go out after 6pm and spent his evenings playing cards with the family. During an entire year he visited the Metropolitan Opera only twice. Dvořák was always happiest at Vysoká, his country estate.

Dvořák left for posterity an impressive collection of compositions: 31 works of chamber music, 14 string quartets, 50 orchestral works and nine symphonies, including such works as the *Slavonic Dances*, whose wealth of catchy melodies has caused them to be condemned as merely light music by some composers, rather like Smetana's *Vltava* (*The Moldau*).

The distinguished musical tradition of Czechoslovakia did not end with the dawn of the 20th century. Leoš Janáček (1854–1928) proved a worthy successor to Smetana and Dvořák. He composed, amongst other works, the world-famous operas *The Cunning Little Vixen*, *Katja Kabanová* and *From the House of the Dead*. Janáček was searching for new forms of expression, for a personal musical language. However, he did not want to compose music which was nothing more than that; he strove to link it to a message of common humanity, a proclamation of his humanistic ideals.

Bohuslav Martinů, who lived in the US from 1940, also has a place in the country's modern musical history. Artistically speaking Martinů was an all-round genius who understood Impressionism as well as jazz. He was one of the first composers to incorporate elements of the latter in his works. His compositions covered a remarkable range comparable only with that of Mozart: no fewer than 400 all told. More important than the number of works he wrote, however, was his unmistakable talent for mixing classical elements with avant-garde features to produce a completely new synthesis of sound. Of all his highly imaginative works, at least the ballet *Spaliček* and the opera *Juliette* are still performed regularly today.

Right, an open-air concert being performed on the Old Town Square (viewed from the tower of the Town Hall).

When anyone mentions Czech literature, most people tend to think in the first instance of *The Good Soldier Schweyk*, the eponymous hero of the world-famous novel by Jaroslav Hašek who is often thought to represent the Czech national character. Václav Havel is well-known as a politician, but how many people can say they have read his dramas and diaries?

World citizens from Bohemia: The origins of the literary tradition in the lands of the Bohemian crown stretch back as far as the 9th century. Seeing his kingdom of Great Moravia threatened by the Franks, and as a sort of cultural offensive against the growing influence from the West, Prince Ratislav summoned the Slavic apostles from Byzantium. The learned brothers Cyril and Methodius who arrived in 863 invented the Old Slavonic Glagolitic script, based on the Slavonic dialect used in the area surrounding their native town, Salonika. The first book to be written in Old Slavonic was thus probably the Bible. Other Old Slavonic texts that can be assigned to this era are the 10th-century *Legends* about St Wenceslas (the Bohemian prince Václav). The Old Slavonic language ceased to be used when Latin was introduced as the liturgical language of the country at the end of the 11th century.

The historic foundations of Czech literature lie in the *Bohemian Chronicles*, the work of the Deacon Cosmas (died 1125). The Latin chronicle recounts the history of the land from the legendary times of the founding father, Čech, until the beginning of the 12th century. In the courts of the Přemyslid kings, encouragement was given to the production of German literature, and the earliest preserved texts in the Czech language were only written in the latter part of the 13th century. During the reign of Charles IV in the 14th century, learning and literature flourished in both German and Czech.

In the 15th century, the social and moral questions addressed by the Hussite Movement gave rise to a great deal of writing in the

vernacular, in the form of treatises and hymns. Hus's own importance for Czech literature not only lay in his vernacular sermons and in his letters; he also set about the reform of Czech orthography, which he laid out in the treatise *De orthographia Bohemica*.

One of the outstanding personalities in Czech literary history was the humanist Jan Amos Komenský (1592–1670), generally known by his Latin name Comenius. He was a teacher, writer and theologian whose influence spread across many countries. The son of Protestant parents, he studied in Heidelberg and became a preacher in the Community of Bohemian Brethren in 1616. He endeavoured to improve the lot of man (in preparation for the Kingdom of Heaven) through his reform of the educational system. Piety, virtue and learning were the cornerstones of his philosophy. His most famous work, *Orbis Sensualium Pictus* ("The World in Pictures", 1654), was for many years the most widely used textbook in Germany. It consists of pictures illustrating Latin sentences.

The reforms of Emperor Joseph II, in particular the abolition of serfdom, prompted a period of national revival which marked the beginning of a new phase in Czech literature. The philologist and historian Josef Dobrovský, together with Josef Jungmann, produced philological works documenting the history of the language as well as a two-volume German-Czech dictionary. *May* (1836), the epic poem by the Romantic poet Karel Hynek Mácha, is regarded as one of the milestones in modern Czech poetry. Outstanding men of letters of this period, which reached its zenith in 1848, included the prose writer Božena Němcová, publicist and poet Karel Havlíček and dramatists Josef Kajetán Tyl and Václav Kliment Klicpera.

Tales of the Lesser Quarter: The transition from Romanticism to Realism was marked by Božena Němcová's novel *The Grandmother*, published in 1855. The Prague writer Jan Neruda (1834–91) is regarded as the founder of the Czech literary feuilleton. He achieved fame as the author of the *Tales of the Lesser Quarter* (1878), a collection of novellas and partly humorous, partly reflective sketches from the Malá Strana. *Pictures*

Left, Jan Amos Komenský (Comenius) (1592–1670) was one of the most important scholars of his time.

of Old Prague, a collection of short stories and imaginative pieces, transport the reader into late 19th-century Prague. The famous Chilean writer Pablo Neruda, the Nobel Laureate of 1971, also published his works under the pen-name "Neruda", in honour of Jan Neruda.

At the turn of the 20th century the classics of international literature dominated the literary scene. Numerous translations of works from world literature, not least from the German classics, helped to raise the general level of education to a higher level and simultaneously paved the way for the integration of Czech into the broader European literary context. In those days a knowledge of German was a *sine qua non* in Bohemia, so many readers were able to claim first-hand knowledge of the works in question.

World literature from Prague: The Bohemian capital, moreover, had traditionally enjoyed a special position in European culture. Apart from the resident Czechs and Germans, a significant Jewish community had evolved, which also made an important contribution to literary history.

It is possible that some natives of Prague, such as Max Brod (who preserved the work of Franz Kafka against his will), or Franz Werfel, are still underestimated today. Even during their lifetimes, however, Rainer Maria Rilke and Franz Kafka were recognised as great writers. Kafka (1883–1924) was almost an exact contemporary of the perennially popular humorist and satirist Jaroslav Hašek (1883–1923), whose main work, *The Good Soldier Schweyk*, is still the best-known book in the Czech language.

The "Golden City" on the Moldau was a centre of literary talent at many points in its history. At the beginning of this century, German and Czech enjoyed equal status as literary languages. A bohemian society in no way inferior to that of Paris established itself in the capital, gathering in coffeehouses such as the legendary *Café Arco*.

Franz Kafka, a Jew, was born on 3 July 1883 in Prague. He seldom left his native city and at the end of his short life was buried there, in the Straschnitz Cemetery. For 14 years Kafka worked as a legal clerk at the Workers' Accident Insurance Institution of the Kingdom of Bohemia, but he regarded his "scribblings" after hours as his "only desire". This prose has turned Prague into a

major landmark on the world literary map.

Although Kafka's diaries and letters fill over 3,000 pages, for many years little was known about his life. The reason lies in the political events between 1933 and 1945 and the subsequent Communist government of the country, which prevented Kafka's work from being made public. The first Czech translations of his writings did not appear until 1957. In 1931, the Gestapo confiscated a large number of Kafka's manuscripts and these must be regarded as lost. Later on, Kafka's three sisters were deported to concentration camps and murdered.

Most of the houses in which Kafka lived in Prague are still standing, including the Palais

Kinsky, in which Kafka's father ran a shop for fashion accessories. Kafka did not leave the centre of the Old Town in Prague until the last years of his life, when illness forced him to a sanatorium.

In contrast to Prague's other German-speaking writers, such as Rainer Maria Rilke and Franz Werfel, who moved in Jewish-German literary circles, Kafka actually sought contact with the Czech population and demonstrated openly his sympathy for the Socialist cause; in later years he supported the idea of a socially-oriented Zionism.

Kafka's work remains controversial and the interpretations of his message are legion.

In his posthumously published novels *The Trial* and *The Castle* he expresses the fears and alienation of 20th-century man by means of his dream-like visions. Of paramount importance in his imagination was a life-long struggle with the dominant figure of his father as well as the perpetual conflict inherent in his relationship with women, in particular Felice Bauer and Julie Wohryzek, both of whom were at one stage engaged to be married to him, as well as Milena Jesenská and Dora Dymant, with whom he spent the last year of his life in Berlin.

Erich Fried, a German Jew, commented on the themes that preoccupied the authors of Prague: "[The German-speaking authors of

Prague] often took as subject-matter the dark events of the time, bringing to life the split personalities. Whether they were Jews or not, they turned their attention to the Golem and other legends and to the teachings of Rabbi Loew, or they wrote about the mysterious cabinet of curiosities of Rudolf II. During the 1920s the Jews probably sensed the dreadful fate which would befall them in 1938, whilst the non-Jews had a premonition of what they would face in 1945. The non-

Left, Jan Neruda, the famous Prague storyteller of the 19th century. **Above**, Egon Erwin Kisch, who made history as a "roving reporter".

Jews and Jews who wrote in Czech, on the other hand, saw Prague only as the Golden City or the Matička ('Little Mother')." Franz Kafka was reputedly the author of the expression "The little mother has claws...!"

The foundation of the independent Czechoslovak Republic in 1918 opened up a range of new perspectives for the country's writers. Some of the greatest achievements of Czech literature date from the 1920s. Among them are the satirical plays of Karel Čapek, the son of a country doctor, who was a friend of the president of the time, T.G. Masaryk. Čapek's best plays describe the problems of a centrally organised machine age. His play *R.U.R.*, first performed in 1921, invented the word "robot", which has passed into international usage. The plot deals with the construction of a man-like machine which functioned more precisely and reliably than a man.

Also included in this category are the works of Jiří Wolker, Josef Hora, Vítězslav Nezval, František Halas and Jaroslav Seifert, who many years later, in 1984, was to become the first Czech writer to be awarded the Nobel Prize for Literature. Seifert was a journalist until 1950, publishing poems from 1920 onwards. Until 1929 he was a supporter of the Communists, but later became an ardent opponent of Stalinism.

Egon Erwin Kisch, a contemporary of Kafka and like him a native of Prague, was the author of works of social criticism. He has gone down in literary history as a *Roving Reporter*, the title of his most famous work. Kisch travelled widely, fighting for the Republicans in the Spanish Civil War and writing about China, Australia and Mexico. He returned to Prague in 1945 and died in 1948.

The German occupation interrupted the history of Czech literature, although the works of Václav Řezáč did break new ground in the genre of the psychological novel. After the Communist takeover in February 1948, Rezac – like many of his contemporaries – declared his support for "Socialist Realism". Until the beginning of the 1960s no works of any great significance were produced. Then political control relaxed slightly, allowing literature to blossom with the novels of Josef Škvorecký, Milan Kundera and Ludvík Vaculík, the short stories of Bohumil Hrabal and Arnošt Lustig as well as the plays of Václav Havel and Ivan Klima. Many of these works have been translated into several languages.

For 20 years after the repression of the Prague Spring in 1968, three distinct literary traditions existed side by side: the "official" authors who were allowed to publish their works with the approval of the State and the Party, and who often achieved vast print runs; the literature of Czech exiles, which had difficulty finding a new international audience; the native *Samizdat*, the works of writers who continued to live in Czechoslovakia but whose writings were banned. The small numbers of copies of their books relied on hand to hand distribution.

It would be unfair to claim that the writers in the first category produced no works of interest and value. Among the most impor-

tant poets were Frantisek Hrubín, Josef Kainar, Vladimír Holan and Miroslav Holub; the prose writers included Ladislav Fuks, Jan Drda, Bohumil Hrabal and Vladimír Páral. It should also be mentioned that works of a number of authors, such as the poet Jan Skácel or Ludvík Aškenázy, were proscribed after 1968 although they had previously enjoyed considerable fame and success.

The most successful of the exiled Czech authors abroad was the prose writer Milan Kundera. Like Kundera, who described his life in Prague in *The Unbearable Lightness of Being*, Pavel Kohout also played an active role in the reform movement of 1968. In

company with many others he was forced to take cover during the next decade; after signing the Charter 77 demanding basic human rights he was driven into exile. His *Diary of a Counter-Revolutionary* describes clearly the determination of many artists not to give way in the face of wrong. Other writers deserving mention are Josef Škvorecký, who distinguished himself by founding in Canada *68 Publishers*, which published the works of exiled authors, and the prose writer Arnošt Lustig, who now lives in the US, the avant-garde poet and sculptor Jiří Kolár, who works in Paris, and the poet Ivan Blatný, who made his home in England and subsequently died there.

The most famous of all the writers banned during this period was the dramatist Václav Havel – also one of the first signatories of the Charter 77. Equally important for Czech literary history, however, is Ludvík Vaculík.

Slovak literature: The literature of Slovakia was closely interwoven with Czech literature until an independent literary language developed from the dialects of Slovakia. After the disintegration of the kingdom of Great Moravia, Slovakia became part of Hungary for a thousand years. As a result, literature here shows strong Latin and Hungarian influences.

The most important names in Slovak literature before the creation of the Czechoslovak Republic were the national revolutionary writer and politician Ľudovit Štúr (1815–56) and the poet Pavol Orságh Hviezdoslav (1849–1921), who also gained fame as a skilled translator.

After 1918 the conditions for the development of an independent Slovakian literature improved dramatically, and the newly acquired freedom was put to good use by a variety of literary trends, ranging from poetic symbolism to decidedly proletarian literature, and categorised by the all-enveloping term "Slovak Modern". The most important group of writers advocating social revolution, including the influential Laco Novomeský, established itself around the newspaper *Dav* (Mass) whose Socialist Realism after 1948 became the official doctrine of Slovak literature.

Above, Franz Kafka and his fiancée Felice Bauer. **Right**, a famous depiction of "The Good Soldier Schweyk".

JAROSLAV HAŠEK

Like his contemporary Franz Kafka, the Prague-born writer who was born on 30 April 1883 lived to be just 40 years old. Jaroslav Hašek worked as a bank clerk, but by the age of 17 he had begun to write his first satirical articles for local newspapers. By the time he was 21, he had become an editor of a number of anarchist publications.

Drafted into the Austro-Hungarian Army, Hašek allowed himself to be captured by the Russians during World War I. While in Russia he joined the Czech liberation army, but then fell into the ranks of the Bolsheviks, for whom he wrote Communist propaganda. Returning to Prague, he devoted himself to writing. His world-famous novel *The Good Soldier Schweyk*, a masterful and wonderfully humorous satire on military life, was published in 1921. Brought to the attention of the international public by the Austrian writer Max Brod, it first came out in English in 1930.

Hašek was a compulsive and accomplished hoaxer and practical joker who hated pomposity and authority. In many ways, the story of Schweyk, a scrounger, liar and undisciplined drunkard, largely reflects Hašek's own eventful life, which ended in a haze of alcoholic apathy (he often only wrote in order to pay his drinking debts). Hašek drew a great deal of inspiration from the world of Prague taverns, where he noted down many a beery truism for use in his works.

Particularly famous is the scene in *The Good Soldier Schweyk* where Schweyk says to his fellow soldiers: "When the war is over you'll see me in my cups in the Chalice again." It guaranteed immortality for the tavern U Kalicha (The Chalice) and provided Prague with a meeting place for locals and visitors hoping to find wit and literary conversation. The venerable Chalice ('with blackened oak panelling and brass hinges on the bar') also formed the central stage in Berthold Brecht's comedy *Schweyk in World War II*.

Readers the world over have smiled at the sly dog trader who took advantage of World War I to gain personal freedom "through idiotic sense-lessness and a clown's mask". Literary critics never tire of pointing out that the hero is not an essential human prototype to be found in every place and every age. Schweyk is the product of a highly specific milieu and a particular period – that of the Austria of the last century. That is why

Schweyk has become living history. F. E. Weiskopf, who lived in Prague at the same time as Hašek, insists that Schweyk is an "historical" character:

"He could only arise in that period of narrow-mindedness, carelessness, good-natured treachery, anachronistic absolutism and national suppression which characterized the Danube monarchy of those days. He could only become the laughable, foolishly artful hero he was in wartime, in this era in which the rotten carcass of state lay in its death throes. And ultimately it was the mischievous, fatalistic sabotage of a Schweyk which destroyed the state itself."

The linking of genuine and feigned denseness, apathy and the submissiveness of the little man with artful cunning, slyness and cynicism was

rejected by Czech intellectuals as being damaging to the national idea of what it meant to be Czech.

Brecht, on the other hand, maintains that it is not the little man himself who is to blame, but the circumstances in which he lived. In his play, the chorus of all the characters insists that:

The times are changing.
The grandiose plans of the powerful
are coming at last to a halt.
And they will walk on like bloody fighting cocks.
The times are changing.
And no force can alter the fact.

A memorial plaque marks Hašek's birthplace in the Školská, House CN. 1325, Novy Město, Prague. ■

Brewery manager: *Do you know the worst thing about all this?*

Vanek: *What?*

Brewery manager: *That with the best will in the world I don't know what I should tell them every week – I know hardly anything about you – we have hardly any contact with each other – and the few odd details I gather, that you go to the laboratory from time to time for a rest – and that you were seen once or twice with Maruschka from the bottling plant – that the engineers did something to the heating in your flat – what use is all that to me? Come on, tell me – what am I supposed to keep on telling them? What?*

The people to whom the brewery manager is supposed to report are the Czech secret police. Vanek, the man he should tell them about, is the playwright and future president of Czechoslovakia, Václav Havel. And even the brewery manager is a real person: he entered Havel's life when the latter was forced to eke out a paltry existence as a brewery worker after his works had been banned from publication and performance. Havel has since used the incident, which occurred in 1975, as the material for his one-act play *Audience*. It has since become his most frequently-performed play.

In this key scene, the brewery manager is endeavouring to turn Vanek into an informer against himself. As a "trained" writer – according to the brewery manager – it would surely not be all that difficult for Vanek to write his own reports about his "subversive" behaviour.

Anyone faced with the task of describing the history and present situation of the Czech theatre will find it impossible to avoid the use of such words as "paradox" and "absurd". The very history of the nation contains a crucial paradox. Lying on the watershed between the western and eastern halves of Europe, the Czech Lands have frequently served as the venue – the "stage" – for historic confrontations: "He who rules Bo-

hemia, rules Europe". The problem was that the rulers were mostly foreigners, and the people themselves were relegated to the rank of spectators. When the Czech people finally developed their own national identity, the theatre played a not insignificant role in promoting it.

As long ago as the Middle Ages the Czechs could boast the beginnings of a national theatre in their native language, but its true roots lie in the period of national revival. The first dramatic performance in Czech took

place in Prague in 1771 – although the actors were German, and unable to pronounce the hitherto despised language properly. In a way it was the Theatre of the Absurd, long before the latter actually made its entrance in theatrical history.

At the end of the 18th century, the first major national play was the dramatisation of *Oldrich and Bozena*, an 11th-century legend. Almost 200 years later, in 1967, the same plot was presented once more, brought up to date by Frantisek Hrubin. The message is simple: Oldrich, a Czech prince, chooses as his wife a girl of humble origins. The prince is portrayed as a wise and just ruler,

Left, Milan Sládek, *The Whale*. **Above**, Prague actor from the Bohemian scene.

who shares the poverty and troubles of his people. The audience can thus immediately identify in the historical subject the contrast with the misery of his own everyday life.

In those days, the ordinary people flocked in droves to the city and formed an enthusiastic audience – thankful to be able to see a play written in their own language. This enthusiasm was the beginning of the Czech national passion for the theatre, which reached its architectural climax in the construction of a National Theatre, which was opened in 1883, and its musical heights in the foundation of a Czech-speaking National Opera Company by the composer Bedřich Smetana.

The foundation of the First Czechoslovak few Czech words to enter the international vocabulary.

The D-34 Ensemble, founded in 1933 by Emil Frantisek Burian, breathed fresh life into Czech theatrical life by virtue of its sensational performances. During the same period, the Liberated Theatre (Osvobozené divadlo) took on a special significance. Its imaginative satirical and musical productions established the reputation of Jan Werich, Jiří Voskovec and the brilliant composer Jaroslav Jezek.

It was not until the early 1960s that the Czech theatre recovered from the severe setbacks it had suffered during the German occupation and the subsequent Communist

Republic saw a second upturn in the fortunes of the Czech and Slovak theatre (the Slovakian National Theatre was founded in 1919). The most important dramatist of the time was undoubtedly Karel Čapek. His brother Josef, an outstanding caricaturist who is remembered for a series of drawings entitled *The Dictator's Boots*, from the time when Hitler was in the ascendant, was also a prose writer, and was mostly responsible for the production of Karel's plays. Some of the most successful examples of their work are *The Insect Play*, *The White Illness* and *The Mother*. In his play *R.U.R.* Capek uses the word "robot" for the first time – one of the takeover. During these years a number of small, adaptable stages arose throughout the capital, breathing fresh life into the musty atmosphere which prevailed: the Divadlo Na zábradlí (Theatre by the Railings), Semafor, Rokoko, the Cinoherní klub (The Actors' Club), and the Divadlo za branou (Theatre behind the Gate). The entire development brought with it a new optimism, which was harshly crushed by the Stalinist countermoves after the Prague Spring of 1968.

Adding to the absurdity of the situation of the Czech theatre during the past two decades was also the fact that its most significant writers – Havel and Kohout – were only able to arrange performances of their works abroad. When, in 1975, an amateur group in České Budějovice (Budweis) attempted to present one of Havel's plays, all the tickets were bought up by the local security police. The only people able to enjoy an evening of subversive drama were the local functionaries of the Communist Party.

Havel himself began his theatrical career as an assistant stage manager at the ABC Theatre, before moving as a dramatist to what was to become his "home" theatre, the "Theatre by the Railings". It had been founded in 1958 as the first small theatre in Prague and quickly progressed to the position of one of the city's most respected experimental

tion and inimitable style inspired a whole generation of mime and helped make Prague a world centre for this form of theatre.

In 1963, the theatre was the stage for the premiere of Havel's first full-length play *The Garden Party,* which also established the author's international reputation. In 1965 the Theatre by the Railings presented a guest performance of the play – in Czech – in West Berlin. It was not long before it was being performed in theatres all over the world.

Jan Grossmann describes the real protagonist of *The Garden Party* as the "mechanism of the spoken word":

"As a variation on the phrase, 'Clothes make the man', it is often claimed that man

stages. Its artistic director, Jan Grossmann, presented productions by international dramatists such as Beckett, Ionesco, Arrabal, Jarry and Mrozek, thus paving the way for the Czech Theatre of the Absurd.

Running parallel to and providing a contrast with drama proper were the pantomime performances of the second troupe of actors under Ladíslav Fialka. Influenced by Debureau and Marcel Marceau, his imagina-

Left, the facade of Prague's Estates Theatre by night. **Above**, performance of Smetana's world-famous opera *The Bartered Bride* in Prague's National Theatre.

does not use the spoken word, but the spoken word uses the speaker. The spoken word is the true hero of the play, for it weaves and entangles the conflict completely at random, determining the actions of the protagonists and creating a new reality by separating itself progressively from the reality it presents." In the face of the predominant "phraseology", the play represents an undisguised challenge to the social ideology of the time.

For the regime, this avant-garde theatre represented a social risk, especially after 1968, when the social climate became noticeably colder. Ewald Schorm, a producer with an established reputation in the film world, was able to steer the theatre through the cultural-political problems of the era by mixing a repertoire of classics (Strindberg, Beaumarchais, Jonson, Ostrovsky, Goethe, Ibsen) with contemporary plays (Hrabal, Albee, Steigerwald). Otherwise there would have been an enforced closure of the Czech theatre, which would have brought in its wake a loss of reputation for the regime.

Today, now that the ghost of the Cold War has been exorcised, Czech theatre stands on the threshold of a completely new era. The first step is a radical change in cultural policy and the break-up of the large theatrical companies, which were generously subsidised by the regime as long as they toed the Party line. Painful as such a discharge of excess ballast may be, it contains the germ of hope for a new beginning. Many private theatrical enterprises are mushrooming, ranging in their output from conventional musicals and operettas tailored to the taste of tourists to totally avant-garde productions.

ning of the 19th century, professional ensembles existed only in the larger towns – Prague, Brno and Olomouc. They existed alongside a lively amateur tradition, comparable with the rural music-making which flourished under the supervision of the so-called minor masters, the cantors of the provincial towns. Between 1830 and 1840, Bohemia boasted more than 130 private theatrical groups.

A large number of today's best dramatists first saw their plays performed by amateur companies in the provinces, whilst the official theatre of Prague ignored local talent. The National Theatre – which to all intents and purposes personified the national con-

line. Painful as such a discharge of excess ballast may be, it contains the germ of hope for a new beginning. Many private theatrical enterprises are mushrooming, ranging in their output from conventional musicals and operettas tailored to the taste of tourists to totally avant-garde productions.

It is a time of searching for authors as well, for the failure of the old system has robbed plays such as those by Václav Havel of their frame of reference, making them virtually unperformable. Czech theatre must decide on a new subject-matter.

Perhaps, once again, it will be the amateur theatre which points the way. At the begin-

sciousness – tended during periods of foreign influence or the Cold War to confine itself to the classics or relatively inoffensive comedies. In the 1880s it was the amateur companies which first performed the works of avant-garde authors such as Ibsen and Hauptmann. Even between the wars, the most important new works received their premiere on small stages.

It is essential that the bourgeois theatrical tradition, repressed under the socialist dictatorship, is encouraged to blossom once more. A first, spectacular indication of this new beginning is the reopening of the Prague Estates Theatre, which since 1948 had borne the name of the playwright Josef Kajetán Tyl (1808–56). In Tyl's play *Fidlovačka* (1834) the song Kde domov muj ("Where is my native land?"), the Czech part of the modern national anthem was first heard.

The theatre, constructed by Count Nostitz, opened in 1786 with Lessing's *Emilia Galotti*. A year later it staged the premiere of the first original historical drama in Czech, a play by Václav Thám, with songs by Břetislav and Jitka which were as significant in those days as they are today. Real stage history was written, however, with the first performance of Mozart's *Don Giovanni* (1787), which went on from here to conquer the opera houses of the world. From 1862 the theatre

edy by Ladislav Klima (1878–1928). Klima, a philosophical existentialist in the tradition of Schopenhauer and Nietzsche, was the victim of social disapprobation because of his sarcasm and obscene language. Under the socialist regime he was regarded as a shocking example of bourgeois decadence. Only during the brief flowering of the Prague Spring did his work see publication.

The development of the Ha Theatre itself is typical of many of the little avant-garde stages throughout the former Czechoslovakia. Founded in 1974 in Prostějov in the Hána (hence the name) as an experimental stage, it moved seven years later to Brno and was placed under the administration of the

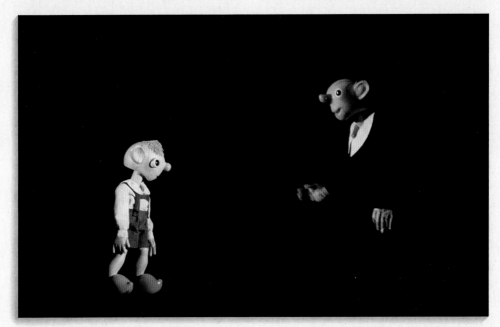

was rechristened the "German National Theatre", regaining its original name, the "Estates Theatre", in 1920. In 1991, after eight years of renovation, the building was reopened once more – naturally enough, to the strains of *Don Giovanni*.

Also waiting to be rediscovered are important writers of the pre-war years. An important step in this direction was taken by the little Ha Theatre (Ha-Divadlo) in Brno, with a new production of *The Human Tragicom-*

Moravian provincial theatre. Like the Studio Ypsilon in Prague – a comparable establishment – it is a typical writers' theatre which produces scripts itself. It is a small theatre, which sees its role as a cultural centre; its programme includes not only drama but also music and poetry readings.

Finally, if you're in Prague with children, do take the opportunity of seeing a performance at the Puppet Theatre. It is the only theatre company with two main comic figures: the narrow-minded father Špejbel, "born" in 1920, and his son Hurvínek, some six years "younger", who is more exhuberant, but also more intelligent.

Left, performance of Puccini's *La Traviata* in the Smetana Theatre. **Above**, the puppet theatre Špejbel and Hurvínek.

"Homage to Prague" is the motto written in mosaic above the main entrance of the Municipal House, a monument to Prague's own brand of Art Nouveau architecture. The building was designed and built between 1906–12 by the architects Osvald Polívka and Antonín Balšánek near the Powder Tower, on the site of the medieval royal palace and thus at the beginning of the traditional Royal Way. It was within its walls that the First Republic was proclaimed in 1918.

The most important Czech artists of the time were involved in the realisation of this city landmark. Karel Spillar provided the design for the mosaic by the entrance; the sculptures illustrating *Humiliation and Renaissance of the Nation* were the work of Ladislav Šaloun; Karel Novák produced the main decorative elements on the facade, including the light-bearing figures of Atlas gracing the balconies. After several years of painstakingly detailed renovation, this stunning Art Nouveau building, which includes several restaurants, six ballrooms and exhibition halls, has been restored to its original glory. The opening of the annual Prague Spring Festival is held in the Smetana Hall.

Particularly eye-catching are the large-scale allegorical portraits in the Primator Hall by Alfons Maria Mucha (1860–1939), the leading representative of the Prague Secessionists and one of the most popular Art Nouveau artists of all nationalities. Mucha worked primarily as a painter and graphic artist, but was also active in arts and crafts. After studying in Vienna and Munich, in 1894 he moved to Paris, where he achieved artistic recognition almost overnight for the posters he designed for the actress Sarah Bernhardt. He was celebrated as a master of the Art Nouveau idiom, giving rise to the so-called "Mucha Style". His sophisticated portraits of women – their hair and garlands of flowers entwined around the face so elaborately that they eventually merge with the

ornamentation of the background or the picture frame – set a new trend.

Jiří Mucha, the artist's son, describes thus his father's commercial success:

"After the phenomenal success of the Sarah Bernhardt posters, which became sought-after collector's items as soon as they were published, the printing firm of Champenois began to produce so-called 'panneaux'. They were really posters too, but without the advertising text. They were printed on good-quality paper or silk, and people either had

them framed like pictures or used them to decorate screens. Within a short space of time, screens already decorated with these pictures were also being produced, and an entire chain of shops sold nothing but the works of Mucha, in every imaginable variation. The decorative panels were all characterised by the long, narrow shape typical of his theatre advertisements. Unfortunately they were not all well made. It was a question of whether my father himself carried out all the corrections. Sometimes the printers were in such a hurry that there was no time for this. In such cases you needed only to glance at the original to realise how many details of

Preceding pages: the Mayor's Chamber in the Municipal House in the New Town, decorated by Alfons Mucha between 1906–11. Left, another Mucha masterpiece. Above, an Art Nouveau doorway.

drawing or colour had been lost in the lithographic process."

Mucha's success seems to have come quite naturally. As his son comments:

"It is typical of the paradoxes which were forever occuring in father's life that he achieved his fame as a result of precisely that aspect of his work which happened to be most fashionable at the time. He was not really aware of this fact himself; in not a single one of his lectures or writings about art does he make even the briefest reference to the way in which he arrived at his style in those days…

Exhibitions in Paris, Munich, Brussels, London and Prague followed, as did a highly-

There is no doubt that Czech Art Nouveau drew its greatest inspiration from Paris. Most Prague artists visited the French capital in addition to the other great artistic centres of the time, notably Vienna and Berlin. Nonetheless, Art Nouveau in Prague developed into an independent artistic form of expression, as witnessed by numerous architectural elements throughout the city. In the early years it represented a reaction against the contemporary predilection for over-emphasising historic forms in architecture.

The main trend-setter as regards the new range of forms was the Prague Academy of Applied Art, which also achieved international acclaim with its contributions to the

praised contribution to the Paris World Exhibition in 1900. In 1904 he travelled to America, where he worked as stage designer and teacher at the Art Institute of Chicago. Shortly before the outbreak of World War I he returned to Prague, where he created during the years which followed his "Slavic Epic", a series of 20 monumental pictures dedicated to Slavic mythology.

In 1913 Mucha designed a magnificently colourful window depicting episodes from the lives of the Bohemian saints for the New Archbishop's Chapel in St Vitus' Cathedral. He was finally laid to rest in the Vyšehrad Cemetery, the pantheon of Czech artists.

World Exhibitions in Paris (1900) and St Louis (1904). Using local folkloric elements, it developed a canon of expression which architects and craftsmen often followed down to the last detail. C. Klouček's ceramic and stucco ornamentation of facades was soon so widely copied that it was to become a characteristic of Art Nouveau buildings in towns all over Bohemia.

In architecture Jan Kotěra, a pupil of the Viennese architect Otto Wagner, was one of the prime influences. He moved on from the originally naturalist conception towards a strong geometric and constructivist formal style. His most impressive works in Prague are the carefully restored Hotel Evropa and the Peterka House, with its elegantly ornamental facade, both on Wenceslas Square.

Apart from the sketches for the Municipal House already mentioned, Osvald Polívka designed the house U Nováků (Vodičkova 36), the building housing the former Prague Insurance Company in the *Národní* 7, the Bank of the Provinces (Na příkopě 20) and the New Town Hall on Mariánské náměstí.

The grandfather of Václav Havel designed and built the Lucerna Palace of Culture on Wenceslas Square as well as the family home on the Rašín Promenade (No. 2000).

With their new design for the Main Railway Station in 1980, the two architects Jan

Congress in the Exhibition and Trades Fair Park. And Hotel Paříž (U obecního domu 1, immediately behind the Municipal House) was declared a national monument in 1984.

The Svatopluk Čech Bridge and the magnificent facades of the Pařížka Street form a remarkable urban ensemble. The bridge was constructed by J. Koula in 1908. Although the shortest bridge in the city, it is certainly one of the most decorative.

The most outstanding sculptors of the era were Ladislav Šaloun, who was responsible for the vast monument to Jan Hus on the Old Town Square, which was unveiled to mark the 500th anniversary of the death of the Bohemian reformer on 6 July 1915, and

Šrámek and Alena Šrámková succeeded in integrating an historic building complex and a modern transport concept. The Art Nouveau building erected by J. Franta between 1901 and 1909 was remodelled around a massive ticket hall and departure area and linked to an underground railway without damaging the original fabric in any way.

Further impressive examples of Art Nouveau architecture are the Koruna House on Wenceslas Square and the steel Palace of

Left, angel above a door in Celetná and the facade of the Hotel Evropa. **Above**, the dome of the Municipal House; decoration in "Carp Street".

Stanislav Sucharda, who created the Palacký Monument on the bridge of the same name.

Art Nouveau is the last era in the history of art claiming to shape all spheres of life by virtue of its unified credo. True Art Nouveau seeks to establish a balance between man and nature by using artistic symbols to add a cosmic dimension to personal experience. The artist could fuse a complex living environment with an idealised creative sphere. The fact that he was attempting to achieve an ideal which has become topical again today may be just one reason why, in Prague, Art Nouveau has lost nothing of its original fascination almost 100 years later.

Since the opening of frontiers after the collapse of the Cold War, protectionists and nature lovers in the Czech section of the Bohemian Forest, in Eastern Bavaria and the Mühlenviertel of Austria have been anxiously watching the fate of the previously inaccessible border regions in the three-country triangle northeast of Passau. The National Park area, made up of the Bavarian Forest and the Bohemian Forest (Šumava), now offers limitless opportunities for development. Memoranda and working papers are headed the *Green Roof of Europe*, *Intersilva*, the *Nature Park Region* or the *Euro-Region*. Institutions and interest groups are clamouring to win support for their proposals to use the tremendous natural potential of the area as the basis for an environment-friendly economic development. There has even been talk of an ecological model region.

The Czech Republic's creation of the Šumava National Park on 20 March 1991 fulfilled one of the important prerequisites for such a scheme. Together with the National Park of the Bavarian Forest in Germany, a total of 200,000 acres (81,000 hectares) of countryside now stands under the strictest protection laws. The area covered by the National Park includes the largest self-contained forest in Central Europe. It is also – uniquely in Europe – an area of over 198,000 acres (80,000 hectares) free of any major roads.

Unspoilt nature: The new Šumava National Park is just one of many areas within the country's boundaries where there are strict limitations on land usage. Reports about the severe environmental damage to the industrial areas, especially in Northern Bohemia, have tended to eclipse the fact that the Czech and Slovak republics form one of the few regions in Europe in which people will still be able to live in unspoilt natural surroundings in 10 years' time: a land in which animals long extinct elsewhere – brown bears, wolves and lynxes – are still found.

Preceding pages: a crisp morning in the High Tatra. **Left,** Slovakian paradise near Nová Ves. **Above,** canoeists can find ideal stretches in both republics.

Despite their relatively small area, the topography of the Czech and Slovak republics is extremely varied. The upland regions include a wide range of scenery, attracting tourists from home and abroad. Cable cars and signposted footpaths lead up to the highest peaks and various recreational centres in the mountains. In order to limit the negative effects of intensive tourism, the authorities have drawn up a strict code of conduct governing visits to the national parks. For example, it is forbidden to leave the marked

footpaths or to light fires or camp except within the specially designated areas.

National parks and nature parks are large areas of untouched or largely unspoilt countryside which are of scientific or general educational importance. Including as they do thousands of lakes and a well-developed network of signposted footpaths, they are rewarding for walkers and other nature lovers. There are tours to suit every taste. In some protected areas nature trails have been laid out (there were almost 100 of these in 1992), marked by a white square with a green stripe. Information boards provide details of local flora and fauna at regular intervals.

The seven national parks: Before 1987, six major areas had been declared national parks. Together with the 1,679 nature conservancy areas within the country, they cover an area of 6,666 sq. miles (17,272 sq. km) – in other words, 13 percent of the total land area. By comparison, the National Parks of the US cover an area of 25,000 sq. miles (65,000 sq. km) – 0.6 percent of the total land area. No country in central Europe can boast larger expanses of unspoilt natural habitats in which flora and fauna are preserved and studied in a scientific manner.

Although most of the national parks are situated within Slovakia, it was in fact in the Czech Lands that the very first attempts were

the Tatrzanski Narododowy National Park of Poland in the north. It covers an area of 300 sq. miles (770 sq. km); the protected area totals 200 sq. miles (510 sq. km). The Polish frontier is not open to traffic at this point. Nonetheless the twin national parks of the High Tatra are administered jointly by both countries.

The Vysoké Tatry (High Tatra) is the highest mountain chain in Slovakia; Mount Gerlachovský (8,496 ft/2,655 metres) and Mount Lomnický (8,422 ft/2,632 metres) are the highest peaks in the country. The topography of this alpine region, with its fissured craggy summits and picturesque mountain lakes, is typical of high-altitude

made to preserve valuable natural habitats. As early as 1838 two nature conservation areas were set up here: the forest areas of Hojná Voda and Žofinský in Southern Bohemia. Twenty years later, the forest conservation area of Boubínský prales was added. After World War II a systematic programme was embarked upon to preserve typical scenery, archaeological sites and topographical formations.

The largest and most important national parks are the High Tatra National Park in Slovakia and the Krkonoše (Giant Mountains) in Northern Bohemia. The High Tatra National Park was founded in 1948 and joins

landscapes and includes glacial valleys, moraines and more than 100 cirque lakes. It is ideal walking country and a popular skiing destination in winter, which means that it can be overcrowded at times. The High Tatra forms the northernmost section of the 750-mile (1,200-km) arc of the Carpathian Mountains. During the Quaternary Era the mountains were largely covered by glaciers; the present topography is the result of glacial erosion. Robert Townson, a Scottish physicist and geographer, studied the region in detail and described it in his book *Journeys through Hungary in 1793* (Slovakia belonged to Hungary at the time).

Brown bears and marmots: The national wild-life protection agency is a fairly recent innovation. The land within the boundaries of the National Parks is subject to fairly heavy tourist traffic (the Polish section of the High Tatra is a fully developed tourist region). Nonetheless, the importance of nature conservancy has been recognised and afforded a high priority.

There is already a ban on the construction of new hotels in the High Tatra, and in some areas there is a general ban on motor traffic. In July and August private cars are prohibited from using the roads to the holiday resorts from Poprad, the most important base outside the National Park. The last stage of

they are protected all the year round. For many years the chamois was considered a threatened species; nowadays they are more common. The chamois living in the High Tatra are a particular species only found here; the increase in tourism poses a threat to their habitat.

Amongst the birds indigenous to the area are pheasant, partridge, wild geese and a number of species of duck. They may be hunted, but rarer large birds, such as golden eagles, vultures, ospreys, storks, eagle-owls, bustards and capercaillies are protected.

The Krkonoše National Park was founded in 1963 and extends over an area of 150 sq. miles (385 sq. km). The region still bears

the journey must be undertaken by bus or train. On sunny days the sky here is a deep and clear blue.

The High Tatra is still the habitat of a large number of species which are extinct in most other European countries, or which are only able to survive in zoos. The mountains harbour brown bears, wolves, lynxes and wild-cats (*felis silvestris*), marmots, otters, wild horses, martens and mink. Most of these animals are hunted, but in the National Parks

Left, this breed of chamois is unique to the High Tatra. **Above**, gathering hay in the Bohemian Forest National Park.

traces of the ice sheets which once covered it. Corries, moraines and glacial valleys are evident, as are the remains of a more northerly flora (e.g. cloudberries). Characteristic species include monkshood, swallowwort gentian, white hellebore etc. The spruce trees planted during the 17th and 18th centuries have been badly damaged by industrial pollution and acid rain. In one of the areas most badly affected by acid rain in the whole of Europe 25,000 acres (10,000 hectares) of pine forest are losing their needles. The stocks of beech are restricted to the lower slopes. The entire National Park area suffers from too many leisure visitors.

Slovakian Paradise: The Slovenský raj National Park was established east of Poprad in 1988. The wild upland landscape extends over 54 sq. miles (140 sq. km) in an area which has been under a protection order since 1964. Wind, water and time have worn away the limestone plateau to form ravine-like gorges with waterfalls, cascades and karst. It is the habitat of many rare and protected plant and animal species.

The region has been made accessible to walkers and climbers by handrails, ladders and bridges (often consisting only of a tree trunk) where necessary. The main attractions of the park include the narrow defile at the rise of the River Hron and the Dobšina ice

caves (e.g. the Demänovské caves) which are accessible to tourists. The past few years have seen a number of hotels and chair lifts built and ski slopes prepared. Nonetheless, the eastern sections of the chain remain very peaceful and show few signs of human intervention. This is ideal walking country, since there are fewer steep gorges than in the High Tatra. Here, too, you may still meet bears, lynxes and wolves. Birds of prey are a frequent sight. You can also fish in the Čierny Vah River and in the large reservoir near Liptovský Mikuláš.

The Lesser Fatra National Park (Malá Fatra) in Western Slovakia occupies an area of 77 sq. miles (200 sq. km) in the northeast-

caves. For keen walkers, Slovenský raj is a true paradise.

The Lower Tatra forms the second-highest mountain chain in Slovakia, extending over a much larger area than the High Tatra. The long main ridge of the range, characterised by dense forest and bare, rounded mountain peaks, is no less than 50 miles (80 km) in length from east to west. It forms the heart of the Lower Tatra National Park (Národný Park Nizké Tatry), which covers a total area of 313 sq. miles (811 sq. km). The highest mountains are Mount Ďumbier (6,477 ft/ 2,024 metres) and Mount Chopok (6,477 ft/ 2,024 metres). There are dripstone caves

ern section of the mountain range of the same name. The highest peaks soar up to 5,469 ft (1,709 metres). A variety of rock types are present, in particular granite, sandstone and dolomite. The park also contains an extremely varied selection of flora and fauna; among the plants are warmth-loving as well as high-altitude species. The lower slopes, interspersed with canyon-like gorges, are ideal walking territory.

Covering an area of only 8 sq. miles (21 sq. km), the Pieninsky narodný Park is the smallest of the seven national parks. It comprises a limestone mountain range dissected by the deeply eroded valley of the River

Dunajec, which has become increasingly popular for rafting trips.

In addition to the seven National Parks, both the Czech and Slovak republics boast an impressive number of extensive conservation areas. The Beskid Conservation Area, for example, extends over an area of 450 sq. miles (1,160 sq. km) and includes the Moravian and Silesian Beskids, part of the Javorníky Mountains and the Vsetinské vrchy. The area is protected for its primeval forests and precious mountain meadows. Also of interest is the traditional architecture of the area.

Conflicting interests: Just as is the case elsewhere, the aims and means of nature and countryside protection have to be defended against the energetic lobbying of economic interests. Slovakia in particular continues to suffer from the economic reform programmes of the Prague government. The attempts to limit armaments production and the export of weapons have already cost a large number of jobs. It must be tempting therefore to compensate such loss by expanding and developing tourism, a course which would inevitably be at the expense of the habitats of rare animal and plant species. It is therefore remarkable that the Slovak authorities in the better developed tourist regions such as the High Tatra have refused to grant building permission for new hotels, and place rigid limitations on private transport.

A model national park region: As plans go ahead for the development of the joint National Park region comprising the Bavarian Forest and the Bohemian Forest (Šumava), it may prove possible to find a compromise between conflicting interests by preserving nature in cooperation with local residents. This is the idea at the heart of the term "Biosphere Conservation Area", which summarises the proposal put forward in July 1991 by the environmental and nature protection agencies of the Czech Republic, Bavaria and Austria as "a united multi-national development concept to be agreed for the entire area". The authors see the "only chance for the Bohemian Forest and the Bavarian Forest in the preservation of the natural potential of the entire region as the basis for an environmentally-oriented continued development within the framework of a model ecological region."

Part of the scheme would include the modernisation or revival of the railway system, and the encouragement of small and medium-sized businesses in an environmentally-conscious way, as well as developing tourist facilities in harmony with the National Park, the natural surroundings and history of the area. Major industrial projects and the promotion of through traffic and goods traffic by the improvement of the road network are thereby rejected.

The opinions of those directly affected are divided. Many village mayors are against the

conservation plan, and are determined to fight it with all the means at their disposal. "They want to send us back to the jungle so that people are forced to leave their homes once more." The opposite view is taken by Peter Pavlik, who was persecuted after the Prague Spring and subsequently found a new home in the depths of the Bohemian Forest. He has transformed a little farmhouse and goat shed into a cheerful restaurant. Just as he once wrote pamphlets against the Prague regime, so he now writes letters to German newspapers: "I beg you, help us to preserve our common natural heritage; there is nothing like it left in Europe!"

Left, strict rules apply to all visitors to the national parks and nature reserves. **Above**, summit experience in the High Tatra.

TWO REPUBLICS

After years of ideological isolation, the Czech and Slovak republics have now emerged as two of Europe's most fascinating travel destinations. While the larger cities are by now well used to the demands of the tourism boom – even if there aren't nearly enough beds in Prague – it often seems that life out in the country has stood still. But even here there are increasing signs of change; and it isn't only the facades, neglected for so many decades, that are suddenly being returned to their former glory.

It is impossible for any guide book to keep up with the pace of developments within the two republics. No sooner is information gathered than another legacy of the socialist era is wiped off the map. The traveller will constantly come across new street names – in many cases they have been reverted to their original names – as well as newly erected place signs; he will also often search in vain for the no longer current names of some of the public facilities such as parks and sports stadiums, or even restaurants and hotels.

Both republics can look back on a long and eventful history lasting over 1,000 years, and thus possess a cultural legacy of great wealth, which in recent years the state has made enormous efforts to preserve. Over 70 historic city centres have had preservation orders placed on them. Many castles and palaces – in Slovakia alone there are no less than 200 – have been declared national monuments, although this status does not yet extend to many of the historically important churches and monasteries dotting the countryside.

For a region with such a wealth of things to see, any description must be selective. The journey begins in the Czech Republic, in the historical Crown Lands of Bohemia, and its magnificent capital Prague. We continue by exploring some delightful destinations in Prague's environs and then follow a large arc from Southern Bohemia to Western Bohemia and its famous spa towns, and Northern Bohemia before travelling east of Prague and into neighbouring Moravia. Having visited its capital Brno, we head off into the countryside once more. The whole process is repeated in Slovakia after a visit to Bratislava. Whichever route you take, you will not only encounter beautiful countryside filled with countless historical and architectural gems, but also lashings of generous hospitality for which both the Czechs and the Slovaks are renowned.

In both the Czech Republic and Slovakia many of the towns have a history not only of Slavic but also of German settlement. In this guide, therefore, some of the Slavic names are followed by their German versions in brackets.

Preceding pages: blooming barley; bucolic bouquet; the blue Beskids. Left, the dream of a romantic holiday comes true.

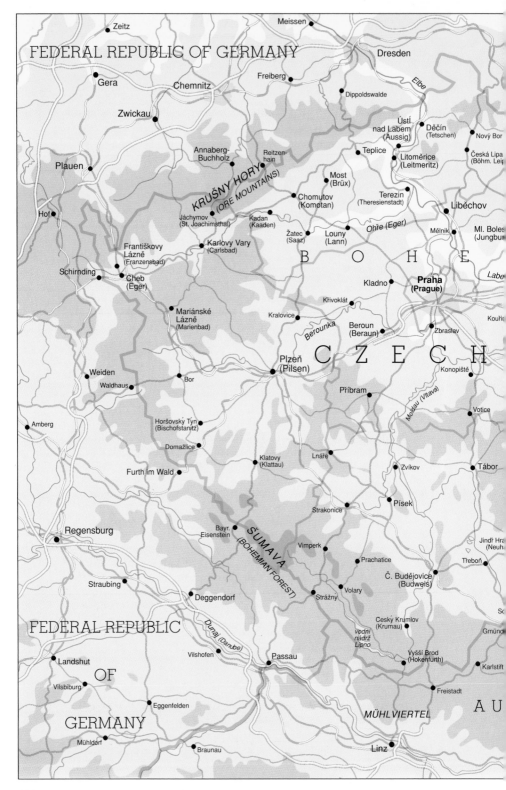

The Czech Republic

48 km / 30 miles

...litz

Lwówek Śl.

Jawor

Wrocław
(Breslau)

Kluczbork

Jelenia
Góra

Brzeg

Frýlant
(Friedland)

Walbrzych

Swidníca

P O L A N D

Opole
(Oppeln)

Liberec
(Reichenberg)

KRKONOŠE
(GIANT MOUNTAINS)

Bystrzyca

Jablonec
n.Nis
(Gablonz)

Vrchlabí
(Hohenelbe)

Trutnov
(Trautenau)

Adršpach
(Adersbach)

Turnov
(Turnau)

Klodzko
(Glatz)

Paczkow

Prudnik

Oda (Oder)

Jičín
(Jitschin)

Hořice

Náchod

Jeseník
(Freiwaldau)

Nové Město
n. Met.
(Neustadt)

Bystrzyca Kl.

Krnov

Racibórz

...I A

A

Hradec Králové
(Königgrätz)

Mladkov

Bruntál
(Freuden-
thal)

Opava
(Troppau)

Ostrava
(Ostrau)

Poděbrady

Pardubice

Šumperk
(Mährisch
Schönberg)

E P U B L I C

Kutná Hora
(Kuttenberg)

Chrudim

Mohelnice

Šternberk

Fulnek

Mor. Trebová
(Mährisch
Trübau)

Olomouc
(Olmütz)

Hranice

N. Jičín
(Neutitschein)

Havl. Brod
Deutsch Brod)

Žd'ár nad
Sázavou
(Saar)

Prostějov
(Prossnitz)

Přerov
(Perau)

Val. Meziříčí

Jihlava
(Iglau)

M O R A V I A

Blansko

Morava (March)

Třebíč

Brno
(Brünn)

Zlín

Telč

Slavkov
(Austerlitz)

Mor. Budějovice

Staré Město

Uh. Hradiště

Pohořelice

Žarosice

Znojmo
(Zaim)

Waidhofen

Mikulov
(Nikolsburg)

Trenčín
(Treutschin)

Trenč.
Teplice

Dyje (Thaya)

Břeclav
(Lundenburg)

Hodonin

...tl

Horn

S L O V A K I A

Wilfersdorf

Jablonica

MALÉ KARPATY
(LESSER CARPATHIANS)

Piešt'any
(Pistyau)

...RIA

Stockerau

Trnava
(Tyrnau)

Nitra
(Neutra)

Vienna

St. Pölten

Devín

131

Viewed from the Castle Hill, the historical centre, whose hundreds of rooftops reflect the golden patina of the midday sun, clings to the gently curving bend in the Vltava. Its banks seem to be only just held together by the filigrane constructions of its bridges: on the one side the Lesser Quarter and on the other the Old Town.

Anybody who gazes over Prague from the parapets of Hradčany Castle must surely consider it to be one of the most fortunate of all European cities; fortunate because its skyline was never touched by the ravages of war and because its essential countenance was never scarred by the addition of any modern eyesores. After years of painstaking restoration, important architectural ensembles such as the Old Town Square have now been returned to their former glory. Today, Prague is a living architectural museum, vividly documenting all phases of development; from its Romanesque origins, to its mighty Gothic churches and monasteries, baroque palaces and right up to its magnificent Art Nouveau boulevards of the "foundation years" laid out towards the end of the last century.

Mozart, Smetana and Dvořak: every year in May, the memory of the Big Three, whose names are so closely linked with the history of the city, is resurrected when the elegant concert halls, churches and palaces open their doors for the "Prague Spring". It is a time when not only great international ensembles perform in the city, but also renowned native orchestras, such as the Czech Philharmonic or the famous National String Quartet. But good music can actually be heard in Prague all the year round: from jazz to punk, every music lover can find what he is looking for here.

The daily life of Prague is best experienced in its pubs. And it doesn't have to be the full-to-bursting U Fleků or U Tomáše, whose reputation is somewhat better than merited; or even the "Chalice" (U Kalicha), the local of Jaroslav Hašek's "Good Soldier Schwejk". No, the best beer, the most fortifying dumplings and the juciest goulash continue to be served in the more cosy, hidden estblishments.

Where does the city's pulse beat? Is it in its historical buildings around which big city and medieval atmospheres seem to fuse? Or in the magical squares, with their continuous mystery plays of light and shade, in which even today one might almost expect to bump into Rabbi Loew's *Golem*? And are they still there, the legendary days of writers and artists; the days when for every normal citizen there were three journalists, four painters and five authors? Or does today the pulse of the city beat stronger on the boulevard of Wenceslas Square with its shopping by day, and its bustling entertainment by night? Today, Prague has many facets, and it is up to every visitor to discover it for himself.

Preceding pages: a classic Prague scene: the Charles Bridge in the early morning. **Left,** no visit to Prague would be complete without a look at Hradčany; here the Matthias Gate.

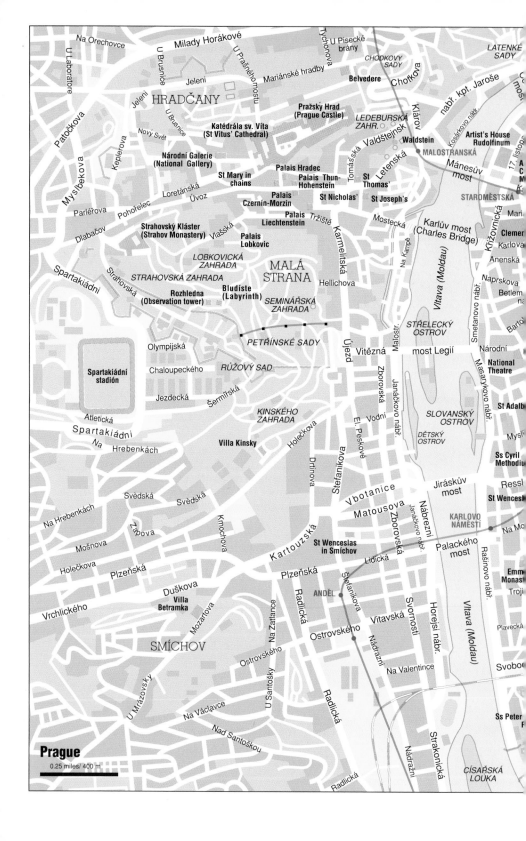

Prague

0.25 miles/ 400 m

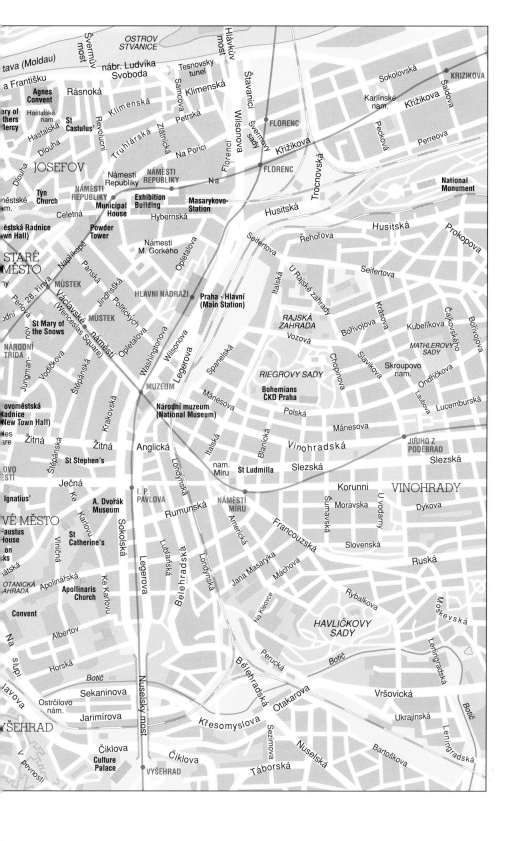

PRAGUE'S OLD TOWN

The dividing line between the Staré Město and the Nové Město – the Old and the New Towns – lies at the far side of **Wenceslas Square**. To right and left, wide pedestrian thoroughfares follow the line of the medieval town wall dating from the time before Charles IV had the New Town built in a semicircle around the historic city centre.

The little street Na můstku leads straight to the heart of the bustling Old Town. After only a few paces the visitor will find himself with a flea market – the traditional **St Gall Market** – to the left, which leads directly into the **Coal Market** one block further on. To the right, in the background, is the silhouette of the **church of St Gall**. Originally Romanesque in style, the church was given its splendid baroque facade between 1690–1700. It marks the hub of the district as it was first planned in the 13th century.

One block further on again lies the **Estates Theatre**, scene of the premiere of Mozart's opera *Don Giovanni* on 29 October 1787. Originally classicistic in style, the building was rebuilt several times; during the past few years it has been the object of a major restoration programme and was rededicated to the public in 1991 – Mozart Year – naturally with a new performance of *Don Giovanni*. Mozart and Prague have reason enough to be grateful to each other. In The Three Golden Lions, a guest house on the nearby Coal Market, the composer prepared for the premiere. He also stayed three times in the Villa Bertramka – now the Mozart Museum – in Smíchov, the southern quarter of the city, where he was the guest of the Dušeks, a family of musicians. The citizens of Prague loved Mozart, and he felt at home and protected in the city. The Oscar-winning film *Amadeus* was largely filmed in Prague. The props used in the film can still be seen in the Barrandov Film Studios outside the city.

The Carolinum, next door to the theatre, was originally a palais purchased by King Wenceslas IV from the Rotlev

family for the Charles University. When Charles IV decided to found the first university in the Empire in 1348, it was his intention that it should serve the entire continent, or – as the Papal Bull confirming the foundation of the university stated – "for all inhabitants of the Kingdom and the surrounding countries, and for the students of all nations who shall flock to the aforementioned town". However, the noble concept of a universal establishment of learning proved difficult to put into practice. The masters of the university council were divided into four "nations" corresponding to the four points of the compass but, after the death of Charles IV, Jan Hus persuaded the new king to allocate the Bohemian nation three votes, thereby ensuring its majority within the administration. Such was their annoyance following this move that many foreign professors and students moved to other universities.

Across the centuries the university expanded to take over other buildings; all that remains of the original Gothic

Left, the House of the Stork on the Old Town Square. **Right**, sweet temptation.

college is an arbour and the magnificent oriel window created by the Parler School. The building is now used for official ceremonies.

The Old Town Square: The square forms the natural centre of the Old Town and the true heart of the city. Occupying pride of place in the middle is the massive **monument to Jan Hus**. It was erected on 6 July 1915 to mark the 500th anniversary of the reformer's death. The surrounding buildings, dwarfed by the towers of the Týn Church, still form an imposing backdrop. At the base of the church towers lies the Týn School, which houses changing exhibitions.

Passing through the building or via the Celetná ul. No. 5, the visitor enters the **Týn Church**, whose treasures include the oldest font in Prague (1414) and a series of baroque paintings, such as the main altarpiece "The Assumption" by the first great master of the Bohemian baroque, Karel Škréta (1610–74). The building, which was erected between 1365 and 1511 on the site of a small Romanesque church of St Mary, served the Hussites as their main place of worship until their crushing defeat by the Catholics at the Battle of the White Mountain in 1620.

Although the varied architectural styles of the surrounding houses blend harmoniously, one or two buildings are nonetheless outstanding. The first of them, "At the Sign of the White Unicorn", is followed by the Týn School and the Gothic **Bell House**. The last in the row is the **Palais Kinsky**, whose fine facade reveals rococo elements. It was built between 1755–65 by Anselmo Lurago according to the plans of the – by then deceased – Bavarian architect Kilian Ignaz Dientzenhofer. In the 19th century, it housed a German school which was attended by Franz Kafka. Today it is the home of the National Gallery's splendid collection of prints and drawings. Of particular note on the north side of the square is House No. 7, once a Pauline monastery.

The smaller part of the square behind the Town Hall is dominated by the magnificent facade of the **church of St**

The astronomical clock was mounted on the Old Town Hall by Nikolaus von Kaaden in 1410.

Nicholas. German merchants erected the first place of worship on this site during the 13th century; the present church was completed in 1735. The architect was again Kilian Ignaz Dientzenhofer, who with his father Christoph was largely responsible for the city's baroque countenance (*see page 156*).

The **Town Hall** is now used only for ceremonial purposes. It is too small to house the administration of the city, especially as the North Wing was burned down in 1945 during the last days of German occupation; a memorial plaque recalls the event.

The building had formed the political hub of the capital since King John of Luxembourg granted the citizens rights of self-government in 1338. The chapel, council chamber and a number of other buildings in the western and northern corners were erected in rapid succession. In 1896 the corner house of U minuty, adorned with antique and biblical murals, was absorbed into the complex. Among the tenants who were served notice to quit was the family of Franz Kafka.

The most notable feature of the exterior is the amazing **astronomical clock**, dating from 1410 and situated to the right of the main late-Gothic portal. This wonderful contraption consists of two clock faces: the calendar, below, moves on a day every time the clock (above) strikes midnight. The signs of the zodiac and the depictions of the months from rural scenes were painted by Josef Mánes in 1864. At the very top is the "Procession of Apostles", which was only installed in the 19th century.

The Southern Old Town: Leading off from U minuty is the Malé nám., the **Little Square**, evocative of medieval Prague. Surrounding the fountain with its pretty Renaissance railings are a number of fine houses, each with its own history. In 1353 in House No. 11, a Signore Agostino of Florence established the first documented apothecary's shop in the city, and during the reign of Emperor Charles IV House No. 1, which bears the twin names "In Paradise" and "At the Sign of the Angel", was the home of a herbalist from Florence.

Most spectacular is the **Rott House** (No. 3), whose cellar was once the lower floor of a Romanesque town house. The first Czech Bible was printed here in 1488; at the turn of the century the new owner, an ironmonger, had the building renovated, painting the facade with the original sign – three white roses – and a selection of his wares.

Past the bend in the Karlova ul., on the right-hand side of the Husova, is the **Clam Gallas Palais**. It is a beautifully restored nobleman's house dating from the high baroque period and now housing the town's archives. Despite the cramped location, the facade is impressive; it is framed by two decorative portals comprising pairs of Titans apparently bearing the weight of the entire world in general and the building in particular. Of unexpected magnificence is the staircase leading up to the audience rooms on the third floor and the frescoes depicting the celestial triumph of Apollo.

In the opposite direction, in other words towards the South, the Husova

The Estates Theatre belonged to the Bohemian estates from 1789 to 1945.

leads to the **House of the Lords of Kunstát and Poděbrady**, whose entrance lies in the Retezova No. 3, and which recalls the only king of Bohemia to be elected by the people. The palais retains its Romanesque features, especially the simple barrel-vaulted rooms on the ground floor and in the cellar.

Further to the left stands **St Aegidius**, the severe Gothic church of the Dominican friars. In marked contrast to its unadorned exterior, the hall church is magnificently appointed inside. Baroque paintings displaying a masterful command of perspective and colour adorn the vaulted ceiling.

Taking the third turning on the right off the Husova, the visitor continues in the direction of the **Bethlehem Chapel**. One of the most important shrines of the Czech people, its self-conscious simplicity serves as a memorial to the inflammatory sermons of Jan Hus, who fulminated against bigotry and love of splendour on this spot. Other great religious reformers also preached here, including Hus's contemporary and fellow rebel Jakobellus von Mies (Jakoubek ze Stříbra), who introduced the administration of the Communion in both forms, and – much later (1521) – the radical Thomas Münzer.

The focal point in the chapel is the pulpit rather than the altar. The walls were used to illustrate the preacher's message in large letters and pictures before a congregation of up to 3,000 faithful. Ironically, after the defeat of the Hussites, the church passed into Jesuit hands; in 1786 it was completely gutted, but from 1950–54 was painstakingly rebuilt in the original style to serve as a national monument.

The **Preacher's House** next door is also open to the public; it contains an exhibition documenting the life and works of the great reformer. On the West side of the square, surrounding a picturesque courtyard, is a well-stocked **Ethnological Museum**. The Naprstkova leads to the Vltava, where – on the far side of the promenade – a little café in front of the **Smetana Museum** offers the best-known view of the Charles

The historical core of the Old Town is dominated by the Týn Church.

Bridge and Hradčany Castle. The museum displays exhibits illustrating the life and works of the famous Czech composer.

Beyond the former millhouses is the **Old Town Bridge Tower** and the square of the "Crusaders of the Red Star". This remarkable fraternity was originally charged with the defence of the bridge and enjoyed high esteem within the city; between 1561 and 1694 the leaders of the order were ex officio the Archbishops of Prague. Their church of St Francis, with its magnificently painted dome, was no doubt designed to vie with the pomp and circumstance of the Jesuits nearby.

The **Crusaders' Square** used to be described as the drawing-room of Prague because of the fine buildings encircling it. Today, heavy through traffic and an apparently never-ending restoration programme on at least one of the historic facades spoil its elegance. You may hardly notice the monument to Charles IV. It was erected to commemorate the 500th anniversary of the founding of the

Coffeehouses are a venerable Prague institution.

university and portrays allegorical representations of the first four faculties at the feet of the founder.

On the far side soars the baroque facade of the **Church of St Saviour**. It forms a part of the sprawling **Clementinum**, which is scarcely noticed by most passers-by despite its size – probably because the nearby Charles Bridge diverts their attention. Nonetheless, the importance of the college established by the Jesuits after they were summoned to Bohemia in 1556 cannot be denied; it represented the bastion of the Counter-Reformation in the Hussite capital. The Society of Jesus took over a former Dominican monastery and a 2-hectare plot of land, which they were determined to transform into a first-class educational establishment with a school, library, printing works and theatre. Their university was soon granted the right to award doctorates and thus gained equal status with the Hussite-influenced Charles University. In 1622, after the Catholic victory on the White Mountain, it was able to absorb the trouble-

some competition and remained for many years the only university in the Czech capital. Today the Clementinum houses a number of libraries, including the **National Library**; the magnificent rooms can be visited upon request.

The Josefov – the Jewish Quarter: Considering the small number of Jews still living in Prague, it is hard to comprehend how enormously important their role in the economic and cultural development of the city used to be. According to records, the first Jewish community was founded here in 1091. In 1255 King Otakar II granted the Jewish Privilege, thus guaranteeing them security within the law for the first time. In return, thanks to their success as craftsmen and traders, the Jews provided the king with a considerable income from the taxes that they paid.

Their relationship with the authorities was always alternating between acceptance and hatred, and they frequently suffered at the hands of Prague's citizens. But Hitler outdid all other animosity with his "final solution", which

he planned to document in a "museum of an extinct race". It was only because of this cynical plan that the synagogues and cemeteries were not destroyed.

The heart of the **Josefov** – named after the tolerant Habsburg emperor Joseph who described the Jews as a "useful element" – grew up after 1250 around the Old-New Synagogue. In 1382 Wenceslas IV pronounced the district a protected ghetto.

Behind the Clementinum, the Platnéřská leads almost back to the Old Town Square. Shortly before this point the visitor should turn left into the Maiselova and left again opposite the Old-New Synagogue into the U starého hřbitova and the **Jewish Cemetery**, where weathered gravestones stand under gnarled trees. At the **tomb of Rabbi Loew**, pious Jews honour one of their great teachers who, during the 16th century, the "Golden Age" of the Jewish community, directed a Talmudic school in Prague. Students of literature know the wise man better as the creator of the Golem, the artificial creature which could be brought to life by mysterious magical practices, arousing a mixture of terror and fear.

At the entrance to the cemetery is the **Klaus Synagogue**, in which old manuscripts and prints are displayed, along with a hall of remembrance containing drawings by Jewish children in the concentration camp at Terezín.

The **Old-New Synagogue** is Europe's oldest Jewish place of worship still in use today. Begun in 1270, the building has an elaborate brick gable and demonstrates unmistakable evidence of the severe Cistercian Gothic style, although a number of elements were purposely altered in order to avoid too much resemblance to the symbolism of the Christian order. Inside, the roof covering the main area is supported by twin columns; only men were allowed access to this part of the synagogue, where readings from the Torah took place. The galleries were added during the 17th century in order to permit women to participate in the acts of worship.

Opposite is the baroque-style **Jewish Town Hall**. Eyes are drawn to the gable

The old Jewish Cemetery was laid out at the beginning of the 15th century.

with its unusual clock adorned with Hebraic symbols: strangely but correctly, the hands turn anti-clockwise. The building still performs its function as the headquarters of Prague's Jewish community; it also houses an excellent kosher restaurant.

The building at the back houses the **"High Synagogue"**, so named because of its location on the second floor; the entrance in the Maiselova leads directly into the lower council chamber, now open to the public as a kosher restaurant. Adjoining is a little park flanked by 19th-century houses with imposing facades and a wealth of ornamental detail.

On the left, by contrast, the ugliness of the Inter-Continental hotel provides a timely warning of the speed at which the delicate harmony of this romantic city can be destroyed by thoughtless town planning. Even if the intention was to create a functional modern building it would have been possible for the architects to find inspiration in the building diagonally opposite. At least its cubist facade strikes a creative accent.

Returning to the Square, the visitor should stroll along the Pařížká (Paris Street). This was created over a century ago within the framework of an arbitrary restoration programme within the Josefov. Its magnificent Art Nouveau facades make it the most spectacular street in the entire city.

Between the Square and the Powder Tower: From the earliest days of the city's history the Celetná was an important trading street. Even though its buildings were frequently rebuilt in accordance with the tastes and fashions of the times (the predominant accent today is baroque), the visitor will be able to discern a number of medieval elements, such as the groin vaulting of No. 2, the **Sixt House** and the wooden roof trusses of No. 3 ("The Three Kings").

On the left-hand side immediately behind the Týn Church, the Štupartská leads down to the **church of St James**. This was originally built by the Minorites during the reign of Charles IV, but it was later the subject of a particularly successful rebuilding in the baroque

The rococo staircase in the Clam Gallas Palais is the work of M.B. Braun (around 1730).

style. The expressive reliefs of the facade and the alteration of the interior to create a theatrical setting provide a fine stage for the frequent organ concerts held on the ornamental and powerful instrument dating from 1705.

Returning to the Celetná, you can continue your exploration of the city along a stretch of the former Royal Way. At the very beginning, almost by the junction with the Square, you will find the **Egon Erwin Kisch Café**, named in memory of the German-speaking Prague journalist who became famous during the 1920s as a roving reporter. Examples of his works can be found in the two bookshops on the left-hand side of the road, or in one of the second-hand shops under the arcades.

A little further on, where an alley joins the main road from the right, stands the corner house known as **"The Black Madonna"**. Its Rondo-Cubist style lends the little square a distinctive note and demonstrates that even in 1912 it was possible to renovate and build anew in the modern idiom without destroying the optical harmony of an entire district.

The end of the Celetná is dominated by the **Powder Tower**. In 1475, King Jagiello had a fortified building erected beside his royal residence, on the site of a defensive gate which had marked the boundary of the Old Town since the 13th century. Badly damaged by the Prussians during the Seven Years' War, it was rebuilt in neo-Gothic style at the end of the 19th century. It was only in the 18th century, when it was used a a powder magazine, that the tower acquired its present name.

Next door – where the former royal court was situated – stands the **Municipal House**. The architects Antonín Balšánek and Osvald Polívka produced the preliminary designs for the Art Nouveau building in 1903; Jan Preisler, Alfons Mucha and Max Švabinský were responsible for the interior, including such exquisite details as the tile pictures, chandeliers, decorative railings and wood panelling. A tour can be combined with a visit to one of the various public rooms. The coffeehouse and restaurant, as well as a wine bar which doubles as a dance hall at night, recall the fact that until fairly recently the house served as the meeting place of the country's so-called Top Ten Thousand. Most concerts in the famous Prague Spring Festival are held in the attractive **Smetana Hall**.

Immediately behind the Municipal House lies another notable building, this time dating from 1907: the **Hotel and Restaurant Paříž** displays a playful mixture of Neo-Gothic and Art Nouveau styles.

The St Agnes Convent: This oasis of tranquillity lies on the banks of the Vltava, off the beaten tourist track yet only a few minutes' walk from the Powder Tower. After years of restoration work, the convent, the oldest Gothic building complex in Prague, was reopened to the public in 1980. It merits a visit, especially on account of its museum of 19th-century Czech Art.

St Agnes was the sister of King Wenceslas I of Bohemia. However, instead of agreeing to a dynastic marriage she took the veil. She founded the **Convent of St Clare** in 1233 and even became the abbess for a short while. A few years later a Minorite Priory was added, but in 1420, during the turbulent Hussite Wars, the entire complex was abandoned. In 1782 it relinquished all pretence of being a convent as a result of the process of secularisation.

The cloister is adorned with plain early Gothic vaulting and simple capitals, but unusually fine and expressive stone carvings are found in the **Chapter Room** and the adjoining Church of St Saviour to the right. The archway is decorated with five crowned heads on each side – men to the right and women to the left. This may indicate that the Přemyslid dynasty extended and used the convent and church as their family chapel and burial place. In the magnificent choir, you will find an elaborate niche where the foundress of the convent was probably going to be buried. The **church of St Francis** is of earlier date, but only the choir has remained more or less intact. Today, freshly restored, it is regularly used as the setting for concerts and lectures.

The Powder Tower is one of the city's main landmarks.

146

THE LESSER QUARTER
AND HRADČANY

At the other side of the Vltava, Prague reveals a very different character from that of the bourgeois Old Town. In the vicinity of the river, the Malá Strana (Lesser Quarter) was previously the home of skilled workers, carters and fishermen; even today, it is a quarter inhabited mostly by ordinary people, students and pensioners. Dominating the area is the residential district on the slopes of Hradčany, where the magnificent palazzi of the aristocracy rise amid wealthy monasteries and churches, the imperial cathedral and, of course, the castle – the seat of the rulers of Prague for over 1,000 years.

The **Charles Bridge** remains the main link between the two halves of the city even today. In view of the traffic – cars, trams and trains – which thunder across the other bridges, the Karlův most is an oasis of calm. Charles IV had the fine stone bridge constructed by his master builder Peter Parler. There had been a stone bridge here before, the Judith Bridge constructed during the latter half of the 12th century and named after the wife of King Vladislav I. But, like its wooden predecessors, it could no longer stand the force of the Vltava and collapsed in 1342.

Charles now wanted to create a permanent link between the two settlements on opposite sides of the river, which in those days were frequently at loggerheads with each other. Begun in 1357, the bridge itself represents the central section of the "Royal Way", along which in medieval times the sovereign walked to his coronation. Today, the Karlův most is a favourite meeting place for half of Prague – local citizens and visitors alike.

Straddling its eastern end is the mighty **Old Town Bridge Tower**, the last work that Peter Parler bequeathed the city. In spite of its slender form and invitingly high archway it was originally designed for defensive purposes, proving its worth in 1648 when the Swedes spent two weeks vainly trying to capture the Old

Town. The west side of the tower was destroyed, but on the Old Town side the gallery of sculptures has survived, including the national patron saint. St Vitus is portrayed protecting the bridge between two kings – Charles IV and Wenceslas IV.

Most of the 30 statues of the saints, which now so dominate the bridge's countenance, were added during the baroque period, although the ensemble was only completed in 1928 with the statue of St Cyril and Methodius. The earliest statue (1683), on the northern central pillar, is that of St John Nepomuk, who was drowned in the Vltava by Wenceslas IV because he spoke out against the latter's religious policies. A pious, and for the moral authority of the Catholic Church a very useful, legend maintains that the king's wrath had been aroused by Nepomuk's brave refusal to break the sanctity of confession by betraying the private secrets of the queen.

Upstream from the bridge, the dramatic weir vividly evokes Smetana's symphonic poem *The Moldau*. Ahead

and to the right, the view is dominated by the Cathedral of St Vitus, crowning the summit of Castle Hill, and at the end of the bridge the Malá Strana is framed between the two **Lesser Quarter Bridge Towers**. The northern tower was built at the same time as the Charles Bridge, but the southern one is a remnant of the old Judith Bridge.

After passing under the arch, visitors should proceed along the Mostecká (Bridge Street) before turning left into the Lázeňská. Continuing past the former hotels "The Spa" and "The Golden Unicorn", you will soon reach the oldest place of worship in the Lesser Quarter, the **church of Our Lady in Chains**, dating from the 12th century. The massive facade combines both Romanesque and Gothic elements. The adjoining Velkopřevoské nam. is bordered by elegant palazzi; the **Maltese Grand Prior's Palace** houses a delightful collection of historical musical instruments.

During the last decade of Communist rule, the palace garden and the island of **Kampa** next door, accessible via a small

bridge over the Čertovká Channel, became the favourite meeting place for the "Flower Children of Prague". They left behind lovingly executed murals in the district of the city known as "Little Venice" on account of its nostalgic water mills and gardens. Their improvised concerts used to be held before an impassive audience of policemen and secret police informers.

Retracing your steps, cross the **Maltese Square**, site of the noble **Palais Nostiz**, also serving as the Ministry of Culture. Turning into the Karmelitská, where the Vrtbovský palác at No. 25 is notable primarily for its terraced garden, the route returns to the Mostecká.

Ever since the 10th century the **Lesser Quarter Square** (Malostranské náměstí) has been the focal point of the settlement under Hradčany Castle. It was the scene of the daily market, and the focal point for trading associations.

The Jesuits transformed the predominantly bourgeois air of this town centre. Exactly as they did when building the Clementinum on the other side of the Vltava, they purchased a large tract of land, had all its buildings razed to the ground – an entire street, two churches and a cemetery – and started building the massive **church of St Nicholas**. Its monumental baroque architecture is a lesson in history. Every detail – from the powerful ceiling frescoes above the forbidding-looking four Doctors of the Church to the elaborately decorated pulpit – expresses the power and absolute authority of the victorious Catholic Church. A comparison with the simple and austere Bethlehem Chapel, in which the heretic Jan Hus preached his sermons, clearly illustrates the full significance of the Counter-Reformation in this Protestant country.

In the immediate vicinity, in the Letenská, which opens on to the square on the northern side, stand the **monastery and church of St Thomas**. The foundation and construction of the Gothic basilica dates from the 13th century; Kilian Ignaz Dientzenhofer gave the church its present appearance, including its imposing facade and the bright interior. The former town hall

A veteran of the times looks on.

(No. 21) was the administrative centre of the Malá Strana until the creation of Metropolitan Prague. It is now the cultural centre **Malostranská beseda**, a popular venue for jazz music.

Neruda Street (Nerudova) is lined with Renaissance, baroque and neoclassical palazzi reflecting the prosperity of the nobility, who chose to build their residences on the approach road to the castle. The house signs in this street help the visitor to get his bearings, especially in the case of "The Three Violins" (No. 12), "The Golden Goblet" (No. 16), "The Golden Horseshoe" (No. 33), "The Black Madonna" (No. 36) and "The Two Suns" (No. 37), once home to the poet Jan Neruda (1834–91), the author of the *Tales of the Lesser Quarter*.

Along the lower section, at No. 5, visitors cannot fail to notice the **Palais Czernin-Morzin** on the left, dating from 1714 and boasting an impressive doorway and a balcony supported by statues of Moors. Built at about the same time was the **Palais Thun-Hohenstein**, diagonally opposite at No. 20. Next door

are the **church and monastery of St Cajetan**, creating an architectural unity typical of the closing years of the 17th century. At its upper end, the Nerudova gives way to a romantic stairway leading to the castle; to the left, the Loretánská leads out to the Loreto shrine and the former poor district, the Nový Svět.

The Santa Casa: Loreto is a pilgrimage village in Italy. It was believed that angels transported the sacred home of the Virgin Mary from the Promised Land to Loreto in the 13th century. When the Catholic Habsburgs tried during the Counter-Reformation to convert their Hussite subjects back to the "true" faith, they used the pious legend to serve their cause. They had replicas of the Santa Casa built throughout the land. The best known and most attractive of these is the **Loreto of Prague** (1626–1750). Unlike the simple original, the shrine became, across the centuries, an entire complex consisting of various buildings with a chapel, cloisters which were several storeys high and the church of the Nativity. Dominating the group is

The Lesser Quarter and St Nicholas viewed from the castle.

the early baroque tower, into which a carillon which chimes every hour was built in 1694. The Loreto's main attraction is the **treasure chamber**, in which are stored the precious votive gifts presented by pious pilgrims to the statue of the Virgin Mary.

The castle quarter: The Nový Svět ("New World") is a picturesque alley leading off the Loreto Square. For many centuries it was the poor district of the Hradčany quarter; today, however, the tiny, lovingly restored cottages with their doll's-house windows and tiny front gardens have made it a popular residential area among local artists.

For a long time, the Castle Square (Hradčanské nám), enclosed by magnificent buildings, formed an independent community, albeit under the control of the lords of the castle. So, beside the stairs leading up from the Nerudova, the former town hall dating from 1598 is adorned with both the imperial and municipal coats of arms. The southern side of the square is dominated by the stucco facade of the **Schwarzenberg Palace**.

Completed in 1563, it is regarded as one of the finest examples of Bohemian Renaissance, and today houses the **Museum of Military History**. Beside the castle entrance, the **Archbishop's Palace** adds an additional note of architectural splendour. Only visitors who chance to arrive on Maundy Thursday will be permitted to view the exquisite **French Gobelin tapestries** and other treasures, for there is no public access for the rest of the year. The **Sternberg Palais** behind contains the National Gallery's priceless collection of non-Bohemian Old Masters.

Hradčany Castle: Prague Castle is now over 1,000 years old; the first Czech rulers, the Přemyslids, established their main residence here, on a strategic site dominating the ford over the Vltava. Bořivoj, the first prince to be mentioned in records, also had a little church built, to replace the pre-Christian burial ground. Since then, succeeding generations of rulers have enlarged the complex with chapels, palaces, defensive structures and residential buildings.

The Castle Steps.

A tour of Hradčany Castle begins in front of the **Matthias Gate** in the first courtyard, architecturally speaking the most recent of the three. To the right, a flight of steps leads up to the former Throne Room; today this is where state receptions are held.

The second courtyard, with its beautiful baroque fountain, is more extensive. To the right is the **chapel of the Holy Cross** built by Anselmo Lurago in 1753. The **cathedral treasure**, including reliquaries, monstrances, crucifixes, and mementos of Bohemian saints and kings, has been on view here since 1961.

Hard left, in the northwest corner, is the **Castle Gallery**, which since 1964 has housed rediscovered works of art collected by the Habsburgs in the 16th and 17th century; above this are the **Spanish Room** and **Emperor Rudolf's Gallery**. Rudolf II, the last ruler to bring imperial glamour to Prague, was an eccentric collector. To the wry amusement of his contemporaries, he showed no interest in politics, but assembled a curious collection of artefacts, includ-

ing stuffed exotic animals, alchemists' tools and objects for use in shamanistic rituals. Although this remarkable collection was dispersed by war and plundering, and at one stage largely removed to Vienna, what remains is still wellworth seeing.

Through the north gate of the second courtyard, a causeway leads across the old moat directly to the attractively landscaped **Royal Gardens**, known today as the Presidential Gardens, open only at weekends. The visitor should head straight for the **Belvedere**, where plans are afoot to restore the former summer residence. In any case, there is an attractive view of the magnificent cathedral across the moat, now transformed into a deer enclosure.

The Cathedral: The **cathedral of St Vitus**, a Gothic basilica 405 ft (124 metres) long and 196 ft (60 metres) wide, was begun in 1344 on the instructions of Charles IV. The first of his inspired architects, Matthew of Arras, was trained in the French Gothic school; his basic design for the cathedral recalls

A smile from the Lesser Quarter.

MASTER BUILDERS

Charles IV, the scion of the Přemyslids who attained the imperial crown in 1355, transformed the city on the Moldau into the political and cultural centre of his vast empire. Under Charles, Prague was dubbed the "Mother of all cities". Gothic Prague, admired by visitors even today, bears the stamp of this native son of Luxembourg. The Charles University, the New Town clustered around Wenceslas and Charles Squares, the Charles Bridge, and – towering above all – the Cathedral of St Vitus – were all part of Charles's legacy.

Peter Parler: On 1356 Peter Parler was summoned to work on the Cathedral of St Vitus as the successor of Matthew of Arras. In choosing this young master builder, Charles provided Prague with a master builder of genius, entirely equal to the task of reflecting his imperialist aspirations. Parler was the son of a German family of builders and sculptors who made a significant contribution to the development of Central European Gothic art and architec-

ture. The family name, Parler stems from Parlier/Polier, the title of the second-in-command of a team of builders. As their master's trademark, the family used an angle bar in the form of an S-rune interrupted in two places.

Peter Parler, the undisputed supreme master builder of the family, was born in 1330 in Schwäbisch Gmünd and buried in 1399 in St Vitus's Cathedral. Charles IV recognised Peter's exceptional talent when he saw him working on the church of the Holy Cross in his home town. The young architect's task in Prague was to prove the most important of his career: the completion of the Gothic cathedral in the Bohemian capital, which in 1344 had been elevated to the rank of archiepiscopal see. The new church was to serve as both coronation cathedral and royal burial place.

Peter Parler's genius can best be appreciated in his design of the choir. The monumental fan vaulting was the first of its kind in Central Europe and became the model for all German vaulted roofs until the end of the Gothic era. Parler assumed sole responsibility for the completion of the main building begun by his predecessor; by allowing light to flood through the upper walls he created a powerful contrast to the relatively dark lower section of the nave. A further trend was set by the cuboid shape of the building, which arose from the juxtaposition of the smaller units representing the various storeys. The angling of the transept towards the imperial palace provided a powerful link between the sacred and secular worlds.

The Old Town Bridge Tower is one of the loveliest and least corrupted examples of this building-block principle. Marking the entrance to the Charles Bridge, its archway clears the entire width of the carriageway and thereby displays the typical Parler characteristic of the use of contrasts.

Peter Parler was also a seminal influence in the field of sculpture. The row of busts in the cathedral triforium represent an important stage in the development of medieval portraiture.

Other documented works of Parler are the All Saints' Chapel in Hradčany Castle, the choir of the church of St Bartholomew in Kolín and the church of St Barbara in Kutná Hora, which contains one of the loveliest examples of fan vaulting in existence.

St Wenceslas in the cathedral, by Peter Parler.

The Dientzenhofers: By the time the Dientzenhofers, the second of the great German families of builders, made their artistic mark on Prague, the importance of the former metropolis had degenerated into that of a provincial backwater in the shadow of Vienna. Whilst the magnificence of the monumental Gothic buildings reflected the glory of the reign of Charles IV, the baroque splendour of a later age stood in crass contrast to the cultural and economic decline that the country had suffered since the disastrous Battle of the White Mountain in 1620. The architectural excesses of the baroque lent the city an illusion of new vitality, but at the same time they testified in stone to the triumph of the Habsburg Counter-Reformation. This impression persists even to this day, when you walk alongside the wall of the Jesuit Clementinum, which seems to tower over the former Royal Way between Charles Street and the Charles Bridge like a massive fortress.

That the powerful ensembles of baroque Prague should nonetheless be regarded as an architectural triumph is due in no small measure to the influence of the Dientzenhofer family. Born in the village of Aibling in Upper Bavaria, the five brothers moved to Prague in order to study contemporary architecture. Whilst four of them left the city over the years in order to return to South Germany, where they left their mark on a number of important sacred buildings, **Christoph Dientzenhofer** (1655–1722) lived the rest of his life in Bohemia, becoming with Fischer von Erlach the joint "Father of Late German baroque". His churches are designed according to the baldachin principle, whereby he blended the Guarini-inspired interaction between space and roof vaulting with the traditional Bavarian pilaster system. Examples of Christoph Dientzenhofer's architectural skill can be found all over Bohemia; his supreme masterpiece is considered to be the church of St Nicholas in the Lesser Quarter of Prague.

His skills were, however, eclipsed by those of his son **Kilian Ignaz Dientzenhofer** (1689–1751), who was born in Prague and is regarded as one of the leading architects of Late baroque. Although he was responsible for a large number of secular buildings (e.g. the Villa America and the Palais Kinsky in Prague), Dientzenhofer the Young-er's main interest lay in the construction of churches. Whilst his father favoured a longitudinal plan, Kilian Ignaz Dientzenhofer preferred a centralised building, which he laid out in the form of a double shell. He developed this principle in Prague in the twin-towered centralised design of the church of St John Nepomuk on the Rock in the Nové Město.

Although the baroque building on the Old Town ring bears only the signature of Kilian Ignaz Dientzenhofer (the paintings are by Peter Asam), the church commissioned by the Jesuits in the Lesser Quarter was the joint work of both Dientzenhofers. The father was responsible for the nave, and the son for the choir and the dome. This jewel of baroque architecture took almost 60 years to complete; it is one of the masterpieces of the era, and its silhouette dominates the skyline of the Lesser Quarter to this day.

The Ursuline church in Kutná Hora and the church of St Mary in Carlsbad (Karlovy Vary) were completed by Kilian Ignaz Dientzenhofer according to plans drawn up by his father. Both buildings represent further highlights of the baroque. ∎

The dome of St Nicholas was the work of Kilian Ignaz Dientzenhofer.

the French models. After his death, Peter Parler and his sons continued the work, but gave the building their own individual stamp.

Since it is impossible to step back and admire the facade from a distance, the visitor can only take it in as a steeply vertical wall. Consequently, entering the vast nave can be disorientating. There are no mysterious shafts of light as in other great cathedrals, for the original glass was replaced by modern panes. At first glance, too, the cathedral seems to lack a unity of style – on the one hand, because of the numerous extensions and additions across the centuries, the last being as recently as 1929, and on the other because the church was planned from the outset not only as a place of worship but also as a coronation church, mausoleum and destination of national pilgrimage. The statues on the triforium record the important personages associated with the cathedral, from Charles IV to contemporary personalities.

The magnificent **chapel of St Wenceslas,** in the south transept, recalls the life and works of the saintly king of Bohemia. Two arches further on, in the chapel of the Holy Cross, a staircase descends to remnants of the walls of early medieval churches and to the Royal Crypt, with the sarcophagus of Charles IV.

Visitors should not forget to glance upwards to admire the lozenges adorning the roof of the choir. The architect Peter Parler displayed a masterly ability to combine revolutionary technical solutions with elegant caprice. This is evident on the south side of the choir, where the interplay of columns and struts and the remarkable complexity of the tracery are especially impressive.

Unusual in both position and execution is the **Golden Door** with its remarkable entrance hall on the south flank. It is the main entrance to the cathedral and it was through here that monarchs passed en route to their coronation. A monarch's journey was not a long one, as the **Royal Palace** lay directly opposite. The visitor enters the majestic **Vladislav Hall** via the Riders'

The Royal Way on the Lesser Quarter side starts in Bridge Street (Mostecká ul.).

Staircase, made wide enough for rulers and guests to enter this throne and tournament room on horseback. The intricate vaulting, spanning the whole width of the hall, makes it one of the most remarkable architectural achievements of the late Gothic era in central Europe.

The **Bohemian Chancellery** was situated in the adjoining rooms. On 23 May 1618, the furious citizens of Bohemia entered the room of the Imperial stadtholders Martiniz and Slawata and threw them, and their secretary, out of the window. Although they all survived the 50-foot drop into the moat, this Second Defenestration of Prague is what sparked off the Thirty Years' War.

Opposite the eastern choir lies the Romanesque **St George's Basilica**. Despite extensions and rebuilding schemes during Renaissance and baroque times, the church has retained its original early medieval appearance and, following a recent renovation, has been restored to its former glory once more. Behind the cathedral, the late Gothic castle fortifications are dominated by the massive **Mihulka Tower**. It contains, amongst other curiosities, an alchemist's workshop; there is also an attractive view over the northern section of the castle complex.

Circumnavigating St George's and then turning uphill to the left, the route continues into the **Golden Alley**, a popular attraction containing antique shops, book shops and even a pub. The tiny houses, tucked into the arches of the battlements, have been the homes of craftsmen, goldsmiths and tailors for four centuries; they were thus conveniently situated to offer their services to their exalted neighbours.

From here, visitors should continue downhill, past the former burgrave's office – now the Children's House – to the **Palais Lobkovic**, housing exhibitions on local history. Through the East Gate, in the shadow of the **Black Tower**, is a terrace with a panoramic view. From here, they can descend the old Castle Steps.

Down below, the route turns right and then right again into a second alley, the

Blossom in the Strahov Park.

Letenská. The first section runs alongside a blank wall, until a gateway suddenly provides access to the lovely gardens of the **Palais Waldstein**, the first baroque palace in Prague, built by the legendary general Albrecht von Wallenstein.

The massive building, now serving as the Ministry of Culture, is not open to the public, but the tranquil garden with its fountains and groups of statues is. Unfortunately, when the Swedes conquered the Malá Strana and with it the palace of their former enemy, they removed the magnificent bronze figures by the Mannerist sculptor Adriaen de Vries. Nonetheless some have been replaced by replicas, including the Laocoon group. The park extends as far as the Garden Room, where the unusual barrel-vaulted ceiling is decorated with illustrations of the Trojan War – an allegorical portrayal of the bloody doings of the owner.

Waldstein Square (Valdšteijnské nám.) is dominated by the broad facade of the palace. Next door stands the **Palais Lebedour** (No. 3). Construction of Palais Lebedour commenced in 1588, as the date carved above the doorway indicates, but the building assumed its present form during the 19th century. Other buildings of note on the square and in the adjacent Waldstein Street are the **Palais Pálffy** (No. 14), **Palais Kolovrat** (No. 110) and, at the far end, the Palais Fürstenberg. Virtually all received their elegant facades during the 18th century; even more attractive are the gardens on the slopes of Castle Hill, which were laid out with great originality by baroque landscape architects.

The Sněmovní ("Parliament Street") leads back to the Malostranské náměstí. At No. 4 is the **Palais Thun**, converted into the local parliament building in 1801. A memorial plaque recalls the fact that the first parliament of the Czechoslovak Republic met here on 14 November 1918 and officially deposed the Habsburg emperors.

Petrín Hill and Strahov Monastery: If you board the No. 22 tram by the National Theatre and travel across the

The Philosophers' Room in the Strahov Monastery Library.

Vltava as far as Hellichova, you will see, just opposite the tram stop, a signpost announcing the Lanova draha and indicating the way to the cable car up **Petřín Hill**.

This ancient cable car runs every 20 minutes, but it is much pleasanter to walk through the orchards and meadows. At the beginning the route passes a monument to the writer Jan Neruda; above the first cable car station, the rambling café terrace of the Vinárna Nebozízek offers a breathtaking panorama. On the summit of the hill are a number of interesting sights: the **Labyrinth of Mirrors**, the **chapel of St Lawrence**, dating from the 12th century, and the **Prague Eiffel Tower** – a small-scale replica of the famous original, but which nonetheless offers a remarkable view over the city.

Another important landmark lies only a few minutes' walk away. By passing through a baroque gateway, you can gain the **Strahov monastery and library**. The oldest buildings in this complex were completed after 1143, but completely destroyed by a fire in 1258. The wars of the next centuries also left their mark, with the result that very little remained of the original Romanesque building. Today the monastery is predominantly baroque in style, but it contains early Gothic and Renaissance elements. Only **St Mary's Church** retains traces of the Romanesque original.

The monastery library is one of the most beautiful and comprehensive historic libraries in Europe. The basis of the collection of over 130,000 volumes, including 2,500 first editions, was established by a perspicacious abbot in the middle of the 18th century. The secularisation under Emperor Joseph II led to the dissolution of a large number of monasteries, but Strahov was spared. The ruler of the monastery at the time took advantage of the dissolutions and purchased a number of collections at low prices. In 1945 the collection was enriched by the addition of works from other monasteries which were being closed down.

Among the greatest treasures are the **Strahov Gospels**, dating from the 10th century (the book on display is only a replica: the original is in safe keeping), and a first edition of *De Revolutionibus Orbium Coelestium*, the work in which Copernicus first expounded his heliocentric theory of the universe in 1543.

The library's true fascination lies in the exquisite form of the two main rooms. The **Theologians' Room**, with baroque frescoes in the stucco cartouches, is particularly attractive. Here you will find a small, barred shrine which contained books banned by the Church's censors. In the middle of the room stand a number of valuable globes from the Netherlands, dating from the 17th century. The **Philosophers' Room** is notable for its rich gold inlay on the walnut cupboards and the elaborate ceiling frescoes depicting the harmony of philosophy, science and religion, by the rococo artist Anton Maulbertsch.

Today the library is a Museum of Czech Literature and Writings. The archives contain 3 million items and include the works of over 1,200 Czech men of letters.

A typical amiable gesture from the late Pan Tau, alias Ota Simánek.

THE NEW TOWN

Wenceslas Square is hardly what one might call beautiful; it is rambling rather than intimate, a long shrill market place rather than a chic boulevard. Its character reflects its original purpose, for it was designed as a horse fair, and was intended to serve as the bustling axis of the Nové Město, the "New Town", which Charles IV had constructed in a semicircle surrounding the Old Town (Staré Město), which was bursting at the seams.

Since the end of the last century elegant buildings have mushroomed in place of the wooden shacks and dilapidated tenement blocks. Prague's revolutions, the great popular uprisings against despotism and foreign oppression, from the Hussite Rebellion to the Velvet Revolution of November 1989, have all begun here; at various times the square has been the stage for displays of national military strength, bitter defeats and jubilant victory parades.

The most prominent building on the square is the **National Museum**. It was constructed between 1885 and 1890 at the instigation of the Bohemian Patriotic Association. It was the Czechs' impressive answer to the German Theatre (now the Smetana Opera House) on the road to the main railway station, which had opened a few years previously to the strains of a Wagner opera. Another reminder of the proud era of Bohemian independence is the equestrian **statue of St Wenceslas**, a massive monument erected in 1913.

As one walks down the square, it loses its civic character and turns into a lively shopping and pedestrian area. Of note on the left-hand side is the modernist **Palais Alfa** (No. 28), built in 1928. One of the finest and most classical examples of Art Nouveau architecture in Prague is the **Peterka House** at the far end of Wenceslas Square. The Czech architect Jan Kotěra built this private residence in just one year (1900).

On the other side of the square are the splendid Art Nouveau Evropa, Zlatá

Preceding pages: the magnificent facades of the Pařížká. Below, a shop with Art Nouveau facade.

Husa and Ambassador hotels. The **Evropa**, dating from 1904, is a popular location for period films. Each floor of the hotel is decorated with floral motifs, mosaics and ornaments. The elegant café was recently meticulously renovated in the original style.

At the far end of the square, next to the row of hotels, stands the Palais Koruna. Constructed shortly before the war, its architecture demonstrates early constructivist elements combined with the decorative features of Art Nouveau.

Na příkopě ("the Moat") is a lively pedestrian street, packed with strollers and shoppers. No. 10 is a magnificent baroque palais; it has a garden restaurant and serves as the venue for cultural events. Each morning the **Čedok Office** at No. 18 sells international air and train tickets; the **Prague Information Service** is next door, at No. 20. The former aristocratic town house at No. 22 today houses a cultural centre with a restaurant and bistro.

Back on Wenceslas Square, the Alfa Passage leads to the **church of Our Lady of the Snows**, founded in 1347. It was actually commissioned by Emperor Charles IV as a coronation cathedral, but as a result of the Wars of Religion which broke out a few years later it only proved possible to complete the chancel. The church became famous as the arena of the radical Hussites. In 1419, incited by their preacher Jan Želivský, they marched to the New Town Hall in order to teach the self-opinionated councillors a lesson and to demand the release of their brethren who were being held in prison.

Národní třída (the "Street of the Nation") is, like Na příkopě, a wide and busy pedestrian area. On the right stands the modern department store Maj; to the left is the enchanting **Kanka House** (No. 16) and the baroque **church of St Ursula** (No. 8), with fine frescoes and statues and a dynamic altar painting of the Assumption. The **Monastery Wine Bar** serves a fine selection of wines and specialities.

The end of the street is dominated by the **National Theatre**. The historic

Catching Christmas carp on Wenceslas Square.

building on the banks of the Vltava is a fine example of Czech neo-Renaissance architecture and embodies the national enthusiasm for culture at the end of the 19th century. On 18 November 1882, the curtain was raised on a gala performance of Smetana's opera *Libuše* – a musical rendition of the myth of the founding of Prague. The adjacent New Theatre is used primarily for ballet, as well as for **Laterna Magika** performances (*see page 173*).

Opposite, enjoying a magnificent view of the theatre and the Vltava, is the **Café Slávia**, the ultimate Prague coffeehouse. It still retains a hint of the turn-of-the-century atmosphere in which tourists and local citizens, fashionable ladies and elegant gigolos gathered to drink coffee and listen to the orchestra.

Down on the Vltava the Slavic Island (Slovanský ostrov), so called because it was the venue of the first Slavic Congress in 1848, is now the site of a popular garden restaurant and cultural events are held here during the evening. The Mánes House of Fine Art on the banks

of the river is worth a visit. The building itself is of interest and reveals the influence of the Bauhaus movement; inside, exhibitions are organised by the Artists' Association. There is also an attractive café with a splendid view of the river.

The Resslova ul. forms the extension of the **Jirásek Bridge**, leading away from the Vltava. At the second crossroads stands the Romanesque **church of St Wenceslas**, the place of worship of the Czech-Hussite Church. Diagonally opposite, the exuberant baroque facade of the **church of SS Cyril and Methodius** was the scene of much blood-letting in the summer of 1942, when the conspirators responsible for the assassination of the hated Reichsprotector Reinhard "the hangman" Heydrich hid in the crypt. After three weeks they were betrayed to the SS, who then surrounded the entire block with 350 men. The three Czechs on guard in the nave managed to hold out for two hours before being killed with hand grenades; the remaining four down in the crypt shot themselves before the Germans reached them. The whole one-sided operation lasted six hours.

Charles Square was planned as the hub of the New City from its inception. Today it is dominated by the mighty **church of St Ignatius** which served as the headquarters of the Jesuits from 1677. The stately **New Town Hall**, where the Hussite Revolution began in 1419, occupies the northern end of the square. The Town Hall remained the political hub for the ordinary people of the New Town until 1784, when the four constituent towns which made up Prague of the time were joined together to form a single administrative unit.

To the south lies the **Faust House**, which has been associated with alchemists ever since the 14th century. Though transformed during the baroque era, the present building actually dates from the 16th century; at that time it was used by the Englishman Edward Kelley, who served as alchemist to Rudolf II. It is said that Kelley was awarded the post after promising the emperor a gold ingot fresh from his laboratory.

A few paces further on stands the **A chimney sweep plies his trade.**

church of St John on the Rock; an extravagant staircase leads up to the entrance, flanked by slightly protruding towers which curve away from the main axis of the building. The dome is adorned with a fresco depicting the Ascent of St John Nepomuk.

The **Emmaus Monastery** to the south of the square deserves even closer attention. Subsequent to its foundation by Charles IV it came to play a significant political and religious role because Mass was celebrated here according to the rites of the Old Slavonic Church – an obvious attempt on the part of Crown and Church to gain influence over the Orthodox Christians of Eastern Europe. Shortly before the end of World War II, many medieval works of art were destroyed when the monastery was bombed; nonetheless, the fine cloisters with their frescoes dating from about 1360 are worth a visit in their own right.

For visitors in need of refreshment, the U Fleků, situated in the Křemencova near the Town Hall is the ideal choice. In summer a folk orchestra plays in the beer garden, but the pub atmosphere is equally convivial inside. Roast pork with dumplings is the order of the day. Every visitor to Prague should make a point of visiting this typical Old Prague tavern at least once; it is to the Czech capital what the Hofbräuhaus is to Munich, or the Preservation Hall is to New Orleans.

Vyšehrad: Above the Vltava stand the ruins of **Vyšehrad Castle**. Legend has it that this was the home of Princess Libuše who prophesied the founding of the city. It became the political and religious centre of the country until, in the 12th century, this role was assigned to Hradčany.

Apart from the St Martin's Rotunda, there is now little intact evidence of the glories of those early years. More interesting is the adjoining **cemetery**, where outstanding personalities of Czech culture and science lie buried. Here the tombs of the composers Antonín Dvořák and Bedřich Smetana, as well as those of the poets Karel Hynek Mácha and Karel Čapek, have become the goal of many an admiring pilgrim.

The National Theatre and the Vltava Bridge.

NIGHTLIFE IN PRAGUE

A visitor setting out to discover the secret charms of Prague after nightfall may well find himself falling into raptures. Bathed in the light of its old-fashioned street lamps, the entire city is enveloped in a veil of romance which encourages long walks. At every corner one is tempted to pause in order to revel in the breathtaking beauty of this historic capital.

The coffehouse atmosphere: During a leisurely walk, perhaps along Charles Street, the visitor will discover numerous little bars and cafés with vaulted ceilings under whose arches he can enjoy an aperitif before dinner. Amongst them will be found the Espresso Bar and the city's first coffeehouse, U zlatého hada. Across the venerable Charles Bridge – during warm summer evenings a favourite rendezvous for lovers, musicians and tourists – you will find the Café de Colombia tucked away immediately behind the archway. No one should fail to stop here to sample the blabla, a brew of coffee laced with local schnapps whose warming properties are appreciated not only in winter. Local citizens and overseas visitors rub shoulders in this small and usually hopelessly overcrowded room; the atmosphere only gains from the enforced intimacy.

Visitors searching for a congenial place in which to while away the evening hours should certainly investigate the elegant coffeehouses. The latter serve not only coffee, but also typical local wines and all other alcoholic drinks except beer; they usually remain open until 11pm. A number of cafés with exceptionally fine Art Nouveau décor also provide live classical music nightly from about 7pm; they include the **Café Slávia**, the **Evropa**, the **Paříž** and the **U Domů**.

Beer metropolis: Beer drinkers can have a field day in Prague with less effort than in virtually any other city in the world. Pubs serving beer enjoy a long, rich tradition here. The brew is known simply as *pivo* in all Slavonic languages;

it is without doubt the national drink of the Czech Republic. A pivnice is an establishment in which one can do more than merely quench one's thirst; here, locals and foreign visitors alike sample a wide range of high-percentage brews accompanied by hearty Czech specialities. Within Prague can be found more than 1,300 inns and taverns. Many of them can look back over a history spanning several centuries. Convivial traditional taverns include the **U Fleků** – a must on the itinerary of every visitor, the **U Pinkasů** – the first Prague tavern to serve Pilsner as well as local lager, the **U Kalicha** – a favourite haunt of the hero of Jaroslav Hašek's famous novel *The Good Soldier Schweyk*, and the **U svatého Tomáše**, whose Gothic vaults have witnessed more than 600 years of brewing history. But here, as in all similar establishments, closing time is 11pm.

Eating Bohemian: Restaurants, on the other hand, and the *vinárnas* – the wine bars which are primarily eating establishments – are open for somewhat longer. Here, in an elegantly informal

atmosphere, the menu shows a preponderance of meat dishes. Fish appears less frequently, according to season. When visiting a restaurant or *vinárna*, it is advisable to book in advance in order to ensure that seats are available. The years of Communism have unfortunately left their mark on service and food standards alike. You are not likely to be disappointed, however, if you visit one of the following restaurants.

U Plebána is a *vinárna* on idyllic Bethlehem Square. Its breast of duck is particularly delicious; the hors d'oeuvres are also a speciality. Another *vinárna*, **U sedmi Andělů**, usually serves a variety of different menus, in a setting as tasteful as the food. In the **U zlaté Studny** you can sample a generous meat dish known as a Moravian Platter. When booking a table, you should insist on being allocated one in the vaulted cellar dining room. Also worth a visit is yet another *vinarna*, the **U Sixtů**. Its attractive décor is one reason for doing so; another is the cuisine, which has a distinctly French accent.

Strict vegetarians may have problems in Prague. Meatless dishes are normally only found in Chinese restaurants. There are a number of these in addition to the well-known **Činská Restaurace**. The guide to the restaurants of Prague obtainable from the Information Office will supply an up-to-date list.

The cultural palette: Apart from the numerous bars, coffeehouses, beer taverns, restaurants and wine bars in the city centre, which no one can fail to spot during any stroll through the capital, Prague can also offer the visitor a remarkable wealth of cultural activities for a city of its size. During the early evening hours you will hear time and again the strains of organ, violin and piano as you pass the many churches, palaces and monasteries. Every day there is a large choice of classical concerts; even the music-loving citizens of Prague, who otherwise seldom venture out at night, flock to pay their respects to well-loved composers and fêted performers.

The many historic buildings provide a magnificent setting with fine acous- **Vltava illuminations.**

tics; not content with simply providing a semi-mechanical rendition of the works on the programme, here the artists can offer their audiences a truly multi-faceted cultural experience. Of particular merit in this respect are the concert halls of the **St Agnes Convent** and the **Smetana Room** in the **Municipal House**.

The theatre: Prague's numerous theatres provide a further enrichment of the cultural palette. There are more than 25 of them all told, although they are of secondary importance for the tourist because of the language problem. Until the Velvet Revolution in November 1989, the theatre represented for local citizens much more than just a pleasant means of passing an evening; it served as a medium which encouraged the development of revolutionary ideas and opposition to government doctrines.

Although state censorship determined the formal repertoire, a finely-tuned level of ambiguous communication beyond the apparent significance of the spoken word arose between actors and audience. It is no coincidence that Václav Havel, a poet and playwright who was a master of this subversive form of language, should have become initially the spokesman of the opposition and subsequently the first democratically elected president of Czechoslovakia**.**

Foreign visitors will find that the **Nová Scéna** and the **National Theatre** offer operatic and theatrical performances not only in Czech. The tiny **Braník Theatre** presents avant-garde pantomime; under the mime specialist Boris Hybner, the programme in the **Gag Theatre** may well bring tears of laughter to your eyes. The **Laterna Magika** rose to world fame following its appearance at the World Exhibition in Brussels in 1958. In line with the official policy of privatisation, it was evicted from its traditional setting on the Národní Třída at the end of 1990. The company now performs in the National Theatre.

Since June 1991, Prague has also been the home of a highly successful English-speaking repertory company, created by theatre enthusiasts from the

Jazz with Milan Svoboda.

United States, Germany and the Czech Republic.

Advance purchase of tickets is recommended in all cases, whether you wish to attend a concert or a theatrical performance.

Jazz and dance: Jazz enthusiasts, on the other hand, can risk a spontaneous visit to a concert. Prague has long been famous for its fine jazz. It goes without saying that this type of music, which has found its second home in the Czech capital, should be performed in a large number of clubs. The most famous of them is the **Reduta**. Also popular with local citizens are the **Jazz Art Club** and the **Viola Club** in the theatre of the same name. Another favourite haunt is the **Press Jazz Club**, which is open until 2am. Its varied programme appeals to enthusiasts of all ages.

It soon becomes clear to visitors wishing to take part in the city's cultural life that Prague can offer a very varied programme of events. Things are a little more difficult if you prefer to go dancing, or wish for entertainment which

continues into the small hours. The choice here is restricted almost exclusively to discotheques and nightclubs. Aficionados accustomed to the flair and modernity of the nightspots of the capitals of Western Europe will, in any case, be disappointed here. The city's handful of discotheques are reminiscent of conservative cafés dansants, offering a mixture of popular and rock music. The discotheques in the larger hotels are more up-to-date, but just as noisy.

They also serve as popular pick-up spots for the local prostitutes. Prague can boast more than 25,000 members of the world's oldest profession – a remarkable statistic in view of the city's total population of barely 1.2 million. Despite this flourishing trade there is no official red-light district; it is thus hardly surprising that upon closer inspection the discotheques of Prague look rather like seedy nightclubs. It seems likely, however, that the situation will be clarified before too long, and that a finer distinction will be drawn between a brothel and a discotheque.

Around Wenceslas Square can be seen posters advertising strip-tease shows and similar seedy amusement. Often recommended is the **Alhambra Club** in the Ambassador Hotel; the programme, a mixture of buffoonery, music, variety and Black Theatre, is more soporific than entertaining. The Jalta Club and the Lucerna Bar offer similar shows.

New on the Prague night scene are the city's casinos. The ubiquitous ladies of the night gather here, escorted by foreign businessmen and a handful of locals with foreign currency to spare – usually taxi-drivers and waiters, counted amongst the wealthiest people in the land – as well as curious tourists and professional gamblers.

Those for whom such frenzied activity is too much, however, need only to retrace their steps to find once more on every corner the nightly enchantment of this loveliest of cities. In the silent alleys of the Old Town or the Lesser Quarter, the din of the discotheques gives way to the chiming of Prague's countless church bells, ringing out in gentle harmony the passing of the hours.

A young flautist at a Christmas concert.

LATERNA MAGIKA

The Socialists regarded the theatre as primarily a service industry which was there to provide the population with cultural entertainment during its leisure hours. They instituted a strict diet of traditional, realistic plays and conservative productions.

At the end of the 1950s, however, an experimental theatre group struck a completely new tone in Czech theatre. The ensemble – initially created by members of the National Theatre solely for the World Exhibition in Brussels, EXPO 58 – was known as the Laterna Magika. It aimed to present visitors to the Czech pavilion with a first-hand impression of life in the socialist republic, its art and its culture. Such was its success that the former cinema of the Adria Palace in Národní třída was placed at the troupe's disposal (today it has moved to the Nova scéna, Národní 40). It has played to full houses virtually non-stop ever since, and has become one of the main tourist attractions in Prague. No doubt one reason for its success is that no knowledge of the Czech language is necessary in order to follow the performance.

The name "Magic Lantern" has been retained to this day. At the heart of the performing technique stands a cinema-like projection procedure in which the actors on stage become directly involved. Through a skilled combination of projections, movable screens and stage props, the plays move between light and darkness, uniting film and theatre, mime and dance into one extraordinary stage experience. The disparate sections never have an independent effect, but work together as a synchronised whole.

At the centre of the spectacle is the visual impression, the dialogue between stage and screen. The protagonists work with additional screens, on to which films or slides are projected. The often confusing actions of the performers on various levels of the stage in combination with the ever-changing projections give the audience the feeling of being in a world in which the laws of time and place have lost their meaning. The traditional theatre genres, such as tragedy and comedy, are fused into a new, poetic drama

of light which has not only entranced countless audiences, but also left its mark on the development of international drama.

The performances of the Laterna Magika are counted among the most original on offer in the Czech capital. Programmes such as *The Magic Circus*, the *Tales of Hoffmann*, the *Odyssey* or the ballet *Minotaurus*, choreographed after a libretto by Dürrenmatt, have lost nothing of their fascination over the years. The founder of the Laterna Magika, the producer Alfred Radok, suffered the same fate as many other artists and men of letters. In 1968 he was forced to flee the country. When he died in exile in Sweden in 1976, the media in his native country did not consider the fact worth mentioning.

As a perfect theatre of illusion the Laterna Magika makes no attempt at a political statement, but it was nonetheless overtaken by the events of the Velvet Revolution. The Civic Forum established its first headquarters here, and it was in the dressing room that Václav Havel wrote the appeal which ultimately forced Milos Jakeš to resign from the office of General Secretary of the Communist Party. ■

The Laterna Magika, the "Magic Lantern", in full swing.

TRIPS FROM PRAGUE

Every year, **Karlštejn Castle**, lying 19 miles (30 km) southwest of Prague on the railway line to Plzeň, is stormed by thousands of tourists in coaches, cars and trains. They achieve what their ancestors in past centuries never managed, for the fortress, protected by massive walls and protruding cliffs, was impregnable to attackers.

But Charles IV did not have Karlštejn built as a military stronghold – strategically speaking, it would have served no useful purpose on this site. It was planned with the sole purpose of safeguarding the holy relics and coronation insignia of the kingdom. In medieval times these relics were of immense significance: they included two thorns from Jesus's crown, a fragment of the sponge soaked in vinegar offered to Him on the Cross, a tooth of St John the Baptist and the arm of St Anne. To possess such treasures was seen as a sign of God's favour, a blessing for the emperor and his subjects. Even if Charles had felt no regard for this precious legacy personally, it would have been regarded as an unpardonable sin if they had not been used to further the greater glory of the emperor and the Holy Roman Empire.

Charles's collection of relics was presented once a year for public worship. On the Friday after Easter, the "Day of the Holy Relics", the people flocked to the Karlštejn, and on 29 November, the anniversary of the death of Charles IV, Mass is celebrated in the chapel of the Cross, where the most precious items are preserved.

It is obligatory for visitors to Karlštejn Castle to join one of the official tours, which are conducted in various languages. Even so, a visit to the castle is an interesting experience, especially if one arrives by car along the Berounka Valley, or – best of all – by one of the frequent slow trains from Smíchov Station in Prague. From Karlštejn Station the castle is a pleasant stroll across the river, through the village itself and uphill through the castle grounds. The tours begin in the **Imperial Palace**, before proceeding to St Mary's Tower, the Great Tower and, highest of all, the chapel of the Cross.

Even the palace, which includes the **Great Hall**, the Audience Chamber and the private apartments of the sovereign and his wife, are lavishly appointed. The ornamentation of the rooms housing the relics, however, is beyond imagination. In the **church of Our Lady**, Charles's court painter, Nikolaus Wurmser, portrayed the emperor with the sacred relics of the Passion beneath a heaven filled with an angelic host. The **chapel of St Catherine**, adorned with semi-precious stones, is where Charles IV spent days and nights in silent meditation. Above the door to the chapel is a portrait of the emperor with his second wife, Anna von Schweidnitz, carrying a massive cross.

The **chapel of the Cross** itself is decorated with over 2,000 semi-precious stones. It is divided into two sections by a golden railing; the precious relics were preserved in the sanctuary,

which only the emperor or the priests were allowed to enter. The walls are covered with over 100 paintings by Theoderich; more relics are set into the picture frames. The themes of these paintings were chosen to provide additional protection for the relics. They include the heavenly host of apostles and saints, who in the central painting are bearing witness to the Crucifixion.

After so much pomp and circumstance, a walk in the attractive surroundings of the castle provides a welcome contrast. The Český Kras, the Bohemian karst, is the setting for many romantic lakes nestling between forests inhabited by a wide range of wildlife. In summer these lakes are used for bathing. The caves of **Koněprusy** can also be visited; in medieval times they functioned as workshops for counterfeiters.

Massacre at Lidice: 25 km (16 miles) to the west of Prague, off the main road to Slany, is the site of a massacre wrought by the SS during World War II on the inhabitants of the little village of Lidice. It was in retaliation for the assassination of the Reichsprotector Reinhard "the hangman" Heydrich by members of the Czech underground on 4 June 1942; the SS had received the false information that Lidice had harboured the assassins.

On the night of 9 June, the SS commander Karl Hermann Frank had all 95 houses burned to the ground. All 192 adult male occupants were shot on the spot; the women were taken to Ravensbrück concentration camp in Mecklenburg, where 60 were tortured to death. The 105 children were transported to Lodz, and 82 of them subsequently died in the gas chambers. After the war, a new village was built next to the ruins of the old. A rose garden was planted and the site was transformed into a memorial to the dead. The little museum to the left of the entrance shows films of the destruction and reconstruction of Lidice.

Mělník and its castle: During the 9th century the Slavic Pšovan dynasty constructed their castle where the Vltava flows into the Labe (Elbe), a good 50 km (30 miles) from Prague. Although to

Fine white wine has been grown on the slopes above the Vltava near Mělník for centuries.

begin with this dynasty was the undisguised rival of the Přemyslids in Prague, the marriage of the heiress Ludmilla with the Přemyslid prince Bořivoj later united the twin territories. From this point onwards the castle, now rebuilt, served as a dowager residence for the princesses of Bohemia. The settlement itself grew into a flourishing trading centre; in 1274 Otakar II granted it royal privileges in accordance with the Decree of Magdeburg.

Under the direction of Charles IV vineyards were established on the slopes above the Labe, a direct result of his coronation as Duke of Burgundy in 1365, from which he returned with vines and vintners. Not only was the red Burgundy-type wine popular at the Imperial Court, but it also brought considerable revenues to the town. The citizens, enjoying their new prosperity, thus sided with the moderate reformers and found themselves on the winning side at the end of the Hussite Wars. As the hosts to three national Utraquist conferences between 1438 and 1432, the town enjoyed the special favour of George of Poděbrady, the leader of the faction, who rose to the position of King of Bohemia. Fortunes declined when his widow died in the Residence of Mělník.

Under a succession of further rulers the castle was rebuilt, fell into decay again and during the baroque era acquired its current character. The prestige it enjoyed in the Middle Ages never returned, however, for the new owners, the Princes of Lobkowitz, preferred to live in their residence in Prague. Even the town's growth stagnated, although the viticulture continued to provide a good income.

The architecture of the castle reflects its historical development quite accurately. Each of the three main wings is characterised by a different style. In the west wing the Gothic influence is dominant, displaying a certain strictness of form; in the north, the Renaissance is clearly evident in the imaginative arcaded walks and ornamental facades, and in the south the opulence of the baroque unfolds. The castle houses a

Konopiště has an English style park with Italian style ornaments.

museum of local history which documents the traditions and folklore of wine production in the area. The culmination of any tour is a visit to the wine bar and restaurant, whose terrace offers a breathtaking panorama of the Labe valley.

The town centre is very picturesque. The market place with its fountain commemorating the grape harvest is framed by a curving arc of arcaded townhouses. The clock tower on the **Town Hall** and the **church of the Fourteen Auxiliary Saints** complete the harmonious ensemble. On the far side of the square, a busy street leads down to the Prague Gate and the impressive remains of the town fortifications.

Konopiště Castle: The E56 road leads in a southerly direction as far as Benešov, where the traveller should turn off to the right towards **Konopiště**. The castle dates from the 13th century. In 1423 – in the midst of war – the two Hussite factions negotiated over liturgical details here. The hostess was Widow Sternberg, who had joined the Hussites after her Catholic husband had fallen in battle. Following the plundering by the Swedish army during the Thirty Years' War, the entire complex – originally built in the Gothic idiom – was rebuilt as a baroque residence. It was Archduke Franz Ferdinand, however – the heir to the Habsburg throne who was assassinated in Sarajevo – who converted it into a fine private palace, which he proceeded to embellish with an extravagant collection of works of art.

Visitors are greeted by a solitary baroque gateway in front of the moat; the high walls are dominated by the **East Tower**. Worthy of particular note inside is the large banqueting hall, with two **Gobelin tapestries** from Paris, and the sketches made for Cervantes' *Don Quixote*. The smoking room, the library and the chapel on the second floor, as well as the countless hunting trophies adorning the corridors and staircases, bear witness to the sophisticated pleasures of the lord of the castle and his guests. The vast castle grounds with their rose garden, ponds and game enclosures are partly open to visitors.

The market place and town hall of Tábor.

Tábor – Bastion of the Hussites: Jan Hus and the Hussites have frequently been mentioned elsewhere in this guide, with Hus himself portrayed as a god-fearing reformer, an eloquent preacher against love of splendour and bigotry, a social revolutionary and a rabid defenestrator. But in Prague – the Bethlehem Chapel and Jan Hus Memorial notwithstanding – reference to this movement, which for centuries determined the history of the country, is vague.

It therefore makes sense to take a trip to **Tábor**, combining the excursion with a roam through the pretty countryside surrounding the capital. In Tábor, every stone recalls the Hussite era. The town itself lies some 56 miles (90 km) south of Prague; it is easily reached via the E 56 trunk road towards České Budějovice (Budweis) and Linz.

Anyone familiar with the Bible will recall that, according to St Matthew, chapter 17, verses 1–9, Mount Tábor was the place of Christ's Transfiguration. The Hussites were thinking of the Transfiguration when, in 1420, they gathered in their thousands near Kotnov Castle. It was five years after the execution of their teacher and a few months after their rebellion in Prague. Able-bodied men as well as women and children gathered to take up arms against the Imperial army and fight Catholic bigotry. The camp required fortifications, and from it grew the new town of Tábor. It was the starting point for the long campaign which culminated in the glorious victories at Vitkov in 1420 and Deutsch-Brod in 1422. However, after their brilliant leader Jan Žižka fell in 1424 and a schism rent the moderate Utraquists apart, the movement gradually waned; the defeat at Lipany in 1434 finally put an end to their hopes of a religious state in Bohemia.

After the war Tábor grew into a busy town. Members of all confessions, including Catholics, were tolerated and the inhabitants coexisted peacefully as Bohemian Brethren, Waldensians and moderate Utraquists. The spirit of rebellion was still alive, however, and whenever the citizens of Bohemia re-

The Bohemians enjoy a good pint and also like their music.

volted against serfdom and usury, the Taborite flag with its black background and red chalice would be seen fluttering amongst the rebels. They were drawn into the defeat at the Battle of the White Mountain in 1620, after which they were forced to pay tribute to the Habsburgs.

Nonetheless the little town still affords a fascinating glimpse of life in this stormy era. From the main road you should turn off to the right and park your car in the car park near the ruined castle. From here you can visit the mighty **Round Tower** and the **Bechin Gate**, which houses a small historical exhibition. The streets were deliberately made narrow and winding for defensive purposes. They climb up to **Žižka Square**, which – like most of the rest of the town – boasts cellars and subterranean passages with sentry posts and storage areas. Since the Czech Nationalist movement discovered its precursors in the proud Taborites in the 19th century, the broad square has been dominated by a monumental statue of the leader of the Hussite legions.

Nearby are the **Roland Fountain** and two simple stone tables, at which the Communion used to be distributed. The lofty tower of the **church of the Transfiguration** dates from Hussite times; it soars above the former Town Hall, now a museum to the Hussite movement, with its huge municipal coat of arms and a two-storey council chamber.

The Pražská ulice starts in the southeast corner of the square and offers a number of attractive Renaissance houses. During the past few years the side streets have undergone a miniature renaissance; artists have established studios here, and a number of new galleries, antique shops and bookshops have opened. The old town wall should also be included in the tour; the northern section is still in good repair. From here you will be able to enjoy a panorama across the **Jordán Reservoir**, created to provide the town's water supply in 1492. It is the oldest construction of its kind in Bohemia.

East of Tábor: Kámen Castle, halfway to Pelhřimov, is also well-worth a visit.

A field of dandelions.

It is no coincidence that it houses a **motorcycle museum**, for the International Motorcycle Federation was formed in 1904 in the inn Na panské in Pacov. In 1906 motorcycles roared along the so-called Pacovský okruh in the first ever motorcycle World Championships.

The architecture of **Pacov** (Patzau) blends with the mountain foothill scenery. Where a stronghold and later a fortress once stood you can now see a Renaissance palace, its former defensive walls transformed into a magnificent promenade.

Pelhřimhov (Pilgram) nestles by the River Bělá. The heart of the old town mirrors its history in the Renaissance and baroque buildings (Early Gothic traces are still found under the facades). A few miles south of Road No 19 lies the village of **Včelnice**, with a glass foundry famous for its red glass, known as "Bohemian Garnet". A particular attraction here is the narrow-gauge railway, which replaced an earlier horse-drawn tram through the forest, linking the town of Kamenice nad Lipou with Obrataň in the north and Jindřichův Hradec in the south.

Southwest of Tábor: The spa town of **Bechyně** has a tradition of pottery making stretching back to the 15th century. It formed the basis for the town's present-day ceramics industry. Since 1884 the town has been the home of a College of Ceramics, from which many famous Czech ceramic artists have graduated.

Following the River Luznice the route returns to the Vltava and the Orlík barrage, which is 37.5 miles (60 km) long. Dominating the central section of the lake, on the west bank, is **Orlík Castle**. Originally an early Gothic fortress, the castle was rebuilt on a number of occasions. It is surrounded by a *jardin anglais* which is a wonderful place for a leisurely stroll. The castle itself contains a display of Empire furniture, weapons, paintings and memorabilia dating from the Napoleonic Wars.

Another popular castle is that at Zvíkov. It enjoys a romantic situation further South, at the confluence of the Otava and the Vltava rivers. **Písek** has a colourful history. A stone bridge dating from 1265, the oldest in Bohemia, crosses the Otava at this point. It formed a part of the Golden Path, the trading route to Bavaria, the *raison d'etre* for the town's foundation. The settlement prospered on the gold-rich sands of the river bed.

Strakonice is often wrongly described as being an exclusively industrial town. In fact, it has preserved many attractive medieval buildings and is the traditional setting for the International Bagpipe Festival. Strakonice achieved fame as the headquarters of the motorcycle company CZM, the fabric company Fezko and a number of well-known producers of industrial machines.

To the north of the town is the moated castle of **Blatná**, an architectural jewel constructed at the end of the 14th century. Unfortunately it is closed for lengthy restoration. The town itself is famous for its rose plantations. Many new varieties were developed here, though the legendary five-petal rose is the work of the horticulturists of Rožmberk in Southern Bohemia.

SOUTHERN BOHEMIA

The writer Jan Neruda described the town of **České Budějovice** (Budweis) at the confluence of the Vltava and the Malse as "Bohemia's Florence".

In 1265 the village, established by German settlers, received its town charter from Premysl Otakar II, and in 1358 Charles IV granted it staple rights. The discovery of silver deposits during the 16th century increased the wealth of the community and made it the economic and cultural centre of Southern Bohemia.

The old town was laid out on the rectangular grid pattern typical of German settlements; the site of the original walls and moat is now a broad belt of parkland. At the centre lies the **Žižka Square**, with the main streets radiating from its four corners. In spite of a certain amount of damage over the centuries, its medieval countenance is clearly visible; the pretty arcaded houses bordering the square have been meticulously restored. Only a few steps from the massive octagonal fountain, graced by a statue of Samson the lion-tamer, one of the paving stones (distinguished by a cross) marks the spot where, in 1478, the 10 men who murdered the local mayor were executed. Legend has it that everyone who steps upon the *bludný kámen*, the "madmen's stone", after 9pm will follow the primrose path to hell.

Within the town itself, it is hard for visitors to lose their way. In the southwest, beyond the baroque **Town Hall** and the **Bishop's Palace** are the ruins of the town fortifications. In the west, the former **Dominican monastery** lies on the defunct arm of the Vltava; it was founded by the King of Bohemia in 1265 and completed during the 14th century as a Gothic ensemble along with the **church of Our Lady of Sacrifice**. Also of note nearby is the former arsenal, built in 1531, and the **Salt House**, whose facade is liberally decorated with masques.

On the Hroznová to the north of the market place, the visitor should make a point of visiting the former Masné krámy. The 16th-century "Meat Banks" have been converted into a restaurant and serve as a favourite rendezvous for experts and aficionados of the famous **Budvar**, the Budweis beer exported to 21 countries throughout the world. Suitably refreshed, one can continue to the **Kneisl House** in the northwest corner and the baroque **church of St Nicholas**. Finally, climb the 360 steps of the Černá věz, the **Black Tower**, a free-standing belfry which soars above the rooftops and affords a bird's eye view of the other places of historical interest within the town.

The view unfolds as far as **Hluboká Castle** some 6 miles (10 km) away. The 13th-century former royal stronghold rises majestically from its rocky perch above the River Vltava. Its design has changed numerous times over the years. Today it resembles nothing so much as Windsor Castle. It is worth visiting for the collections of wood carvings, porcelain, tapestries, paintings and furniture collected by the Imperial princes of

Left, the smoking room in Hluboká Castle north of České Budějovice (Budweis), one of the most-visited castles in the republic. Right, canoeing it through the Bohemian Forest.

Schwarzenberg. The castle riding school and the elegant conservatory form the **Southern Bohemian Gallery of Art**, housing an exhibition of southern Bohemian Gothic and Flemish art. The permanent display is supplemented by regular travelling exhibitions of a high standard.

The hunting lodge lying a mile or so to the southwest is also of interest; its attractive house and grounds contain a **Museum of Forestry and Hunting** as well as a zoo.

Třeboň and surroundings: Extensive woodland, meadows, peat bogs, artificial canals, ponds and lakes are characteristic of the countryside surrounding Třeboň. Many of the lakes were dug during the 16th century; the largest, covering an area of more than 1,235 acres (500 hectares), is **Rožmberk Lake** to the north of the town. The lakes made Třeboň the fishery centre of Bohemia, and the local carp are still considered a delicacy. Every three years, a non-stop carp angling competion is held over a period of three days. To the north of Rožmberk Lake is the romantic **Svět Lake**, where you can hire a sailing boat or go for a trip on a steamer.

The healing powers of the peat moors were exploited during the last century in medicinal baths and sanatoria. The town fortifications, including the old town gates and walls, have largely survived and enclose a medieval town centre where many houses date from Gothic and Renaissance times. The rich variety of manuscripts and books in the castle archives has made them famous throughout the literary world.

Also of interest is the village of **Chlum** near Třeboň, famous for its glassmaking; the blown and cut glass products are exported all over the world. The little town of **Jindřichův Hradec** is worth visiting, since attractive religious buildings and a large number of late Gothic, Renaissance and baroque houses have been preserved. The medieval **castle** was enlarged and given its Renaissance countenance by Italian architects in the 16th century. The Gothic chapel of St George contains a cycle of

Communal fishing in one of the many lakes near Třeboň.

frescoes depicting the famous legend. Here, too, the skills of an ancient craft are practised: a local workshop still produces hand-knotted Gobelin tapestries.

The route from České Budějovice leads in a southeasterly direction along the Malse to **Trocnov**, the native town of the Hussite leader Jan Žižka. The former gamekeeper's house has been turned into a museum. Only a few miles further on lies the village of **Římov**, surrounded by a Way of the Cross marked with 25 little chapels decorated with exquisite wood carvings and sculptures. Near the village the valley has been dammed to create a reservoir serving two-thirds of Southern Bohemia. No bathing is allowed; for once the prohibition is accepted without demur as the area offers a large number of attractive alternatives.

The rooms in **Žumberk Fortress**, southeast of Trhové Sviny, containing the castle's original furniture, provide visitors with an evocative picture of life in these ancient castles, when the flickering of pinewood torches was the only

illumination and open fires the only means of heat.

The venerable village of **Nové Hrady**, near the Austrian border, was built during the 13th century. Particularly interesting is the exhibition of mysterious black glass, known as hyalite. It was produced by the glassblowers in the surrounding foundries.

Following the main road to the southwest of České Budějovice, the **Zlatá Koruna Monastery** ("The Golden Crown") lies a few miles north of Český Krumlov. Chief attractions are the extensive library and the triple-naved basilica dating from the 14th century. Legend has it that the linden tree in front of the monastery produces leaves in the shape of a hood, recalling the unfortunate Cistercian monks whom Žižka hanged from its branches after he had set fire to the monastery buildings. Přemysl Otakar II founded the religious community here in 1263 in order to protect his royal interests in the region against the incursions of the noble Vítkovci (Wittigo) family.

Famous Bohemian crystal is produced in Chlum near Třeboň.

Český Krumlov: Český Krumlov (Krumau) has retained its medieval character better than any other town in Southern Bohemia. Every alleyway and every hidden corner invites the visitor to tarry awhile. The entire town has been declared a historic monument and, although restoration work during the past decades has made only slow progress and some architectural treasures are still crying out for renovation, a leisurely exploration is recommended.

In 1240, the Vítkovci dynasty built their castle overlooking the Vltava; they were followed by three families of German nobles: the Rosenbergs (1302–1611), the Eggenbergs (1622–1717) and the Schwarzenbergs (1717–1945). The original fortress was rebuilt as an aristocratic palace, from which the lords of the castle administered their economic and political interests throughout Southern Bohemia. German colonists settled on the far side of the bend in the river Vltava and were awarded a town charter in 1274. Silver deposits in the nearby Bohemian Forest brought wealth to the noble rulers and diligent burghers alike; even when the mines were exhausted during the 16th century, the town was able to retain its prosperous air.

In the middle of the Old Town lies the Ring, bordered by charming Renaissance houses and the richly decorated **Town Hall**. To the south and west you can see sections of the original fortifications, topped by the slender tower of the **church of St Vitus**. The latter contains Gothic wall paintings and an elaborate early baroque altar. Of particular interest in the east are the Curacy and the **Town Museum**. Forming part of the former Jesuit College (now in use as a hotel) is a theatre completed in 1613.

The suburb of Latrán on the other side of the bridge across the Vltava boasts the **Convent of the Minorites and the Sisters of the Order of St Clare**. Both communities used the adjoining Corpus Christi church. A long-established brewery occupies a 16th-century arsenal. The **castle** sprawls high above the town – less extensive than Prague Castle, but no less attractive thanks to its moat, now

Sightseers in Česky Krumlov (Krumau).

188

the home of a colony of bears. The Upper Castle was designed as a feudal residence; the **Hall of Masques** is decorated with wall paintings and the **Chinese Cabinet** contains a collection of exquisite porcelain from the Chang Dynasty. The massive tower belongs to the earliest period of the medieval castle, although the cap and arcade were added in 1590.

A bridge flanked with statues of saints leads across to the baroque **Castle Theatre**, built in 1767. The castle gardens contain an open-air theatre with a revolving stage which hosts a wide range of imaginative productions during the summer season.

To the Lipno Reservoir: Like Rožmberk Castle, **Vyšší Brod Monastery** was founded by Vok von Rožmberk before the middle of the 13th century, along the trading route to Austria. The community soon prospered. Before World War I its estates comprised more than 100,000 acres (4,000 hectares). Part of the monastery was returned to the Cistercian order in 1990.

The road to the Lipno Dam on the Vltava passes through **Hořice na Šumavě**. This village was traditionally famous for its Passion plays, performed by the local residents (largely of German extraction); the plays were staged even through the war years. The tradition broke down after the Germans were expelled, but now the community is endeavouring to revive the tradition. The little medieval town of **Horní Planá** (Oberplan) lies directly on the shores of the lake. It is the birthplace of the poet and painter Adalbert Stifter (1805–68). The house where he was born now contains a small museum.

The **Lipno Reservoir** is 27.5 miles (44 km) long and up to 10 miles (16 km) wide in places. A steamer service links the lakeshore communities of Lipno, Frymburk, Černá v Pošumaví and Horní Planá. For many years, a considerable stretch of the long strip of land between the lake and the Czech-Austrian border was fenced off with barbed wire, which enabled it to retain much of its original charm. A footpath leads from Nová Pec

Reflections of Jindřichův Hradec near the Austrian border.

to the **Plešné Lake**, above which a monument to Adalbert Stifter stands sentinel on a high cliff.

Unspoilt nature in the Bohemian Forest: The Bohemian Forest (Šumava), especially the sections adjoining Germany and Austria, are less suited to a touring holiday than to a peaceful stay in unspoilt natural surroundings. The **Schwarzenberg Canal** is a remarkable construction dating from the end of the 18th century. In times past it served as a means of transporting felled logs; today it links the sleepy villages of the Bohemian Forest and isolated farmsteads. A yellowing postcard outside a wooden chapel near the border states: "This was once the flourishing village of Schwendreut, now gone with the wind. It was built upon a hill which used to be covered with dense forest and which the forest will now reclaim once more."

The Iron Curtain was the death-knell of the border regions. Now, with the creation of a national park area spanning the national frontiers, new life is blossoming in the area. For some years now it has attracted country lovers keen to save the lovely old farmhouses from decay. Thanks to them a number of the typical 17th-century wooden cottages are still standing, and the wooden chapel on the hillside near **Stožec** has been faithfully restored. In the Upper Vltava Valley the visitor can observe encouraging signs of careful tourist development designed to attract visitors seeking peace and quiet in restful surroundings. They can walk at leisure through the forests (though some sections of the Bohemian Forest are under strict protection and not accessible to tourists).

South of Vimperk (Winterberg), at the foot of Mount Boubín (4,358 ft/ 1,362 metres), lies the **Boubínský Prales Forest**, a conservation area since 1933. Some of the trees here are 400 years old; the rare flora and fauna of the region attract botanists and zoologists.

Zlatá stezka (The Golden Pass) was the name of the trading route from Bohemia to Bavaria. During the Middle Ages it brought considerable prosperity to the towns in the Bohemian Forest.

The highpoint of the trip for these country ladies.

Volary (Wallern), the best-known resort in the area, was founded by settlers from Tyrol. Even today you can see the occasional wooden chalet with sloping roofs weighted down with stones so typical of alpine regions.

Vimperk (Winterberg), also along this route, is the gateway to the Bohemian Forest. In 1264 Přemysl Otakar built a fortress above the Volynka Valley to protect the trading route. The town is noted for its printing works, founded in 1484. It produced elaborately decorated missals, Korans and other books. Fine examples are on display in the municipal museum and the Bohemian Forest Gallery in the castle, along with an exhibition of cut glass characteristic of the region. Above Vimperk, the cross-country ski tracks lead to Zadov and Churánov, the winter sports centres of the Bohemian Forest.

All the old routes of the Golden Pass converge on the little town of **Prachatice** (Prachatiz), where the luxury goods, cloth and weapons were stored until their sale or onward transport had been arranged. The most important trading commodity was salt; until the 17th century the town was the biggest repository of salt in Bohemia. When the Habsburgs introduced a salt monopoly and diverted the salt routes through České Budějovice (Budweis) and Gmünd, Prachatice declined into an economic and cultural backwater. Remains of the 14th-century town walls are still standing today. There is also a Gothic church housing a number of treasures, and a Town Hall constructed in 1570 and reconstructed during the 19th century with elaborate sgraffito decorations. The grammar school on the market place was where Jan Hus, a native son of neighbouring **Husinec**, was educated.

At the end of the 16th century Wilhelm von Rosenberg (Rožmberk) commissioned **Kratochvíle Castle** in the Renaissance style some 12 miles (20 km) from Prachatice. His brother, Peter Vok, embellished the property with a park, surrounded by a wall and bastion. Today the castle serves as an exhibition centre for Czech cartoon films.

he
**ohemian
orest in
winter.**

WESTERN BOHEMIA

In many respects, the historical and cultural development of Bohemia mirrors that of the capital Prague; the area was always subject to both Slavic and German influences. This is particularly true of Western Bohemia. A journey through this scenically attractive region can be combined with a tour of the world-famous spa towns described in the next chapter.

Plzeň (Pilsen) is the second-largest town in Bohemia, with a population of 180,000. It is famous for the local beer, *Prazdroj* (Pilsner lager, *see page 198*). Plzeň rose to international importance soon after receiving its charter from King Wenceslas II in 1295. Lying at the confluence of four rivers – the Mže, the Radbuza, the Úhlava and the Úslava – and at the crossroads of four long-distance trading routes, the town rapidly established itself as a trading centre; in addition, the locally mined raw materials (kaolin, mineral ores and hard coal) helped to make it a centre for crafts and industry.

It was in Plzeň that the first Czech book, the *Kronika Trojánská*, was printed and published in 1468. From 1420, following the voluntary departure from the city of the Hussite military leader Jan Žižka, Plzeň was loyal to the Catholic emperors. To show his thanks, Emperor Sigismund relieved the town of all feudal dues; Plzeň thus acquired the privileges of a tax haven and entered a new era of economic prosperity. In 1599, when the plague was rampant in Prague, Emperor Rudolf II moved his official residence here for nine months. The entire court and all foreign representatives were forced to follow suit, and once more the town boomed.

The stormy period of industrialisation during the 19th century was accompanied by the expansion of Plzeň to a cultural centre for the surrounding region. The first theatre opened here in 1832; today, Plzeň boasts three major dramatic stages, including a Children's Theatre and a **Marionette Theatre**

where Josef Skupa, creator of the legendary puppets Špejbl and Hurvínek (*see page 107*), once worked.

Plzeň is also the home of the famous Škoda Works, founded by the engineer and industrialist Emil von Škoda at the end of the 19th century. The enterprise grew from the modest base of a small machine factory to become one of Europe's greatest industrial complexes, known for its arms production in both World Wars. The company was for decades the town's largest employer, and would probably have continued to expand according to the values of Western capitalism had the American troops under General Patton, who liberated the town in 1945, not subsequently withdrawn in accordance with an agreement with the Soviet army.

The Gothic heart of the city takes the form of a rectangular chessboard, with a large square, known today as the **Square of the Republic**, in the centre. The middle of the square is occupied by the early Gothic parish **church of St Bartholomew**, whose spire (330 ft/103

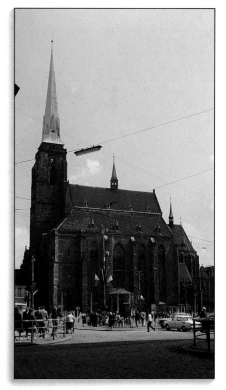

metres) is the tallest in Czech Republic. The interior is decorated with murals dating from before 1400. Dominating the high altar is a Gothic statue, the **Plzeň Madonna**, completed in about 1390. With its flying buttresses and pendant keystone, the **Sternberg Chapel** on the southern side of the choir is a typical example of Late Gothic architecture. The **Town Hall**, built in the style of the Renaissance between 1554 and 1558, is decorated with extravagant sgraffito ornaments, making it by far the most conspicuous building on the entire square. When Rudolf II came to the city, he resided in the **Emperor's House** next door.

House No. 234, opposite the main entrance to the church, dates from the Middle Ages. Since its renovation in 1770 it has been considered one of the finest baroque buildings in Bohemia. The architectural magnificence continues around the square and along the narrow alleys of the **Old Town**, where the facades of the houses are decorated with fine frescoes and sgraffito, the work of Mikulá Ale, an esteemed Czech artist of the 19th century. In the midst of all this splendour, only the solitary **Plague Column,** erected in 1681, recalls that even the wealthy citizens of Plzeň were not spared the dreaded pestilence.

In the southeastern corner, the Frantiskanska ul. leads to the former monastery with its pretty **chapel of St Barbara** and its Late Gothic frescoes illustrating the lives of the saints. In the northeast of the Old Town, by the Perlova, are the former butchers' stalls, recently converted into an exhibition hall and concert auditorium. The water tower nearby is 450 years old; a few yards further on, in the Veleslavinova ul., the **Museum of Beer Brewing** is also worth a visit: it is the only such museum in the country.

The environs of Plzeň: During the Middle Ages a community of Cistercian monks settled near **Plasy**, some 9 miles (15 km) north of Plzeň. They built a vast monastery complex, one of the largest in Bohemia. The most impressive building is the convent itself, which was

The main square in Plzeň's old town is the largest town square in Bohemia.

constructed on oak stilts because of the marshy conditions. The two-storey **Royal Chapel** is a particularly fine example of the Gothic mason's art.

Following the course of the Střela in an upstream direction, the traveller reaches **Rabštejn nad Střelou**, the smallest town in Central Europe, which boasts just 40 inhabitants. It perches on a rock above the swiftly flowing river, which is spanned by a magnificent 14th-century Gothic bridge. From the 13th century a well-fortified castle protected this important crossing on the long-distance trading route to Saxony and Northern Europe; the remains of the stronghold can still be seen today.

The little town of **Manětín** lives up to its reputation as the best place to see baroque architecture in Western Bohemia. It lies some 19 miles (30 km) from Plzeň. The town grew up around a hunting lodge, which was totally destroyed by fire in 1712. The town received a complete facelift during the 18th century, hence its baroque countenance. Surrounding the palace – the work of the Italian architect Giovanni Santini who was responsible for many such projects in Bohemia – are many examples of baroque sculpture. Also worth mentioning are the fine paintings by the Czech master Peter Brandl, hanging in the town's two churches.

Some 5 miles (9 km) southeast of Plzeň lie the ruins of the former **castle**, mentioned in records as early as 976. After the foundation of the town of New Pilsen, the site of the fortress was rechristened Old Pilsen; it later came to be known as **Starý Plzenec**. The castle was built by the Přemyslid dynasty as a cultural and administrative centre; it included fortifications with a 32-ft (10-metre) wall – a section of which is still standing today – and the oldest intact monument in the Czech Republic, the **Rotunda of St Peter**, which dates from the second half of the 10th century.

A few miles further on, rising on a hillside to the east of the village of Stáhlavy, stands **Kozel Palace**. The splendid classical-style building nestles in magnificent woodland; the main

The large salon in Kozel Castle near Plzeň.

PILSNER LAGER

Few Czech products are as famous as its beer. The brewing tradition in Bohemia extends over many centuries – in Prague, the oldest written record of the brewer's art is found in a document dated 1082. And yet, the capital does not produce the country's best beer; that honour is uncontestably held by Plzeň (Pilsen).

Although the Prazdroj Brewery was founded as recently as 1842, the tradition of brewing beer in the town stretches back much further. When Plzeň was founded in 1290, the town was granted the right to brew its own beer. Numerous exhibits in the Museum of Beer Brewing, which has been established in a Late Gothic malthouse in the Veleslavinova ul., testify to a thriving brewing industry in the Middle Ages. Before the new brewery was opened, beer was still brewed in various private houses scattered through the town.

Like every other beer, Pilsner is produced by heating ground malt with water and hops before allowing the liquor to ferment at low temperature by the addition of a special yeast, the *saccharomyces carlsbergensis*. Despite all this, the flavour of Pilsner lager remains unique and many attempts have been made to discover the secret. The water used in the brewing process clearly plays an important role in the determination of quality and taste; the local water is very soft and has an exceptionally low level of salinity. The secret of the beer's success lies in the preparation of the malt; only barley with a low protein content is used. But the characteristic taste and headiness of the beer is achieved by the addition of first-class, oast-dried hops from Žatec. All these basic ingredients have been employed in foreign breweries; nonetheless, to date not a single one has succeeded in producing an authentic-tasting Pilsner Urquell.

Another secret must lie in the cellars in which the beer ferments and matures. They were driven deep into the sandstone cliffs and extend over a distance of 5 miles (9 km). Throughout the year, they maintain a constant temperature of 33–35°F (1–2°C). The walls of the cellars in which the beer is kept for two to three months are coated with a fungus similar to penicillin. Many "spies" have tried to kidnap the fungus from the cellars of Plzeň in order to introduce it to the cellar walls of their own breweries. So far, nobody has been able to find a suitable habitat; sooner or later it died.

Fourteen years after the brewery was set up, local lager was sold for the first time outside the country. The citizens of Vienna were the first to try Pilsner Urquell; by 1865, three-quarters of the brewery's total production was destined for export. From 1 October 1900, a "beer train" left Plzeň daily for Vienna. Somewhat later, a similar train travelled regularly to Bremen; there the lager was loaded on to ships for transportation to America. Today the Prazdroj Brewery alone produces 28.6 million gallons (1.3 million hectolitres) of beer each year. If you visit the brewery in Prazdroj Street, which lies to the east of the inner city, you can study brewing techniques at your leisure. Having done so, you should treat yourself to a glass of the delicious brew in the adjoining bar. Be careful, however; the alcohol content of Pilsner lager is unusually high, and many a visitor has overestimated his personal capacity.

Who would ■ say no?

Pilsner Urquell

section was completed between 1784 and 1789. Several years later a number of additions were made, in accordance with plans drawn up by the master architect Ignác Palliardi. Nowadays the palace houses an exhibition of 18th and 19th-century art. It is worth making a short detour to view the **Empire Theatre**, which has been maintained in the original style.

From Plzeň to the German border: The E53 from Plzeň leads south to the little town of **Švihov**, where there is a magnificent moated castle built in a mixture of Gothic and Renaissance styles. It houses a comprehensive collection of medieval weapons.

The town of **Klatovy** (Klattau), a few miles further on, is known as the gateway to the Bohemian Forest. It is also famous as a horticultural centre specialising in the cultivation of carnations. The **Black Tower** soars to a height of almost 256 ft (80 metres) above the Renaissance-style Town Hall and the market square. Its airy gallery affords a wonderful view of the historic town walls and the surrounding hills. Those with a sense for the macabre can gaze at the mummified corpses of Jesuits in the catacombs beneath the early baroque Jesuit **church of St Ignatius**. A veritable treat for the eyes is the so-called **White Tower**, a free-standing belfry belonging to the early Gothic **church of St Mary**.

Visitors should also take a look inside the former chemist's shop (*lékárna*) on the Town Square, which still contains its original, baroque shop fittings; as such is it unique, and is listed in the UNESCO catalogue of historic monuments.

The beautiful countryside of the central Bohemian Forest also deserves protection. Particularly attractive is the valley of the thundering **Vydra torrent**, which is 4 miles (7 km) long, and which lies a few miles southeast of Klatovy. Beyond Susice, where the river flows more quietly, stand the ruins of **Rábí Castle**, built in the mid-14th century to protect the local gold-panning industry. This, the most powerful ruined castle in Bohemia, was captured twice during

A bubbling stream deep in the Bohemian Forest.

the Hussite Rebellions; it was later destroyed by fire and finally abandoned.

At the centre of the western section of the Bohemian Forest is **Železná Ruda**. The main sight of this small town is a little church topped by the onion-shaped domes typical of High baroque architecture in the region. In the immediate vicinity is a ski circus as well as a cable car to the summit of **Mount Pancíř** (1,214 metres/3,885 ft).

Shortly before the German border, the ancient trading road turns in a southwesterly direction towards the Bavarian towns of Furth im Wald and Regensburg, cutting through the **Chodsko** region. The Chods – the name is derived from the Slavic word for "patrols" – are a Slavic ethnic group whom the rulers of Bohemia allowed to settle in the district some 1,000 years ago; their task was to defend the border and to offer protection to travellers and traders. They accomplished this with such efficiency that they were awarded special privileges, which they continued to enjoy until the region came under the rule of the Habsburgs after the Battle of the White Mountain in 1620.

To this day, on the weekend following 10 August, the Chods make their annual pilgrimage to the **Svatý Vavřinček** mountain, where they take part in an age-old festival of song, dance and bagpipe music. The Chods still wear their traditional costumes, and are also noted for their production of exquisite handicraft, particularly pottery and wood-carving.

The town of **Horšovský Týn** is another Chode settlement. It was protected by a mighty fortress, built during the second half of the 13th century. Some parts of the early Gothic castle are still standing. Following a devastating fire in the mid-16th century, the fortress was rebuilt in the style of a Renaissance palace. It is surrounded by an extensive landscaped park.

Domažlice (Taus), the capital of the Chodsko region, lies only a few miles from the German border crossing at Furth im Wald. The town was established around 1260 as a customs post.

The Chods celebrate their annual festival in Domažlice every August.

The fortifications are still visible in places; the **Lower Gate** (Dolní brána) leads directly on to the long, narrow market square of this pretty little town, fringed by attractive arcaded houses of various periods. A massive belfry rises up above the **Deanery church**; every evening, an ancient Chode trumpet melody rings out from its panoramic viewing platform.

The **castle** itself was built during the 13th century; it was later completely destroyed by fire and rebuilt in 1728. Of the original fortress, only the **Round Tower** remains today; it houses collections from the **Chodsko Regional Museum**. The **Jindřich Museum**, named after the well-known composer and expert in Chode folklore, provides an introduction to the particular character of the customs and culture of the area. There is also an interesting and comprehensive display illustrating the traditional craft of glass painting.

Visitors wishing to learn more about the folklore of the Chodsko should pay a visit to the surrounding villages.

Drazenov, Mrákov and **Újezd** are typical of the local architectural style; particularly attractive are the traditional Chode log cabins.

There is plenty to see on the E50, which runs in a westerly direction from Plzeň (most drivers move too fast to appreciate the sights and villages). The first town along the route is **Stříbro**, founded in 1240 in the vicinity of a silver mine. Parts of the Late Gothic fortifications are still visible, including a Gothic bridge with a Renaissance tower, and Renaissance-style houses – especially the town hall – surrounding the market place.

It is worth making a short detour to the south to visit the important monastery at **Kladruby**; its cathedral is the work of the architect Giovanni Santini.

A few miles before the border stands **Přimda**, originally built in the Romanesque style during the 12th century as a look-out fortress. In former times the little township beneath the castle was inhabited by the Chods. **Tachov**, a former royal town, is considered to be

The Bohemian Forest in autumn.

the centre of the region. Remains of the medieval town wall and a goodly number of fine old houses testify to its illustrious past.

To northwestern Bohemia: From Stříbro you can turn north along the main road leading up to Cheb in the northwest of Bohemia, a route which provides access to the Bohemian spa towns described in the following chapter.

Cheb (Eger) – "the lovely town on the bend in the river" – always lay right in the firing line of two opposing cultures. The town bears traces of a turbulent history, originating in the 10th century when the Slavs built a stronghold on the rock overlooking the ford. Soon afterwards, German merchants settled around the fortress, founding the town of Egire which acquired market privileges in 1149. A young duke of Swabia carried off and subsequently married Adelheid, the fair maid of the castle. In 1167, as the Emperor Frederick Barbarossa, this man became ruler of the fortress and township and embarked upon an ambitious scheme to enlarge its base. He held court here on three occasions; his son often celebrated Christmas here, and even his grandson, the Emperor Frederick II, despite his preference for Apulia, summoned his vassals to this imperial palace on five occasions. Thus **Cheb Castle** is not only the oldest well-preserved building in the Czech Republc; it has also repeatedly served as a stage for European history.

The town achieved fame on one other occasion after this. During the period when the country was subject to Habsburg rule, it fell into the hands of the Bohemians. Albrecht von Wallenstein, the brilliant Bohemian general in charge of the Imperial army stationed his troops in Cheb during the Thirty Years' War. In the interests of a united Germany with himself as its supreme authority, he was considering the possibility of negotiating peace with Sweden – a course of action which would have saved many hundreds of thousands of lives and prevented the devastation of vast tracts of land. He demanded that his officers, who were under oath of loyalty

The old apothecary in Sušice.

202

to the Emperor, swear allegiance to him personally. The Emperor saw this as an act of high treason and declared the general an outlaw. The Irish cavalry officer Walter Devereux led an attack on Wallenstein on 25 February 1634; the general's troops were overpowered and Wallenstein himself was assassinated in his house by the market square.

Cheb today is a much quieter place. The market place is the focal point of this little town of some 20,000 inhabitants. Surrounding the square (named after King George of Poděbrady, the first Hussite sovereign of Bohemia), beneath the arcades of the half-timbered houses, are a number of pretty shops and cafés. Some of the buildings are particularly striking: the former **town hall**, a splendid example of baroque architecture, dominates the eastern side of the square. The **Schiller House** next door was where the famous dramatist stayed whilst gathering material and impressions for his famous *Wallenstein* trilogy. The **Hotel Hvězda** on the corner offers a restaurant and bar as well as overnight accommodation.

The broad market place is graced by the Roland Fountain on the south side and the **Hercules Fountain** to the north. In the centre is the Spalícek, a collection of market stalls (formerly constructed of wood, which could be extended as required). Of special interest are the **Schirnding House** behind, which boasts a high gable, and the **Gabler House**, which was originally Gothic in style. Tucked away at the top of the square is the **Municipal Museum** – the house in which Wallenstein was assassinated.

On the southwestern and northern periphery of the Old Town, comfortably reached on foot through the picturesque alleyways, lie five interesting churches. All were built by religious communities which took up residence in the town during the 13th century. To the south lie the Gothic **church of Our Lady of the Ascension** and the baroque **church of St Clare**; to the north are the churches of **St Wenceslas** and **St Nicholas**, the portal and towers of which display elements from the original Romanesque period. The latter was sub-

stantially altered by that master of the German baroque, Johann Balthasar Neumann, who was born in Cheb in 1687, and went on to design many outstanding secular and religious baroque buildings all over southern Germany. The **church of St Bartholomew** lies directly on the River Ohře; from here it is only a few steps to the fortress.

The **Black Tower**, the massive keep of lava stone, is perched on steep cliffs overlooking the river dominating the Romanesque **castle complex**. The showpiece of the castle is the painstakingly restored two-storey **Romanesque chapel**. It looks unassuming enough from the outside, and the gloomy lower floor which housed the guards and servants confirms the initial impression. The airy upper floor, however, which was also reached by a wooden bridge from the palace proper, is a miniature gem of Late Romanesque architecture. Graceful columns with exquisitely carved capitals support the elegant ribbed vaulting of the ceiling – a fitting setting for the emperor and his retinue.

Fine residences line the market place in Cheb (Eger).

THE SPA TOWNS OF WESTERN BOHEMIA

Nowhere else in the country will the tourist find his needs better catered to than in the venerable spa towns of Western Bohemia; not even Prague has greater experience in dealing with the requirements of the more demanding guest. Here visitors can still immerse themselves in an atmosphere belonging to the long-vanished era of the Austrian empire. Since the Velvet Revolution of 1989 it has acquired even greater nostalgia value.

Sadly, the architectural sins of the more recent past are not so easily undone; here and there, grey concrete buildings characteristic of the Communist period rise between the faded "imperial yellow" of the residences and sanatoria.

Karlovy Vary: Karlovy Vary, formerly Carlsbad (Charles' spa), is the oldest of the Bohemian spa towns. Legend has it that Emperor Charles IV discovered the healing spring on which it is centred quite by chance, whilst chasing a stag on a royal hunting expedition from his nearby castle of Loket. The exhausted animal sprang from a cliff straight into a bubbling hot spring, with the baying hounds undaunted close on its heels. Despite the scalding temperature of the spring, the emperor's personal physician declared that it possessed healing properties. In 1349 Charles founded a settlement here; and in 1370 he granted the town its municipal charter.

But it wasn't until the latter part of the 17th century, following a period of devastating fires and damage during the period of Swedish occupation in the Thirty Years' War, that the town's golden age began. Under the generous patronage of the Habsburgs, Carlsbad rose to supremacy as the most elegant spa town in the world, offering every refinement essential for fashionable amusement at the time. Competitions and plays, gossip and political intrigue, exhibitionism and witty conversation were its hallmarks. Everyone wanted to be a part of the scene. The sins and vituperations of the nights of riotous drinking and extravagant parties were washed away by morning constitutionals and bathing in the healing waters.

Crowned heads and fêted men of letters alike were attracted by this heady mixture. Peter the Great put in an appearance on two occasions – under the pretext of engaging in lively discussion with Leibniz over the progress of science and art in Russia. Among the many visitors to the spa were great men of letters such as Gogol, Goethe and Schiller, and composers from Bach to Wagner, but Carlsbad also attracted new tycoons of Europe, who tended to stay in the high-altitude Sanatorium Imperial. Aristocratic visitors tended to prefer to stay in the velvet-and-plush Grand Hotel of the former confectioner Johann Georg Pupp. Even Karl Marx took the waters in Carlsbad; in fact, the town provided the mordant social critic with plenty of inspiration for several chapters of *Das Kapital*.

World history was also made in Carlsbad. Matters reached a head in 1819, when the frenzied times of the

French Revolution and the Napoleonic Wars gave way to the Congress of Vienna. The Austrian Chancellor, Prince von Metternich, invited representatives of those German states he considered to be "reliable" to join him in determining the "Carlsbad Decrees". These represented a joint agreement to repress all attempts at greater civil liberty within Europe, an aim which would be achieved through the use of police informers and censorship. Metternich and his decrees were largely responsible for the tension that ultimately led to the European upheaval of 1848.

In the spas' heyday the journey to Carlsbad – by carriage through the Bohemian Forest and then down into the narrow Teplá Valley – was much more difficult than it is now. But at least there was no shortage of parking spaces, and the lords and ladies were not forced to abandon their carriages by the roadside. Today, vehicles are prohibited from entering the historic spa district itself. The easiest approach is from the south; if you are lucky you may be able to leave your car by the bend in the Teplá, or even on the promenade by the river.

The row of stately buildings begins on the left bank of the river with the **Art Gallery** and a magnificent **casino**. Together with the **Parkhotel**, the **Grand Hotel Pupp** is impossible to overlook as it extends across several blocks along the esplanade. Its main entrance, much less conspicuous, is set back on a square where the Teplá takes a bend to the right. Behind the hotel, a cable car climbs some 640 ft (200 metres) to the **Friendship Heights** where there is an observation tower and the restaurant "Diana". The station half-way up is the starting point for a number of clearly marked walks such as the tranquil footpath to the Petrova Výšina ("Peter's Heights") and the steep cliff known as Jelení skok ("Stag's Leap"), at the top of which a bronze chamois stands sentinel. From the numerous clearings in the woodland, the wanderer can enjoy a fine view of the town and the surrounding hills.

Returning to the valley, a favourite walk is along the Stará louka (Alte

Spa Colonnade in Karlovy Vary.

Wiese), an avenue containing the most elegant and expensive shops in town. Particularly tempting is a factory outlet selling locally-manufactured Moser glass and porcelain; the beauty of the factory's vases and dinner services has made them world famous. Here, too, you can buy other typical souvenirs from Karlovy Vary, including the legendary Lázeňské oplatky (Karlsbader Oblaten) – wafers which have enjoyed popularity for over a century – and Becherovka, a brand of bitters prepared since 1805 from 19 herbs in accordance with a traditional recipe drawn up by the Imperial Count's personal physician, Dr Frobzig. The appropriate antidote in cases of excessive consumption is "Carlsbad Salts", also locally produced and offered for sale in every shop; they are a powerful laxative.

On the opposite bank of the river, which can be comfortably reached from any point by one of the many little footbridges, stands another famous hotel, the **Kaiserbad** – built before the turn of the century by Viennese archi-tects in the style of the French Renaissance. Nearby is the **Municipal Theatre**, built in 1886 and carrying on a theatrical tradition that has been in the town since 1602.

The Promenade leads to the market place. Hopefully future renovation work on the market place will take into account the mistakes of the past, the most glaring examples of which are the hideous **Pump Rooms** opposite. The magnificent **church of St Mary Magdalene** is well worth a visit; completed in 1736 on the orders of the Knights of the Cross, it is a further fine example of the work of the Bavarian architect Kilian Ignaz Dientzenhofer. It invites comparison with his famous church of St John on the Rock in Prague.

The focal point of the spa town is the **Mill Colonnade**, built between 1871–79 by Josef Zítek, who was also responsible for the National Theatre in Prague. Here one can sample one of the four thermal springs upon which the town's fame rests. There is no need to extend the tour to include the other spa and

Drink cure under the colonnades.

medicinal bath complexes further to the north, unless you want to indulge in long-term therapy in what is the largest balneological establishment in the country. Instead, take the left-hand fork, which leads to the **Russian church**, completed at the end of the last century. By following the steep incline up the Savodá třída – Park Road – bordered by huge and ancient trees and charming villas – you can quickly escape the noise and bustle of the promenade and look down on the spa quarter with its hotels and baths.

The basis of the treatment at Karlovy Vary is its 12 thermal springs, each boasting a high mineral content. They gush out of the earth at high pressure, at a rate of almost 660 gallons (3,000 litres) per minute. The best-known spring – Vřídlo, the "bubbly one" – produces, each day, more than 660,000 gallons (3 million litres) of water at a constant temperature of 163°F (73°C). The most important part of the cures is drinking the water; baths, too, are believed to be beneficial. In former times only baths were prescribed and the patients were obliged to lie in the water for two days and two nights without interruption. Today's cures are less rigorous, and treatments, whether they are for metabolic disorders, digestive complaints, chronic malfunction of the liver and gall bladder, infectious hepatitis, diabetes or gastric and duodenal ulcers, by no means precludes taking advantage of all the leisure facilities and attractions that this lively spa town provides.

Karlovy Vary also has plenty to offer on the cultural side. As well as theatre and opera performances, exhibitions and promenade concerts, the summer film festival (*see page 212*) provides exciting variety. The festival has established a notable reputation as a stage for young film-makers from Central and Eastern Europe; as such, it attracts increasingly large audiences.

Jáchymov: Jáchymov (Joachimsthal) lies in the foothills of the Ore Mountains (Erzgebirge), a few miles north of Karlovy Vary on the road to Chemnitz in Germany. The first settlement was

The Café Elefant in Karlovy Vary

founded here in 1516 following the discovery of rich silver deposits; three years later, the town acquired a royal charter. The founder of Jáchymov, Imperial Baron Schlick, was granted the privilege of minting the famous Joachimsthaler guilders. The latter were soon recognised as international currency, giving their name to the *Thaler* – the silver coin formerly used in Germany and Austria – and ultimately to the leading monetary unit of the modern world, the dollar.

Even in the 16th century, Jáchymov, then with a population of some 20,000, was the second-largest town in Bohemia after Prague. At times, as many as 1,000 miners were employed underground. After just over a century of intensive exploitation, however, the silver seams were exhausted; by 1671, even the mint had to close down. The little town, having lost its *raison d'être*, was given a new lease of life by the worldwide scientific revolution. For a while, the people of Jáchymov eked out an existence manufacturing porcelain and glass. The dyes were extracted from pitchblende, a waste product of silver mining. In 1896, however, the French physicist Antoine Becquerel discovered radioactivity in these mineral deposits. Shortly after that, the physicists Marie and Pierre Curie demonstrated the existence of the elements polonium and radium, which they were able to isolate from the heaps of waste.

Joachimsthal became the site of the first radium baths in the world. A small baker was the first to open a jerry-built bathing establishment. The next complex was more elaborate, and by 1906 the town was recognised as a medicinal spa town.

Today the little town's main source of income remains its medicinal baths and cures. The healing properties of the radioactive waters from the mines, which bubble forth from galleries more than 1,600 ft (500 metres) below the earth's surface at a pleasantly warm temperature, have been found particularly efficacious in the case of disorders of the locomotive and nervous systems and vascular disease.

The spa buildings are concentrated in the south of the town, surrounded by woodland and lying some distance from the road. The **Radium Palace**, the magnificent spa rooms built in 1912 in the Secese style (the Czech variation of Art Nouveau), contains a concert hall and a number of elegant restaurants. In the nearby park stands a fine monument to the scientific pioneer Marie Curie-Sklodowska, erected by the grateful citizens of Jáchymov. The modern spa rooms, the Akademik Běhounek, are named after one of the illustrious physicist's pupils; they, and further recent buildings, testify to the town's economic expansion.

To the north, the **Old Town** marks the historic centre of the mining community. Characterised by its octagonal tower and terraced gables, the Late-Gothic **Town Hall** dominates the central square. The long, narrow market place is bordered by a number of distinguished, well-preserved houses in a mixture of Gothic and Renaissance styles. Despite frequent renovation, the

Marble elegance in the historic Grand Hotel Pupp.

For two weeks in summer, usually in July, the Film Festival brings an international flair to the little Bohemian spa town of Karlovy Vary. Since 1950 the festival has been held biennially, attracting film makers and cinema enthusiasts from all over the world. It is the second-oldest festival of its kind in Europe – younger than Venice, but founded before those of Cannes, Locarno and Berlin.

Paradoxically, the origins of the Karlovy Vary Festival lie in neighbouring Mariánské Lázně. Immediately after the Czech film industry was nationalised in 1946, the first festival was held there. Originally there was no element of competition, but in 1948 a jury, at first drawn just from within the country, began to judge the films that were shown; from 1950 an international committee judged the films and the festival became linked to an annual theme.

During the early years the festival also included short films and cartoons, and for a while there was also a special section for films from the Third World. The competition also introduced a new category for first films by young directors.

From the beginning, the Karlovy Vary Festival showed a strong bias towards films on social themes. At the same time, it offered cinematographers from socialist and developing countries the chance to present themselves on an international stage. The quality of the films chosen confirmed the value of the concept: among the prize-winning works were *Auschwitz*, by the Polish director Wanda Jakubowská (1948), *No Peace under the Olive Trees* by the Italian director Santini (1951), *The Children of Hiroshima* by Japan's Kanet Schindó (1954), the Soviet film classic *Nine Days in a Year* by Michail Romm, *Diary of a Lady's Maid* by Luis Buñuel (1964) and Saura's brilliant film version of Lorca's *Blood Wedding* (1980). On the negative side, it was clear that the organisers were often guided by ideological rather than artistic motives in their choice of films. Nonetheless, the Karlovy Vary Film Festival was the only one in the former Eastern bloc to achieve the highest international "A" rating.

The 27th festival in 1990 was held under very different conditions within Czechoslovakia. On this occasion, the organisers had moved away from the previous, rather pompous framework. Nevertheless all the national film critics were unanimous that the festival did not gain in quality. Only the retrospective on Czech film production during the 1960s and some examples of the later works of Miloš Forman compensated for the lack of interesting new films.

In 1992, the festival was organised, as planned, as an exposition of European films, including previously unseen Czech productions. But at the time of writing it is difficult to say what path the festival will take in the future. The Czech Ministry of Culture is responsible for the event, and just as is the case with all other institutions, it will take some time after the division of the country in January 1993 for clear policies to emerge. Further doubts stem from the fact that Karlovy Vary alternated its role as a forum for East European film with Moscow, which may now decide to hold its festival on an annual basis. As things stand at the moment, the next Karlovy Vary Film Festival is due to go ahead as scheduled in 1994. ■

Poster advertising Chabrol's *Quiet Days in Clichy*.

parish **church of St Joachim** is worth a visit. The former mint behind the town hall now houses a **Museum of Mining and Numismatics** and provides an interesting insight into the town's history. To gain the best overall view of the town, the visitor should take the chair lift to the top of the **Klínovec** (3,980 ft/ 1,244 metres), the highest mountain in the Ore mountains and a spectacular vantage point.

Loket Castle, some 6 miles (10 km) southwest of Karlovy Vary on a minor road to Cheb, is a favourite destination for an outing and worth the detour. The royal fortress is built on a high cliff overlooking a bend in the River Ohře, which explains the appropriateness of the name *Loket*, "Elbow". The first documented reference to the stronghold was in 1239; the oldest section of the building still standing, a Romanesque-style rotunda, was probably built towards the end of the 12th century. The main tower is constructed of granite blocks; the gateways and the margrave's residence were added during the 14th century.

Additional points of interest include an attractive collection of locally manufactured glass, porcelain and pewter. There is also a Goethe Museum. Protected by the castle, the settlement has survived until the present day. The medieval houses grouped around the market square charm visitors.

Frantíškový Lázně: Frantíškový Lázně (Franzensbad), lying a few miles north of Cheb (*see previous chapter*), is the odd one out among the spas of Western Bohemia. With its 24 icy mineral springs, the town was conceived in a unified style at the end of the 18th century. Taking the waters here, or undergoing a course of baths in the radioactive moorland mud, is beneficial in treating coronary and rheumatic disease and a wide variety of gynaecological complaints. The little spa town has an international reputation.

The healing water comes from the Ohře, an acidic spring whose curative properties were well known even in the 16th century. It was a local physician, Dr Vinzenz Adler, who introduced the

Loket Castle
and a girl
without a care.

spa to an international public at the beginning of the 19th century. Emperor Franz I of Austria discovered the benefits of the spring and gave his name to the newly-built town.

The town centre is laid out on a regular grid pattern and surrounded by spacious parks, containing the springs, spa rooms and baths. The Národní třída, the "National Street", is bordered along its entire length by attractive turn-of-the-century houses. The House of the Three Lilies at No. 10, one of the first boarding houses, is 100 years older. Standing off centre in the southwest corner is the Nám. mírů, the main square with colonnade, meeting rooms, gas baths and the elegant **Frantisek Spring Pavilion**, which was built in 1832. Adjoining it on the west side, in **Dvořák Park**, is the Bath House I and the massive wooden pavilion housing two further springs, the **Luisin pramen** (Luisenquelle) and the **Studený pramen** (Kalter Sprudel).

In the vicinity are two Glauber's salt springs, the source of an efficacious laxative which, together with the spring water, constitutes one of the spa town's principal export commodities. The other springs are to the southeast near the **Hotel Imperial**, still one of the best addresses in town, which enjoys a splendid location and can be reached by a pleasant walk. To the north and east is the **Municipal Museum**, the theatre and the **Music Pavilion**, the setting for frequent promenade concerts.

Only 4 miles (6 km) from Františkový Lázně lies a bizarre landscape. The peat moor of **Soos-Hájek** has been declared a nature conservation area. Poisonous carbon dioxide issues from funnel-shaped hollows; the bubbling mud, like a landscape in a science-fiction film, recalls the volcanic origins of the region. This is even more in evidence in the nearby **Komorní Hůrka nature reserve**, where traces of the region's last volcanic eruption during the Quaternary Period can still be seen.

Mariánské Lázně: Situated at an altitude of some 1,920 ft (600 metres) in a protective arc of wooded hills stretching to the north, west and east,

Františkovy Lázně (Franzensbad) has been a spa town since 1793.

214

Mariánské Lázně makes a good base for a tour through Western Bohemia, not only for its favourable geographical location but also for its well-developed tourist infrastructure.

One of Europe's most scenic spas, Mariánské Lázně's long list of famous visitors includes the English king Edward VII. The town possesses over forty mineral springs, whose highly saline waters are today used for the treatment of bladder disorders, respiratory problems, heart ailments, rheumatism and blood and skin diseases.

The Premonstratensian monks from nearby **Teplá** must have been aware of the healing properties of the water when they established the village of Auschowitz near the springs in 1341, creating a sort of *dépendance* of their abbey, which lay some 8 miles (13 km) to the east. In 1710 the abbot had a pilgrims' lodge built to provide shelter for the steadily growing band of invalids who came in search of a cure. At the same time, the springs were tapped; the monks decanted the water into barrels which they sold for a handsome profit to prosperous cities and noblemen's estates. In 1749 an inventive apothecary at the abbey found a convenient way of cutting the transport costs by evaporating the water and marketing the much more convenient Teplá Salt.

The mineral baths were added a few decades later. The water from the "Stinking Spring" (Stinkquelle) – named for its high hydrogen sulphide content – proved particularly efficacious, and thankful patients dedicated votive pictures to the Virgin Mary. The obnoxious spring's name was replaced by "Mary's Spring" (Marienquelle). In 1818 it became officially known as the "Spa Town of the Austrian Monarchy", although it didn't receive its town charter until 1868.

Mariánské Lázně is full of fascinating stories. In 1820, at the age of 74, Goethe drove over by coach from Karlovy Vary. He returned the following year, the constant companion of the charming Baroness Ulrike Levetzov, who was only 19 years old. Their relationship developed into a passionate romance, but

Ballroom dancing in Mariánské Lázně's Main Colonnade.

when the potential mother-in-law refused to give her consent to a marriage, Goethe withdrew and never visited the spas again.

Goethe was only the first of many writers and composers to be inspired by the springs of Mariánské Lázně. He was followed by Frédéric Chopin, Richard Wagner and the dramatist Henrik Ibsen. In 1833, the violinist Ludwig Spohr composed his romantic waltzes entitled *Memories of Marienbad*, and in the 1960s Alain Resnais made the film classic *Last Year in Marienbad*, which rapidly gained cult status.

A popular venue for international congresses and symposia, Mariánské Lázně has developed into the most comfortable and modern of all spas, expanding far beyond its modest origins. Today the southern approach leads through several miles of uninspiring modern suburbs before the elegant spa district unfolds. On the left-hand side, the central avenue, **Hlavní třída** (former Kaiserstrasse), is bordered by a variety of shops, attractive restaurants and a number of large hotels, including the Bohemia, which underwent renovation a few years ago and now combines Art Nouveau elegance with modern facilities and comfort.

On the right, the spa gardens extend towards the horizon across gentle hills. On its southern boundary stand two fine buildings dating from the turn of the century – the **New Baths** and the former pump rooms, now known as the **Casino** and used as a cultural centre. (The casino proper, with an excellent restaurant and bar, lies a good 300 yards further to the south, at the entrance to the spa district.) From here you pass the **Ambrožův pramen** (Ambrosiusquelle), the **Central Baths**, the **Mud Baths** and the **Mariin pramen** (Marienquelle).

Ascending the hill, the road passes the **church of the Assumption** before reaching the spa promenade. The rotunda housing the **Křížový pramen** (Kreuzbrunnen) was built in 1818 when the town was first recognised as a spa. The **New Colonnade** is a fascinating (both optically and technically) cast-

The Rudolf Spring in Mariánské Lázně.

iron structure. The filigree struts forming the framework of the finely proportioned **Promenade Hall** were produced by a Moravian foundry in 1884–89; they lend the open construction with its lively ceiling frescoes a wonderful sense of lightness. Completed in 1988, the computer-controlled **Singing Fountains** – a series of playful water sculptures immediately in front – are unconvincing by comparison.

Climbing up to the next terrace, you reach the **Goethe House**, which recalls the spa's illustrious visitor. Today the neoclassical building serves as municipal museum. The square in front is dominated by the old-fashioned **Hotel Kavkaz**. Its rooms appeal to lovers of faded elegance who are prepared to ignore the dripping taps, musty carpets and warped window frames.

A stroll along the northern perimeter of the park will lead past a number of other hotels and bath houses and then back to the upper end of the Hlavní třída. It is worth checking the programme at the **Municipal Theatre**.

Nature-lovers will also find plenty to enjoy in the immediate neighbourhood of the town. There are many delightful woodland walks along a total of 70 km (40 miles) of signposted paths.

A few miles northwest of Mariánské Lázně lies **Lázně Kynžvart** (Bad Königswart), another little spa town, known for its therapeutic, iron-rich, acidic waters, and specialising in the treatment of child illnesses. The town, which came into the possession of the dukes of Metternich in 1630, is dominated by a massive castle. In 1690, the dukes proceeded to erect a mighty baroque palace over the old castle walls. Chancellor Metternich then had the building converted into the Empire style at the beginning of the 19th century.

Goethe and Beethoven both stayed here. Today's visitors can enjoy the castle's valuable collections which include such diverse treasures as Egyptian mummies, oriental and Gothic paintings as well as a display of curiosities. The castle is surrounded by an extensive English-style landscaped park.

Goethe with Ulrike von Levetzow; he was 70 and she was only 19.

NORTHERN BOHEMIA

Northern Bohemia is a region of great scenic beauty as well as a treasure chest of history and culture. It is an area famous for growing fruit, hops and wine, but it is also a mining district with smoking chimney stacks and factories. The observant traveller crossing the countryside on the southern slopes of the Ore Mountains (Erzgebirge) will stumble upon many contradictions.

Leaving behind the spa towns described in the previous chapter, the next stage of the tour strikes out from Karlovy Vary in a northeasterly direction towards **Klášterec nad Ohří** (Klösterle), on the River Ohře (Eger). This ancient little town was originally the possession of the Benedictine order; the Bohemian king Přemysl Otakar II later presented it to the aristocratic Cumperk family. The Renaissance **castle** acquired its pseudo-Gothic countenance after being gutted by fire in 1856; today it houses an extensive porcelain collection with exhibits ranging from Chinese antiquities to contemporary items.

Another interesting town is **Kadaň** on the Ohře. The medieval town square with its arcades, elaborate gabled roofs and stone portals is especially attractive. The **town hall,** with its Gothic tower and pretty oriel window, was rebuilt in the baroque style following a fire, as was the church opposite, also originally Gothic. On the southern slopes, overlooking the river, stands the former **monastery**, now the municipal archives. Apart from a large number of Gothic remains and baroque additions, it boasts cellar-like vaulting and the sarcophagus of the monastery's founder, Johann Hassenstein von Lobkowitz.

No visit to Northern Bohemia, the cradle of hop-growing, would be complete without sampling the local beer. A pleasant aroma and a spicy resinous quality characterise the type of hop grown in the area surrounding the town of **Žatec** (Saaz). Fertile soil and favourable climatic conditions guarantee the supremacy of hops from this region,

grown here since the 10th century. Today 60 percent of the total production is destined for the export market.

Chomutov (Komotau) offers a number of architectural sights, including the historic town square which has an unusual arcade and the 16th-century Collen-Luther House. A number of magnificent medieval chambers have been preserved. The little **church of St Catherine** in the vicinity is a fine example of the early Gothic style.

The medieval town of **Most** (Brüx), lying on the trading route from Bohemia to Saxony, has become a thriving mining community. A new town has gradually replaced the original settlement. The relocation of the Gothic **Deanery church** in 1975 was an impressive technical achievement. For the first time in Europe, a total mass weighing 12,000 tons was moved in one piece. Only the altar, 56 ft (17.5 metres) high and 26 ft (8 metres) wide, was dismantled.

Of particular interest is the nearby **Jezeří Castle**. The remarkable architectural ensemble includes baroque build-

ings, a Renaissance palace and a Gothic fortress. Nonetheless, since 1973 the entire complex has been the subject of violent controversy. The coal lobby demands that the castle be demolished and the rock upon which it stands blown up, since they stand in the way of mining the brown coal. Cultural historians and ecologists object violently to these plans, and geologists have pointed out that if coal mining goes ahead the entire mountain would suffer from a landslide.

The castle in **Duchcov** (Dux) is the former residence of the von Waldstein family. It contains a rare collection of historic gems. At the end of the 18th century, Giovanni Giacomo Casanova wrote his memoirs here. The district town of **Teplice**, housing the **Krušno-horské divadlo Theatre** and an interesting museum, is the oldest spa town in Bohemia. The baths, with their radioactive springs, are used to treat circulatory disorders and malfunctions of the motor system. Recommended is a visit to one of the town's many welcoming restaurants, wine bars and cafés.

The Labe (Elbe) Valley: Litoměřice (Leitmeritz) and its hinterland are often described as the Garden of Bohemia; fruit and vines flourish here. The former Royal City also offers the visitor a wealth of historic sights and architecture. The town is characterised by its Renaissance and baroque buildings. Setting the scene are the chalice-shaped roof of the **Mráz House** and the **town hall**, of Gothic origin but rebuilt in Renaissance style. The town's skyline is dominated by **St Stephen's Cathedral**. Visitors should also make a point of visiting the **Gallery of Northern Bohemia**.

This attractive region has had its fair share of suffering at the hands of history. A particularly harsh fate befell the town of **Terezín**. It was founded in 1780 by Emperor Joseph II as a bastion against the Prussians and named in honour of Empress Maria Theresa. During the last war, the German occupying forces established the notorious concentration camp of Theresienstadt here. A memorial recalls all those who suffered and died (*see box page 51*).

Most (Brüx) has its fair share of environmenta problems.

222

A few miles further upstream lies **Roudnice nad Labem** (Raudnitz), site of a baroque castle. An interesting gallery is housed in the former riding school. **Mount Říp** rises above the gentle hill landscape to the south. According to legend, Čech, founding father of the nation, and his entourage paused on the mountain's summit and, enchanted by the view, decided to settle in the region. The romantic **St George's Chapel** on the mountain was built in honour of a celebration marking the victory of Prince Soběslav over Emperor Lothar in the Battle of Chlumec in 1126.

Downstream from Litoměřice, the next town is **Ústí nad Labem** (Aussig). Its well-developed industry has made it the economic centre of the region. Enjoying a favourable location on the medieval Salt Road and at the confluence of the Bílina and the Labe, Ústí nad Labem became a Royal City in the 13th century. The approach to the city is marked by **Střekov Castle**, perched on a high basalt cliff overlooking the Labe just outside the city. Many famous personalities have visited this fortress; in 1842, Richard Wagner composed his opera *Tannhäuser* here.

The town centre has a number of other interesting sights. Since a bomb attack during World War II, the tower of the Gothic **church of the Assumption** has had a small list. The entire building has had to be underpinned and is regarded as one of the architectural curiosities of Europe. The neighbouring baroque ensemble, comprising the **church and monastery of St Adalbert**, has been restored and now serves as a concert and exhibition hall. In 1972 an organ with 3,572 pipes was installed.

In the vicinity of Ústí nad Labem is **Tiské skály**, a romantic labyrinth of bizarre sandstone rock formations. A few miles further upstream, **Velké Březno Castle** is worth visiting for its interior, which retains its original features, and an attractive 12-acre (5-hectare) park. Also worth mentioning is the village of **Stadice** in the **Bílina Valley**, the setting for *Kosmas*, the first Czech chronicler's account of Přemysl Oráč,

Hops from Žatec (Saaz) give Czech beers their special flavour.

the founder of the ruling dynasty of Bohemia. According to the legend, Princess Libuše summoned the simple farmer to Prague to share the throne. In memory of the event, the inhabitants of Stadice are said to have supplied hazelnuts for the royal table. Today the town square, with its ancient memorial stone, is a national monument.

Interesting in a very different way is the toxic waste tip in **Chabařovice**, to the west of the town. There are no precise details concerning the exact contents of the tip, which was commissioned in 1905. It is suspected that the contents of the entire Mendeleyev periodic table are represented here, offering the possibility of hitherto unknown compounds. The American government provided funds for the disposal of 40,000 tons of highly toxic hexachlorobenzol.

Děčín (Tetschen) Castle, situated on the Labe just before the German border, was occupied until recently by the Soviet army; following the 1968 invasion, they established a permanent garrison here. Although the soldiers have now

withdrawn, to date only the rose garden in the castle grounds has been made accessible to the public. Concerts are held here on summer evenings.

Nature lovers have a special affection for the area surrounding Děčín. Two Swiss artists, the painter Adrian Zingg and the engraver Anton Graff, were so enchanted by the beauty of this landscape that when they surveyed the picturesque rocky cliffs, deep ravines and narrow defiles they felt themselves transported back to their native land and lost their desire to return home. That was in 1776; since then, the area surrounding Děčín, and in particular the sandstone region near **Hřensko**, has been dubbed "Bohemia's Switzerland". One of the thrills of the area is a trip through the foaming spray of the mountain torrents in a narrow boat – with a local wild water expert at the helm, of course. Also popular is a detour to **Pravčická brána**, a remarkable natural rock formation in the sandstone plateau around Hřensko.

The sandstone mountains were formed 130 million years ago; the region is in grave danger from today's air pollution. One crumbling sandstone block weighing about 800 tons is poised threateningly above the main road from Hřensko. It will probably have to be blown up in to avoid the risk of a major catastrophe.

The district known as **Česká Lípa** (Böhmisch Leipa) is rich in unusual natural phenomena. These include the **Sloupské skály cliffs**, occupied by the sandstone castle of Sloup, and the **Panské skály cliffs**, which consist of thousands of basalt pillars. Observed from the air they resemble a honeycomb; from the side, they look more like organ pipes, which explains their nickname: *varhany*, "The Organ".

Southeast of Česká Lípa, the mighty ruin of **Bezděz Castle** soars heavenwards; it is one of the most important examples of Bohemian Gothic defensive architecture. It was never rebuilt and includes an early Gothic chapel. Emperor Charles IV had the **Máchovo Lake** created near the castle. The lake is known for its carp, but it is also a popular resort area with sandy beaches and pleasantly warm water temperatures.

The Labe (Elbe) near Litoměříce (Leitmeritz).

The Jizerské Mountains (Isergebirge):
With a population of 100,000, the town of **Liberec** (Reichenberg) is famous for its cloth production, which was begun in the Middle Ages by Flemish weavers. The long weaving tradition led to tremendous prosperity in the middle of the last century, when a succession of textile factories were established. Today, a number of well preserved historic buildings still testify to the town's Golden Age. More than 40 of them are national monuments. Among the most important is the **Renaissance palace**, whose chapel is noted for its beautifully carved altar and coffered ceiling. Impressive, too, is the **Town Hall**; built in the style of the Dutch neo-Renaissance, it was designed by the Viennese architect Frans von Neuman and has definite similarities with the New Town Hall in Vienna.

A wonderful view of the town and the **Jizerské Mountains** beyond can be enjoyed from the central of the three towers. On the **Old Town Square** beneath, the 16th-century **Deanery church of St Antony** was rebuilt in neo-Gothic style in 1879. From here the narrow Větrná ulice (wind alley), with its beautiful 17th-century half-timbered **Wallenstein Houses**, leads through to the **Small Square** (Malé nám.).

The **Museum of Northern Bohemia** is situated in the north of the town. It contains an impressive collection of handicraft (tapestries, furniture, pottery and glass) as well as a historical and folklore section. It should be mentioned that between 1938 and 1945, Reichenberg was the largest town in the so-called Sudetenland. It was also the home of Konrad Henlein, the Sudeten German leader who demanded the Anchluss with the Reich and subsequently became the Gauleiter of Sudetenland and civil commissioner for Bohemia.

Some 12 miles (20 km) north of Liberec stands the forbidding fortress, **Frýdlant (Friedland) Castle**, with its impregnable round tower. It was built in 1241, on a rock above the Smědá, by a knight named Ronovec; later owners had it converted into a Renaissance castle. After the Bohemian uprising of 1619, the Lutheran lord of the castle, Christoph

von Redern, sided against the Habsburgs; his fate was sealed after defeat at the Battle of the White Mountain. In 1620 Albrecht von Wallenstein bought the estate and made the castle his home.

As a token of his gratitude to his diligent general, Ferdinand II elevated Wallenstein to the rank of duke. But the moment of glory was to be short-lived; in 1634 Wallenstein was assassinated and the Friedland estate passed to Count Gallas, another general in the imperial army. His heirs opened the castle to the public; one of the first castle museums in Europe was created almost 200 years ago in response to the considerable interest in the glamourous Duke of Friedland that Schiller's dramatic trilogy *Wallenstein* had aroused. The Lower Castle, with its meticulously renovated Renaissance facade, is linked by the Knight's Bridge to the original Gothic fortress. The latter contains luxuriously appointed salons and halls as well as a well-stocked art gallery.

Also worth visiting is **Sychrov Castle**, 12 miles (20 km) south of Liberec. It

Bohemian Glass

There is evidence that even during the Bronze Age the settlers of what is now the Czech Republic manufactured glass in the form of beads for necklaces and bracelets. During the Middle Ages, at about the same time as they produced the first glass drinking vessels, they learned how to make windows, panes of glass and wall mosaics.

In 1370, under Charles IV, artists created the monumental mosaic on the South Portal of St Vitus's Cathedral, depicting scenes of the Last Judgment. The magnificent windows of the church of St Bartholomew in Kolín date from about 1380. Domestic use of glass included the manufacture of bottles and flasks, in a greenish or brownish colour. By the turn of the 15th century there were eight glassblowers' foundries in Bohemia, five in Moravia and a further eight in territory which belonged to Bohemia at the time. The glass factory in Chřibská (Kreibitz), a town in the Lusatian hills, was first mentioned in 1427. It exerted a considerable influence on the development of the glass industry.

During the 16th century the rough-and-ready glassware produced in the Bohemian Forest no longer satisfied the refined tastes of the worldly aristocrats in the first years of Habsburg rule. Following the Venetian glass-blowing tradition, production moved towards thin glass in the harmonious forms of the Renaissance. After 1600, cylindrical tankards served as a basis for the famous enamel painting. Between 1600 and 1610 the gem cutter Caspar Lehmann from Uelzen (1563–1622) experimented with the cutting of glass at the court of Rudolf II in Prague. The manufacture of cut glass did not become widespread in Bohemia until about 1680. Nowadays, Bohemian crystal is exported all over the world.

The classic form of the Bohemian baroque wine glass with a cut pedestal foot, and the many-faceted beaker of fine, thin glass was traditionally adorned with ornate floral bouquets, garlands or grotesque decorations. After 1720 the range was enlarged by the addition of gilt glass and the black engraving in the style of Ignaz Preissler (1676–1741). Along with the local cut and polished glass, Bohemian chandeliers with cut glass prisms were also much sought after. During the 18th century crystal lustres were exported to the courts of the King of France and the Tsar.

After a period of decline at the end of the 18th century, Bohemian Hyalith glass with its coloured enamel decoration established an independent reputation. Around 1800 the range of glass was further enlarged by the trend towards less ornate, finely polished and engraved Empire and Biedermeier glassware. The thick-walled coloured glass discovered by Friedrich Egermann in about 1820 revived interest in the craft further: black hyalite glassware, agate glass, Lithyalin glass and new uses for ruby glass all became popular. The status of Bohemian glass was boosted during the 19th century by the manufacture of mirrors and tableware as well as glass coral. The latter survived until recent times in Jablonec nad Nisou (Gablonz) under the trade name JABLONEX. Even during the 20th century the names of Loetz, Lobmayer and Jeykal ensured the continued worldwide reputation of Bohemian crystal by virtue of their adaptation of the fantasy, colour and metallic effects characteristic of the Art Nouveau style. ■

Art Nouveau glass from Bohemia.

was built at the end of the 17th century, but did not acquire its romantic Gothic appearance until the last century. Today's visitors to the castle tread in the footsteps of two of the greatest Czech composers, Antonín Dvořák and Josef Suk, who were frequent guests.

One of the most prominent landmarks in the region is undoubtedly the elegant tower of the television transmitter on the summit of **Mount Ještěd**. It can be reached by cable car, and the tower restaurant offers a panorama across the Krkonoše and the Jizerské mountains.

Bohemian Paradise: Adjoining the district to the south lies the nature reserve **Český raj** (Bohemian Paradise), where between Turnov (Turnau) and Jičín the massive sand deposits left by a sea covering this land during the Cretaceous Period have remained until this day. Near Jičín, there is the famous nature reserve of **Prachovské skály**, with its bizarre sandstone cliffs, vertical walls and deep, narrow grottoes.

Founded by Václav (Wenceslas) II, **Jičín** is an old royal city which at various times belonged to a number of Bohemian noble dynasties. After the Battle of the White Mountain, it fell to Wallenstein who incorporated it in his Friedland estate. He wanted to make Jičín the political and cultural centre of his empire, but he could only partially realise his plans. Be that as it may, this period was the most important in the town's history.

The only town gate still standing is the 50-metre (150 ft) **Valdická brána**, built in 1568. It provides a fine view of the tree-lined avenue leading to the park of **Libosad** in which Wallenstein had an attractive pleasure palace built for himself and his retinue. Further to the north are the towers of the Carthusian monastery which he founded; it was converted into a prison in 1783. Next to the gate, the **church of St James** was also built on the orders of Wallenstein, but was only completed in the 19th century; the general's daughter is buried within. The town square is surrounded by beautiful Gothic, Renaissance and baroque houses. On the southern side stands

eople have een skiing n the rkonoše Giant lountains) ince 1894.

Waldstein Palace, built by Italian architects between 1624–34. It was here, in 1813, that the "Holy Alliance" of the Allies against Napoleon was sealed.

The region is also characterised by its remarkable volcanic features, for example the basalt cliffs which rise above the bizarre ruins of the Gothic castle in **Trosky**. Further on the road to Turnov is the remarkable cliff town of **Hrubá Skála**, with the ruins of another medieval castle nearby.

The area retains considerable economic significance because of the presence of extensive deposits of Bohemian garnet and other precious stones. **Turnov** (Turnau) is internationally famous as a centre of gem polishing and the production of garnet jewellery. The district museum with its collection of precious stones is well-worth seeing.

Following the Jizera valley to the north of Turnov, the visitor will soon arrive at the town of **Železný Brod** (Eisenbrod), which is world-famous for the manufacture of ornamental glass. The town gets its name from the iron ore which has been mined here ever since the 17th century. A number of old wooden buildings are preserved, including the **belfry** next to the church of St James. Železný Brod is a good base for excursions into the Český raj.

Jablonec nad Nisou (Gablonz), the principal town in the Jizerské mountains, stands in the shadow of the highest peak in the area, the **Černá hora** (3,469 ft/1,084 metres,) and is primarily important for its glass and jewellery production. During the 16th century the area was settled by German glassblowers because the wooded slopes of the Jizerské mountains provided them with copious supplies of charcoal, needed for their craft. During the 18th century they rose to fame with their glass imitations of pearls and precious stones, and the community experienced an economic boom. Today the **Glass Museum** documents the little town's glorious heyday and the history of this traditional craft (*see page 226*).

Walkers and skiers find ample recreation possibilities in the Jizerské mountains in summer and winter alike. Especially popular is the annual cross-country ski competition known as the Jizerská padesátka ("The Iser Mountain Race"), which starts in the resort of **Bedřichov**.

The Krkonose: To the East rise the mountains of the **Krkonoše** – the "Giant Mountains" – which as the highest mountains in Bohemia form the natural boundary between the Czech Republic and Poland. The mountain crest extends over a length of 22.5 miles (36 km); the highest peak, at 5,126 ft (1,602 metres), is the **Sněžka** (Schneekoppe). Weathering and ice have produced a succession of strangely shaped seas of rock and bare pillars of stone, providing a fitting scenario for the fantastic stories of Rübezahl and other legendary characters. Almost the entire region was declared a national park in 1963; together with the adjoining area across the Polish frontier, it forms one of the largest nature conservancy areas in Europe.

The domestic buildings of the Krkonoše display a unique variety of styles, demonstrating the skill of the carpenters in this mountainous region. Also of note are the **museums** in Vrchlabí (Hohenelbe), Jilemnice, Vysoké nad Jizerou and Trutnov (Trautenau). They house extensive folklore collections and natural exhibits.

The main winter sports centres, with ski lifts, cross-country ski tracks and downhill pistes are **Špindlerův Mlyn** (Spindlermühle), **Pec pod Sněžkou** and **Harrachov**. The international ski-flying championships, the *Turné Bohemia*, are held here each year. The highlight of the winter sports season in Harrachov is the ceremonial entry of Rübezahl, the legendary ruler of the Krkonoše, at the beginning of March. The costumed parade fills the streets with an atmosphere of festivity and celebration.

East of **Trutnov**, the area surrounding **Police nad Metují** and **Teplice nad Metují** is well known by mountaineers. Erosion of the sandstone cliffs has resulted in an intricately-shaped skyline, resembling the silhouettes of towns. Particularly popular are the **Adršpašsko-teplické skály**, but the more remote **Broumovské stěny** also offer spectacular views. The little town of

Liberec (Reichenberg) – here the town hall – has been a centre of the textile industry since the late Middle Ages.

Broumov is the ultimate backwater. The Benedictine monastery here – just one of the works of the Dientzenhofers in this part of the country – is a superb example of baroque architecture.

On the journey from the Krkonoše to **Hradec Králové** it is worth stopping in **Dvůr Králové**. A zoo, later expanded into a safari park, was established here in 1946. The park is stocked with a wide range of animals, including rare species such as the white rhinoceros; visitors can view the animals from the safety of a bus. A few miles to the south lies the spa town of **Kuks**, which is notable for the impressive baroque statues of Matthias Bernhard Braun surrounding the **church of the Holy Trinity**.

The origins of **Náchod** lie in a Gothic watchtower built to protect the long-distance trading routes. A succession of historical figures left their mark here: George of Poděbrady, Albrecht von Wallenstein, the Trčka family and the Piccolominis. Náchod was also the native town and periodic place of work of the writer Josef Škvorecký. The sur-rounding region provides the background for his well-known novel *The Cowards*.

South of Náchod, **Rozkoš u České Skalice** – the largest reservoir in Bohemia – provides opportunities to bathe. In **Nové Město** it is worthwhile visiting the castle and the market place, which is fringed by Renaissance-style town-houses. Another interesting destination is **Opočno**, the location of a magnificent Renaissance castle with arcades.

The Orlické Mountains (Adlergebirge): Two rivers, the Tichá Orlice and the Divoká Orlice, both free of industrial pollution, flow through the little towns of Letohrad, Lanskroun, Litice, Jablonné and Žamberk. Providing the backdrop are the **Orlické Mountains**, a relatively low chain of mountains covered in spruce. They reach a maximum altitude of 3,696 ft (1,155 metres). Below, in the picturesque valleys, glitter countless lakes. The most popular one lies near **Pastviny**, north of Letohrad; the best-known ski centres, with lifts, are **Deštné** and **Říčky**.

Rychnov n. Kněz Castle contains an exhibition dedicated to the entire region. The town itself, a regional centre, was traditionally the home of clothmakers and weavers; its textile manufacturing industry is still very important.

From here you can make pleasant excursions into the mountains or to the large number of castles concentrated in the immediate vicinity. Particularly recommended are **Častolovice** and **Doudleby**, as well as the imposing baroque castle in **Litice**.

Among the little towns in the foothills of the Orlické mountains, **Žamberk** (Senftenberg) has the most historical importance. During the 17th century, Magdaléna Grambová introduced the art of **lace making** to the town from Italy. The traditional family workshops gradually expanded, until there was a flourishing industry in the town; even today, local residents find no shortage of customers for their wares. The **municipal museum** has a permanent exhibition dedicated to lace production; the town also has a training centre for lace workers.

Left, the source of the Labe. Right, downhill skiing in the Krkonoše.

EASTERN BOHEMIA

From Prague the national road No. 333 leads to **Kutná Hora** (Kuttenberg). This attractively situated town is today a rather sleepy little regional centre, but back in medieval times it was the most important town in Bohemia after Prague. As the centre of silver mining and the royal mint, the town generated such enormous wealth that it placed the Bohemian kings among the most influential rulers in Europe, and they frequently resided here. At the insistence of Jan Hus, Wenceslas IV signed the "Kuttenberg Decree", a major reform of the constitution of Prague University in favour of Czech nationals. With the victory of Jan Žižka's troops over the emperor's army of mercenaries before the city gates in 1422, Kutná Hora entered the annals of the Hussite Wars.

Approaching from Prague, the traveller's first impression upon entering the town is of the richly decorated stone fountain on the Rejskovo nám. The attractive baroque **church of St John Nepomuk** lies on the Husova třída, leading into the Palackého nám, bordered by fine Renaissance houses and, along with the **old town hall**, forms the heart of the Old Town. A short distance to the east, the **church of Our Lady on the Ore Heap** recalls Kutná Hora's economic foundations.

The late-Gothic **Stone House** (Kamenný dům) on Nám 1. máje is of particular interest. This unusual townhouse was constructed by an unknown master builder towards the end of the 15th century; most of the statues are ascribed to Brixi, a famous stone mason from Wroclaw. The building underwent major renovation at the beginning of this century and today serves as the municipal museum.

On the way down to the River Vrchlice lies the Gothic **church of St James**, with a 262-ft (82-metre) high tower. During the baroque period an onion dome was added; at the same time the interior acquired its share of baroque

features. Next door lies the "Inn of Valais", originally built as the **Royal Mint** in about 1300. Florentine craftsmen minted the silver coins which served as legal tender throughout Europe: the "Prague Pennies". The cellars house an extensive exhibition documenting this medieval trade. In about 1400, Wenceslas IV had the East Wing redesigned as a royal residence. Forming part of this complex is the **St Wenceslas Chapel**, demonstrating a surprising blend of architectural styles: under the Gothic ribbed vaulting, and framed by medieval winged altars, the Art Nouveau artist František Urban has executed a series of paintings narrating the legend of St Wenceslas.

The Barborská ul. leads south past the "Fort" – also formerly used as a mint – and the powerful Jesuit college to the Gothic **cathedral of St Barbara**. The mine owners of Kutná Hora financed this magnificent place of worship and dedicated it to their patron saint. Peter Parler began the building work in 1388, but the project was not completed until

1558. Apart from the valuable frescoes in the **Smíšek Chapel**, the many references to the cultural and economic history of the city are of particular interest. The spaces between the vaulting of the choir roof are decorated with the coats of arms of the craft guilds of the town. On the west wall of the south aisle, workers in the city's mint are depicted; a wall statue portrays a miner with tools and lamp.

Situated 2 miles to the northeast of Kutná Hora, **Kačina** is the finest Empire palace in all of Bohemia. Built between 1802–22, it is surrounded by an attractive English-style park, which contains a large number of rare trees. The attractions of the palace itself include the library and the theatre, as well as an agricultural museum.

In the nearby town of **Kolín**, the Old Town is laid out on a grid pattern of equal squares, a piece of town-planning characteristic of the Germans who settled here at the beginning of the 13th century. The **cathedral of St Bartholomew** was begun a little later; Peter

PARDUBICE STEEPLECHASE

" **I** t was a gloomy, foggy day – typical English weather. Early in the morning we drove in a carriage decorated with twigs gathered from fir trees onto a field behind the viaduct. In the distance we could discern through the mist horsemen in formal attire, grooms, roughriders and stable lads; some of the horses bore sidesaddles. At half-past eleven the sun broke through the mist, and the temperature rose. In the distance we could see the bright red riding habits of the master of hounds and his two assistants, together with the pack. The bells tolled noon, and the nobility gathered together." Thus Josef Pírka, a photographer from Pardubice, described the start of the hunt in the 19th century.

The hunt soon developed into tournaments in which speed was what counted. Following the English pattern, the huntsmen followed each other in hot pursuit; their goal was usually a church tower (steeple). This led to the founding of the Pardubice Hunt Club in 1848, and on 5 November

1874 the signal was given for the start of the first race across a specially prepared course.

The Great Steeplechase in Pardubice is one of the most difficult and dramatic horse races in Europe; for that reason, to win in Pardubice or in the Grand National in Aintree is every jockey's dream. Racing fans, punters and tipsters gather in their thousands on the last Sunday in March at Aintree and on the second Sunday in October in Pardubice; some try to attend both events.

The two races, however, are completely different. Characteristic of the Grand National is the English love of order. The horses run on a closely mown grass track, completing two virtually identical laps with almost 30 artificial obstacles through an English park; the terrain is as flat as a snooker table. The course is 7,770 yards (7,216 metres) long and the race is over within a matter of minutes.

The Pardubice course, by contrast, reflects the very different personality of the Czechs: no grass, no artificial barriers, but hedges, sand and water-filled ditches and rough ground with 31 obstacles. The course is 7,456 yards (6,990 metres) long. In the entire history of the two races, so far only one jockey – the English professional G. Williamson – has succeeded in winning at both Pardubice and Aintree. He gained the trophy in Pardubice four times, between 1890 and 1893, but in Aintree he won on just one occasion – in 1899.

Rather like Beecher's Brook at Aintree, the speciality of Pardubice is the Taxis Ditch, the fourth obstacle. Whoever stumbles here has already lost the race. During the 1880s it was mooted that the "Big Ditch", as it was then known, should be made less difficult, but the Count of Thurn und Taxis, the Postmaster-General of the Royal and Imperial Monarchy, defended the ditch, and in his honour it was renamed the Taxis Ditch. No less tricky are the Irish Bank – a natural embankment, 6 ft (2 metres) high and 6 ft wide, with small ditches in front and behind the obstacle, the Snake's Ditch and the deceptive "Gardens".

In 1990, the centenary of the steeplechase, the Popkovicky skok proved to be the acid test. It was really only a miniature Taxis Ditch, but it was here that the two favourites had to bury their hopes of victory in the true sense of the word.

The leap over Taxis Ditch.

Parler subsequently added a magnificent choir. With its radiating chapels illuminated by elaborately traced windows it is one of the loveliest churches in Bohemia. The town once housed one of the largest Jewish communities in the land. Today, the only traces of Kolín's former ghetto are a semi-ruined **synagogue** and a medieval **cemetery**.

In 1757 Kolín was the site of a major battle in which the imperial forces, under Field Marshal von Daun, defeated the army of Frederick the Great, forcing the Prussians to withdraw from Bohemia.

Each June a rousing **brass band festival** is held in memory of František Kmoch, a composer who was also a native son of the city; brass bands from all over the world are invited.

Further down the Labe lies the spa town of Lázně **Poděbrady** (Bad Podiebrad), whose most valuable asset is the iron-rich mineral spring discovered at the beginning of this century. The spa subsequently became famous for the treatment of coronary and vascular complaints. Renowned, too, is the Bohemian **lead crystal** from the glass foundries of Poděbrady. The town's other claim to fame is as the birthplace of the first Hussite king of the Bohemians; George of Poděbrady was born here in the castle in 1420.

Following the E67 in an easterly direction, travellers cannot fail to notice the Gothic castle of **Karlova Koruna** ("Charles's crown") in the little town of **Chlumec nad Cidlinou**; it is the work of the Italian architect Giovanni Santini. Chlumec went down in history as a centre of the Peasants' Revolt, which occurred here in 1775. A memorial some way outside the town bearing the popular Czech proverb "Fallen like a Peasant at Chlumec" recalls their defeat.

Continuing eastwards, the route passes the pretty little castle of **Hrádek u Nechanice**, which lies a few miles north of the E67.

Hradec Králové (Königsgrätz) grew up on the site of a prehistoric settlement at the confluence of the Labe and the Orlice. During the 14th century it became the dowager property of the queens

of Bohemia. Dating from this period is the brick Gothic **cathedral of the Holy Ghost** (sv. Ducha), which in 1424 served as the temporary burial place of the Hussite leader Jan Žižka. As a centre of the reform movement, two years after the Battle of Lipany, in which the Hussites were defeated, the town was bold enough to defy Emperor Sigismund. The **White Tower** (Bílá vêz), boasting the second-largest bell in Bohemia; the baroque **church of St Mary**; the Jesuit College and the **Bishop's Palace** all date from the 16th century.

Northwest of Hradec lies the dreamy little town of **Chlum**, also known for the battle fought here in 1866 in which the Prussians defeated the Austrians and their Saxon allies. The 300 graves and gravestones scattered between the villages of **Hořiněves**, **Číštěves** and **Sadová** are a moving legacy of the battle. On an eminence near Chlum is a neo-Gothic charnel house and a memorial to the fallen.

The second most important town in Eastern Bohemia, and for many years the rival of Hradec Králové, is **Pardubice**. The Renaissance-style town centre reflects its Golden Age under the aristocratic Pernštejn family. Among the many architectural attractions of the town are the Late Gothic **Green Gate**, the church of St Bartholomew and the church of the Annunciation. The **castle** was originally built as a fortress and later converted into a palace; it now houses the collection of the **North Bohemian Gallery**.

Today, Pardubice is a modern town with an excellent university for chemistry and technology. Nearby is the **Semtín chemical plant**, which produces the explosive Semtex. The main local event is the annual **steeplechase** held in Pardubice for the first time in 1874 (*see page 236*). Also in the immediate vicinity lies **Kladruby** – location of a famous **stud farm** where Spanish and Italian throroughbreds, the so-called Kladruby Greys, are bred. In the mid-16th century the first horses were supplied for the Pernštejns' estate by Emperor Maximilian II.

The little wooden church at Slavanov near Nachod.

South of Pardubice, the countryside becomes more varied, with dense forests covering the hills. Every July the town of **Chrudim** attracts puppeteers from all over the world, who come for the **marionette festival** (Loutkarská Chrudim). The **Museum of Puppets** occupies the former Soap Boilers' House – a magnificent Renaissance building .

The Renaissance castle in **Slatiňany**, a few miles further south, houses a remarkable gallery of paintings, engravings and sculptures dedicated to horse breeding.

The idyllic artificial lake of **Seč** in the upper reaches of the Chrudimka is surrounded by hills. The scenic beauty of the region has been protected by the designation of nature conservation areas, such as that surrounding **Polom**, which retains the essential character of the primeval forests which once covered the area. Also typical is the rural architecture, examples of which are displayed in the **Vysočina open-air museum** west of **Hlinsko**.

To the east of Chrudim, passing through a varied hilly landscape, the route leads to **Vysoké Mýto** (Hohenmauth), a romantic little town still bearing traces of the original grid pattern (around the market place) as well as three town gates dating from the 13th century.

Further along the E442 is **Litomyšl** (Leitomischl). From earliest times this town has been a trading and cultural centre, and has played a dominant role in the Czech national revival during the last 200 years. Today, a **Renaissance castle** stands on the site of the former fortress; this was one of the many magnificent residences of the Pernštejns, who even installed a theatre within its walls. Also of interest in Litomyšl is the **Presbytery Church**, the **college**, the **Piarist Church** and the main square. The latter is bordered by stately baroque, Renaissance and Empire buildings and was once one of the main centres on the trading route from Bohemia to Moravia. Although the town has lost much of its historical, economic and social significance, it has not lost all of its former glamour. Famous musicians and guests from all over the world flock here each year for the **Festival of Opera and Classical music**, for Litomyšl was the birthplace of Bedřich Smetana. The brewery houses a museum of Czech music and a special exhibition illustrating the life and works of the famous composer.

The local district town of **Svitavy** (Zwittau) lies to the southeast of Litomyšl. In the vicinity are a number of other villages. Of particular interest is **Moravská Třebová**, which has a magnificent Renaissance-style town hall, an imposing fortress and a palace.

The Sázava Valley towards Brno: There is a motorway linking Brno (Brünn) with Prague, but travellers who prefer a more leisurely pace, or who like to travel by train, are recommended to follow the alternative route along the thickly forested **Sázava Valley**. Further downstream the river is tamed by a number of locks; in the upper reaches, however, particularly the section between **Světlá** and **Ledeč**, it finds its own way, tumbling from rapid to rapid.

The writer **Jaroslav Hašek**, author of the world-famous novel *The Good Soldier Schweyk*, lived and died in the shadow of the fortress in **Lipnice nad Sázavou**, to the west of Deutsch-Brod. He was buried in the local cemetery and his house has been turned into a fascinating memorial museum. Within the castle itself, an informative exhibition recalls the master of humour and satire.

The little villages surrounding **Havlíčkův Brod** (Deutsch-Brod) are the home of glass-blowers and miners. It is a poor but attractive region. The town itself was rechristened in 1945 after the Czech poet and satirist Karel Havlíček Borovský; the old name, however, recalls the German miners who settled by this ford (*Brod*) from the 13th century. A fine portal of the Gothic **church of the Assumption** still stands; the oldest bell was cast in 1300. The baroque church of the Holy Family (*svaté Rodiny*), fine townhouses dating from the same period and the rococo facade of the Krenovský dům set the tone of the Old Town. A bizarre skeleton adorns the tower of the town hall.

BRNO

Brno (Brünn), the capital of Moravia, nestles in attractive rural surroundings at the confluence of the Svratka and the Svitava rivers. Over 30,000 years ago, settlers of the Aurignacian culture made their home in this congenial place, and a few centuries before the dawn of the Christian era, Celtic tribesmen founded a town here, which they called Brynn. The Slavs, who arrived here in the 6th century, changed the name to Brno; in about 800 they built a fortress on Mount Petrov. The earliest documented records of the castle date from the 11th century; it is cited as the seat of a margrave of Moravia.

The stronghold guarded the crossroads of the trading routes to the Baltic and the Black Sea; a flourishing community soon grew up in its protective shadow, expanding during the 12th and 13th centuries under the influx of new citizens from Germany. In 1243 it was granted a municipal charter by Wenceslas I. The town's importance grew considerably under Charles IV; from 1350, the Moravian provincial parliament met here and local assizes were held. It was not until 1462, however, that Brno was finally proclaimed the capital of Moravia in place of Olomouc (Olmütz). Charles IV issued a decree that all traders following the Royal route from Austria to Poland via Moravia had to stop in the town and offer their wares for sale. This encouraged science and the arts to flourish too, a trend most strongly reflected in the foundation of new monasteries.

First textile factories: Cloth manufacturers set up factories in Brno towards the end of the 18th century; the flourishing sheep farming in the surrounding grazing land provided the raw materials, and the fast-flowing rivers and local coal deposits provided the energy. Soon cloth woven in Brno penetrated the important markets of the Habsburg empire and even established itself in Western Europe in competition with rival fabrics produced in England. Before long, Brno was being called "the Manchester of Moravia".

The demolition of the town fortifications during the 18th century provided space for a major rebuilding scheme including generously laid-out parks and boulevards. The architects Adolf Loos and Bohuslav Fuchs (the founder of Czech functionalism) were responsible for shaping the town's modern configuration. The best examples are found in the gracious 19th-century residential districts outside the park belt. The **Villa Tugendhat** in the Černá pole district was built in 1930 after a design by Ludwig Mies van der Rohe. In 1928 an exhibition of contemporary art and culture in the Pisárky district of town received attention from the international press. The exhibition halls erected for this event today form the centre of the **International Trades Fair complex**, which hosts the International Machine Fair in autumn and the International Consumer Goods Fair in spring. As well as textiles, Brno has emerged as a major centre of the machine building and electronics industries; these fairs are very important for the country's exports.

The Old Town: The site of the original Slavic fortress is occupied by **St Peter's Cathedral** (Dóm na Petrově). Built in the High Gothic style, the cathedral suffered severe damage when the town was besieged by the Swedish army during the Thirty Years' War. During the 18th century it was renovated in the baroque style. At the beginning of the 20th century it was renovated again, in the neo-Gothic style, and acquired twin towers. The church contains a number of notable frescoes and sculptures, including the massive Gothic sculpture "Madonna with Child".

One particularly interesting detail is the exterior pulpit on the north side of the church. From here, in the 15th century, the fanatic Italian Franciscan monk John of Capestrano harangued the faithful gathered on the square below. The church bells are rung twice daily – at 11am and again at noon. This tradition dates from 1645, when the Swedish troops under General Linart Torstenson laid siege to Brno. The leader of the

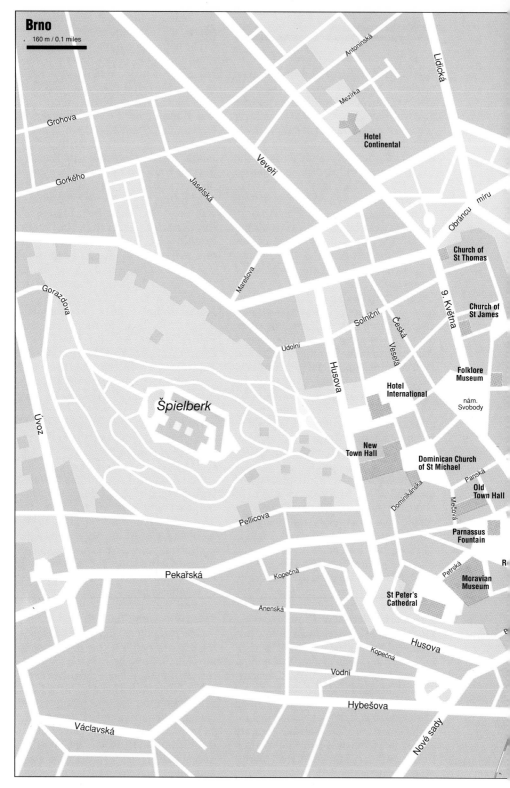

Brno

160 m / 0.1 miles

Antonínská

Lidická

Grohova

Mezírka

Hotel
Continental

Veveří

Gorkého

Jaselská

Obráncu míru

Marešova

Church of
St Thomas

Gorazdova

9. Května

Solniční

Church of
St James

Česká

Udolní

Veselá

Folklore
Museum

Úvoz

Husova

Hotel
International

nám.
Svobody

Špielberk

New
Town Hall

Dominican Church
of St Michael

Panská

Dominikářská

Old
Town Hall

Mečová

Pellicova

Parnassus
Fountain

Petrská

R

Pekařská

Kopečná

Moravian
Museum

Anenská

St Peter's
Cathedral

Husova

Kopečná

P

Vodní

Hybešova

Václavská

Nové sady

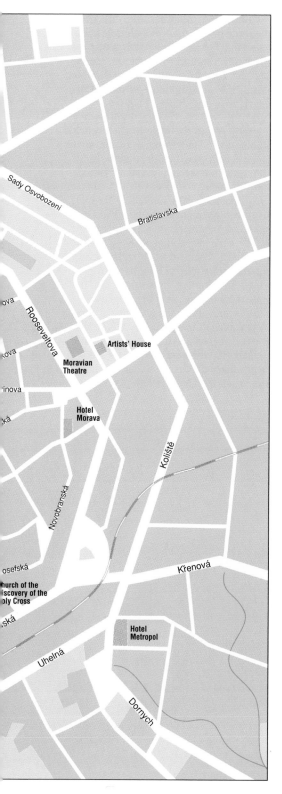

army had laid a wager that he would scale the town walls by noon, or else he would withdraw. Hearing of this oath, the beleaguered citizens, no longer able to resist the force of the Swedish attack, had the bells of St Peter's chime 12 o'clock when it was only 11am. The town was saved.

The winding Peterská ul (Cathedral Street) leads down to the secular centre of the old town, the former **Herb Market** (Horni trh), dominated by the **Trinity Column**. The market square is always an animated spot, with stalls and stands grouped around the elaborate **Fountain of Parnassus**, a baroque fantasy of mythical figures and allegorical representations of the four seasons.

At the point where the Peterská ul. opens on to the square, the most striking building complex is the Museum of Moravia (Moravskémuzeum), housed in a succession of medieval palazzi. The famous **Venus of Věstonice**, at 30,000 years the oldest extant Stone-Age clay figure, forms the *pièce de résistance* of a comprehensive archaeological and scientific exhibition. Also worth a visit is the art gallery, containing works by Rubens and Cranach as well as Moravian painters from the 15th century to the present day. In the southeast corner lies the Reduta, opened in 1670 and thus the oldest theatre in the town.

In the north, only a few steps away along the Radnická ul., stands the oldest secular monument in Brno, the **Old Town Hall**. Dating from the 13th century, it is famous for its entrance by the famous master builder Antonín Pilgram. The Town Council held its meetings here until the end of World War II. Guarding the passage through to the courtyard is the **Dragon of Brno**, which according to local legend once gobbled up all the virgins in the city. In fact, it is a stuffed alligator, presented by a passing group of Turkish jugglers to Archduke Matthias, who visited Brno in 1608 to drum up support for a conspiracy against his brother, the Emperor Rudolf II. Before leaving he decided to donate the creature to the city fathers, who displayed it in a place of honour in front of the Town Hall.

Following the Mecova ul. the visitor reaches the former fish market. Here stands the baroque **Dominican church**; the former monastery next door has served since 1945 as the New Town Hall. The Renaissance building erected above the cloister was used as long ago as 1582 as the assembly hall for the Moravian estates.

Further to the north, surrounding the Nám. Svobody ("Freedom Square"), lies the **Lower City**. The square served as the lower market place of the medieval town; all that remains from this period today is the former merchant's residence in the southwest corner, dating from 1596 and boasting a fine entrance and inner courtyard. The **church of St James** (Chrám sv. Jakuba) was rebuilt following a devastating fire during the 15th century. Under the window on the south face of the high tower, Antonín Pilgram placed a little manikin who points his naked backside at the Cathedral – the church of the wealthy inhabitants of the Upper Town – embracing a pretty girl as he does so.

Continuing in an easterly direction, the route passes the Jesuit church, dedicated in 1734 and regarded as the finest baroque church in town, before reaching the ring of parkland. To the left stands the contemporary **Janáček Opera House and Ballet Theatre**, to the right the Mahen Theatre, built over a century ago in the style of the French Renaissance and famous as the first stage in Europe to be lit by electric light. Behind stands the lovely **Artists' House**, built in 1911.

Špilberk Castle, dominating the town from a high plateau, is the most conspicuous landmark. It was built about 1270 on the instructions of King Otakar Přemysl II because he thought the old Slavic stronghold on Mount Petrov provided insufficient protection. By the time the Swedish army began its memorable siege during the Thirty Years' War, Italian military architects had transformed it into a virtually impregnable citadel. It withstood attack by troops from many countries; as late as 1742, Frederick the Great failed to storm the

Brno is dominated by its Cathedral of St Peter and Paul.

246

fortress. Eventually Napoleon was successful in 1809.

From the 17th century the castle was one of the most feared prisons in Europe. Among the incarcerated were unrepentant heretics, peasant revolutionaries and members of the aristocracy who had fallen into disfavour at the imperial court, such as the Croatian pandour leader, Baron Trenck. The tolerant Emperor Joseph II had it closed in 1783, but after the French Revolution the Habsburgs reopened it, to house their many political opponents; the Italian poet Silvio Pellico, for example, spent 15 years in Spilberk.

At the foot of the fortress lies the former Augustinian monastery with its church of the Assumption, containing a charming pietà ascribed to Heinrich Parler the Younger and dating from ca. 1385. The monastery was the home of the father of genetic science, the abbot Gregor Johann Mendel (1822–84); it was in the monastery's garden that he pursued his research into inherited characteristics in plants, in particular peas.

Mendel established a tradition of education and learning in the city. Today, its six ancient establishments of higher education within the city have over 20,000 students. Viktor Kaplan, the inventor of the hydraulic turbine, lectured at the **Technical University**, and the founder of the **College of Music** was the composer Leoš Janáček; his works are the focus of the annual autumn festival of classical and contemporary music.

In the vicinity of Brno: On 2 December 1805, the armies of three emperors faced each other in the Battle of Austerlitz, 12 miles (20 km) east of Brno: the victorious French forces under Napoleon confronted the allied regiments of Austria and Russia under Emperor Francis II and Tsar Alexander I. On **Mount Žuráň**, two trees mark the position of Napoleon's command post. From here he directed 741,000 men and 250 cannon against an army which was far superior in numbers. Some 40,000 men fell in the ensuing battle. In 1911 a monument was erected in their memory on top of the Mohyla míru Heights near the village of

Prace, where the slaughter was thickest.

After the battle Napoleon set up his headquarters in the baroque Slavk**ov** (**Austerlitz**) **Castle** nearby. It was here, on 6 December, that he signed the peace treaty acknowledging his supremacy as the most powerful ruler in Europe. Each year, on 2 December, the **battlefield of Austerlitz** becomes the arena for a reconstruction of the fight. Thousands of enthusiasts flood in from France and other European countries to take part in the Battle of the Three Emperors.

The Moravian Karst: North of Brno, between **Blansko** and **Sloup**, lies the **karst region** of Moravia (Moravský Kras), a landscape of romantic gorges and some 400 caves both large and small, carved out of the solid limestone by underground rivers.

There is a spectacular view down into the **Macocha Abyss**, 440 ft (138 metres) deep. A marked footpath leads down the virtually vertical walls to the twin lakes at the bottom. Those with a poor head for heights are recommended to visit the Punkevní jeskyně caves by boat. The breathtaking magnificence of the vaulted roofs is heightened by the forests of stalactites and stalagmites. The largest cave is the **Kateřinská** (concerts are held here to take advantage of its unique acoustics). The Balcarka caves are particularly stunning. The **Sloupsko-šošůvské jeskyně** cave complex, on the northeastern edge of the karst region has been the site of a number of interesting archaeological finds; the **Kůlna cavern** bears traces of human occupation some 100,000 years ago. The settlement in the **Byčí skála** cavern dates from the Palaeolithic era, and remains of a royal burial place from the 7th–6th century BC have also been found.

Evidence of early iron smelting furnaces can be found all over the Moravian karst region. The rich iron ore deposits and the ease with which charcoal could be obtained made the area a valuable source of raw material for the armament industry in the Greater Moravian kingdom. Not only swords and armour but also iron tools and jewellery were manufactured.

The International Trade Fair complex.

MORAVIAN WINE

Although the vintners of Southern Moravia like to maintain that Noah planted the very first vine after the Flood (and thereafter drank wine for 300 years, thus providing incontestable proof of wine's beneficial effect on health), it seems likely that grapevines were brought to Moravia by the ancient Romans. By the time of the Kingdom of Great Moravia, wine was certainly produced in the region, for excavations of settlements dating from this period have revealed evidence of grapes. Wine production in Moravia must therefore be at least 1,100 years old.

The wine-growing regions of Southern Moravia extend over an area of more than 65,000 acres (26,000 hectares). They lie at the northern limits of the wine-growing region of Central Europe. Moravia has neither the intense sunshine of Dalmatia nor the tranquil and humid climate of the Moselle or Rhine valleys. For this reason, vines are grown only on south-facing slopes in hilly districts protected from frost and wind, and predominantly on dry, sandy soils. Despite all this, Southern Moravia produces light wines which are often sweeter than those from the famous wine-producing areas of France.

Among the Southern Moravian vintners, a deeply rooted tradition of professional integrity and diligence are passed on from generation to generation. During the first weeks after the grape harvest, the cellarmen supervise the process of maturation until the *burčák*, the new wine, is ready. It is allowed the "cook", as this process is known, for only a couple of hours before the vintners themselves drink a good litre of it each, on the pretext that it will cleanse their blood and provide them with the life-giving energy of the soil and the sun.

Months will pass by before the wine has settled in the barrels and it is time to taste it. Unless a vintner decides to treat a novice to his "three-man wine" – when one person actually drinks the brew while the other two hold him firmly to stop him from shuddering violently and falling to the ground – a wine tasting is a dignified procedure. "Remember it's not water!" scold the vintners when visitors quaff the brew too quickly. Before taking the first little sip one should take in the colour and savour the bouquet. After the first reaction to the unexpected sharpness, let the full taste slowly develop on the tongue. The entire procedure is repeated several times standing in front of a number of barrels, until the preferred wine is determined.

Two of the oldest and most famous wine cellars are Valtice and Prímětice, near Znojmo. Both were established during the baroque era and boast magnificent cross vaulting. The arches were built so wide that the lord of the manor could drive in in his coach and even turn round. Another impressive cellar is in Satov, also near Znojmo; its walls are adorned with amusing frescoes.

During the 16th century the Archbishop of Olomouc received his supplies of red wine from the village of Pavlov near Mikulov. And for many years the wine served in the Town Hall cellars in Vienna came from the community of Satov. Jan Amos Komensky was a guest in Blatnice, and even Napoleon was a fan of the wine of Archlebov; he celebrated his famous victory at Austerlitz with a Southern Moravian vintage. ■

Grape-picking in Southern Moravia.

SOUTHERN MORAVIA

There are a number of routes from Brno into the rural heart of Southern Moravia. The tour described here runs in a clockwise direction around the region. It starts by taking the E461, which leads due south from Brno towards the Austrian border, following the Svratka to the lower reaches of the River Dyje (Thaya). The rolling landscape here is reminiscent of Italy; to the south rise the **Pavlovské vrchy mountains**, with Devon limestone cliffs and the **Pálava nature reserve**, famous for its rare steppe flora. In times gone by the silhouette of the Pavlovské vrchy served as a landmark for merchants; today, it is reflected in the waters of the **Nové Mlýny reservoir**.

Just to the north of the Austrian border, in a wine-growing area, is **Mikulov** (Nikolsburg). Since the 16th century this pretty little town has been connected with the name of the dukes of Dietrichstein-Mensdorff. Their castle, dating from medieval times, was rebuilt on a number of occasions and ended up as a baroque palace. One of the main attractions here is the so-called "tenner" barrel dating from 1643, which has a capacity of 270 gallons (1,010 litres). Mikulov has preserved a large number of features from the past. An old synagogue in the oriental style demonstrates the importance of the local Jewish community. The lovely **chapel of St Sebastian**, on the Svatý Kopeček, the "holy mountain", dominates the scene.

The castle in **Lednice**, a few miles to the east on the River Dyje, is visited by up to half a million tourists each year. It was built in the English Gothic style and is surrounded by an attractive *parc à l'anglaise*. Also of interest are the cast-iron framed greenhouses dating from 1834, the 192-ft (60-metre) **minaret**, replicas of historic churches and the **Janohrad**, an artificial ruin. Further south, the little town of **Veltice** has a well-known vintner school, and the 17th-century former palace of the Dukes of Liechtenstein is famous for its wine

cellars. Also well-worth visiting is the parish church of the Assumption, whose altarpiece of the Holy Trinity is a Rubens original.

To the south of **Břeclav** (Lundenburg), an important railway junction, excavations have revealed a vast Old Slavic defensive settlement which was an important centre of the Kingdom of Great Moravia. The **archaeological museum** here merits a visit.

Southwest of Brno: The little town of **Ivančice** was the birthplace of the famous Art Nouveau painter Alfons Mucha. Although he spent much of his life in France, in nearby **Moravský Krumlov** Mucha reveals to what extent he remained faithful to his Czech homeland. His famous *Slovanská epopej* – 20 vast canvasses depicting themes based on Slavic history and mythology – is exhibited in the **Knights' Hall** of the Renaissance castle.

The road rejoins the River Dyje as it irrigates the fertile Znojmo plain to the southwest of Brno. The main crops in the valley are fruit and vegetables; the slopes are reserved for the production of fine wines. The town of **Znojmo** (Znaim) was the first community in Moravia to receive its town charter, in 1226. It has successfully preserved its medieval character over the succeeding centuries. The city walls still stand, along with numerous houses and churches from the Gothic, Renaissance and baroque eras. Beneath the market place (Nám. Míru) there is a vast cellar for the storage of wine; the square itself is dominated by the fine Gothic tower – all that remained of the Town Hall at the end of World War II. The **castle** occupies the site of a former 11th-century border fortress dating from the Přemyslid kingdom. It now houses the **Museum of Southern Moravia**. The Romanesque **round church of St Catherine** contains a series of wall paintings dating form the early 12th century.

After the end of the Cold War the magnificent tract of land on the banks of the Dyje was deemed deserving of protection as a joint Austrian-Czechoslovakian national park. Numerous footpaths and tracks lead through the Dyje valley; the entire region is a paradise for nature lovers, anglers and walkers.

The Upper Dyje Valley: Further upstream, the Dyje has been dammed to create a vast reservoir. One mile from the barrier itself, perched on a crag above **Vranov nad Dyjí**, stands the magnificent **Castle of Frain**. Originally built as a fortress, it was later converted into a splendid baroque residence. It is worth joining a tour just to see the splendid baroque **Ancestral Hall**, not to mention the castle chapel and the lovely audience rooms. The whole building has been wonderfully restored.

A fine castle stands sentinel over the little town of **Jaroměřice** (Jarmeritz), equally famous for its lovely bridge across the River Rokytná. The castle includes its own theatre, in which the premiere of the first Czech opera, *L'origine de Jarmeritz en Moravie*, (The history of the town of Jarmeritz in Moravia) was performed in 1730. The work was composed by František Václav Miča, a valet who had been commissioned by the lord of the castle to assemble a servants' orchestra. He even arranged a number of ambitious productions of Italian operas. The tradition is perpetuated to this day in the **annual festival of classical music** held in Jaroměřice each summer. Then the extensive castle grounds and the pretty little town are thronging with international visitors.

West of Brno: **Třebíč** (Trebitsch) is known primarily as an industrial town, but its **Basilica of St Procop**, dating from the 13th century, is well worth a visit. The triple-naved building is the most important example of the transition from Romanesque to Gothic architecture within the lands of the Bohemian crown. The basilica forms a part of a monastery in which the **Abbot's Chapel** also contains a magnificent series of 13th-century wall paintings. Part of the monastery was converted into a palace during the Renaissance; today it houses the **Museum of Western Moravia**, including unusual collections such as a picturesque selection of crib figures.

Market place with fountain in the roman† border town o† Slavonice.

In the town centre, only a handful of houses and doorways remain from the Gothic era; a hint of the Renaissance is visible in the gables of the monumental townhouses. The **Malovaný dům** was adorned with sgraffito by the Venetian merchant Francesco Calliardo; the "Black House" dating from 1637 bears an allegorical depiction of Virtue, and many other buildings display fine decorative features.

Nestling amidst woodland near **Náměšt' nad Oslavou**, a charming little town west of Brno, lies a vast **Renaissance castle** which served Tomáš Garrique Masaryk, among others, as a summer residence. Today a precious collection of Gobelin tapestries is displayed here. In the neighbouring village of **Kralice nad Oslavou** there is a memorial museum dedicated to the *Kralická bible*, the Czech Bible, produced during between 1579 and 1593. The scripture is linked with the Community of the Moravian Brethren, who rose to fame as religious reformers in Bohemia during the Middle Ages.

Telč (Teltsch) is undoubtedly one of the most beautiful towns in the whole Czech Republic. Dating from the 16th century, the central square is surrounded by historic houses linked by continuous arcades. After the Great Fire of 1530, the entire town was rebuilt in a unified Renaissance style. The region was originally covered by marshes, but during the 12th century the founding fathers of the city had these drained. By the beginning of the 14th century Telč had been awarded royal privileges; still standing within the old town centre are various Late Gothic gateways and a large number of fine old houses which date from this period. Most important among the town's religious buildings is the **church of the Assumption**, built during the 15th century.

The sprawling **Renaissance palace** stands immediately next to the market place. It was built to replace the original fortress at the end of the 16th century, at the behest of the lords of Hradec, who were inspired by their frequent trips to sunny Italy. They added columned ar-

Southern Moravian costume.

cades, audience rooms with statues, paintings and stuccoed walls and ceilings in the Italian manner.

The visitor approaching via the Prague motorway, or planning to return to the capital by the same route, should make a point of breaking his journey in **Jihlava** (Iglau). The town was founded in 799 on a former trading route; it rose to prosperity during the 13th century when extensive silver ore deposits were discovered in the vicinity. In 1249 the town received its charter; 20 years later the citizens were awarded staple rights and permission to mint their own coins. In the **Court of Appeal of Iglau**, the ultimate authority in mining law for the entire Holy Roman Empire, cases were tried according to the "Iglau Mining Laws", which were regarded as binding in many parts of the world even centuries later.

When silver mining was abandoned some 300 years later, cloth production became the principal driving force behind the town's economy, a complex industry which was introduced by Flemish weavers and dyers. Jihlava is, however, particularly proud of its reputation as a centre of the arts; the town's most famous native son is the composer Gustav Mahler.

Remains of the town walls, and the *Nám. Míru*, whose area of almost an acre (3,700 sq. metres) makes it the largest town square in Central Europe, bear witness to the town's historical importance. On the east side of the square, bordered by townhouses with painted arcades, stands the **Town Hall**. Dating from 1426, it provides access to the catacombs, constructed during the Middle Ages as storerooms and defensive passages. The previously mentioned miners' court met in the corner house at No. 7/63; the mint was housed in the building opposite. Also on this square was the headquarters of the clothmakers' guild; it now serves as a museum. The parish **church of St James** is the real jewel among an array of interesting churches. Begun in 1257, the building was completed at the end of the 14th century. Dating from the same period is the exquisite statue of St Catherine.

The Bohemian-Moravian Mountains:

North of the motorway from Prague to Brno extend the Bohemian-Moravian Mountains. It is a landscape of wooded slopes reflected in the waters of countless lakes. Those who follow the route from Prague along the Sázava Valley (*see preceding chapter*) will pass through Deutsch-Brod before coming to **Žďár nad Sázavou**. The town serves as the starting point for a visit to the **Zdarské vrchy nature reserve** on the crest of the Bohemian-Moravian ridge. Here the visitor will find expanses of primeval forest, Ice-Age peat moors and more than 280 lakes both large and small. In this remote region you will find the last evidence of many of the country's oldest and most interesting traditions, and in the villages the old wooden farmhouses, the so-called *dřevěnice*, can still be seen. On **Mount Žákova** (2,512 ft/ 785 metres), by the source of the Svratka, the local inhabitants welcome spring by ceremoniously opening the well. The associated celebrations are a delight.

Following a branch line of the rail link to Brno, the traveller comes to **Nové Město na Moravě**, famous for the **Horácké Museum** and its 16th-century castle. The town is a good base for walking expeditions through the mountains, which have been the setting for world championship skiing.

The enchanting **Pernštejn Castle** perches above the **Nedvědička valley**. Its massive walls have survived the vicissitudes of time remarkably well. The old stonework, the untouched rural surroundings and the relative lack of tourists combine to produce an undeniably romantic atmosphere. However, you may find your visit coincides with that of film crews and production teams, for the castle is a popular setting for authentic cloak-and-dagger films. Many fairy tales are also produced here.

Visitors should also visit the **Porta coeli** ("Gate of Heaven") monastery in **Předklášterí** near Tišnov, a few miles before Brno. Founded in 1233, the complex includes a majestic church with a cross vaulted roof. The cloisters and the chapter house are among the finest works of Gothic architecture in Moravia.

Pernštejn, one of the largest and best-preserved castles in the Czech Republic.

NORTHERN MORAVIA

Northern Moravia has 2 million inhabitants, virtually all of whom are concentrated in the two conurbations around Olomouc and Ostrava; the remaining regions are rural in nature and sparsely populated. In the south lies the fertile Haná plain (Hannakei), with Olomouc at its centre. Passing through the Moravská brána, the Moravian Gate, the traveller reaches the northeastern industrial area centred upon Ostrava. To the north, the Jeseníky Mountains form a natural boundary; in the southeast the Moravian and Silesian sections of the Beskid Mountains separate the region from Slovakia.

Olomouc: The town of **Olomouc** has a long and colourful history. The first written references to this settlement in the shadow of a Slavic fortress were in 1055. Eight years later, Olomouc was elevated to the rank of diocesan town. Its spiritual rulers awarded the community municipal and staple rights and encouraged the diligent Premonstratensian order to settle here along with German craftsmen and merchants, so that the town soon became the capital of Moravia. It was occupied for a number of years by Swedish troops during the Thirty Years' War, an event which was to mark the beginning of the town's slow decline. Brno, its rival in Southern Moravia, then became the provincial capital; in 1778 the university was also transferred there. Olomouc remained stuck with its reputation as a bastion of Catholicism loyal to the ruling Habsburgs, surrounded by an increasingly rebellious hinterland. For this reason the town was often referred to as "The Salzburg of Moravia".

This may explain why so many historic buildings have survived in the **Old Town**. On the Nám. Míru, the former Upper Square, the most conspicuous is the magnificent **Town Hall**. To the former town clerk's office were added a splendid banqueting hall and the Late Gothic **chapel of St Jerome**; during the Renaissance came the elaborately decorated external staircase and the loggia. A particular attraction is the **astronomical clock** dating from 1422, whose figures move in a similar manner to the apostles on the town hall clock in Prague. Characteristic is the massive 18th-century **Trinity Column**.

Half a dozen baroque fountains grace the Old Town. Two of them stand on the **Square of Peace**; others are to be found on the Lower Ring, immediately adjacent to the south side of the square, and to the north, on the square in front of the **church of St Maurice**. Construction of the latter, a hall church housing a fine baroque organ, began in 1412; it was the place of worship of the common citizens. The episcopal church was the **St Wenceslas Cathedral**, which dates from 1107, and which later acquired a 13th-century Gothic cloister that was decorated with a fine series of murals in about 1500. The **cathedral treasury** can be viewed in the crypt.

Litovel (Littau), to the northwest of Olomouc, is often nicknamed the "Venice of the Hannakei". It is a pretty little

Preceding pages: a view of the Moravian-Silesian Beskids. **Left,** a church near Střilky. **Right,** costume from Uherské Hradiště.

town spread across the six arms of the River Morava. Its principal historic monuments include a Gothic chapel, St Mark's Church and the **Plague Column** erected in 1724. There is an interesting local museum with displays of traditional folk costumes and prehistoric archaeological finds. Worth visiting in the hills to the west of the town is 13th-century **Bouzov (Busau) Castle**. After suffering extensive damage during the Thirty Years' War, in 1696 the fortress and the attached estates were taken over by the Teutonic Order, which had the building converted into a magnificent palace at the beginning of this century. A further local attraction are the caves of **Javoříčko**.

The Jeseníky Mountains, to which the town of **Šumperk** serves as gateway, are rich in scenic beauty. A little further north lies the spa town of **Velké Losiny**, scene of one of the last witch trials in Europe; an exhibition of instruments of torture recalls the fateful event. The best base for a tour of the region is without doubt the spa town of **Karlova Studánka**, to the east. From here you can follow a variety of walking routes into the mountains. Particularly rewarding, if testing, is the path leading to the summit of the **Praděd**, the highest peak in the Jeseníky Mountains (4,771 ft/ 1,491 metres): the view stretches right across into neighbouring Poland. Another interesting path on the other side leads towards **Petrovy kameny**, passing – if you believe the old legend – the scene of the Witches' Sabbath of the Walpurgis Night.

Through the Moravian Gate: Lipník nad Bečvou, to the east of Olomouc, has preserved its medieval town centre and 15th-century fortifications. Also of interest are the Renaissance castle and the Gothic church, which was rebuilt during the Renaissance and the baroque periods.

A footpath leads from the town along the far bank of the River Becva to the 13th-century **Helfsteyn Castle**, one of the most imposing ruins in the country. Fencing displays, performed in costume, are frequently held in the castle court-

Fine oriel windows in Olomouc (Olmütz).

yards. A few miles south of Hranice lies the spa of Teplice nad Bečvou. The town is popular not so much for the rather stale-tasting warm water produced by its springs as for the **Zbrasovské aragonitové jeskyňe caves**, which contain mighty stalactites and miniature lakes, emitting mysterious vapours.

Fulnek is worth visiting for its castle, built in a mixture of baroque and Renaissance styles. It is also the site of the monument to Jan Amos Komenský, better known to foreigners under his Latin name, Comenius, who lived here from 1618 to 1621.

Shortly before Opava lies the lovely palace of **Hradec nad Moravicí** (Grätz), built on the site of a 10th-century Slavic fort. Following a devastating fire, the complex was rebuilt in the Empire style and subsequently rechristened "The White Castle". Great composers such as Paganini and Franz Liszt stayed here at the invitation of the music-loving Prince Lichnowsky. The **Beethoven Weeks** commemorate two visits by the German master in 1806.

The name of **Opava** first cropped up in records in the 12th century. The town was the capital of the German-settled Silesian duchy of Troppau from the 13th century right the way up to 1918. Amongst the town's sights are the remains of the former town wall and the Gothic churches of St Mary, the Holy Ghost and St John. From 1618, the tower on the so-called "Butterfly House" (Schmetterlingshaus) was where travelling merchants stopped with their wares, which they were required to offer for sale for a period of three days. The entrepreneurial spirit of Opava has been maintained to this day; it is regarded as a model for the development of privatisation within the newly capitalist Czech Republic. Because of its German roots, many inhabitants still have relatives or contacts in Germany.

Ostrava, with 350,000 inhabitants, is the third-largest town in today's Czech Republic, but its history reaches back into the mists of time. Traces of a camp left by mammoth hunters have been discovered on Landek Hill. However,

View from the garden of Hradec nad Moravicí (Grätz Palace), in which Beethoven often stayed.

its turbulent modern history began at the beginning of the last century, when extensive coal deposits were discovered. This led to a massive boom in the town, which became the centre of iron and steel smelting and heavy industry. Since then, Ostrava has been the privileged bearer of the ambiguous nickname "The steel heart of the Republic".

Other industrial towns sprang up around Ostrava. Pitheads and vast factory complexes scar the landscape and noxious smoke, rarely filtered, belches forth into a leaden sky, casting a grey veil across what was once attractive foothill scenery.

The monuments worth seeing, such as the 17th-century Town Hall on **Masaryk Square**, a little wooden church in **Ostrava Hrabová** dating from the 16th century, and the Renaissance palace surrounded by a magnificent park in **Karviná**, struggle bravely to maintain their attractions in the face of this perpetual pollution

In the Beskid foothills, on both banks of the River Ostravice, lies the twin town of **Frydek-Místek**. It was founded in the 13th century as a Moravian border town. Frydeck boasts a castle rebuilt in the baroque style.

The Beskids: The little town of **Hukvaldy**, boasting a wildlife park and shady avenues of chestnut trees, lies on the northern slopes of the Beskid Mountains in the shadow of a romantic ruined castle. The famous Czech composer Leoš Janáček was born here.

Worth visiting nearby for its Gothic church and the well preserved Renaissance buildings surrounding the market place is **Příbor**, the town where Sigmund Freud first saw the light of day.

Only a few miles to the south lies **Štramberk**, overshadowed by the tower of a medieval castle which looks more like a mosque. The town itself is one of the loveliest in the entire country, a maze of winding narrow streets. The local culinary speciality is the delicately spiced cone-shaped waffles known as *štramberské uši* ("Stramberg Ears"), a name referring to the time when the town was overrun by the Tartars. The

Štramberk in the Moravian-Silesian Beskids.

neighbouring town of **Kopřivnice** is famous as the home of the Tatra automobile production plant. Further to the West, **Nový Jičín** is a Gothic jewel with historic townhouses, a Gothic church and a castle.

The **Beskid Mountains** of Moravia and Silesia form a natural boundary to the Slovakian Republic. The **Valašsko** (Wallachia) lies in the Western Beskids – without doubt one of the most fascinating regions in the Czech Republic, especially for authentic folklore (a far cry from the performances offered in restaurants and nightclubs). Old customs are still treasured and the local people are welcoming. For sports enthusiasts the Beskids offer a wide range of activities throughout the year, from mountain walks in summer to ski tours and downhill skiing in winter.

The town of **Rožnov pod Radhoštěm** provides an excellent base from which to explore. In the **Open-Air Museum of Wallachia** you can witness life as it used to be lived all over this part of the country, and hear the tinkling bells of the traditional horse-drawn carriages and the strains of dulcimer and violin playing the folk music of Wallachia. The buildings which comprise the park were collected from the immediate vicinity and rebuilt within the museum park. Later on, perfect replicas of other houses were added. In this way an entire little town of wooden buildings has been recreated, with a landvogt's residence and a pretty church where services are held. The inn Na posledním groši serves satisfying meals.

The newest section of the park includes a water-driven sawmill, a water mill and a smithy which echo to the sounds of paddle wheel, saw and hammer. The weekends are devoted to specific traditional customs. Music and dancing are performed in local costumes and traditional crafts, from wood carving to pottery, are offered for sale.

From the nearby Ráztoka Valley it is possible to take a chair lift to the summit of the **Pustevny** (3,340 ft/1018 metres), a popular local mountain whose flanks are dotted with typical Wallachian

Relaxing at day's end.

wooden houses and a number of mountain hotels. It is worth taking the hour-long ridge walk to the **Radhošt'** (3,613 ft/1,129 metres), dominated by a majestic statue of the Slavic god Radegast. According to legend, those who touch the statue's stomach are bound to return here one day.

The castle in the district centre of **Vsetín** in the Bečva valley houses an exhibition portraying the customs and traditions of the area. Within easy reach to the southeast lies the winter sports and mountain walking paradise of **Soláň**. Equally attractive are the idyllic hamlets and exquisitely built wooden mountain huts. Sheep graze on the mountain slopes, and horses and oxen still draw the plough.

The **Lysá hora** (4,237 ft/1,324 metres) is the highest peak in the Beskids. It lies to the east and can easily be scaled from the little town of **Ostravice**. The ascent, which takes several hours, is amply rewarded by the enchanting view. On a clear day you can see the peaks of the **Malá Fatra**, the Lesser Fatra range in Slovakia. During the winter months, Lysá hora is a mecca for downhill and cross-country skiing enthusiasts.

Further to the east lie the remote mountain villages of **Dolni** and **Horní Lomná** – as yet an undiscovered part of Moravia. Both communities are famous for their folklore festivals. The high-altitude valley, enclosed on three sides, preserves its primeval forests in the form of a nature reserve.

Another centre of the Valašsko is the little town of **Vizovice**. The romantic castle, built on the site of a 13th-century monastery, contains a painting gallery with works by Dutch, Italian and French masters; there is also a collection of fine china.. Vizovice is famous for its distillery, which produces the plum schnapps slivovice (Slivovitz). At harvest time – and at other seasons of the year – the entire town is filled with celebrations and rejoicing.

Zlín is often described as a town in the country. Originally of no particular importance, it enjoyed a boom towards the end of the 19th century, when Tomáš

The nave of the Cistercian monastery church, Velherad.

Bat'a had the idea of producing here the *Bat'ovky*, simple and inexpensive shoes of linen. The enterprise soon expanded to become a shoe manufacturer of world-wide fame. The town itself is a typical example of inter-war development, constructed in a unified functionalist style. Here great modernist architects such as Le Corbusier and Franz Gahura realised their concepts for residential and commercial districts. In 1949 the town was rechristened Gottwaldov, after the first Communist president of Czechoslovakia. In 1990, after the Bat'a heirs' claims of ownership were recognised, the old name was readopted.

The spa town of **Luhačovice**, to the east of Uherské Hradiště, basks in an atmosphere of peace and relaxation. Ten mineral springs, in particular the Vincert Spring, provide relief from disorders of the upper respiratory system. The composer Leoš Janáček is among those who have come to convalesce in this romantic little town.

On the trail of Great Moravia: In the valley of the **River Morava** (March), in the heart of Moravian Slovakia, lies the town of **Uherské Hradiště** (Hungarian Hradisch), founded in 1257 by Přemysl Otakar II to protect the trading routes. The name indicates that it was here, on the border of Upper Hungary (most of which now lies in the region of Slovakia), that a large group of Protestant refugees from Hungary made their home. They injected fresh life into the town. The Gothic town hall, a number of lovely churches, most of them rebuilt in the baroque style, and the **apothecary** on the market place, reconstructed in the rococo idiom, all testify to Uherské Hradiště's glorious past. The town's principal attraction, however, is the Staré Město on the West Bank, now a suburb but very probably once the site of **Velehrad**, the legendary capital of the first Slavic empire within the territory which today forms the Czech and Slovak Republics.

During the last century, traces of an early Slavic settlement were discovered here; it was not until a systematic excavation was undertaken in 1948 that ex-

A happy reaper.

perts were able to establish with certainty that this had been an important town, if not the very capital, of the Kingdom of Great Moravia. During the 9th and 10th centuries its rulers established close links with Byzantium and, with the help of the Slavic apostles Cyril and Methodius, began the Christianisation of Central Europe. Supporting such an assumption are the location (near the Moravian Gate, at the crossroads between the Amber Road – one of the most important North-South routes in Central Europe) and the East-West trading route along the Morava valley. Thousands of urn graves dating from the 6th and 7th centuries have already been examined; living quarters and a two-storey cathedral have also been unearthed, and it is well known that Velehrad, with its 3-mile (5-km) fortifications, was well protected against attack from the landward side. Nonetheless, the archaeological investigations continue, and the results to date can be visited in a new, specially created museum, the **Památník Velké Moravy**.

The name of the capital of Great Moravia has been preserved a few miles to the west, in the **Cistercian monastery of Velehrad**. It was founded in 1205 by the Margrave of Moravia, a brother of the king, Přemysl Otakar I. Its basilica, completed in 1238, is dedicated to the two Slavic Apostles. Each year, on July 5, the joint festival of the two saints, the monastery – now used as a sanatorium – is the focus of a colourful folkloric pilgrimage.

The **Haná Plains** (the Hannakei) extend northwards towards Olomouc. The principal town is **Kroměříž** (Kremsier), which boasts a beautiful historic centre that has been declared a national monument. The central square, **Riegrovo náměstí**, stands on the site of an Old Slavic settlement. In 1110 the market town passed into the possession of the bishops of Olomouc and remained with them for centuries. Even a number of short-lived occupations by the Hussites had no effect on the the town's religious orientation. Awarded a municipal charter in 1266, the little town's advanta-

Kroměříž (Kremsier): th colonnade in the Bishop's Garden.

geous location on the Morava trading route attracted a large number of new residents. A castle and a cathedral were built. Both the German colonists and an active Jewish community, which since the Late Middle Ages had boasted its own chamber of trade and even a town hall, had an impact on the continued development. The **church of St Maurice**, begun in the 13th century, was finished in about 1500.

In 1643, during the Thirty Years' War, the town, the castle and the cathedral were burned to the ground by invading Swedish troops, but it wasn't long after the cessation of hostilities that reconstruction began. Under the supervision of Italian architects, work commenced on the remodelling of the fortress to create a magnificent **palace** in a combined Renaissance-baroque idiom. Today the visitor can inspect not only the meticulously restored apartments, but also one of the most important art collections in the country, housing works by Titian, Lucas Cranach and Pieter Brueghel, amongst others: *King Charles of England and Queen Henriette* was painted by Antony van Dyck.

A flower garden was created just outside the estate gates; it is a stunning example of baroque garden planning. The **Květná zahrada**, a public park, is an oasis of calm in this lively city. The **music festival** in August and the subsequent film festival, **Ars-Film**, is one of the liveliest times to be in the city.

Following the Morava to the south of Uherské Hradiště, after 12 miles (20 km) the road comes to the little town of **Strážnice**. It's a sleepy place for most of the year, except for the end of June when it suddenly comes to life on account of the **International Folklore Festival**. Costume groups arrive from all over Europe and beyond, to take part in the singing and dancing competitions. In the castle itself there is an interesting folklore museum.

Twelve miles further on, **Hodonin** is an industrial town that wouldn't be worth mentioning if it were not for the fact that it is the birthplace of the country's founder president, Tomáš G. Masaryk.

The imperial hall in Bučovice Castle.

Even today, Slovakia is regarded by the international tourist industry as an unknown quantity. But what a country! With a wealth of natural sights second to none – vast tracts of unspoilt woodland, high mountain peaks, hundreds of glacial lakes, five national parks, castles, ravines, waterfalls – for adaptable, nature-loving visitors willing to restrict their material needs, Slovakia is a romantic, still relatively inexpensive holiday destination *par excellence*.

Slovakia covers an area of 19,000 sq. miles (49,000 sq. km), which makes it larger than Switzerland; within the most popular holiday region, the High Tatra Mountains (up to 8,480 ft/ 2,650 metres), an area of 300 sq. miles (770 sq. km) has already been designated as a national park where no further tourist development is permitted. With its canyons, waterfalls and caves, it is ideal walking territory. What's more, there are the extensive forests of the Low Tatra (the habitat of bears, wolves and lynxes); 100 or so castles to explore; and traditional spa towns such as Piest'any in which non-walkers can unwind and hikers can recuperate.

Slovakia has a glittering future as a tourist destination.The only thing to threaten it is the perpetuation of the fallacy that Slovakia is a cheap tourist country offering too few material comforts for the pampered visitor from the West. In fact, after the Velvet Revolution, tourism in Slovakia underwent a fundamental change. Before then, 93 percent of tourists came from the former socialist countries; in 1991, this figure was down to 70 percent. Many of the lost customers were Czechs, Poles and Yugoslavians drawn by the magnetic pull of the West rather than the call of the wild. This means that the so-called "Ossis" have stopped coming, whilst the "Wessis" have not yet arrived.

The situation is unlikely to remain like this for long, for Slovakia is undergoing a rapid process of change. Since the country's independence in January 1993, it has automatically become a major tourist destination in its own right. As privatisation progresses, old hotels are being returned to their former owners, and new premises sold to energetic entrepreneurs. Overseas tour operators are becoming increasingly aware of the delights offered by this once so remote part of Europe.

Although still scarred by the legacies of socialism, the national capital Bratislava, with its lovely Old Town and a range of cultural activities, is rapidly rediscovering its traditional identity as one of the cultural hubs of Europe. But other towns in the region also have historic centres, invariably painstakingly restored.

Preceding pages: Štrbské Pleso in the High Tatra; Spiš Castle is the largest such edifice in Slovakia. **Left,** wooden dwellings near Zuberec in the Tatra foothills.

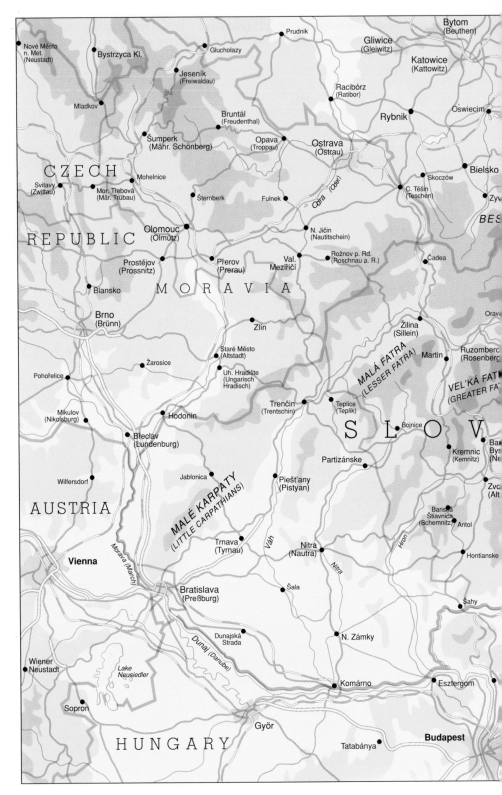

Bytom
(Beuthen)

Prudnik

Gliwice
(Gleiwitz)

Katowice
(Kattowitz)

Nové Město
n. Met.
(Neustadt)

Bystrzyca Kl.

Głucholazy

Jeseník
(Freiwaldau)

Racibórz
(Ratibor)

Mladkov

Bruntál
(Freudenthal)

Rybnik

Oświecim

Šumperk
(Mähr. Schönberg)

Opava
(Troppau)

Ostrava
(Ostrau)

C Z E C H

Mohelnice

Bielsko

Svitavy
(Zwittau)

Mor. Třebová
(Mär. Trübau)

Šternberk

Fulnek

Skoczów

C. Těšín
(Teschen)

Žyv

Odra (Oder)

BES

Olomouc
(Olmütz)

R E P U B L I C

N. Jičín
(Nautitschein)

Prostějov
(Prossnitz)

Přerov
(Prerau)

Val.
Meziříčí

Rožnov p. Rd.
(Roschnau a. R.)

Čadca

Blansko

M O R A V I A

Orava

Brno
(Brünn)

Zlín

Žilina
(Sillein)

Ruzomberc
(Rosenberg

Staré Město
(Altstadt)

Žarošice

MALÁ FATRA
(LESSER FATRA)

Martin

Pohořelice

Uh. Hradiště
(Ungarisch
Hradisch)

VEĽKÁ FAT
(GREATER FAT

Mikulov
(Nikolsburg)

Hodonín

Trenčín
(Trentschin)

Teplice
(Teplik)

S L O V

Břeclav
(Lundenburg)

Bojnice

Kremnic
(Kemnitz)

Ba
Bys
(Ne

Wilfersdorf

Jablonica

Piešťany
(Pistyan)

Partizánske

Banská
Štiavnica
(Schemnitz)

Zvc
(Alt

A U S T R I A

MALÉ KARPATY
(LITTLE CARPATHIANS)

Antol

Morava (March)

Trnava
(Tyrnau)

Váh

Nitra
(Nautra)

Hontianske

Vienna

Nitra

Hron

Bratislava
(Preßburg)

Šaľa

Šahy

Dunaj (Danube)

Dunajská
Strada

N. Zámky

Wiener
Neustadt

Lake
Neusiedler

Sopron

Komárno

Esztergom

Győr

H U N G A R Y

Tatabánya

Budapest

276

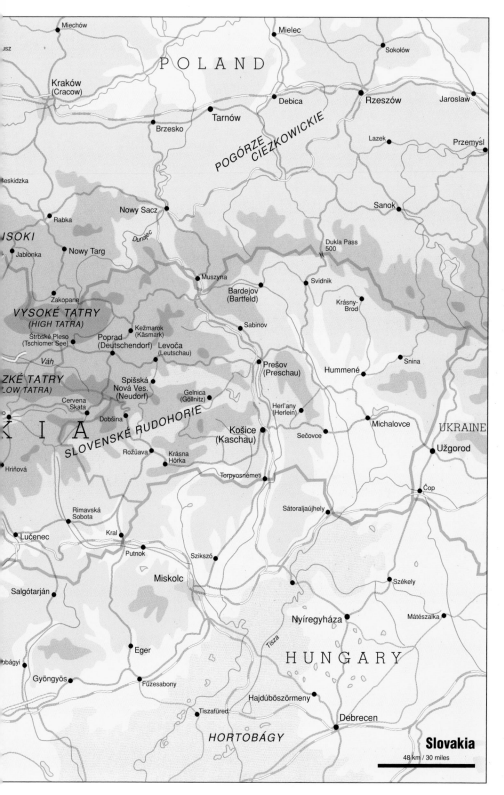

POLAND

Miechów
Mielec
Sokołów
Kraków
(Cracow)
Debica
Rzeszów
Jarosław
Tarnów
Brzesko
POGÓRZE CIEZKOWICKIE
Lazek
Przemyśl
Beskidzka
Nowy Sacz
Sanok
Rabka
ISOKI
Jabłonka
Dunajec
Nowy Targ
Muszyna
Dukla Pass
500
Zakopane
Svidnik
Bardejov
(Bartfeld)
Krásny-
Brod
VYSOKÉ TATRY
(HIGH TATRA)
Kežmarok
(Käsmark)
Sabinov
Štrbské Pleso
(Tschiomer See)
Poprad
(Deutschendorf)
Levoča
(Leutschau)
Váh
Prešov
(Preschau)
Hummené
Snina
ZKÉ TATRY
OW TATRA)
Spišská
Nová Ves.
(Neudorf)
Gelnica
(Göllnitz)
Cervena
Skata
Herl'any
(Herlein)
K I A
Dobšina
Michalovce
UKRAINE
SLOVENSKÉ RUDOHORIE
Košice
(Kaschau)
Sečovce
Hriňová
Rožňava
Krásna
Hôrka
Užgorod
Torpyosnémeti
Čop
Rimavská
Sobota
Sátoraljaújhely
Lučenec
Kral
Putnok
Szikszó
Miskolc
Székely
Salgótarján
Nyíregyháza
Mátészalka
bbágyi
Eger
HUNGARY
Gyöngyös
Füzesabony
Hajdúböszörmeny
Tisza
Tiszafüred
Debrecen
HORTOBÁGY

Slovakia

48 km / 30 miles

BRATISLAVA

Even in prehistoric times the fertile plain around Bratislava on the southern slopes of the Little Carpathians attracted settlers. The site boasted a further advantage in its strategic position at the intersection of two long-distance trading routes near the Hungarian Gates Gorge, where the Danube valley cuts between the Alps and the Carpathians. The Amber Road linked the centres of civilisation on the Mediterranean with those around the Baltic, and the Danube provided a means of transporting goods from Western Europe to the Black Sea.

A Celtic tribe, the Boii, made themselves a base in a fortified settlement near Bratislava. They minted coins and were active traders. After a short period of occupation by the Germanii, the Romans established camps along the southern bank of the river. The fortified natural boundary marked the limits of their empire, the *limes*, although they did build outposts on the far side of the river as well.

During the 4th century the invasion of the Huns put an end to Roman rule, but neither the aggressive mounted tribes nor the Langobards and Avars who succeeded them left any traces of their stay. This, however, was not true of the Slavs whose migration brought them to the region from the 6th century. In 623 they founded a tribal union covering the whole of what now constitutes the Czech and Slovak Republics, and during the 9th century the amalgamation of the Slavic principalities of Moravia and Nitra created the Kingdom of Great Moravia, in which the area surrounding Bratislava played a crucial role.

Hungarian rule: The defeat of an army of Bavarian and Slavic troops in 906 marked the beginning of Hungarian rule. It was a historical turning point, described in chronicles as the Battle of Brezlauspurg. The name, which reveals the origins of the German for Bratislava, *Pressburg*, can be traced back to Braslav, the Slavic ruler of the town. The Slavs soon reached a compromise with the new rulers, who were able to strengthen their position of supremacy despite temporary re-conquest by the Czech Přemyslid dynasty and attacks by the German Empire.

The kings of Hungary granted Bratislava its municipal charter in 1217 and encouraged foreign workers to settle in the area. The arrival of Italian craftsmen and Jewish and Arabian traders soon turned Bratislava into an international city. During the dispute over the Austrian succession the population decided to offer their support to Hungary rather than Austria. The King of Hungary, Andras III, demonstrated his grateful thanks by making Bratislava a free city on 2 December 1291 – an act which unleashed an unprecedented economic and cultural boom. The Gothic city, which has survived at least in outline until the present day, thus arose, protected by massive walls.

The banks of the Danube benefited from the construction of a harbour; tolls and taxes on the principal exports – wine and cloth – were dropped. An independent municipal administration, free election of judges and religious tolerance attracted new residents. Among the 5,000 citizens were a large number of Jews, who lived in their own district. Additional privileges, such as the right to mint coins and staple rights, the elevation to the rank of Free Royal City in 1405 and the founding of the Academia Istropolitana, the first university in Hungary in 1467, encouraged further prosperity.

The Turkish invasion came out of the blue; the Turks conquered the heartland of Hungary and the capital city of Buda. Consequently the Hungarian National Assembly chose Bratislava as its temporary capital in 1535. Originally intended as an interim solution, the situation lasted right up until 1784; in fact, no fewer than 11 kings and 8 queen consorts had been crowned in St Martin's Cathedral by 1830.

The coronation of Maria Theresa: One of the queens was Maria Theresa, the Empress of Austria and Queen of Hungary, under whose rule Bratislava blossomed once again. The former fortress

Bratislava: evening view of the Danube with the silhouette of the castle.

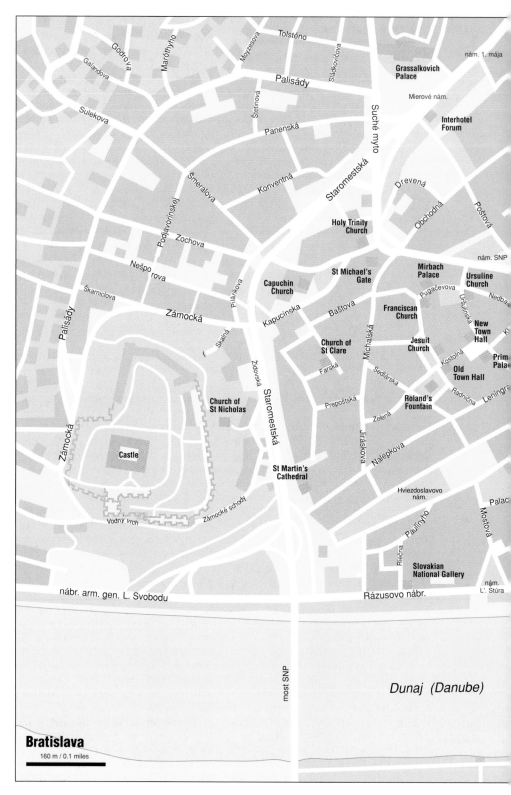

Godrova

Galandova

Sulekova

Marôthyho

Moyzesova

Tolstého

Palisády

Panenská

Šmeralova

Štetinová

Konventná

Staromestská

Podjavorinskej

Zochova

Nešporova

Škarniclova

Palisády

Zámocká

Pilárikova

Skalná

Židovská

Staromestská

Zámocká

Church of
St Nicholas

Castle

Vodný vrch

Zámocké schody

nábr. arm. gen. L. Svobodu

most SNP

Bratislava

160 m / 0.1 miles

Suché myto

Drevená

Obchodná

Poštová

Holy Trinity
Church

nám. SNP

St Michael's
Gate

Mirbach
Palace

Ursuline
Church

Nedba.

Capuchin
Church

Pugačevova

Kapucínska

Baštova

Franciscan
Church

Ursínska

New
Town
Hall

Church of
St Clare

Michalská

Jesuit
Church

Kostolná

Prim
Pala

Farská

Sedlárska

Old
Town Hall

Radnična

Leningra

Prepoštská

Roland's
Fountain

Zelená

St Martin's
Cathedral

Jiraskova

Nalepkova

Hviezdoslavovo
nám.

Palac

Paulínyho

Mostová

Riečna

Slovakian
National Gallery

nám.
Ľ. Stúra

Rázusovo nábr.

Dunaj (Danube)

nám. 1. mája

Grassalkovich
Palace

Mierové nám.

Interhotel
Forum

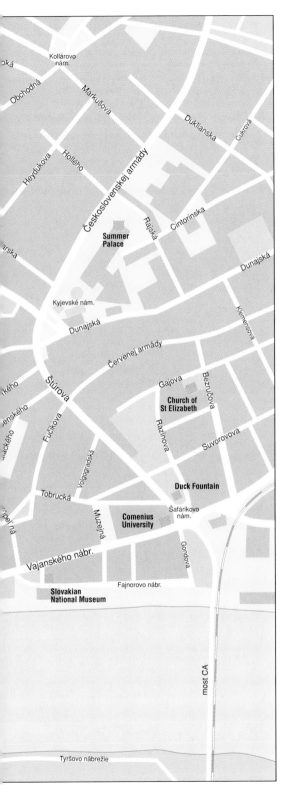

was converted into a magnificent palace, and whilst the Old City was being modernised in line with the baroque elegance fashionable at the time, the first factories were opened in the suburbs. Based on a long tradition of craftsmanship, Bratislava soon became a rapidly expanding industrial centre. The founding of the Danube Steamship Company in 1830 and the opening of the railway link with Vienna in 1848 revolutionised trade and business.

One more revolution was to shake the city, however. Under the pressure of the Hungarian Estates Council, the Emperor signed a treaty in Bratislava on 11 April 1848 granting Hungary autonomy, with its own government and parliament. One year later the Emperor Franz Joseph I declared the treaty null and void, but in 1867 the Habsburg monarchs were forced to accept a compromise.

The capital of Slovakia: Under the leadership of Ľudovít Štúr, the Slovakian opposition was still on the Hungarian side in March 1848. However, they were soon forced to recognise that the revolutionaries, too, were only interested in pursuing a policy of Hungarian nationalism. For many, a new orientation became essential: exiled in America, Slovakian and Czech immigrant groups agreed on the foundation of a common state. On 1 January 1919 the troops of the Czechoslovak Republic marched into Bratislava. The town, in which about half of the residents were Slovakian, became the capital of Slovakia.

The first experience of living with the Czechs was not encouraging; between 1938 and 1945, the Slovaks even attempted independence with their own state under Fascist rule. On 4 April 1945, Soviet troops liberated the city from the Germans. During the second half of the 20th century Bratislava finally became a Slovakian city; today the Slovaks virtually have their capital to themselves.

An ambitious rebuilding and restoration programme has transformed the city. However, not all the developments have been positive; while the historic city centre has survived largely intact, Bratislava still bears all the scars of 40 years of Communist planning and control. The sights can be savoured in the course of three leisurely walks.

To the Cathedral and the castle: The 14th-century **St Michael's Gate** is the only medieval town gateway still standing. The tower, which was given its baroque cupola in the 18th century, is surmounted by a statue of the archangel. Even visitors not wishing to tour the **Museum of Historic Weapons** should climb to the top, for the panorama from the platform provides a good view of the Old Town. It is worth making a short detour by the outer gateway beside the little bridge across what was once the town moat; house No. 28 contains the historic apothecary's shop "At the sign of the Red Crab" and an interesting **Museum of Pharmacy**. Continuing along the Michalská, you pass a fine Renaissance house at No. 7, built in 1648 for the town councillor Andreas Segner, whose family coat of arms still graces the entrance; an interesting modern "espresso gallery" has been established in the inner courtyard. Many visitors miss the unobtrusive **St Catherine's Chapel**; those who enter are greeted by an attractive Gothic interior.

A few steps further on, house No. 4 contains a handicrafts shop and a Hungarian bookshop. The baroque mansion opposite is open in the evening, when its vaulted ceiling reverberates to the sounds of disco music.

The atmosphere in the adjoining palazzi is much more sedate, for they now serve as the university's library. The **Royal Hungarian Chamber**, a magnificent baroque palace, was where the Hungarian Estates Council met from 1802–1848. It was before this assembly that Ľudovít Štúr made his stirring speech advocating equal rights for all peoples within the Austro-Hungarian monarchy. A memorial plaque recalls the deeds of this forerunner of the Slovakian freedom movement.

Beyond this point the Michalská leads into the Jiráskova. The garden pavilion of the **Palais of Leopold de Pauli** was the setting for the celebrated concert début of Franz Liszt, when he was just

Between 1541-1784, Bratislava was the capital of Hungary and was called Pozsony.

nine years of age. In 1762 another infant prodigy, the six-year-old Wolfgang Amadeus Mozart, enchanted the local *haute volée* in the **palais of Marshal Pálffy** in the Jiráskova 10. This distinguished building was for a while the Party college; ironically enough, after the revolution it served as the administrative headquarters for the movement Public against Violence, the Slovakian counterpart of the Civic Forum in Prague. In 1467, on the other side of the road in the Jiráskova 3, King Matthias Corvinus founded the Academia Istropolitana, the first Hungarian university. Today the building houses the **Academy of Fine Arts**: a key centre in the Velvet Revolution. The café opposite is a meeting place for students, intellectuals, artists and supporters of avant-garde movements.

This lively street was one of the town's main thoroughfares even in medieval times. In those days it was named the "Ventura Alley" after a family of Italian tradesmen who lived there. It ends by the **rococo palace of Count Erdödy**.

Turning right into the Panská, you reach **St Martin's Cathedral**.

Even the basic design of St Martin's Cathedral is unusual. The tower, surmounted by a golden crown and glittering glassy roof tiles, formed a part of the medieval fortifications. For this reason the entrances had to be placed along the side walls. It is a triple-naved hall church which was finally dedicated in 1452 after a construction period of over 100 years. The interior is dominated by Gothic fan vaulting, which shows the influence of the Viennese architectural style. A pillar within the choir is adorned with the coat of arms of King Matthias Corvinus. The donor of the church received the bones of St John the Evangelist as a gift from the Turkish Sultan Mahmud I; today these are housed in a chapel in the north transept specially designed by Georg Raphael Donner between 1732 and 1734. The same master also created the baroque high altar and the lovely **equestrian statue of St Martin** which adorns the head wall of the south transept.

From 1563–1830 the cathedral of St Martin was the site of the coronations of the kings of Hungary. During the 18th century it was rebuilt at their behest, and baroque exuberance replaced the simple Gothic style of the interior. In the cathedral treasury above the canons' chapel on the north side of the tower, some original traces can still be seen. Of particular note is an exceptionally fine monstrance dating from 1449.

One of the most glaring eyesores in modern Bratislava is the urban motorway that cuts straight between the old city and the **castle** and then crosses the Danube by means of the **bridge of the Slovakian National Uprising**. It is a remarkable construction indeed, but the observer is tempted to ask himself whether it was really necessary to sacrifice part of the historic town centre, including a Jewish synagogue, to make space for it.

Once at the other side, the visitor mounts **castle steps** (Zámocke schody) to the fine Gothic gate. On the way it is worth making a short detour to visit the Dom U Dobrého Pastiera, the "House of the Good Shepherd", which lies at the junction of Židovská ul. and Mikulášska ul. It is a delicate house with a fine yellow stucco facade, which was built in 1760 in the pure rococo style; each storey consists of a single room; it now houses the historic **Clock Museum**.

The massive building of the Hrad rises above the city and the river. As early as the 9th century, the Slavs built a border fortress to protect the ford at this point on the Danube. It was extended over the following centuries by the Hungarians. The Habsburgs recognised the strategic importance of the site as one of the outer defences protecting Vienna from the Turks, and between 1635 and 1649 they had the high walls with the protruding corner towers constructed upon a square ground plan by the master fortress builder Carlone. Even Maria Theresa still kept the Hungarian crown jewels within the castle walls.

The castle burned down a total of three times, the last occasion being in 1811, after which it was not restored

A restorer works a Renaissance house in the Michalská ul.

284

until 1953. A glimpse into the corners of the **Hunger Tower** and the **Torture Chamber** (full of bats) provides a vivid impression of the cruel fate suffered by many of those incarcerated in their walls. Highly symbolic is the location of the city's new landmark, the building of the **Slovakian National Committee**, immediately below the castle courtyard.

The best way to return to the starting point is along the northern side of the cathedral. During the Middle Ages the canons from the cathedral chapter lived in the Kapitulská (Priests' Alley). They were permitted to sell their own wine and were exempt from paying taxes. Accordingly, many of the houses in this quiet street are elaborately decorated, including the **Provost's Palais** at No. 19, the **Collegium Emmericianum** at No. 20 and the **Canon's House** at No. 15, which boasts a Renaissance facade and a baroque doorway.

An ever popular interlude in any tour of the city is the fish restaurant U zlatého kapra (The Golden Carp) in the Prepoštská. The next lane to the right

Bratislava offers great culinary variety.

leads to the **convent of St Clare** with its simple Gothic church, which now serves as a gallery for Gothic paintings and sculptures as well as forming an elegant setting for classical concerts. The reason why the strange pentagonal tower stands on the perimeter wall of the church is that it was the only way in which the nuns were able to circumvent the strict building regulations applicable to a begging order. After the Klariská the visitor should turn right into the narrow Baštová, previously known as Executioner's Alley. The incumbent of this honoured municipal post resided at No. 5. Passing the arsenal at No. 2, one quickly arrives at St Michael's Gate once more.

To the Danube Esplanade: The second walk starts from the point where the first one ended. Opposite the Baštová is a romantic, winding street lined with lovingly restored houses which leads towards the eastern section of the Old Town. The **Franciscan church** on Dibrovo nám. is the oldest church in the city; it was completed in 1297 and the

unadorned choir still dates from this period. On the side altar stands a remarkable Late Gothic sandstone pietá. St John's Chapel on the north side, dating from 1380, is another masterpiece of the Gothic mason's art. The church was extended several times at later dates; during the 18th century it was even adorned with a Loreto chapel similar to those found in Prague. The light-hearted rococo **Mirbach Palais** opposite was originally the residence of a wealthy brewery owner; today the building forms part of the **Municipal Art Gallery**.

Fringed by noble townhouses, the beautiful **Main Square** has formed the bustling hub of urban life since medieval times: it served simultaneously as market square, parade ground and place of execution. Its centre is occupied by a huge fountain depicting Roland.

Bratislava is a religious centre, which explains the large number of churches in this part of town. Among the most magnificent is the **Jesuit Church** standing on the northern side of the square; at the time of the Counter-Reformation it was changed from Protestant to Catholic and subsequently acquired an imposing new appearance. The fine rococo pulpit and the **St Mary's Column** in front are both witnesses to the zeal of the architects.

The **Old Town Hall** next door is the result of the amalgamation of a number of private houses. As long ago as the 14th century it was known as the Gothic "House with the Tower", and from that time onwards became the seat of the municipal administration. The vaulted passageway leads into an attractive courtyard; even the Gothic chapel has been carefully restored. The building acquired its predominantly Renaissance appearance in the 16th century and the present tower was built in baroque style in 1732, the old one having been toppled by an earthquake. Inside, the visitor will be impressed by the beautiful coffered ceiling of the council chamber as well as the baroque stucco and frescoes adorning the courtroom. The building also houses the city archives and a library. In addition, since 1948 the entire complex together with the adjoining **Apponyi Palais** has served as the **Municipal Museum**.

It is impossible to overlook the Zelený dom (Green House), an old tavern in which the town's golden days were duly celebrated. After admiring the lovely Art Nouveau palais next door, enjoy an espresso in the elegant interior of the **Café Roland**.

Between the Town Hall and the Jesuit church a little street leads directly to the elegant **Bishop's Palace**, built between 1777 and 1781 for the Archbishop of Esztergom. It served as winter residence for the first prince of the church and the holder of the highest religious office in Hungary. The building is open to the public today as the Municipal Art gallery, which permits the visitor to venture into the **Hall of Mirrors** where the Treaty of Bratislava was signed on 26 December 1805 after the Battle of Austerlitz.

In former times the town moat ran between the Old Town and the Danube. When the fortifications were removed

The courtyard of the town hall.

by Maria Theresa, the space was used for public buildings. The top end of the lengthy Hviezdoslavovo nám. is dominated by the **Slovakian National Theatre**, in front of which stands the massive **Ganymede Fountain**. Diagonally opposite, the **Carlton Hotel** still retains an air of the Roaring Twenties. From the Carlton, the Mostová ul. leads past the Reduta, the home of the **Slovakian Philharmonic Orchestra**, and down to the bank of the Danube and the modern monument to Ľudovít Štúr, the creator of written Slovakian. This was previously the site of the Coronation Hill, where newly crowned kings would solemnly promise to protect the city against all foes.

On the right-hand side of the road running along the river bank is the **Slovakian National Gallery**, housing paintings from the past 200 years. Further downstream stands the **Komenský University**, the most important institute of higher education in Slovakia, and the **Slovakian National Museum**, which offers an important archaeologi-

Medieval carvings on the door of St Martin's Cathedral.

cal collection. Also here is the landing stage for passenger ships to Vienna, Devín and Budapest.

The modern town: Bratislava has an equally dynamic present. The city's pulse beats fastest on the northeast side of the Old Town, on the Námestie SNP (the Square of the Slovakian Uprising). During the Velvet Revolution, tens of thousands of citizens braved the cold here. Even today, the square is the arena for protest meetings and hunger strikes. At other times it is the haunt of little groups of schoolgirls, licking ice-creams as they huddle together during breaks between lessons.

To the south of here lies **Kiev Square**, lined with department stores, hotels and fine Art Nouveau buildings. To the north is the tree-lined pedestrian area, the Poštová, which crosses the busy Obchodná shopping street. This is always a chaotic spot. Pedestrians take little heed of the warning bells of trams, which have difficulty making progress in the confusion, and the atmosphere is frenzied. The visitor may well decide to

take refuge in one of the nearby cafés or restaurants.

At the end of the Postová lies the Mierove námestie, location of the Grasalkovič palác, a magnificent rococo-style summer residence built for the princes and presidents of the Royal Hungarian Council. Above a sweeping circular staircase is the **Spanish Room** where Franz Josef Haydn and his orchestra performed in 1772. Next door stands the luxury hotel **Forum**, with cafés, restaurants and a casino.

Further to the north is the city's prosperous villa quarter containing fine turn-of-the-century houses. The terrain climbs towards the **Slavín**, the huge monument to Soviet soldiers who fell in World War II. The church Kostol na Kalvárii used to stand nearby, but the authorities decided to demolish the church tower in order to make the monument more prominent.

Beyond the city gates: Clearly signposted footpaths lead to the hilly **Horský Park**. Koliba and the television tower on the summit of the Kamzik offer magnificent views of Bratislava; this eminence can easily be reached by means of the trolleybus No. 213, and has the additional advantage of an excellent restaurant at the top.

The **Malé Karpaty**, the Little Carpathian Mountains, which extend in a northerly direction from Bratislava, are the city's nearest recreational area. Vineyards nestle betweeen wooded hillsides; wine tastings are available almost everywhere. A number of picturesque wine-growing villages punctuate the **Wine Route**, including **Jur**, **Limbach**, **Pezinok** and **Modra**.

The restaurant **Pezinská Baba**, in the middle of the woods, is famous for its excellent wine and homemade specialities. Nearby stands a cottage, the Chata na Bielej skale, the former holiday home of the Communist leaders. Trout and carp from the Netherlands were flown in specially for the dignitaries, while they themselves went hunting for moufflons, wild boar and deer. Deer are still common; even packs of wolves occasionally roam these vast forests.

Slovakian zither players.

Excursions into the past: Further excursions in the immediate vicinity are offered by **Červený kameň Castle** and the **Palace of Smolenicky zámok**, which displays a number of interesting architectural details and fine interiors.

But the most mysterious place in the environs of Bratislava is undoubtedly **Devín Castle**, which lies some 6 miles (10 km) upstream and can also be reached by river boat. The precipitous rock overlooking the confluence of the Morava and the Danube has been built upon for at least 5,000 years. According to legend the first castle was built here by Devoina, the daughter of the Duke of Moravia: it is first mentioned in records of the kingdom of Great Moravia during the 9th century. The present fortress dates from the 13th century, although this was rebuilt in the 16th century by the Hungarian king of Poland and prince of Transylvania, Stephen Bathory. In 1809 it was almost completely destroyed by Napoleon's troops.

But even in the late 20th century, Devín Castle continued to have its uses:

The Little
Carpathians
are an
important
vine growing
area.

those who failed in their attempt to flee into nearby Austria were condemned to see their hopes of a better life end in the castle prison. The barbed wire and gaol did not disappear until after the critical days of November 1989. In July the Slovaks celebrate an **annual festival of peace** in the ruins.

An alternative excursion follows the southern bank of the Danube to the unusual archaeological site of **Gerulata**. Only 15 minutes' drive from Bratislava, this Slovakian enclave just before the Hungarian border clusters around the three villages of **Rusovce**, **Jarovce** and **Čuňovo**. It was the only region within Slovakia which formed part of the Roman Empire for any length of time. Extensive excavations have shed new light on Roman culture and its interaction with neighbouring people in this far-flung province.

The banks of the Danube are still a miniature paradise for anglers and lovers of riverside flora and fauna. Many traditional inns and taverns offer fish specialities and potent wines.

WESTERN SLOVAKIA

Trnava (Tyrnau), a diocesan town, lies in a fertile, vine-clad valley only 28 miles (45 km) to the northeast of Bratislava. It can be reached by means of the D61 motorway as well as by train.

In 1988 the town celebrated its 750th anniversary and, in honour of the event, it received meticulous restoration. The architectural variety of Trnava reflects its significance as one of Hungary's religious and cultural centres during the long period of Turkish rule within the southern part of the country, and explains why it has been dubbed "Slovakian Rome".

In 1238 Bela IV, the king of Hungary at the time, awarded the settlement its municipal and market privileges, placing it directly under the jurisdiction of the crown. The extraordinary advantages associated with its status and its favourable location at the intersection of two long-distance trade routes encouraged Trnava's rapid growth and prosperity. In 1543 the town became the religious centre of all Hungary when the Primate of the Hungarian Church, the Archbishop of Esztergom, took refuge here because his own town and most of the rest of the country had been overrun by Turks. The foundation of a university less than a century later marked the transformation of the trading centre into a cultural metropolis. The transfer of the university to Buda in 1777 and the return of the Primate to Esztergom after its liberation in 1822 would have probably resulted in Trnava's sinking into provincial oblivion once more, had Slovakian intellectuals not moved the seat of the "Company of Academics" to the town in 1792. This was the most important scientific and literary association in Slovakia, which at that time was still under Hungarian rule.

Topped by its massive twin towers, the **cathedral of St Nicholas** dominates the panorama of the Old Town. In 1380 the present Gothic church was built on the site of a Romanesque basilica; it was subsequently extended on several occasions. The **university church of St John the Baptist** was constructed by Italian masters commissioned by the Jesuits. In only eight years, between 1629 and 1637, they completed the largest religious building in Slovakia. Together with the **Archbishop's Palace**, it sets the architectural tone on University Square.

Soaring above the long, narrow market place is the **Town Tower**, 220 ft (69 metres) high. The elaborately stuccoed facade of the classicistic **Town Hall** dates from 1793 and bears witness to the unshakeable optimism of Trnava in a time of threatened slump, as does the **Municipal Theatre** of 1831. Also worth closer inspection are a number of beautiful private houses in the Hollého ul. and the Kapitulská ul., as well as the well-preserved town walls with the protruding bastions to the east and west of the Old Town.

Into the Váh Valley: Piešt'any (Pistyan) lies 22 miles (35 km) along the Váh Valley following the main road No. 61 to the north. A statue in the spa quarter bears testimony to the great expecta-

Preceding pages: the restaurant in the noble spa hotel at Piešt'any. Left, into the Váh Valley. Right, in the spa gardens at Piešt'any.

tions of this world-famous spa town; it depicts a man throwing away his crutches. Some 700,000 gallons (3.5 million litres) of hot mineral water, at a temperature of 152°F (67°C) gush out of the earth here every day; patients with rheumatic complaints appreciate the sulphurous mud. There are first-class hotels and spa facilities available, and the nearby **Slňava Dam** offers good opportunities for water sports. The town is delightfully peaceful and provides a good base for excursions into the surrounding countryside. Because of the protection provided by the hills, the climate here is unusually mild.

From the 17th century increasing numbers of visitors flocked to the spa, and in 1827 the Hungarian count Erdödy, whose family owned the entire town until 1940, decided to make capital of its advantages. Spa halls and parks were created on the north bank; the southern **Bathing Island** with the **Napoleonic Baths** and the town's principal spring, the **Pramen Adam Trajan**, was linked directly to the town by means of the colonnade bridge. Under the aegis of Alexander Winter, the private citizen who took on the general lease for the spa facilities, a number of Art Nouveau sanatoria were built. The enterprising businessman not only transformed Piešt'any into a favourite meeting place of the fashionable world, but also encouraged a social conscience. In 1893 he founded a "workers' boarding school" and persuaded public health bodies to fund spa visits for the first time. During the past decades the municipal authorities have confirmed the town's international reputation by building modern spa facilities and the **Art Museum**.

It seems that a fondness for sitting in warm mud has a long, indeed ancient, tradition. Evidence of Neanderthal settlement has been found here. Even the local love of the arts, expressed during the **international music festival** each summer and the open-air exhibition of plastic arts in the spa gardens, has ancient roots: in 1939 a farmer found the **Venus of Moravany**, a small sculpture carved from the tooth of a mammoth,

Fresh from the Slovakian garden.

which is one of the oldest sculptures ever found.

Near **Čachtice**, situated 6 miles (10 km) further north, a vast castle rises threateningly out of the valley. It was formerly the residence of Countess Elisabeth Bathory. Court documents record that the "White Lady", as the countess was known, was responsible for the murder of 300 young girls. She believed that bathing in their blood was beneficial to her snow-white skin. The story has inspired a number of horror-film producers.

Trenčin, a lively little town with a long history, lies further upstream. As long ago as the 6th century, the Slavs built a fortress on the huge rock overlooking the Váh Valley. History here goes back even further, however, as the Roman inscription on the rock testifies: Dated 179 AD, it records the victory of the locally stationed Roman legion over a tribe of Germanii; it is the oldest written record ever found in Slovakia.

A settlement soon developed in the protective shadow of the fortress, and was awarded market rights in 1412. From 1302 the Hungarian magnate Matuš Čák had the complex remodelled into a prestigious, well-fortified castle, from which he ruled over the whole of western Slovakia. John of Luxembourg and his son, the future Emperor Charles IV, chose it on several occasions as the site for negotiations with the kings of Poland and Hungary. King Sigismund strengthened the bulwark against the Moravian Hussites. From the 17th century, the Counts Illésházy – who had received the town and its fortress in fief from the Habsburgs – rebuilt the complex in accordance with the latest theories of defensive architecture. Their descendants donated the entire fortress to the town in order to avoid the immense maintenance costs.

A castle chapel with a rotunda and the central **Matuš Tower** are all that remain of the medieval structure. The entire complex is extensive and includes an arsenal, casemates and an oubliette as well as the **Trenčin Gallery** with a collection of old master paintings.

Vlkolínec, a village built entirely of wood.

The Gothic **parish church** was built in the shadow of the castle rock. It possesses a perfect example of a charnel house, and an elaborate alabaster altar adorns the baroque burial chapel of the Illésházys, added at a later date.

The central axis of the Old Town is formed by the Mierové nám (Peace Square), fringed by well-kept private dwellings dating from Renaissance and baroque times. The brightly coloured frescoes in the Early baroque **church of St Francis** are charming. The town gate with its octagonal tower provides access to an unusually large 19th-century synagogue, which reminds the visitor that the town's expansion into a cloth centre and fashion capital was a direct result of the efforts of the once flourishing Jewish community.

The **Thermal Baths of Trenčíanske Teplice** lie barely 9 miles (15 km) further to the north along the Váh in the tributary valley of the Teplica, which is bordered by wooded hills. The hot springs, high in sulphur and chalk content, provide relief from rheumatism and neurosensory diseases; they were known during Roman times and the Middle Ages as Aqua Teplica but were seldom visited. It was the enterprising Joseph Illésházy who had a pretty summer residence built here in 1729 and who subsequently attracted High Society to the emerging spa town. In 1750 the fashionable **Hotel Kaštiel** opened its doors; it was a Grand Hotel built in the style of Renaissance castles. Under the direction of private individuals, bath houses, pump rooms and elegant restaurants were built beside the 11 springs. The most original contribution was provided by the architect Franz Schmoranz, who delivered an **oriental bath house** in Moorish style. The owner of the spa town, Iphigenie d'Harcourt, discovered the imaginative sketch at the Paris World Exhibition in 1878 and commissioned the architect to build the *hammam* as an intimate bath house with luxurious, individual cabins. Today it is used as the men's changing rooms for the adjoining Sina spa house.

The cradle of Slovakia: The romantic **Nitra Valley** lies to the east of the Váh Valley and can be reached either by crossing the mountains from Trenčin, or by going back along the Váh and taking the main road from Trnava. The venerable town of **Nitra**, the oldest town settlement in the Czech and Slovak Republics, lies on a broad bend in the river. It is an attractive setting and must already have been inhabited for several generations when, in 829, the Slavic feudal lord Přibina persuaded Archbishop Adalram of Salzburg to dedicate a court chapel here. From this point onwards, the history of the place is easier to follow: Mojmir I, Prince of the Empire of Greater Moravia, conquered the town shortly afterwards and extended it considerably. In 880, after the message of Christianity had been spread across most of the country by the two "Slavic apostles" Cyril and Methodius, still regarded as the patron saints of the Slovakian people, the pope elevated Nitra to the rank of the first diocesan town in Slovakia. Under Hungarian rule in the 11th century, the town entered its Golden Age.

The **castle** served the bishops, who were simultaneously the local feudal lords, as administrative seat. Even today it is still the residence of Bishop Ján Chryzostom Korec, who established a reputation for himself within the Slovakian Opposition. All the alleys leading uphill from the town open on to the **Square of Slovakian Cooperation**, dominated since 1750 by a column dedicated to the Virgin Mary and recalling the two cholera epidemics of the previous decades. A stone bridge lined with statues of saints leads to the first gateway and the courtyard, where a restored tower recalls the medieval stronghold.

The single-nave **Gothic cathedral** was extended on several occasions; in 1720, following a radical remodelling in the baroque style, it was adorned with original frescoes. A much older Early Romanesque church was discovered in 1930; the master builders of the intervening epochs had walled in this architectural jewel. The upper classes and senior clergy lived in the Upper Town, literally in the shadow of the towering castle. The craftsmen and traders joined together to form a community within the Lower Town.

After seeing the castle, take the Východná, which leads downhill to a quiet square. The **Great Seminary** appears to hover between the baroque and classicistic styles; today it houses the **local museum** with a fine collection of archaeological exhibits; the **Diocesan Library** next door houses the famous **Nitra Codex** dating from the 11th century. Opposite stands the classical-style **Canons' House**. The builder added an athletic-looking Atlas to one corner; the alert citizens soon recognised that the statue fulfilled no structural purpose and consequently christened him Corgoň, the Rascal. Following the Samova ul., the visitor arrives in front of the Franciscan monastery, today the **Museum of Agriculture**. The adjoining church contains some fine wood reliefs illustrating the life of the founder of the order.

The underpass beside the Studenie Gallery and the **Academy of Art** was once the only access to the castle. Beyond the square, the Saratovská ul. forms the central axis of the Old Town. Only two blocks further on and standing in the centre of the Mierové nám. (Peace Square), **St Michael's Chapel** recalls the town's two cholera epidemics. The surrounding cafés and the garden terrace of the Hotel Slovan provide a welcome chance to relax. The rest of the Lower Town can easily be explored during a gentle stroll. Turning towards the southwest, the visitor will discover a series of 11th-century frescoes in the attractively simple Romanesque **chapel of St Stephen**. The most notable buildings in the Gudernova ul. are the baroque ensemble formed by the Grammar School and the Piarist church, which possesses a remarkable double tower. To the east, on the former main square of the medieval Lower Town, the architectural tone is set by the modern **Andrej Bagar Theatre** and the Town Hall.

The slopes of the **Tribeč Mountains** to the north of the town provide ideal wine-growing conditions; the vineyards are interspersed with traditional roadside inns and attractive restaurants such as the Zoborská perla. The summit of the **Zobor peak** (1,880 ft/588 metres) provides a magnificent panorama across the town and the valley.

Half-way between Nitra and Bratislava lies the pretty little town of **Galanta**. It is the home of the legendary Esterházys, who collected castles and palaces as other people collect postage stamps. It is not surprising, therefore, that their native town, despite its population of only 15,000, should boast no fewer than four castles. The oldest, in the centre of the built-up area, dates from the Renaissance; another, in neo-Gothic style, houses the **Museum of Local History**.

On the return journey, less than 12 miles (20 km) before Bratislava, lies the community of **Senec**, whose two lakes, crystal-clear and undeniably romantic, never fail to enchant visitors.

Downstream along the Danube: This southwest corner of Slovakia bears strong traces of Hungarian influence; in some villages, Hungarian is even the main language. Travellers who want to

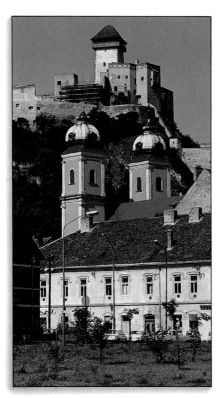

A view of Trenčín.

learn more about the cultural and historical influences of the region may be tempted to make a detour across the border to Hungary, to Esztergom or even to Budapest.

Behind Bratislava, to the right of the trunk road No. 63, are lush and lovely river meadows. Unfortunately from **Samorin** they have been ruined by the construction of the reservoir and power station at **Gabčíkovo**, a scheme which has sparked off a major international row between Slovakia and Hungary: the Hungarians maintain that the completion of the dam and the diversion of the river along a canal will result in enormous damage to the environment, and have demanded that the Danube be made an internationally protected area.

It is advisable to bypass the scene of the controversy by following the road No. 63, along which the town of **Dunajská Streda** offers the first interesting opportunity for a break. The name of this town means "Wednesday on the Danube", which alludes to the fact that since the 16th century this regional centre has been permitted to hold a market every Wednesday. The **Zity kaštiel**, the baroque "Yellow Castle", is a well-stocked **museum of local history**; it, and the Gothic **church of the Assumption**, decorated with medieval frescoes, are both worth visiting. The recent discovery of hot springs has given new impetus to local hotellerie and gastronomy. The nature conservation area Zlatná na Ostrove, shortly before Komárno on the Danube, is still the habitat of the Great Bustard (*otis tarda*), the largest European scavenging bird resident in the steppes.

The history of **Komárno**, which lies at the confluence of the Váh and the Danube, mirrors almost exactly the rise and fall of the royal and imperial monarchy. The native town of Franz Lehár, whose music reflects with such light-hearted elan the many national influences at work in his homeland, has been divided since 1918. The Danube serves as the frontier – just as it did in Roman times when the *limes* ran along its course, and later during the Turkish attacks on the fortress. Worthy of particular note

among the many fine churches is the **Orthodox Pravoslav Church**, which boasts an exceptional collection of icons and liturgical items.

The highlight of any visit to Southern Slovakia could well be a stay in **Patince** or **Štúrovo**, the idyllic spa towns lying downstream along the Danube. The region enjoys the highest average temperature in the whole of Slovakia; moreover, it seldom rains here. Additional attractions lie in the area cradled by the arm of the Danube, in the solid comfort of the hotels and guest houses, and – a particularity of Southern Slovakia – in the so-called *Pussten*. These are a particular type of traditional Hungarian restaurant, where violinists, playing genuine Gypsy music, accompany the serving of flambéed specialities and fine wine. In Štúrovo you can even try out an unusual form of transport – the *kompa* ferry, which carries tourists across to the other bank of the Danube, to the ancient town of **Esztergom** with its famous cathedral presided over by the Hungarian bishops.

A stork with a view.

CENTRAL SLOVAKIA

Central Slovakia can be subdivided according to its clearly defined geographical areas. The mountains of the Lower Tatra gradually give way on all sides to gentle river valleys and rolling hills. There are no major conurbations in the region, but in the south in particular a number of mining communities developed as a result of the lucrative deposits of copper, silver and gold.

Old mining communities: The most interesting of these mining towns is undoubtedly **Banská Bystrica** (Neu–sohl). The Slavic inhabitants of the sleepy hamlet of Bystrica were seized by gold fever during the 13th century, when gold, silver and copper deposits were discovered before their very doors. Encouraged by the royal privileges, German miners flocked to the new eldorado from nearby Zvolen (Altsohl). The community soon prospered and was awarded a town charter in 1255. The Fugger dynasty from Augsburg saw the potential of the mines and stepped in, investing vast sums of capital. At the beginning of the 16th century James II, nicknamed "The Rich", acquired a large proportion of the mines, both in the town and the region, for his family business, thus establishing what was actually a monopoly on European copper production. The Fuggers and their partners made Neusohl their administrative capital, thus enabling the town to achieve huge profits not only from the extraction of the ore, but also from processing, related crafts and international trade in precious metals. In those days, however, the profits were anything but fairly distributed. In 1525 the miners came out on strike.

It was from Banská Bystrica, on 29 August 1944, that the message for the Slovakians to start their revolt against the Nazis went out over the radio. Since then, the old market place has been called the **Square of the Slovakian Uprising** (SNP for short). This has always been the focal point of the busy little town. Despite some rebuilding in

the Renaissance style, most of the houses surrounding the square have retained many original Gothic elements. The **Thurzo House** in the southeast corner of the long, narrow square is the most magnificent of all, for it served as the official headquarters of the mining company. Today it houses the **Museum of Municipal History and Folklore**. The **Benicky House** diagonally opposite is notable for its elaborately decorated facade with a loggia supported by elegant Tuscan columns.

The **Clock Tower** points the way to the **fortress**, a collection of buildings which gradually evolved into a single complex. The residence of the governor appointed by the king to oversee the mining operations also served as a storehouse; it later became known as the "Matthias House", for the Hungarian king Matthias Corvinus stayed here on a number of occasions. The Gothic gateway tower and the **Miners' Church** completed the castle complex; the barbican was added at the beginning of the 16th century.

In **Zvolen**, too, you will find many buildings recalling its own Golden Age. The settlement received its town charter in 1244 and became prosperous with the mining of its silver deposits. It is not the town itself which is of particular interest, however, but the magnificent **castle**. It was built in 1382 by King Ľudovít the Great, who planned to use it as a base for his hunting expeditions. King Matthias Corvinus also fell in love with the beautiful setting and made the hunting lodge his favourite residence. During the 16th century the Thurzos replaced the elegant lightness of the original building with massive defensive features; the Esterházys finally turned it into an imposing palace. The castle now serves as a museum for a remarkably valuable collection of medieval Slovakian art.

In the town itself, little remains of the workshops that once made this an important centre of woodcarving. However, traditions are kept alive by the **International Folklore Festival** which takes place every July.

Banská Štiavnica (Schemnitz) traces its origins back to a mining village established in about AD 1000. During the 12th century, German miners added a number of pit shafts to the open-cast seams. The village subsequently expanded into a national mining centre. In 1244, Banská Štiavnica received its charter as a free Royal city. Here, too, the Fuggers ensured that they retained the lion's share of the mining and, during the 15th and 16th century, the town became the most important supplier of silver in all Hungary. Widespread investment and high profits allowed for technical improvements in mining technology, which were soon emulated on a worldwide scale. Explosives were first used in Banská Štiavnica in 1627; the introduction of mechanical pumps was also an invention of local mining engineers, who from 1735 were trained in a special university college.

The most interesting buildings in the town are the former houses of the wealthy mine owners; their Renaissance-style architecture, built upon Roman- **A quaint Easter custom.**

esque or Early Gothic foundations, reflects the enormous prosperity that Banská Štiavnica achieved. Most of them are situated around the central Trojičné nám. (Trinity Square), dominated by its baroque column.

The Miners' Court used to meet in No. 47; its verdicts were based on the Schemnitz Mining Law, which was codified in 1217. Today the building houses an informative **Museum of Mines**, where the industry of the Middle Ages is documented with tools, rock samples, models and a shaft leading some 230ft (70 metres) underground. Nearby stand the Renaissance building occupied by the former Chamber of Mines, the notable **parish church of St Nicholas** and the Old Town Hall.

Above the Old Town rises the **Castle**. During the 13th century a Romanesque church occupied the site, but with increasing prosperity in the 16th century the citizens converted the strategically located place of worship into a fortress with thick walls and five towers. The nave became a castle courtyard.

Historically speaking, **Kremnica** (Kremnitz) is one of the most important towns in Slovakia. Mentioned in records as a Slavic settlement from the 12th century, the town owes its rapid expansion and elevation to a Free Royal city in 1328 to the extensive gold and silver deposits in the nearby Kremnica Mountains. Even today, precious metals are still extracted from its pits.

From 1335, following the awarding of special privileges by the King of Hungary, Charles Robert, the town was permitted to mint its own gold ducats – a tradition maintained by the mint in the Horná ul. until recent times. Such was the town's prosperity that it repeatedly attracted the attention of envious conquerors; even the Hussites plundered it during their punitive expedition of 1434. Nonetheless, the town has been able to maintain its traditional countenance. The spacious Nam. 1. mája (Square of 1 May) is bordered by several dozen fine houses, mostly built during the 14th century and extended in contemporary style during the Renaissance. The

A Slovakian wedding procession.

Municipal Museum in No. 7 provides the visitor with an insight into the colourful history of the town. The square, built on a slight slope, is bordered by the **castle**, which from the 13th century served both as administrative headquarters and as a secure repository for the precious metals. The embankments and bastions surround a Gothic church and the forbidding castle keep.

A host of castles: Apart from its picturesque towns, the region boasts a large number of fortresses and palaces. Totalling no fewer than 70, some of them are in good condition whilst the others survive only as ruins. **Bojnický zámok Castle**, west of the town of **Prievidza** (Priwitz), is popularly considered the finest in the whole of Central Europe. Some historians claim that it was founded about AD 1000, during the reign of King Stephen of Hungary. The castle changed hands frequently over the years. The Lords of Pálffy assembled a unique collection of paintings here. Directly below the castle walls there is a popular thermal bath; the cas-tle grounds contain the largest zoological gardens in Slovakia.

South of Martin, **Blatnický hrad Castle** dominates the lovely **Gaderská dolina valley**. Hidden away in a large stretch of continuous woodland, it appears all the more imposing when seen at close quarters. The castle is first mentioned in records dating from the 13th century. Access to the complex is gained by a footpath; no cars are permitted.

The course of the Váh is rich in castles. **Budatín Castle** lies at the confluence of the Kysuca and the Váh, just to the north of the town of **Žilina** (Sillein). Having grown up at the intersection of important medieval trade routes, today the town remains the busiest traffic junction in all Slovakia. Of particular interest is the little church of St Stephen, one of the oldest Romanesque churches in Slovakia, whose interior is adorned with a number of striking frescoes. Žilina makes a good base for exploring the attractive region of **Orava**, in the northernmost corner of Slovakia. A well-developed tourist infrastructure has

Oravský hrad stands sentinel above the Orava River.

arisen around the Orava reservoir (Oravska nadrž). The romantic **Orava Castle**, boldly perched on a limestone crag above the river, was built to guard the trading route to Poland and was thus fortified on a number of occasions. Today it houses a museum of local history.

The entire region is famous for its traditional folk music and extravagant **traditional costumes**. Your best chance of seeing these is to be invited to a wedding, which can last for three days or more. Traditional crafts such as embroidery, ceramics and pottery, as well as the painting of furniture, also retain their place in modern society. To the south of Žilina, **Čičmany** is famous far and wide for its richly embroidered costumes and its wooden houses decorated with colourful motifs.

Into the mountains: To the east of Žilina the visitor can follow the romantic Vrátna valley through Terchová and on to Vrátna, from where a cable car trundles up to the main ridge of the **Lesser Fatra** (Malá Fatra), beneath the highest peak of the range, Veľke Kriván (5,606 ft/1,709 metres).

The **Lower Tatra** (Nízké Tatry) is a paradise for walkers and ski enthusiasts. In the western section, the long succession of peaks makes it possible to hike along the crest, where the breathtaking views amply repay the effort involved. The descent into the valley is punctuated by mountain huts where it is possible to obtain milk and simple lamb dishes. One of the most rewarding hikes is the traverse from Šturec or Krížna in the **Greater Fatra** (Velká Fatra) to Chabenec and on to the **Chopok**, the main ridge of the Lower Tatra.

In the town of **Liptovský Mikuláš**, the **Museum of Slovakian Karst** provides a foretaste of the wonders of nature to be experienced in the fabulous **Demänovské jaskyňe caves**, 7 miles (11 km) to the south. Their chambers and galleries are magnificently orna–mented with stalactites and stalagmites and are linked by a whole series of underground lakes, streams and waterfalls. On the southern flank of the Chopok ridge, the village of **Tále** is a good base for less experienced walkers.

The gentle ski slopes in the foothills of the **Bystrá dolina valley** are ideal for novices. The village also offers playgrounds, an open-air swimming pool, restaurants and accommodation in hotels, a motel and a campsite.

At 6,722 ft (2,049 metres), **Mt Ďumbier** is the highest peak in the Lower Tatra. The ascent from **Čertovica** in summer or winter is equally rewarding: there is a magnificent view across the mountains of Slovakia from the Polish to the Hungarian frontier, from the Beskids to Branisko.

The eastern section of the Lower Tatra, between Čertovica and the **Popová ridge**, is an unspoilt wilderness. The main crest is covered by extensive forests. The only reminder of civilisation is a hideous transmitter on the summit of the **Krakova hoľa**. There are few mountain huts providing accommodation for tourists; the marked footpaths, however, pass a succession of hunting lodges, for the entire region is rich in game. This remote corner of the continent is even inhabited by bears.

Many rare flowers in Slovakia are protected.

EASTERN SLOVAKIA

No other region of the former Czechoslovakia offers the visitor a more varied and colourful combination of natural beauty and historic sights than Eastern Slovakia. Although the inhabitants of Spiš, Šariš, Zemplín, Gemer and Košice all feel themselves to be Eastern Slovaks, there are clear differences in both dialect and folklore. The variations are most clearly reflected in the architecture of the towns and villages.

Košice (Kaschau), idyllically situated in the foothills of the Slovenské Rudohorie (Slovakian Ore Mountains), is the principal city in Eastern Slovakia. Founded by Saxon settlers, the community was awarded special privileges by the King of Hungary in 1244; in 1342 it was proclaimed a Free Royal City and from 1369 it was the first city in central Europe to be allowed to bear its own coat of arms. The town became wealthy as a result of its international trade with Hungary and Poland; the university, founded in 1657, turned it into a cultural metropolis. The Golden Age lasted only until the 18th century, when internal strife, the Turkish Wars and finally the split from Hungary marked the beginning of a period of economic decline.

The historic town centre is a national monument. **St Elizabeth's Cathedral** rises above the central Nám. Slobody (Peace Square); it is considered to be one of the most beautiful Gothic churches in the country. The north door, the *porta aurea,* dating from 1460, frames a statue of the patron saint; the magnificently carved high altar, completed a few years later, describes 12 scenes from the life of the saint.

The free-standing **belfry**, Urbanova věža, and the cemetery chapel, dedicated to St Michael, complete the architectural ensemble of the square. For modern citizens of Slovakia, Košice is the town of the Slovakian "magna carta", and the home of the Košice government protocol, which was proclaimed in the Committee House here on 4 April 1945, **The pedestrian precinct in Košice.**

and which provided the basis of Czechoslovakia's postwar constitution.

The Communist leadership decided to turn Eastern Slovakia into an industrial region. In the vicinity of Košice a vast iron and steel works was constructed, although there were lamentably inadequate supplies of water and iron ore. It proved to be the most blatant and, ecologically speaking, the most catastrophic false investment in the history of Czechoslovakia. The only positive step taken by the former regime was its expansion of the education system. The Technical University of Košice produced a large number of good steel and mining engineers.

In the northeastern corner of the region lie Prešov (Preschau) and Bardéjov (Bartfeld), attractive towns which in medieval times enjoyed privileges as free royal cities, forming the Pentapolis League with Košice, Levoča and Sabinov. Fine Gothic and Renaissance houses with ornately decorated gables grace the Town Square of **Prešov**, now an important centre of Slovakian and Ukranian culture, possessing both a Slovakian and a Ukranian theatre. The most attractive building is the **Rákoczyho palác**, the residence of Prince Rakoczy, which until recently housed exhibits from the Museum of the Bolshevik Slovakian Soviet Republic.

In **Bardéjov** near the Polish border, the medieval city centre, dating from the town's founding year (1219), has survived to this day. Almost all the fortifications, constructed during the 15th century, can also still be seen. The houses surrounding the central square reflect the town's heyday in Gothic and Renaissance times. The **Town Hall** dates from 1509; today it serves as municipal archives and museum. The Gothic **church of St Aegidius** boasts eleven magnificent altars as well as numerous paintings and statues. The neighbouring spa town of **Bardéjovské kúpele** has operated as a spa since the 13th century. Its waters are famous for their efficacy in treating stomach disorders and illnesses of the digestive tract. It is the most important spa town in Slovakia after Piešt'any.

Vernacular churches: The remote mountain villages of Eastern Slovakia are known for their traditional **wooden churches**. Most of them were built during the 18th century and reveal an imaginative mixture of baroque and archaic elements. They frequently stand on some sort of eminence, their towers rising above the rooftops of the village. Their interiors bear witness to a Byzantine influence; many contain an iconostasis. The portraits of saints on the folding triptychs are mostly the work of anonymous local artists and craftsmen and depict religious subjects in accordance with classical models. The minor figures, however, are modelled on simple people, displaying the common features and ordinary clothing of the times. Also worthy of note are the decorative wall and ceiling paintings, the altars, pews and missals. There are 24 such churches in Eastern Slovakia and they are national monuments.

In a hilly region further to the south, on the **River Ondava**, lies the **Domaša Dam** – a good tip for a longer stay. The

The famous Madonna of Košice, in St Elizabeth's Cathedral.

reservoir is popular among anglers and offers water sports facilities of all kinds.

Among the natural sights of the region are the Morské oko mountain lake in the **Vihorlat mountains** and the lovely **Zemplínská Šírava Lake**, also known as the East Slovakian Lake. Its enchanting location on the southern slopes of the Vihorlat ensures favourable climatic conditions. The bathing season lasts for almost five months of the year, and there is an annual average of nearly 2,200 hours of sunshine. The passenger boats crossing the lake afford delightful outings to the pretty villages lining the shores. The restaurants have an excellent reputation; apart from fish and game, they serve local specialities of the region.

A caver's paradise: The scenery of the **Slovenský kras mountains**, surrounding the mining town of **Rožňava** in the south of the region, is characterised by caves, gorges and karst landscape. The vaulted roof of the **Domica cave** is covered with bizarre coloured stalactites. You can take a boat trip along this underground river, through the eerie world of different colours. Equally impressive are the vast columns of ice in the **Dobšinská ľadová cave**, north of the town of **Dobšina**. It lies adjacent to the **Slovenský raj**, the "Slovakian Paradise", an area of natural beauty marked by canyons, gorges and waterfalls. Particularly spectacular is the **Kyseľ Canyon**, which over a length of 3 miles (5 km) drops a height of over 1,000 ft (350 metres). The most impressive of all, however, is the **Veľký Sokol**, also 3 miles (5 km) long and with walls rising up to 1,000 ft (300 metres) above the river, which in one place is only 3 feet across. On the edge of the Slovenský raj, the River Hornád forces its way through a 6-mile (11-km) gorge (only traversable by boat).

Further to the west, the town of Švermovo provides a convenient base for hikes into the eastern end of the Lower Tatra range, specifically the ascent of the 6,391ft (1,948 metre) high Kráľova hoľa.

A cultural entity: Culturally speaking, northeastern Slovakia is a largely independent region. Known to the Slavs as **Spiš**, it was christened Zips by the German migrants who settled in the area from the 11th century onwards. In 1271, 24 towns within the region joined forces to form a league of free cities, choosing the royal town of Levoča (Leutschau) as their capital. Five years later they were emulated by the "Seven Mountain Towns of the Zips" surrounding the Free Royal City of Göllnitz. They prospered on their mining, trade and crafts, but the towns' history was a turbulent one. In 1412, the Emperor Sigismund pawned 13 of them to Poland for a few thousand silver pence, then refused to buy them back. The remaining towns came under pressure from the Hungarian nobility, and the Catholic Church attempted to force their inhabitants to convert to the one true faith. In 1769 the Habsburgs conquered the entire region, annexing it for their empire. It was not until 1876, however, that the Hungarians finally put an end to all autonomy.

The magnificent Gothic and Renaissance churches of the region bear wit-

Peppers thrive in the warm climate of Eastern Slovakia.

ness to this history, as do the elegant belfries, fine town halls, sprawling farms and mighty castles. Many of these monuments have been turned into museums, but a considerable number of the churches were sadly converted or even demolished by the Communist regime. Nonetheless, the centres of the cities of the Spiš have maintained their medieval countenance. Four of them have been declared national monuments: Levoča, Kežmarok, Poprad, Spišská Sobota and Spišská Kapitula.

Levoča contains a unique work of art by the local master craftsman Pavol: a **Gothic wooden altar**, no less than 58 ft (18 metres) high. It stands in the 14th-century parish **church of St James**, the second-largest gothic church in Slovakia, which is situated on the Mierové nám (the Peace Square), a spacious square bordered by splendid patrician houses. The lovely Renaissance Town Hall was completed in 1559 and is adorned with a massive belfry and a series of fine frescoes, depicting bourgeois morality.

Kežmarok (Käsmark) is notable for its Romanesque-Gothic parish church of the Holy Cross, its Protestant wooden church and a fortress which was later converted into a palace.

In the **church of St Aegidius** in **Poprad**, a series of 15th-century frescoes, in particular an enchanting panorama of the High Tatra, the mountains dominating the town, has been carefully preserved. In the **Spišská Sobota** district there are historic townhouses and a Gothic parish church. Exceptionally fine examples of popular architecture are found in the remote villages of the Levoča Mountains and the valley of the River Poprad.

The northern Spiš region includes the magnificent **Pieninský narodny National Park**, where the **River Dunajec** carves its way through the Pieninský Mountains. One of the most exciting ways of exploring the river is to take a wild water trip on a raft in the company of a rafter from the Górale, a people living on both sides of the national frontier between Slovakia and Poland.

House facade in the cloth town of Bardéjov (Bartfeld).

THE HIGH TATRA

The most popular tourist region in Slovakia is a nature reserve: the Tatra National Park (Tatranský národní park). By following carefully laid-out paths visitors can observe and experience a natural wilderness without damaging it. Almost all the mountain peaks in the park are accessible, and from almost any point in the park it is possible to enjoy unforgettable views of the main mountain ridge.

Extending about 40 miles (64 km) along the Slovakian–Polish frontier, the High Tatra (Vysoké Tatry) is the highest mountain range in the Central Carpathians. Although the range is much lower than the Alps and therefore lacks the permanent snowfields and glaciers, it nevertheless possesses a distinctly alpine character. The mountain slopes are covered with pine woodlands up to an elevation of 6,600 ft (2,500 metres), above which the alpine zone begins. The High Tatra supports a rich variety of fauna, including bears, chamois, marmots and eagles.

Around 300 peaks are identified by name and elevation. Until an earthquake blew off its top in the 16th century, the highest peak in the range was the Slavkovský štít, with an elevation of more than 8,850 ft (2,700 metres). Evidence of the catastrophe can be seen in the massive outcrops of rock which were hurled into the Veľká Studená dolina valley. The highest mountain in the Tatra now is the Gerlachovský štít (8,737 ft/ 2,663 metres).

The highest peaks were originally over 9,600 ft (3,000 metres); during the Ice Age glaciers up to 640-ft (200-metres) thick wore away the summits and rent deep clefts in the mountain mass, thus forming the impressive hanging valleys, lakes and rock walls which characterise the Tatra today. Glacial remains can still be found on the north faces, where the sun never penetrates. In some places you will also come across large patches of snow which do not melt, even on the warmest summer days.

Wonders of nature: The 35 mountain lakes in the Slovakian Tatra have been left behind by the retreating glaciers. They are commonly referred to as "sea eyes", because the ancients believed that their deep, crystal-clear waters were directly linked with the sea. Some fill the hollows left in the rock by the ice sheets; others are contained by rock dams formed by the deposition of rocks and stones. The largest of the mountain lakes, the Veľké Hincovo, has a surface area of almost 50 acres (20 hectares) and is over 160 ft (50 metres) deep.

The jewels in the crown of this mountain range are the picturesque waterfalls. The spectacular Kmeťov Falls in the Nefcerka Valley thunder 256 ft (80 metres) into the depths below; the vast Studenovodské vodopády and the Skok Falls in the Mlynická dolina valley, as well as the Obrovský Falls in the Studenovodská dolina Valley are a magnificent natural spectacle.

Ideal climate: But the Tatra Mountains have much more to offer than just scenic beauty; the towns and villages and the bracing mountain climate are equally inviting. The massif towers above the surrounding mountains, forming a watershed and creating a microclimate unique in Central Europe.

The setting was ideal for the establishment of sanatoria for the treatment of tuberculosis, asthma, respiratory complaints and nervous disease, all of which respond well to the oxygen-rich air. A stay in the Tatra is beneficial even during the cold, wet season, for the intensity of the healing ultraviolet rays is largely dependent upon the purity of the air. Even during the main tourist season, when in the Alps there tends to be a lot of haze, the skies in the High Tatra are generally clear. There is a partial ban upon the use of private cars, which means that the range is largely spared pollution from exhaust fumes, smoke and water vapour. Above the tree line, after the fog or rain has cleared, there is virtually no trace of water evaporation. The number of hours of sunshine here is as high as on the sunny plains of southern Slovakia, and amounts to between 1,800 and 2,000 hours per year.

Preceding pages: the Gerlachovský štít is the highest summit in the High Tatra. Left, climbers in the High Tatra.

Characteristic of the region are sudden climatic changes. Whilst the valleys are buried under a thick layer of cloud, the upper slopes of the High Tatra often enjoy brilliant sunshine. The cold air, which is relatively heavy, sinks into the valleys and the warm air, which is less dense, moves up to the higher altitudes. Among the climatic characteristics of the Tatra region are a number of strange phenomena: a mirage effect caused by the mountains, flashes of lightning from an otherwise clear sky and föhn winds of up to 94 mph (150 kph). Even sand from the Sahara desert, brought by the high-altitude trade wind, is deposited on the snow-covered peaks of the High Tatra. A particular attraction is the ever-changing play of light at dawn and during the evening.

A paradise for trekkers: For those who want to hike in the High Tatra, the autumn is probably the best time of year for a visit. Although the days a shorter, the skies are at their most brilliant blue, and the forested slopes are a riot of colour. The highlight of exploring the High Tatra is to climb through the wild, romantic valleys, past mountain lakes and across strangely formed rock terraces. The 220 miles (350 km) of clearly marked footpaths provide even inexperienced walkers with access to the mountains. The main ridge of the High Tatra is only accessible for experienced climbers; it extends for a distance of over 16 miles (26 km) from Ľaliové sedlo to Kopské. The northern slopes in particular are steep and cold, and present a tremendous challenge to mountaineers.

Even in winter, the High Tatra and the neighbouring White Tatra (Belanske Tatry) to the east are attractive destinations, for they offer ideal conditions for cross-country and downhill skiing. The guesthouses, however, are often fully booked during the winter sports season, so prior reservations (or plenty of patience) are necessary.

The Tatra Mountains are easily reached from other parts of the country and offer a sensitively developed tourist infrastructure, with accommodation ranging from top-class hotels to moun-

An autumn hike up Mount Rysy.

tain huts offering shared mattresses on the floor. A hundred years ago no direct roads led to this remote mountain district. Today it can be reached via the scenic route Cesta Slobody ("the freedom trail"), which links the main tourist centres – Štrbské Pleso, Starý Smokovec and Tatranská Lomnica. Buses and an electrified railway line provide additional means of transport.

Starting points: Tatranská Lomnica is an ideal base for a visit to the region, since many walking tours actually begin here. Visitors who prefer not to exert themselves unduly can take one of the two cable cars to the Salnaté pleso, which lies at an altitude of 5,600 ft (1,750 metres). The **Hotel Encián** and the observatory invite one to stay longer; additional cable cars provide a link with the highest peaks of the range. The picturesque village itself houses the **Tatra National Park Museum**, where – apart from exhibits illustrating the region's folklore – the visitor can admire the largest collection of flora from the Spišská Magura. From Tatranská

Lomnica one can continue to **Tatranská Kotlina** and visit the impressive **Belanská jaskyňa caves**. Nearby **Ždiar** is a typical Slovakian hill community extending 4 miles (7 km) along the slopes of the Spišská Magura. On Sundays and during folk festivals the locals wear their traditional costumes.

Štrbské Pleso, the highest village in Slovakia, also makes a good base. It is the starting point for a number of interesting routes, including the popular climb to the top of Mount Rysy, whose summit provides a magnificent view of the entire Tatra range. Another much-visited destination is Mount Kriváň (8182 ft/2,493 m), further to the west; the goal of many national pilgrimages.

Routes through the mountains: Every visitor to the Tatra makes for the **Cesta Slobody**, the "Freedom Trail", undoubtedly the loveliest mountain road in Slovakia. For more than 44 miles (70 km) it runs parallel to the mountains from Podbanské in the west, through Tatranská Lomnica to Podspády and Javorina, from where it continues across

Mount Kriváň is one of the most spectacular peaks in the range.

the border into the Polish Zakopane. Less convenient, but every bit as attractive, is a journey by **train** from Poprad to Tatranská Lomnica and on to Štrbské pleso; the carriages chug slowly and laboriously through the craggy mountain landscape and stop beside virtually every barn.

The main footpath through the mountains, the so-called **Magistrale**, provides the best way of getting to know the region. The route is marked in red, is well maintained along its entire length and traverses the area between Podbanské in the west and Tatranská Kotlina at an average height of 4,160–6,400 ft (1,300–2,000 metres).

The first section passes along the shores of the Jamské pleso lake to Štrbské Pleso, continuing to Popradské pleso and up the famous zig-zags to the summit of **Ostrava**, on over Mount Tupá, beneath Končistá and Gerlachovský štít to **Sliezsky dom**. From here the marked route runs along the slopes of **Mount Slavkovský štít** and past the Sesterské pleso lakes to the **Hrebienok**.

Skirting the mouth of the **Studen–ovodská dolina valley**, the path continues past the waterfalls and uphill to Lake Skalnaté pleso as far as the cable car leading up **Mount Lomnický štít**, which at 8,635 ft (2,632 metres) is the second highest mountain in the range. Then it's on to Veľká Svist'ovka and down into the **Zelené pleso valley**. Near the Bielé pleso, the path starts to climb once more to the **Kopské sedlo**. Another path then traverses the ridge of the Belanske Tatry and leads the hiker down to Tatranská Kotlina.

Mountain challenges: Hiking along the Magistrale is an unforgettable experience, even for less practised walkers – especially when one combines the main walk with short detours to the nearby summits and valleys. But when attempting to climb a mountain it is imperative that the time it takes (shown on the signposts) is taken into account. The Tatra is not only a region of great beauty; it can also be a region of great danger. Many visitors overestimate their strength, abilities and knowledge of the area and pay for their foolishness with an accident, frost bite or even death. Not only individuals, but also groups are at risk. Before undertaking an ambitious touring programme, it is absolutely essential to check with the mountain rescue association, which has a branch office in every larger village. These are some of the most popular routes from west to east:

1. From **Podbanské**, Tri studničky or the **Furkotská chata** mountain hut hike up to **Kmeťov** and the **Vajanského vodopád** waterfalls in the shadow of **Mount Kriváň**. Two further routes of interest in this area lead over the Kôprovské sedlo mountain crest to Lakes **Hincovo pleso** and **Popradské pleso**, and the **Furkotská Valley** with the Wahlenbergové plesá lakes.

2. From **Štrbské pleso** in the Furkotská valley climb up Mount Kriváň and descend into the **Mlynická dolina valley** (ski area established in 1970), passing the **Skok Waterfall**, the **Vyšné Kozie** and **Capie pleso** mountain lakes. From there a route continues up the **Mengusovská dolina valley**, and past

Tatranská Lomnica at the foot of Lomnický štít.

318

the **Popradské pleso** mountain lake, which is the starting point for the ascent to the summit of **Mount Rysy**, beneath which is the highest mountain hut in Slovakia. The trail to **Vyšné Hágy** over Mount Ostrva is also pleasant.

3. From Vyšné Hágy walk to the **Batizovské pleso** lake. Then either continue westwards past the Popradské pleso to Štrbské pleso, or eastwards to Sliezsky dom and from there to **Tatranská Polianka**.

4. From Tatranská Polianka hike to Sliezsky dom and then continue from the **Velické pleso** mountain lake up to the **Poľský hrebeň** (Polish Saddle), before descending through the **Svišt'ová** and **Bielovodská dolina** valleys to **Javorina**. From Sliezsky dom one can also hike to the top of the Hrebienok. Another attractive route leads from the Batizovské pleso mountain lake to Vyšné Hágy. Experienced walkers under the direction of a guide might also consider tackling the routes up **Gerlach-ovský štít** or the **Vychodná Vysoká** from Sliezsky dom.

5. From **Starý Smokovec** take the cable car up the Hrebienok, and from there follow a not too arduous but a long climb up the **Slavkovský štít**. An alternative is to follow the **Veľká Studená dolina** valley to the **Zbojnická chata** hut and then continue via Prielom and Poľsky hrebeň to the Sliezsky dom. Another beautiful route leads to the **Studenovodské vodopády** waterfalls and to the **Téryho chata** mountain refuge, which is run by Belo Kapolka, a well known writer.

6. Set off from **Tatranská Lomnica** to the Studenovodské vodopády waterfalls and up the Hrebienok, beneath the cable car to the **Skalnaté pleso** mountain lake and on to the **Hotel Encián**; from the hotel, either climb up to the **Hrebienok waterfalls** or descend into the lovely valley occupied by the **Bielé pleso** (white lake) and the **Zelené pleso** (green lake) and return to Tatranská Lomnica. Very experienced mountain walkers will also enjoy the challenging route from Bielé pleso to Tatranská Kotlina.

A cosy evening after a long day's hike.

TRAVEL TIPS

GETTING THERE

BY AIR

THE CZECH REPUBLIC

Prague is firmly on the international air grid, so many airlines now fly from New York to Prague and in the case of ČSA, the Czech national carrier, the flight is non-stop. ČSA also flies from Chicago via Montreal as well as from Toronto. Prague is directly linked to virtually every European capital.

Prague Ruzyně airport lies 20 km (13 miles) northwest of the city. There are public bus services to the centre, as well as taxi and hire cars. The state travel agency Čedok runs a shuttle bus service between the airport and the city's Interhotels between 11am and 4pm.

ČSA also operates a similar service between the airport and the city terminal (Vltava Travel Agency, Revolucní 25. Tel: 231 7395, 2146). It runs every 30 minutes, Monday–Friday 5.30am–6.30pm, Saturday and Sunday 6.30am–6.30pm. The journey takes 30 minutes and costs 15 crowns. The buses also stop at the terminal station *Dejvická* of the green Metro line A.

For further information contact one of the ČSA offices located either in Prague or abroad (*see Useful Addresses*).

SLOVAKIA

Bratislava was served by a limited number of international flights before the division of the country in January 1993, although all ČSA flights to the city went via Prague. At the time of going to press it is not known when and how ČSA will be broken up, although it looks like maintaining its full operations at least until the end of 1993. Slovakia will form its own national airline and Bratislava will become an international airline destination in its own right. At present, visitors can fly into Prague and get the connecting flight, or fly into Vienna International Airport and then drive or take the train; Bratislava is only 56 km (35 miles) away from the Austrian capital. The charter holiday business looks certain to take off in Slovakia, with charter companies flying to a number of destinations, including the town of Poprad at the foot of the High Tatras.

BY RAIL

THE CZECH REPUBLIC

There are direct train connections to Prague from Germany and Austria. From Stuttgart and Munich, the journey takes approximately 8 hours, from Frankfurt 10 hours, Berlin 6 hours, Hamburg 14 hours and Vienna 6 hours. Generally speaking, "Eurorail" and such passes may be used only on the Czech sections of international routes, not on the domestic network. There is no through service from the channel ports. The service from Paris is known to the French as the Paris–Praha Express and to the Czechs as the Zapadní Express. It leaves from the Gare de l'Est at 11pm and goes via Frankfurt and Nuremberg, arriving at Prague at 5.53pm the following day. The Donau Kurier from Cologne leaves at 7.58am, requires a change at Nuremberg, and reaches Prague at 9.55pm. All trains from Southern Germany and Austria come in at the Main Station (*Hlavní nádraží*). Trains from the direction of Berlin come to halt at the Masaryk Station (*Masarykovo nádraží*) or at Prague-Holešovice Station.

Travellers coming from Germany and wishing to see the spa towns of Western Bohemia can take the train to Cheb (Eger) from Nuremberg and there change over to other forms of transport. Other rail destinations in the Czech Republic as well as Slovakia can be reached via Prague. Travellers who do not have a ticket from the capital city to their ultimate destination may purchase one at the main train station in Prague. Domestic and international tickets can be purchased in Western currency at:

Čedok, Na příkopě 18, Prague 1, or directly at the railway station in crowns.

Further information pertaining to rail travel can be obtained in Prague from 7am–3.30pm, tel: 236 4441; and 6am–10pm at the main station, tel: 235 3836; also Prague Smichov, Tel: 2161 5086.

SLOVAKIA

There are regular train services to Bratislava from Prague, Vienna and Budapest. The journey from Vienna is the shortest and most convenient means of entering Slovakia by train; the international train services between Budapest and points west run through Slovakia.

BY ROAD

THE CZECH REPUBLIC

Travellers arriving from Germany can reach Prague via the following main border crossings from:

Baryreuth via Schirnding/Pomezí
Nuremberg via Waidhaus/Rozvadov
Regensburg via Furth im Wald/Folmava
Passau via Phillipsreuth/Strážný

Munich via Bayrisch Eisenstein/Železná Rudá
Berlin via Zinnwald/Cínovecb

If you're entering the Czech Republic from Austria (from west to east):
Salzburg via Linz Summerau/Horni Dvořistě
Vienna via Gmünd/České Velenice or Grametten/ Nová Bystřice

SLOVAKIA

Travellers arriving from Austria can best reach Bratislava by taking the motorway from **Vienna** via Hainburg. Those arriving from Hungary will take the road from **Budapest** along the Danube and either cross the border at Komárno or continue along the Hungarian side of the border past Gyor. The most direct link to Bratislava from the Czech Republic is the motorway down from **Brno** via Kúty.

Although there are nowhere near as many private cars as there are in Western Europe, drivers still have to reckon with delays, particularly in the Czech Republic. The main roads are generally in good condition, but the many lorries using them can make progress very slow, especially by day.

All drivers are required to be in possession of a valid national driver's licence, car registration documents and a car nationality sticker. The international green insurance card should also be taken along. At the border "citizens of foreign countries" are handed a special vehicle licence which is to be filled out and then shown with the other documents. If the driver is not using his own vehicle, he must provide written consent from the vehicle's owner. Caravans, trailers and boats require no special customs documents. Controls at the border crossings are often very thorough, so be prepared for long waits, particularly during the high season. This situation does not yet apply to the new international border between the Czech Republic and Slovakia; a customs union has been established enabling the free transportation of goods.

Nowadays, unleaded petrol (95 octane) is obtainable at most larger filling stations. Note: neither petrol nor diesel bought in the country may be taken out in reserve canisters. If you're travelling by night you should make sure you have enough petrol, as it may be impossible to find a filling station open.

By and large, the international traffic regulations apply in both republics. The motorways are toll-free. Maximum speed limit within city boundaries is 60 kph (37 mph). On expressways it is 110 kph (69 mph), and on country roads 90 kph (56 mph). If you get caught exceeding the speed limit you can count on paying a fine of about 500 crowns. Driving while under the influence of alcohol is absolutely prohibited.

Children under 12 years of age are not allowed to sit in the front seat. Seat belts must be fastened outside the built-up areas.

Breakdown: It's a good idea to purchase International Travel Cover from your own automobile association prior to your intended journey.

The headquarters of the Czech Breakdown Service can be contacted any time of the day or night in Prague at Limuzská 12a, tel: (02) 154 or 773 4553. The service is free to those with the necessary insurance cover. The police number in Prague is 158, or you can call the tow-away service "Yellow Angel" on 154.

There are a number of 24-hour garages which will do quick repairs: Prague 10, Limuzská 12, tel: 773 455; Prague 4, Macurova 1640, tel: 791 9157; Prague 8, Lodzská 14, tel: 855 8381.

Members of the AA or other automobile association can contact: Autoturist, Prague 1, Ječná 40. Tel: 293 723.The agency Pragis Assistance, a non-stop emergency for tourists and motorised visitors, can be reached by calling (02) 758 115. Such services normally have people who speak English or German or at least can tell you the way to the next garage.

BY BUS

There is a large choice of organised coach tours from Germany and Austria. Such journeys generally offer two nights' accommodation as well as a tour programme. Czech buses regularly ply the routes from Frankfurt and Nuremberg, Munich and Vienna. An operator that travels from Frankfurt to Prague several times a week is: **Deutsche Touring**, Am Römerhof 17, 6000 Frankfurt 1. Tel: 069-79 03 248. If you are in Munich, a Czech operator runs a service to Prague every Saturday (returns Fridays). A single journey will cost you DM 57; tickets can be obtained from: **Autobus Oberbayern**, Lenbachplatz 1, 8000 München 2. Tel: 089-55 80 61.

From Vienna, there is a bus service running on Sunday and Wednesday to the health resort of Piest'any. It costs 215 Austrian Schillings; further information can be obtained from Čedok.

The terminus is the Prague-Florenc bus station. Information regarding national connections can be obtained daily 6am–8pm by calling this station on 221445-9 (only Czech spoken). The staff at **Autoturist** (Tel: 290 956, 295 096, 204 300) and **Bohemia Tours** (Tel: 232 3989) are better at coping with non-Czech speakers.

Information concerning both national and international bus connections from Prague can be obtained in Prague by calling: 221445. There are also bus services to Prague from all large cities in the Czech Republic (Brno, Plzeň) as well as Slovakia (Bratislava).

BY BOAT

It is possible for visitors to enter the Czech Republic by boat along the Elbe (Labe) River from Dresden via Schmilka-Hřensko. For those wishing to enter Slovakia by boat, Bratislava is neatly placed for the river ships plying between the Danube cities. From April to October, a daily hydrofoil service runs between Vienna and Bratislava. At other times of the year it runs only on Thursday, Friday and Saturday. For boat services from Vienna, contact: **DDSG-Danube Cruises**, Handelskai 254, A-1021 Vienna. Tel: 21-75-00.

Travel Essentials

For citizens of most European countries as well as the United States and Canada, no visa is required for either republic. Nationals of other countries are advised to contact their respective Czech or Slovak embassies or consulates for information (*see Useful Addresses*).

CUSTOMS

Customs controls are quite rigid. In order to avoid misunderstandings, bone up on regulations beforehand. Upon entering the Czech or Slovak republics, you'll be given a leaflet explaining the customs regulations. There is now a customs union operating between the Czech Republic and Slovakia. At the time of going to press, however, it was not clear how long the "open" rules on the border would last.

IMPORT

All items of personal use may be taken in duty-free; any electronic, photographic and filming equipment should be listed together with serial numbers and presented to the customs for confirmation. The list must be declared again upon departure. All items of personal use taken in to the country, must also be taken out.

You are allowed the following items for your own consumption (goods restricted to persons 18 years of age or older): 250 cigarettes, 50 cigars or 250 grams of tobacco, 2 litres of wine, 1 litre of spirits. Foreign visitors are permitted to take gifts into the country whose total value does not exceed 3,000 crowns.

EXPORT

The following items can be taken out of the republics duty-free: 2 litres of wine, 1 litre of spirits, 250 cigarettes, 50 cigars or 250 grams of tobacco, items purchased in the republic the total value of which does not exceed 1,000 crowns, articles that have been purchased in hard currency in TUZEX shops (make sure you save your receipts), cut glass, porcelain, souvenirs and other gifts when their value is not disproportionate to the amount of money you have officially changed and the reasonable cost of your staying in the country. Proof of such expenses can be provided by your hotel bill or an invoice from your travel agents.

In other cases, the export of goods can only go ahead with a customs permit, which costs between 3–150 percent of the price of the goods.

To export some items, it is not only necessary to have a permit but also to pay an additional fee. The list of these items, and of those whose export is forbidden, can be obtained at every border crossing. Antiques more than 50 years old can only be taken out with a special permit which can be very difficult to obtain.

MONEY MATTERS

CURRENCY

The unit of currency is the crown (koruna or Kčs), which is divided into 100 halér. There are 10, 20, 50, 100 and 1,000 crown notes and 1, 2, 5 and 100 crown coins as well as 5,10, 20 and 50 halér coins. In August 1992 the exchange rate was approximately 6 crowns to £1 sterling. There is no limit to the amount of hard currency that may be taken in or out of the country but crowns must not to taken in or out. In January 1993 the Slovaks started to print their own currency, the Slovak crown, which was to come into circulation as soon as possible. The exchange rate with the Czech crown was expected to be 1 to 1, at least for the immediate future.

Eurocheques can be exchanged everywhere in the country and even on the border for a maximum of 6,500 crowns. Sometimes what looks like an exceptionally good rate may be accompanied by an inordinately high commission. Travellers' cheques are only accepted by banks and credit cards only by certain shops and hotels. It is possible to change back your crowns, but in this case it is necessary to have an exchange receipt.

BLACK MARKET

While it is possible to exchange money on the black Market just about anywhere in Prague, the practice is officially forbidden and offenders will be prosecuted. One should therefore not be tempted by any offers, particularly as one might also end up being cheated: the worthless Polish Zloty notes look conspicuously like Czech crown notes.

EXCHANGE

In most shops and kiosks, payment is made in crowns. Shops and hotels accepting credit cards will normally have the requisite signs on the door.

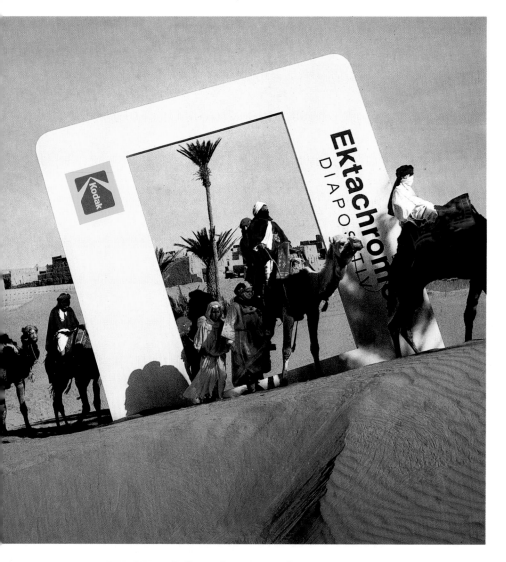

THE COLOUR OF LIFE.

A holiday may last just a week or so, but the memories of those happy, colourful days will last forever, because together you and Kodak Ektachrome films will capture, as large as life, the wondrous sights, the breathtaking scenery and the magical moments. For you to relive over and over again.

The Kodak Ektachrome range of slide films offers a choice of light source, speed and colour rendition and features extremely fine grain, very high sharpness and high resolving power.

Take home the real colour of life with Kodak Ektachrome films.

LIKE THIS?

OR LIKE THIS?

A KODAK FUN PANORAMIC CAMERA
BROADENS YOUR VIEW

The holiday you and your camera have been looking forward to all year; and a stunning panoramic view appears. "Fabulous", you think to yourself, "must take that one".

Unfortunately, your lens is just not wide enough. And three-in-a-row is a poor substitute.

That's when you take out your pocket-size, 'single use' Kodak Fun Panoramic Camera. A film and a camera, all in one, and it works miracles. You won't need to focus, you don't need special lenses. Just aim, click and... it's all yours. The total pictur

You take twelve panorami pictures with one Kodak Fun Pan ramic Camera. Then put the camer in for developing and printing.

Each print is 25 by 9 centimetre Excellent depth of field. True Kodak Gold colours.

The Kodak Fun Panoramic Camera itself goes bac to the factory, to be recycled. So that others too can capture one of those spectacular phooooooooooootoooooooooooooos.

International exchange rates are published daily in the newspapers and displayed at banks and exchange bureaux. There is no shortage of places to change your money in the city centre. Banks are normally open from 9am–noon and 2pm–4pm.

GETTING ACQUAINTED

GOVERNMENT & ECONOMY

From January 1993 the federal state of Czechoslovakia ceased to exist. The revolution which took place in November 1989 brought the old quarrels between the two republics once again to the forefront. Acting without the direct mandate of the people, strong political movements in both republics negotiated the division of the country during the course of 1992. The Czech Republic has opted to go for more rapid change under a programme of economic reforms based on the principle of the free market. Slovakia, on the other hand, has opted for more gradual reform; its economic problems are the greatest because the development of its industrial base occurred only relatively recently, and most of this at the whim of the central authorities in Prague. An example of the misplaced industrial strategy of the Communists are the steel works at Košice. But there are many who believe that economic prosperity in Slovakia will be even harder to achieve without the Czechs.

GEOGRAPHY

The **Czech Republic** encompasses an area of 78,864 sq km (30,450 square miles); **Slovakia** an area of 49,035 sq. km (18,933 square miles).

The republics form part of Central Europe and are situated at a latitude between 48°- 51° north and at a longitude between 12°-22° east. **Prague** is the Czech Republic's capital; **Bratislava** is the Capital of Slovakia. The Czech Republic shares its borders with Germany and Austria and Poland; Slovakia has Austria, Hungary, Poland and the Ukraine as neighbours. Brno is the capital of Moravia, which is part of the Czech Republic.

PRAGUE

The Bohemian metropolis is situated on the River Vltava (Moldau), spread out between seven hills. It lies between 176–397 metres (575–1,300 ft) above sea level, at 50° North and 14° East; about the same latitude as Frankfurt, Land's End and Vancouver. The city has a population of 1.2 million (1991) living over a total area of 497 sq. km (190 sq. miles). The historical part is made up of the Old Town (Staré Město), the New Town (Nové Město, Hradčany and the Lesser Quarter (Malá Strana), and boasts over 500 towers and steeples. Prague is divided into 56 districts which are administered from town halls.

BRATISLAVA

The capital of Slovakia lies on the Danube, where the river has cut a broad path through the southern tip of the Little Carpathian Mountains. The Hungarian border is only 20 km (13 miles) to the southeast, and Vienna 56 km (35 miles) to the west. Of particular interest to the visitor is the Old Town, containing a large number of remarkably beautiful buildings dating from a variety of periods. They reflect the city's fortunes through 11 centuries of direct or indirect Hungarian rule. The Castle stands some 80 metres (250 ft) above the river and dominates the Old Town from its position at the other side of the Vienna motorway. Bratislava is much smaller than Prague, with a population of just over 400,000, but is nonetheless a major road and rail junction as well as river port. This importance is likely to grow as the city establishes itself in its new role as capital of an independent Slovakia.

POPULATION

There are over 10 million people living in the Czech republic and around 5 million in Slovakia. There is a sizeable German minority living in the Czech Republic and the largest minority in Slovakia is that of the Hungarians living in the south and making up nearly 11 percent of the population. There are also Polish and Ukrainian minority groups.

CLIMATE

Hot summers punctuated by occasional periods rainfall and long, dry winters are typical of the moderate continental climate found in both the Czech and Slovak republics. Considerable climatic variations are due primarily to differences in elevations. For example, whereas the annual precipitation in Prague measures 476 millimetres, in the High Tatra the average amounts to 1,665 millimetres per year. From a climatic point of view, the best times to visit Prague are the spring and autumn. May, when the gardens and parks are in full bloom, heralds the classical music festival "Prague Spring", while the mild autumn with its stable weather offers the best prospects for extended strolls around town.

RELIGION

After World War II religion – as was its fate in other Communist countries – was stripped of all official significance. Religious services were only permitted within certain limitations. In the wake of 1989, however, chapels and churches throughout the two republics are in the process of being restored and revived.

Of the 18 different religious denominations represented in the country, Roman Catholicism has the most adherents, especially in Slovakia. There has recently been a large increase in the growth of sects, which attract young people in particular.

ELECTRICITY

The electricity supply in both republics is mainly AC 220 volts, although very occasionally there are outlets supplied with just 120 volts.

BUSINESS HOURS

Most **shops** are open weekdays 9am–7pm, with speciality stores open from 10am–6pm. Smaller shops frequently close their doors for a couple of hours during lunchtime. On Saturdays shops close at noon or 1pm with the exception of large department stores, which often remain open until 6pm.

BANKS & EXCHANGE BUREAUX

In general most banks are open 8am–noon Monday–Friday. Larger branches, however, may stay open until 5pm.

Exchange bureaux are open 8am until at least 7pm; some even remain open until 10pm. Most hotels will exchange money around the clock, but be aware that their rates are slightly higher than at a regular exchange bureau or bank.

HOLIDAYS

At least until the division of Czechoslovakia in January 1993, the dates of national holidays were as follows:
1 January: New Year's Day
Easter Monday
1 May: May Day
5 July: Feast Day of SS Cyril and Methodius
6 July: Anniversary of the death of Jan Hus
28 October: Day of the Republic
25–26 December: Christmas

Various Christian holidays, for example the Feast of Corpus Christi and The Assumption of the Virgin Mary, are celebrated in different regions but are not considered national holidays.

COMMUNICATIONS

THE MEDIA

NEWSPAPERS, MAGAZINES & BOOKS

Foreign news publications are available at the kiosks located in hotels as well as in many bookshops. It has recently become possible to purchase locally-published German and English language weekly papers in Prague and at various border-crossings. The Tourist Information Centre stocks restaurant guides and general information brochures in a number of different languages.

If you're looking for books written in German, French, Russian or English, your best bet is to make a trip to one of the international bookstores in Prague. An increasing amount of Western literature is also available in Bratislava.

RADIO & TELEVISION

Radio and television in the two republics are still under state control. Channel 4 (medium waveband 255) broadcasts an entertainment and information programme in both English and German. Radio 1 (the channel still has a tendency to float), organised and moderated by a young team in Prague, is one of the very first private radio stations to have emerged.

Since 1990 the television station OK 3 has been translating its programmes into German, English and French. In areas near to the borders it is also possible to tune into German and Austrian TV channels.

POSTAL SERVICES

Stamps can be bought in post offices or at newspaper kiosks. Enquire about current postal rates for letters and postcards once you're in the country as they tend to go up frequently. Within Europe a stamp for a postcard presently costs 3 crowns, a letter 5 crowns; sending mail overseas costs 6 crowns for a postcard and 10 crowns for a normal letter up to 10 grams.

In the larger centres, you'll find red letter boxes just about everywhere you look. The larger post offices are open from 8am–7 pm Monday–Friday and from 8am–noon Saturday; smaller post offices are generally only open from 8 am–1 or 3 pm at the latest Monday–Friday.

TELEPHONE

There are two different kinds of telephones in operation (provided they are not out of order). The first kind accepts only 1 crown coins and be used only for making local calls. Although the second type will accept 1, 2 and 5 crown coins, they are rather impractical for long-distance calls due to the fact you must constantly feed change into them. Taking this into account, if you want to make a long-distance call your best bet is to dial from either a post office or hotel: bear in mind that hotels will charge a 20–30 percent commission for this service.

TELEX, FAX & COMPUTER SERVICES

In most of the larger hotels you can both send and receive a fax or telex. In addition to this, many first-class hotels also offer office services which include access to various computers and printers. Telegrams can be sent from every post office, or over the phone (Tel: 127).

EMERGENCIES

CRIME

The crime rate is significantly lower than that of Western European countries. However since 1990 the incidence of offences like robbery, fraud and larceny have increased measurably, particularly in Prague. It's therefore a good idea to deposit any valuables in the hotel safe and if possible to park your car at a supervised car park.

In case of an emergency either consult with your hotel reception or contact the police directly by dialling 158.

If you should have the misfortune to either lose or have your personal documents stolen, get in touch immediately with your embassy representative (*see Useful Addresses*).

MEDICAL AID

Western visitors will be treated in any city clinic or hospital. All costs incurred – including those for medical treatment and hospital stays – must be paid in foreign currency. In contrast to this policy, medication is paid for in crowns. It's a good idea to take out a medical insurance policy that will cover you while travelling before setting out on your journey.

Emergency Numbers
Emergency 155
Ambulance 373, 333
Dental Emergency Service 374
Fire Brigade 150
Police 158

Chemist shops are open during normal business hours. In case of an emergency after hours, you'll find the address of the nearest chemist on emergency duty posted in the window. You should, of course, bring with you any special medications that you know or suspect you may need while visiting the country.

GETTING AROUND

Despite increasing competition from the private sector, for information about where to go and how to get there and bookings the national travel agency **Čedok** remains the largest and most efficient agency. It maintains several offices in **Prague**: Na příkopě 18, tel: 212 7111 (information, international tickets, exchange bureau); Vácslavské nám. 55, tel: 227 096 (tours and stays in the spa towns). In **Bratislava** the Čedok office is located at: Stúrova 13. Tel: 52 081, 55 280. After the division of the country in January 1993, Čedok was to continue its function in both republics; at the time of going to print, however, it was not known whether it would maintain its old name in Slovakia. For addresses of Čedok abroad, *see Useful Addresses*.

PIS, the Prague Information Service, also provides tourists with all necessary information. However, one does have to be patient. It may take a while for you to get someone who speaks English, and even then it is not guaranteed that this someone will be able to answer your questions; he may have to go and ask someone else. This kind of scenario is repeated almost everywhere in Prague, whether you're trying to hire a car or buy a ticket.

The PIS main office is located in the Hradčanská Metro station; more centrally situated is the office at Na příkopě 20. Tel: 544 444. In July 1992 the office on the Old Town Square still had no telephone; a further office is to be found on the B-level of the Main Station. The **Bratislava Information Service** (BIPS) has two branches, in Leningradská 1 (Tel: 33

715) and in Wolkrova 6 (Tel: 33 56 97). Here you can not only find out about everything that is going on in the city, but also book tours, interpreters and translators. Room reservations are possible through the Interhotel Bratislava, Hviezdoslavovo nám. 5 (Tel: 33 31 85-7, Fax: 31 46 45).

Detailed information can also be obtained from the private travel agencies (*see Useful Addresses*). Drivers can obtain service and information from: **Autoturist**, Opletalova 29. Tel: 223 544.

DOMESTIC FLIGHTS

From and to the Prague Airport:
Brno, Bratislava, Karlovy Vary, Košice, Ostrava, Sliač, Piešťany and Poprad. For information regarding flights not mentioned here contact a representative at one of the ČSA offices (*see Useful Addresses*).

Visitors must pay for domestic flights with foreign currency.
From and to Bratislava Airport:
There are flights offered daily to Prague, Košice and Poprad.

Note that since January 1993, flights operating between Slovakia and the Czech Republic have no longer been considered domestic, but international.

BY RAIL

Both the Czech Republic and Slovakia maintain a well-developed railway network. Riding either first or second class is quite comfortable as well as relatively inexpensive, even when punctuality may leave a little something to be desired.

Information regarding current prices is available directly at railway stations. Train timetable information can be obtained around the clock in Prague by dialling 02-26 49 30, or between 7am–3pm Monday–Friday on 02-235.

BY BOAT

During the summer tourist season (1 May–15 October) sightseeing cruises are offered along the Vltava (Moldau) departing from Prague. For further information call 02-293 803. You'll find tour boats moored near the Palacký Bridge. Tel: 298 309. During summer there are also steamers which depart from Bratislava and travel in the directions of Vienna and Budapest along the Danube River during the summer season. If you're really in a hurry, you can cruise these stretches in just a few hours on board a Raketa (Rocket) Boat. Because ticket prices and schedules change constantly, it's best to enquire directly at one of the local travel agencies or actually at the quayside.

PUBLIC TRANSPORT

CITY TRAFFIC

Tickets for the various means of public transport are available at kiosks and automatic ticket machines. Every time you transfer on either a bus or tram it is necessary to have a new ticket stamped. The exception to this rule is when you're using the underground system in Prague; here you can transfer as many times as you want within a time limit of 90 minutes. At the present all tickets cost 4 crowns, but children and senior citizens ride free.

Buses connect suburbs to city centres or provide services over longer distances. Prague is the only city with an underground system. Other cities rely on buses and trams, which although slow and antiquated do provide the visitor with the opportunity of to getting to know a city.

PRAGUE'S UNDERGROUND

The modern underground system links the centre with the suburbs and provides for convenient changes inside the city. It is a remarkably clean and quick means of public transport. The 3 lines have been developed with an eye towards expediency and by transferring it's possible to conveniently reach just about all the important tourist attractions located within the city. Underground stations are designated with a large "M" (*see map page 329*). Trains are in operation from 5 am until midnight. The 24-hour ticket for 8 crowns is an especially good deal for visitors intent on seeing as much as they can in a relatively short period of time. The transport system is bolstered by the old-fashioned trams, especially in the Nové Město. A good way to establish your bearings is to take a ride on the number 22.

TAXIS

With the exception of night buses, after midnight taxis constitute the sole form of public transport available (especially in Prague). You'll find a number of taxi stops in the Czech capital's city centre as well as in front of larger hotels. Even if the taxi driver seems reticent, insist that the taximeter is running before starting out. Official taxis can be recognised by their taxi signs and by the licence number posted inside the vehicle. They can be easily ordered by telephone in Prague under the number 02-203 941 or 202 951.
Brno: 05-25 404 and 25 606
Bratislava: 07-50 851 and 50 852
Drivers often turn out to be very friendly individuals with an intimate knowledge of their city. Many have other professions, but can earn more by driving taxis. They may be engaged for a half or entire day to drive passengers into and around the surrounding countryside. Having first established that the car is

in relatively good order, the driver seems to know his way around and can perhaps even speak a bit of English, it pays to do a little bargaining until a mutually acceptable price is reached.

PRIVATE TRANSPORT

DRIVING

There are about 73,793 km (46,120 miles) of road in the Czech and Slovak republics. Of these, only 403 km (252 miles) are motorways running between Prague, Brno and Bratislava, and Trnava. Main trunk roads are designated with the number 1–99. In both republics the use of double brake lights is prohibited and there is a mandatory seat-belt law. Traffic regulations are essentially similar to those in operation in other Western European countries. Keep in mind that it's a good idea to pay attention to no-parking signs as the traffic police will not hesitate to fine you should you ignore them.

RENTAL CARS

You can rent a car from the agencies Herz, Avis and Europcar at Pragocar, located in Prague. Credit cards are accepted and you have to be at least 21 years of age. It goes without saying that prospective drivers must be in possession of a valid driver's licence. Rental rates including mileage begin at around £20 per day.

For further information, contact Pragocar, Štěpánská 42, Prague 1. Tel: 02-235 2825, Telex: 122 641. In addition to this agency, it is also possible to rent a car from the Inter-Continental Hotel: To make a reservation tel: 02-231 9595 in Prague.

Those wishing to go with Avis or Hertz can book from home as this generally works out a lot cheaper. To rent a car you have to be at least 21 years of age and in possession of a valid driver's licence. Credit cards are accepted.

Pragocar with its fleet of Škodas offers the cheapest terms. The Škodas not only have the advantage that Czech mechanics can repair them in their sleep, but also that they are not the most desirable of booty for car thieves. The Škoda costs about £15 a day and 15 pence per kilometre, or about £30 a day for unlimited mileage; for a weekend from 1pm on Friday to 9am on Monday they come at the bargain price of around £50 including 600 free kilometres. Because Pragocar is also represented in Karlovy Vary (tel: 017/22833-4), you can pick up a car in one town and deposit it in the other. This is not possible with other agencies.
Pragocar: Ruzyně Airport, tel: 36 8 707; Hotel Atrium, tel: 284 2043; Hotel Intercontinental, tel: 231 9595; Hotel Forum, tel: 419 0213; Opletalova Street 33, tel: 222 324; Pankráč, tel: 692 2875.
Czech Auto Rent: also offer cheap deals. Hotel Palace, Panská 12, tel: 236 1637; Hotel Prezident Nám. Curieových 100, tel: 231 4812 ext: 119.
Hertz: Ruzyně Airport, tel: 312 0717; Hotel Atrium, tel: 284 1111; Karlovo nám, tel: 290 122.
Avis: Hotel Atrium, tel: 284 2043.

HITCHHIKING

Hitchhiking is a popular form of getting around especially among younger people. Soldiers also make use of this cheap mode of transport. Both local and foreign hitchhikers are a common sight on the roads and are quickly offered a ride by passing motorists.

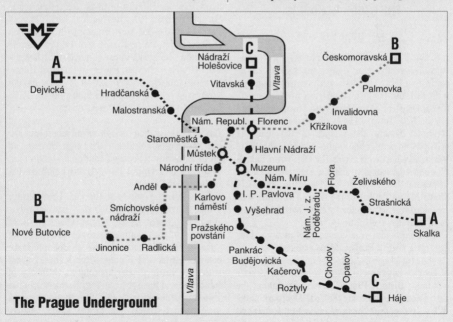

The Prague Underground

THINGS TO DO

Sport Tourist and various other tour agencies organise a variety of riding, canoe, ski and hiking programmes in nearly every region of both the Czech and Slovak republics. For further information concerning outward-bound activities, *see Sport section*. Details are available at any Čedok agency (*see Useful Addresses*).

TOUR GUIDES & INTERPRETERS

Čedok agencies and the various tourist information centres located in individual cities (for example PIS in Prague and BIPS in Bratislava) all offer foreign language-speaking tour guides to both travel groups as well as to independent travellers for day excursions or several-day trips. They can also furnish you with an interpreter or translator upon request. It is not unusual in Prague to "rent" a tour guide who then accompanies you on foot through the city. The price for an hour of this particular kind of service is about 70 crowns per person.

THE CZECH REPUBLIC

PRAGUE

It is not difficult to find your bearings in Prague, especially as the most important sights can be reached on foot. The city's small centre (Prague 1) is divided into the historic quarters of Malá Strana (Lesser Quarter), Staré Město (Old Town), and Nové Město (New Town). The latter is centred around Wenceslas Square and extends to the road Na příkopě. Adjacent and to the north is the Staré Město, which extends across the Old Town Square (Staroměstské náměstí) and the right bank of the Vltava and the Charles Bridge. The picturesque Malá Strana lies on the left of the river. Two other self-contained districts are the Josefov (Jewish Quarter) and Hradčany, the Castle Quarter.

It's a good idea to allow yourself at least three days for a visit to Prague. Many agencies including the state travel agency Čedok not only organise tours of the city but cultural events as well. The 3-hour city tour "Historic Prague" is run throughout the year. Departure points are the Čedok bus park in the Bílkova 6 (opposite the Intercontinental Hotel) and

the hotels Panorama, Forum and Atrium.

Private tours of the city are organised by the Prague Information service (PIS), as well as travel agencies AVE and Pragotour (*see Useful Addresses*), and tours of Hradčany are organised by Informacní stredisko prazského hradu, Prague 1 (Hradcany), Vikárska 37 (on the northern side of St Vitus' cathedral); Tel: 2101/3368.

The following daily tour programme is designed to aid visitors who are only in Prague for short stay but who prefer to make their own way around rather than join an organised tour.

Day 1: We suggest that your first day's sightseeing is spent strolling through the winding streets and alleyways of the Old Town to the Jewish Cemetery and the Old Town Square. The day can be concluded not far from the Powder Tower with a classy dinner at the Hotel Paříž.

The tour commences at Wenceslas Square and leads via the Na můstku right into the Old Town, and the main sights to be seen here are as follows: the Flea Market – Old Town Hall – Old Town Square with the Jan Hus Monument – Karlova ulice – Clam-Gallas Palais – Husova ulice – Bethlehem Chapel – Náprstkova ulice – Bank of the Vltava with the Smetana Museum – Old Town Bridge Tower and the Crusaders' Church – Clementinum and the Church of St Saviour – Platnéřska ulice – Maiselova ulice – Jewish quarter with the old Jewish Cemetery, Klaus Synagogue, Old-New Synagogue and the Jewish Town Hall.

The visitor can now pause for lunch and has the choice between the Kosher restaurant in the former lower council chamber of the Town Hall, the wine bar U Golema (Maiselova 8) or the restaurant U Barona (Pařížská 19). After lunch go back along the Pařížská to the Old Town Square with the Church of St Nicholas, Palais Kinsky and the Týn Church. Then into Štupartská ulice – Church of St James – Celetná ulice – Powder Tower – Municipal House. Reward yourself at the end of a long day of sightseeing with a sumptuous dinner in the Paříž Restaurant (tel: 232 2051) next door.

Day 2: The second day of sightseeing might lead you over the Charles's Bridge to the Lesser Quarter and up to Hradčany. This day's tour could be brought to a close in a typical Lesser Quarter pub serving both beer and meals.

The starting point is at the Old Town Bridge Tower. Having walked across the Charles Bridge, you'll be greeted by the Lesser Quarter Bridge Towers. The tour continues into the Lázeňská ulice – the Church of St Mary in Chains – Velkopřevorské náměstí – Island of Kampa – the Maltese Square with the Nostiz Palais (housing the Ministry of Education and the Arts), and into Karmelitská ulice with the Vrtbovsky palác (No. 25). Along Mostecká ulice (Bridge Street) and to the Lesser Quarter

Square with the Church of St Nicholas. Here it's time for a break, before the walk up to the castle. There are the two pubs, the U Glaubiců and the U Schnellů, or the café in the middle of the square.

Then into the Neruda Alley and up to the Hradčanské náměstí and on: Loretánská ulice – Loreto Shrine – Novy Svět – back to Schwarzenberg Palais – Archbishops' Palace – Prague Castle with St Vitus' Cathedral and the Royal Palace – St George's Basilica – Mihulka Tower – Golden Alley – Lobkovic Palais – Black Tower – Old Castle Steps – Valdštejnská ulice. And there we reach the Valdštejnská Hospoda (Tomášská 16, tel: 536 195), our tip for a hearty Bohemian meal. If you don't get a place there, we suggest you go down the Tomášská to the Lesser Quarter Square, turn left at the corner to arrive at the venerable pub U Svatého Tomáše in Latenská 12, (tel: 530 064).

Day 3: The third day's excursion could take you across Wenceslas Square and the New Town, with the National Theatre, the Vltava Quay and Charles Square. Dinner is a choice of either good, solid Bohemian food in U Fleků, or refined Russian dining in the Volha.

The tour begins at the equestrian statue of St Wenceslas in front of the National Museum and continues down Wenceslas Square past the classic Art Nouveau hotels – Evropa, Zlatá Husa, and Ambassador – the Alfa Palais (No. 28) and the Peterka House (No. 12) to the Koruna Palace at the end. Do an about-face and amble back along the other side of the square until you've reached about the half-way point, and then left into the Jindrísska ulice with the Hotel Palace; then along the Panská ulice – Na příkopě – Powder Tower and back to Wenceslas Square. Then continue into the Jungmannovo náměstí with the Church of St Mary of the Snows – Národní třída with the Maj department store – Kanka House (No. 16) and the Church of St Ursula (No. 8). For lunch, the monastery wine cellar offers a selection of tasty wines and dishes, or failing that there is the pub U Medvídků just around the corner (Na Perštyně 7, opposite the Maj department store).

The end of the Národní třída is completely dominated by the National Theatre. The Café Slávia stands opposite. Now walk upstream along the bank of the Vltava. Our route: Slavic Island – Mánes House – Jiráskův Bridge where the Vltava cruisers pull in and where there is a small pub with terrace called "Vltava" – Resslova ulice – the Church of St Wenceslas – the Church of SS Cyril and Methodius Church – Charles Square with the "Faust House"; the Church of St John on the Rocks is located to the south, opposite the Emmaus Monastery; back via the Church of St Ignatius and the New Town Hall which provides a counterpoint to the Faust House.

Especially in the late afternoon the U Fleků is the perfect place to sit back and take the load off your feet (turn left by the Town Hall into the Myslíkova and take the second right into the Křemencova). But

for those who don't like the noise here, perhaps a better choice is the Volha (Myslíkova 14, tel: 296 406. Open: 11am–12 midnight).

FURTHER SIGHTS

Apart from visiting its historical sights, there are plenty more interesting things to see in Prague. Here are some proposals:

Prague Zoo is situated in Prague 7, Troja, and can be reached by the Metro line C, getting out at the station Nádrazí Holesovice and continuing on the 112 bus. A visit to the attractive zoo can also take in the nearby Troja Castle. Founded in 1931, today the zoo is home to 2,000 animals of 600 species. The breeding of the famous Przewalski horse is of international importance: Prazská zoologická zahrada, Prague 7 Troja, U Trojského zámku 3. Opening hours: October–March 7am–4pm; April 7am–5pm; May 7am–6pm; June–September 7am–7pm.

The Botanical Gardens are part of the university and are to be found in the Nové Město not far from the Church of St Nepomuk on the Rocks: Botanická zahrada, Prague 1, Na slupi. Open: 7am–7pm.

Prague Observatory, Prague 1, Petřín 205 (next to the the cable car station on the Petřín Hill. Open: daily except Monday: January, February, October, November, December 6–8pm; March, September 7–9pm; April, August 8–10pm; May, June, July 9–11pm.

AROUND PRAGUE

Čedok organises a number of day-long excursions into the environs of Prague. The tours include: Castles in Bohemia, Southern Bohemia, Gothic architectural jewels in Bohemia, Attractive Central Bohemia, Vineyards of Bohemia and cruises on the Vltava. The buses depart from the Panorama Hotel at 8am, the Forum Hotel at 8.10am, the Atrium Hotel at 8.20am and from Čedok, Bílkova 6 at 8.40am. Tickets may be purchased from the hotel receptions as well as from Čedok: Prague 1, Bílkova 6, tel: 231 8855; Na příkopě 18, tel: 212 7111; Prague Ruzyně Airport, tel: 367 802.

For those with their own car there is a host of attractions in the vicinity of the Czech capital, all of which are easy to reach. Here is a selection:

Průhonice: Renaissance palace with botanical garden, reached via the motorway to Brno. The palace contains one of the largest herbarium collections in the world.

Konopiště: Palace with rose garden, bathing pool and English-style park. The original 14th-century castle was converted in the 18th century and served as a hunting lodge for the Austrian archduke Franz Ferdinand until his assassination in Sarajevo. There is a weapons collection with over 5,000 pieces.

Slapy Dam: A popular summer excursion for the people of Prague, located in the Vltava valley to the south of the city.

Karlštejn: Built by Charles IV in 1348 as the representative residence of the king and the depository of the crown jewels. Situated to the southwest of Prague, it is considered to be one of the most beautiful castles in Europe. It can be reached from the motorway in the direction of Plzeň as far as Baroun.

Koněprusy: Caverns near Karlštejn castle, discovered in 1950. Remains of prehistoric man as well as a coin forging workshop dating from the 15th century.

Křivoklát: 15th-century castle set in an extensive area of forest which has been adopted by UNESCO in the programme "Man and the Biosphere". In the summer there are performances of music and theatre.

Rakovník: One of the oldest towns in Central Bohemia in the middle of the hop growing area. Its historic centre contains a number of important monuments.

Kladno: Historic mining town to the northwest of Prague (past Ruzyně Airport). There is a baroque palace with a museum of mining.

Lidice: A memorial to Nazi massacre of 1942 in which all menfolk were shot and women rounded up and taken away to Ravensbrück concentration camp. The surviving children were dispersed through Germany to be renamed and raised as Germans. In an action that formed part of the Germans' brutal reprisals for the assassination of the deputy leader of the SS, Reinhard "the hangman" Heydrich, by the Resistance, the village was burned to the ground. Situated between Prague and Ladno.

Veltrusy: Baroque Palace with original interior. It contains a collection of Asian porcelain, crystal and tapestries. It can be reached by following the E 55 in the direction of Teplice.
Nearby is the village of **Nelahzeves** with the house in which Antonín Dvořák was born.

Mělník: A wine producing town at the confluence of the Vltava and the Labe (Elbe), whose origins go back to the 9th century.

Mladá Boleslav: Home of Škoda cars. Přemyslid castle dating from the 10th century. Ancient centre containing interesting examples of avant-garde blocks of flats from the 1930s. It lies to the northeast of Prague along the E 65.

Přerov nad Labem: Open air museum of vernacular architecture. Located to the east of Prague on the E 67 towards Poděbrady.

Kutná hora (Kuttenberg): In the 13th and 14th century this town became the economic centre of Bohemia on account of its silver mines, and was the site of the royal mint. The Brass Music Festival "Kmochs Kolín" takes place here in June. The imposing Church of St Barbara was designed by Peter Parler. It is situated some 10 miles to the southeast of Kolín.

Český Sternberk: One of the best preserved castles in the country, dating from the 13th century. Its location on a clifftop above the River Sazava made it impregnable for centuries. Musical performances are held here in the summer. It lies to the southeast of Prague along the E 50.

BRNO

Visitors based in the Moravian capital of Brno have a number of interesting sights in the vicinity, which include:

Slavkov (Austerlitz): It was here, in 1805, that Napoleon defeated the Austrians under Franz I and the Russians under Alexander I at the so-called "Battle of the Three Emperors".

Pernštejn Castle: This fairy-tale castle is one of the largest and best-preserved in the entire Czech Republic.

Moravian Karst: An extensive system of caves, grottoes and underground streams, most impressive around Blansko in the north of the region and including the spectacular Macocha Abyss.

SLOVAKIA

BRATISLAVA

Bounded by the Danube to the South, the historical city centre is easy to get around. The urban motorway, which connects the city to Vienna in the west, Brno and Prague in the north and Central Slovakia in the east, divides the Old Town from the Castle. But it can be crossed by bridges and subways and so both parts of the city can easily be explored on foot. For trips out to the suburbs there are trams and trolley buses. One should allow at least two days to see the sights of Bratislava. We propose two round tours of the Old Town, followed by a stroll through the New Town.

Day 1: From St Michael's Gate to the Cathedral and up to the Castle. From the gate, walk up the Michalská, past the University Library to arrive in the Jiáskova with the Palais Leopold de Pauli and the Palais of Marshal Pálffy, as well as the Academia Istropolitana. At the rococo palace of Count Erdödy turn right into the Nálepkova as far as St Martin's Cathedral. The castle is reached via its impressive staircase.

Return via the north side of the cathedral through the Kapitulská with the Provost's Palais (no 19), the Collegium Emmericanum and the Canon's House. There is a good fish restaurant in the Prepoštská, the U zlatého kapra (the Golden Carp). Pass the Convent of St Clare and turn right through the narrow Bastová to arrive at St Michael's Gate once again.

Day 2: From St Michael's Gate via the Town Hall and the Bishop's Palace to the Danube Promenade. Opposite the Baštová, the narrow Zámočnická leads to the eastern part of the Old Town. We come to the Dibrovo náměští with the Franciscan Church and the Palais Mirbach. From there the route continues to

THE KODAK GOLD GUIDE TO BETTER PICTURES.

Good photography is not difficult. Use these practical hints and Kodak Gold II Film: then notice the improvement.

Move in close. Get close enough to capture only the important elements.

Frame your Pictures. Look out for natural frames such as archways or tree branches to add an interesting foreground. Frames help create a sensation of depth and direct attention into the picture.

One centre of interest. Ensure you have one focus of interest and avoid distracting features that can confuse the viewer.

Use leading lines. Leading lines direct attention to your subject i.e. — a stream, a fence, a pathway; or the less obvious such as light beams or shadows.

Maintain activity. Pictures are more appealing if the subject is involved in some natural action.

Keep within the flash range. Ensure subject is within flash range for your camera (generally 4 metres). With groups make sure everyone is the same distance from the camera to receive the same amount of light.

Check the light direction. People tend to squint in bright direct light. Light from the side creates highlights and shadows that reveal texture and help to show the shapes of the subject. If shooting into direct sunlight fill-in flash can be effective to light the subject from the front.

CHOOSING YOUR KODAK GOLD II FILM.

Choosing the correct speed of colour print film for the type of photographs you will be taking is essential to achieve the best colourful results.

Basically the more intricate your needs in terms of capturing speed or low-light situations the higher speed film you require.

Kodak Gold II 100. Use in bright outdoor light or indoors with electronic flash. Fine grain, ideal for enlargements and close-ups. Ideal for beaches, snow scenes and posed shots.

Kodak Gold II 200. A multipurpose film for general lighting conditions and slow to moderate action. Recommended for automatic 35mm cameras. Ideal for walks, bike rides and parties.

Kodak Gold II 400. Provides the best colour accuracy as well as the richest, most saturated colours of any 400 speed film. Outstanding flash-taking capabilities for low-light and fast-action situations; excellent exposure latitude. Ideal for outdoor or well-lit indoor sports, stage shows or sunsets.

INSIGHT GUIDES

COLORSET NUMBERS

You'll find the colorset number on the spine of each Insight Guide.

the Hlavné námestí, with the Jesuit Church, the Town Hall and the Fountain of Roland. The Kostolná ulice leads to the Bishop's Palace. Further towards the Danube is the Slovakian National Theatre and one block further is the Danube Promenade with the Slovakian National Gallery and the Slovakian National Museum.

Day 3: A stroll through the New Town. In the northeast of the Old Town is the Square of the Slovakian National Uprising, the actual city centre. It is bounded in the south by Kiev Square and in the north by the Poštová pedestrian precinct, which is crossed by the Obchodná shopping street. From the Hotel Forum one can visit the elgant villa district of Bratislava, with fine late-19th century houses and the Slavín Monument. The hill provides beautiful views of the city and the Danube Valley.

AROUND BRATISLAVA

The environs of Bratislava offer a number of attractions, of which the following are only a selection:
Devín Castle: Situated 10 km (6 miles) to the west of the city at the confluence of the Morava and the Danube, this famous ruin can also be reached by river boat. There has been a castle on the site ever since the days of the Kingdom of Great Moravia. The present building dates from the 13th century, and the hill on which it stands offers magnificent views of the surrounding countryside. It is the site of an annual folklore festival held in July.
Senec: Lying 24 km (15 miles) to the east of Bratislava on the main road nr. 61, this is a popular resort with its own artificial lake. On the way is the excellently preserved baroque palace at Bernolákovo.
Železná studnička: A centuries-old mineral spa situated 5 km (3 miles) to the north of Bratislava.
Stupava: 18 km (11 miles) to the north of the city, Stupava boasts a Renaissance palace as well as a fascinating pottery museum and the remains of a Roman camp.
Malé Karpaty (Little Carpathians): These hills are famous for the cultivation of wine. Wine villages are strung out along the road nr. 502, the most famous of which are Juri pri Bratislave with its Gothic church of St George, Pezinok with its Gothic parish church and Renaissance palace, and Modra with its vintners' school and research institute.
Komárno: Situated at the confluence of the Váh and the Danube 104 km (65 miles) to the southeast of Bratislava, this old port is well worth a visit on account of its beautiful old town and impressive fortifications, which are best viewed from the river.

HEALTH CURES

The Bohemian spas were famous as long ago as the Middle Ages. The reputation of Bohemia in this regard is based on the large number of medicinal springs (over 3,000) and mineral waters, therapeutic mud and natural vapours. In the Czech and Slovak republics today there are a total of 57 recognised health spas, 36 of which are in Bohemia and Moravia and 21 in Slovakia. They all have in common a long spa tradition, offering the very latest healing procedures and a good healthy climate.

High season is from 1 May–30 September; the off season from 1 March–30 April and 1 October–14 November; the winter season from 15 November–28 February (Christmas and New Year's Day excluded). Listed are the major spas (together with the conditions they treat):

THE CZECH REPUBLIC

Karlovy Vary (Western Bohemia): stomach and intestinal ailments, gall-bladder trouble, diabetes.
Mariánské Lázně (Western Bohemia): kidney and urinary disorders, metabolic disease (gout and diabetes), disorders of the digestion system, general problems with the respiratory tracts, diseases of the spine.
Jáchymov (Western Bohemia): diseases of the spine and locomotor system, neuropathy, metabolic disease (gout).
Frantiskovy Lázně (Western Bohemia): gynaeco-logical diseases.
Poděbrady (Central Bohemia): heart problems and circulatory disturbance (especially for children).
Teplice (Northern Bohemia): problems with the locomotor system, vascular disease.
Třeboň (Southern Bohemia): problems with the locomotor system.
Luhačovice (Moravia): general problems with the respiratory tracts, disorders of the digestion system, diabetes.

SLOVAKIA

Piešťany: chronic rheumatism, neuropathy.
Trenčianské Teplice: problems with the locomotor system.
Štrbské Pleso (in the High Tatra): asthma and other allergies.
Bardejovské Kúpele: disorders of the digestion system, general problems with the respiratory tracts, metabolic diseases.
Sliac: heart problems and circulatory disturbance.
Nový Smokovec: general problems with the respira-tory tracts.

Apart from the Čedok offices, further information about the individual spas can be obtained from: **Balnea**, Pařížská 1, Prague 1. Tel: 232 3767 or 292 868; **Slovakoterma**, Radlinského 13, Bratislava.

A visit to the Czech Republic or Slovakia could be combined with a visit to one of the countless festivals or other cultural events that take place throughout the year. Here is a selection (approx. dates only):

THE CZECH REPUBLIC

March, Karlovy Vary: Jazz Festival.

May–September, Karlovy Vary: Colonnade Concerts (daily except Mondays).

April, Prague: Interkamera – an international photography and technology exhibition.

May/June, Prague: Prague Spring Music Festival.

May–August, Luhačovice: Music Spring; International Music Summer.

June, Prague: Concertino Praga – debut performances from a variety of young, talented musicians.

May, July, Mariánské Lázně: International Music Festival

June, Kolín/Central Bohemia: International Brass Music Festival "Kmochs Kolín".

June, Poděbrady: International Brass Band Festival.

June, Teplice: Shostakovich Festival.

June (end of the month), Strakonitz/Bohemian Forest: Folklore Festival.

June–July, Stražnice/Southern Moravia: International meeting of various folk groups, in ethnic costume, celebrated by traditional dancing and music.

June–July, Luhačovice: Janáček Festival.

June–September, Teplice: Castle Music

July, Karlovy Vary: International Film Festival – the traditional forum for Eastern European films.

July, Chrudim/Eastern Bohemia: Puppet Festival.

July, Znojmo/Southern Moravia: Royal Festival – medieval tournaments and events.

July, Zelezný Brod/Eastern Bohemia: Folklore Festival.

July–August, Třeboň: Culture Summer.

August, Mariánské Lázně: Chopin Festival

August, Domažlice/Western Bohemia: Chode Festival, a festival of the culturally independent border people with dancing, music and even bagpipes.

August, Mariánské Lázně: Chopin Music Festival.

September (the middle of the month), Žatec/Northern Bohemia: Žatec Hops Festival.

September, Karlovy Vary: Antonín Dvořák Autumn Festival.

September/October, Teplice: Beethoven Festival.

September/October, Namest na Hane/Northern Moravia: Harvest Festival.

October, Jáchymov: Music Festival.

October, Pardubice/Eastern Bohemia: Big international steeplechase – one of the most gruelling and notorious steeplechase competitions in the world.

December/January, Prague: Prague Winter – a theatre and music festival.

June (the second half), Roznava/Eastern Slovakia: Hungarian Folklore Festival.

June (end of the month), Svidník/Eastern Slovakia: Ukrainian Festival.

June (last weekend of the month), Terchova/Malá Fatra: Janosik Festival in commemoration of the man referred to as the Slovakian Robin Hood.

July/August, Vychodna/Central Slovakia: The most colourful and lively festival of ethnic costumes and folklore throughout all of Slovakia.

October (end of the month), Bratislava: International Jazz Festival.

FOOD DIGEST

The cultural differences between the Czech Republic and Slovakia were largely created by the outside influences that historically dominated the respective regions – the primarily Habsburg-Germanic influence on the Czechs and Moravians as opposed to the Magyar-Hungarian influence on the Slovaks. The division is reflected in the food, although the Bohemian, Moravian and Slovakian cuisines can all be characterised by the word "hearty". The national Czech dish is roast pork served with cabbage and dumplings. Main meals customarily begin with a bowl of soup, followed by a hefty main course including meat and is finished off with pudding, fruit or a soufflé-like concoction accompanied by a sweet sauce. A variety of duck and fish dishes number among the national culinary specialities. In Slovakia goulash features prominently, alongside other typically Hungarian specialities. While the Bohemians tend to drink beer (*pivo*) with their meals, the people of Slovakia and Moravia prefer wine produced within their particular regions. The finishing touch to an enjoyable meal is frequently a good swig of Becherovka or Slivovitz.

As eating and drinking are significant activities for native Czechs and Slovaks, the portions served in restaurants are correspondingly large – and relatively inexpensive.

Since the beginning of 1991 many restaurants have fallen into private hands. In conjunction with this development and in contrast to nationally-owned dining establishments, prices have become competitive. A higher bill is offset by more attentive service. Despite the fact that tips are generally included in the price of a meal, it is customary to round up the total when you settle the bill. Because prices are comparatively low, overly enthusiastic tourists have a tendency to leave more than a 100 percent tip! This gesture, though generous, is inappropriate and locals will not be pleased.

No matter where you want to dine, it's wise to call in advance and reserve a table.

PRAGUE

There's no question about it: in Prague you can eat a lot and sometimes even quite well. Fans of plain old home-cooking frequently consume roast pork and beef, goulash and duck served with either dumplings or cabbage twice a day. A main dish ordered in a beer pub or in one of the relatively inexpensive wine bars/*vinarna* (serve more than just wine) will seldom cost more than about £2. The meal is naturally washed down with a glass or more of beer on tap. Apart from ready-meals (*hotová jídla*), the menu also includes "meals to order" (*jídla na objednávku*) such as steaks and roasts. These are freshly prepared and tend to be expensive.

RESTAURANTS

Apart from the pubs and wine bars (listed in separate sections), the city has many excellent restaurants. The following is a list of establishments in the different districts of the city where we found particularly good food and value for money.

LESSER QUARTER

Valdštejnská hospoda, (Waldstein Inn), Prague 1, Tomášská 16. Tel: 536 195. At the foot of Hradčany. Traditional decor, game specialities, not expensive. Open daily 11am–3pm, 6–10.30pm.
U tři pštrosů, Dražického nám. 12. Tel: 536 007. Next to the Charles Bridge. Traditional decor and Bohemian cuisine, upper price range. Open daily 11am–3pm, 6–11pm.
U čerta, Narudova 4. Tel: 530 975. Stylish, with waiters who speak English and German, reasonably priced. Open: daily noon–3.30pm, 6–11pm.
U Malfrů, Malézké nám. 11. Tel: 531 883. French restaurant since 1543 serving superb cuisine. French Prices. Open: daily 9am–2am.
Nebozízek, Petřínské sady 411. Tel: 537 905. At the middle station of the funicular up Petřín Hill. Large terrace, elegant restaurant with a view of the Vltava and the Old Town.

OLD TOWN

U tři Gracii, Novotného lávka 5. Tel: 265 457. Moravian wines and Moravian cuisine.
Ve Skořepce, Skořepka 1. Tel: 228 081. Traditional atmosphere, reasonably priced. Open: Monday–Friday 11am–10pm, Saturday 11am–8pm. Closed: Sunday.

U sedmi andělu, Jilská 20. Tel: 266 355. Antique interior, middle of the price range. Open: daily except Monday noon–3pm, 6–11pm.
U Rudolfa II., Maiselova 5. Tel: 232 2671. The smallest of Prague's wine bars with good food based on traditional recipes. Affordable. Open: daily 10am–10pm.
Paříž, U Obecního domu (directly behind the Powder Tower). Tel: 232 2051. A beautifully restored restaurant with Art Nouveau furnishings. Upper price category.
Opera Grill, Karoliny Světlé 35. Tel: 265 508. International cuisine. Open: daily except Saturday and Sunday 7pm–2am.
U Sixtů, Celetná 2. Tel: 236 7980. Traditional Bohemian cuisine in a cellar. Open: daily noon–1am.
U zlaté Studny, Karlova 2. Tel: 220 593. Moravian wines and cuisine. Open: daily 11am–3pm, 5pm–midnight.

NEW TOWN

Adria, Národní třída 40 (on Jungmann Square). Tel: 62637. Summer terrace but still reasonable. A café adjacent. Open: daily 10am–10pm.
Volha, Myslíkova 14. Tel: 296 406. Excellent cuisine from the Black Sea/Caucasus region. Middle of the price range. Open: daily except Saturday and Sunday 11am–midnight.
Vltava, Rašinovo nábřeží (right bank of the Vltava where the cruisers pull in). Tel: 94964. Terrace on the Vltava and a cosy room for bad weather. Reasonably priced and generous portions. Open: daily 11am–10pm.

INTERNATIONAL RESTAURANTS

Alex, Prague 1, Revoluční 1. Tel: 231 4489. German specialities. Open: daily 11am–1am.
ASIA, Letohradská 50, Prague 7. Tel: 370 215. Asian cuisine. Open: 11am–11pm. Closed: Saturday and Sunday.
Berjozka, Prague 1, Železná 24. Tel: 223 822. Russian specialities. Open: Monday–Saturday 11am–11pm.
Čínská restaurace, Vodičkova 19, Prague 1. Tel: 262 697. Chinese cuisine. Open: noon–3pm, 6am–11pm. Closed: Sunday.
Gruzia, Prague 1, Na příkopě 29. Specialities from Gruzinskaya. Open: daily 11am–7pm and 6pm–1am.
Habana, Prague 1, V Jámě 8. Tel: 260 164. Specialities from the Caribbean and Cuban cocktails. Open: noon–4pm and 6pm–midnight. Closed: Sunday.
Jadran, Prague 1, Mostecká 21. Tel: 534 671. Balkan specialities and wines. Open: daily 11am–10pm.
Jewish Restaurant, Prague 1, Maiselova 18.
Mayur, Prague 1, Štěpanská 61. Tel: 236 9922. Indian specialities. Open: noon–4pm, 6–11pm. Closed: Sunday.

Pampa, Prague 6, Karlovarská 1/4. Tel: 301 7731. Argentinian restaurant. Open: noon–4pm, 5.30pm–midnight. Closed: Sunday.

Peking, Legerova 64, Prague 2. Tel: 293 531. Chinese cuisine. Open: 11.30am–3pm, 5.30–11pm. Closed: Sunday.

Pelikán, Prague 1, Na příkopě 7. Tel: 220 782. Elegant surroundings in the pedestrian precinct. Open: daily 11am–11.30pm.

Praha Expo 58, Prague 7, Letenské sady 1500. Tel: 377 339. Beautiful view of the Vltava and the Old Town; terrace café in the summer. Open: daily 1.30–3pm, 6–11pm.

Rostov, Prague 1, Václavské nám. 21. Tel: 262 469. Bohemian specialities, tables outside in the summer. Open: daily 1–3.30pm, 5–11pm.

Rotisserie, Prague 1, Mikulandská 6. Tel: 206 826. The menu includes a variety of steaks. Open: 11.30am–3.30pm, 5.30–11.30pm. Closed: Sunday.

Savarin, Prague 1, Na příkopě 10 (in the arcade). Tel: 22 20 66.

Sofia, Prague 1, Václavské nám. 33. Tel: 264 986. Balkan specialities. Open: daily 11.30am–3pm, 6–11pm.

Thang Long, Dukelských hrdinů 48, Prague 7. Tel: 806 541. Vietnamese cuisine. Open: daily noon–3pm, 5–11pm.

Trattoria Viola, Národní 7, Prague 1. Tel: 266 732. Italian cuisine. Open: daily 11.30am–3pm, 5.30–11pm. Closed: Saturday and Sunday during July and August.

BOHEMIAN SPECIALTIES

Barrandov Terraces, Prague 5, Barrandovská 171. Tel: 545 309, 545 409.

Černý kůň (Black Horse), Prague 1, Vodičkova 36. Tel: 262 697. Traditional Prague cuisine, Pilsner beer. Open: daily 11am–1pm.

Halali-Grill, Prague 1, Václavské nám. 5. Tel: 221 351. Game dishes.

Hanavsky Pavillon, Prague 7, Letenské sady 173. Tel: 325 792. Open: daily 8.30pm–12.05am, terrace in summer noon–8.30pm.

Lví dvůr (Lion's Den), Prague 1, U prašného mostu 6, (in the Prague Castle complex). Tel: 535 386. Open: 10am–5pm. Closed: Monday.

Myslivna, Prague 3, Jagellonská 21. Tel: 277 416. Game specialities. Open: daily 11am–11pm.

Obecní dům (Municipal House), Prague 1, Nám. Republiky 1090. Tel: 231 9754. French restaurant in Art Nouveau, Pilsner Bier. Open: daily 11am–11pm.

Rybárna (fish restaurant), Prague 1, Václavské nám. 43. Tel: 227 823. Open: 11am–10pm. Closed: Sunday.

Savarin, Prague 1, Na příkopě 10 (in the arcade). Tel: 222 066.

Slavie, Prague 1, Narodní 1. Tel: 265 760. Nextdoor to Prague's most famous coffeehouse the Slavin. Open: daily 11am–11pm.

Slovanský dům (Slavic House), Prague 1, Na příkopě 10. Tel: 224 851. Largest restaurant complex in Prague. Open: 11am–midnight. Closed: Sunday.

Theatre Restaurant, Prague 1, Národní 6 (National Theatre). Open: daily 11am–4pm, 5pm–midnight.

U kalicha (The Chalice), Na Bojišti 12, Prague 2. Tel: 290 701. Open: daily 11am–11pm. A venerable institution. Many tourists.

U krále brabantského (The King of Brabant), Prague 1, Thunovská 15. Tel: 539 975. A good stock of wine. Open: 1–11pm. Closed: Sunday.

U Lorety, Prague 1, Loretanské nám. 8. Tel: 536 025. Elegant Prague restaurant opposite the Loreto Church; garden terrace in the summer. Open: daily 11am–3pm, 6–11pm.

Vikarka, Prague 1, Vikářská 6. Tel: 536 497. Famous pub at the Castle, popular amongst Czech artists.

Vysočina, Prague 1, Národní třída 26. Tel: 225 773.

SNACK BARS

From 7am until 6pm what in the Czech Republic are referred to as "bufety" offer a selection of dishes appropriate to the time of day. The food is filling as well as inexpensive; standard fare includes sandwiches, sausage salad and meatloaf. A typical *bufety* is a self-service operation. Over time a real snack-bar culture has developed as sausage and waffle stands have cropped up on various squares and streets.

PUBS IN PRAGUE

If you believe statistics, each resident of Prague downs about 150 litres of beer per year. The usually hopelessly over-crowded pubs and inns attest to the fact that little of it is drunk in privacy at home. Czech beer is probably the finest beer in the world. Its quality is largely thanks to the famous "Bohemian hops", which have been culivated in Northern Bohemia ever since the Middle Ages. The hop centre is Žatec (Saaz). In Prague both light (*svetlé*) as well as dark (*tmavé*) beer is poured. The most famous beers are *Pilsener Urquell* from Plzeň and *Budvar* from České Budějovice. But the beer from Prague's Smíchov brewery is also very good, and then there is the strong dark beer brewed on the premises at U Fleků. Another strong beer comes from the Prague district of Braník.

There are more than 1,500 pubs in Prague alone. Some of these can look back on a history that is literally centuries-old, while others have just got established during the past few years. Whatever their age, they all have one thing in common: during the Communist regime all the pubs and inns located in Prague became arenas for social interaction. Accompanied by a good "pivo" politics were discussed and individual desires were philosophized, explained, complained about and laughed over.

The traditional pubs are beloved by students,

intellectuals and plain old working-class people alike and the clientele at most places is always quite mixed. But the historically interesting taverns tend to be the preserve of tourists. What you will find there, however, are hoards of tourists, usually members of organised tours., witness the beloved pub U Fleků – one of the very oldest in the entire city – which pulls customers with live music and cabaret. The waiters here are fluent in a number of languages and perform heavy labour in the true sense of the word. Each year they approximately 6,000 hectolitres of the dark, house-brewed beer. Some 960 seats are tucked among the Gothic arches and in the garden, enjoying the cabaret and live music. Things are just about as lively in the pub U svatého Tomáše. Tasty dark beer is also on tap here and during the peak season tour groups storm the old vaulted cellar of this former monastery brewery.

Each historic Prague tavern has its own folklore. One popular anecdote is the story of how the world-famous Pilsen beer managed to make its way into Prague and how ultimately, it managed to remain there. The story goes that in the year 1843 Pinkas, a master tailor, met up with a coachman by the name of Salzmann who let him have a taste of Pilsen Beer. The master tailor found the brew so delicious that without much further ado he opened up his own pub. And thus even today Pilsen Beer is served in the U Pinkasů. The U Mědvidku and the U Labutě are two traditional pubs less haunted by tourists. While taking a walk through the quieter streets in the Old Town, call in at the little *pivnice* on the corner of Jilská and Vejvodova. The pub's two vaulted rooms are divided into smoking and non-smoking sections, definitely a plus for those who prefer to savour their roast pork and *pivo* without having to swallow clouds of cigarette smoke at the same time.

Good, hearty meals are also available in pubs. Menus generally include roast pork and beef accompanied by sauerkraut and dumplings as well as goulash and a variety of game dishes.

It doesn't matter whether you end up in a little, *pivnice*, or find yourself in one of the tourist-infested strongholds of beer culture; everywhere you go, the closing time is 11 pm. Keeping this in mind, it may be a small comfort to know that many pubs open their doors again at 7am in the morning.

Bránický sklípek, Prague 1, Vodičkova 26. Tel: 260 005. 14° beer from Braník.

Černý Pivovar (Black Brewery), Prague 2, Karlovo nám. 15. Tel: 294 451. 12° Pilsener Urquell.

Na Vlachovce, Prague 8, Rudé armády 217. Tel: 840 576. 12° Budvar.

Plzeňský dvůr, Prague 7, Obránců míru 59. Tel: 371 150. 12° Pilsener Urquell.

Rakovnická pivnice, Prague 5, S.M. Kirova 1. Tel: 542 531. 12° Bakalar beer from Rakovník.

Smíchovský sklípek, Prague 1, Národní 31. Tel: 268 172. 12° beer from Smíchov.

U Bonaparta, Prague 1, Nerudova 29. Tel: 539 780. 12° beer from Smíchov.

U Černého vola, (The Black Bull), Prague 1, Loretánské nám. 1. Tel: 538 637. 12° beer from Velké Popovice.

U dvou kocek (The Two Cats), Prague 1, Uhelný trh 10. Tel: 267 729. One of the most popular of Prague's pubs: Pilsner Urquell.

U dvou srdcí (Two Hearts), Prague 1, U lužického semináře 38. Tel: 536 597. 12° Pilsener Urquell.

U Fleků, Prague 1, Křemencova 11. Tel: 293 246. The malthouse and brewery date from 1459. 13° dark beer still brewed on the premises, accompanied by traditional Prague cabaret.

U Glaubiců, Prague 1, Malostranské nám 5, 12° beer from Smíchov.

U medvídků (The Bears), Prague 1, Na Perštyně 7. Tel: 235 8904. This traditional restaurant offers Southern Bohemian and Old Czech specialities, accompanied by 12° Budvar.

U Pinkasů, Prague 1, Jungmannovo nám. 15. Tel: 261 804. A popular pub that has been pulling Pilsener Urquell since 1843.

U Schnellů, Prague 1, Tomášská 2. Tel: 532 004. 12° Pilsener Urquell.

U Sojků, Prague 7, Obránců míru 40. Tel: 379 107. 12° Pilsener Urquell.

U supa (The Vulture), Prague 1, Celetná 22. This pub dates back to the 14th century and serves Braník Special.

U sv. Tomáše (St Thomas's), Prague 1, Letenská 12. Tel: 530 064. 12° beer from Braník.

U zlatého tygra, (The Golden Tiger), Prague 1, Husova 17. Tel: 265 219. 12° Pilsener Urquell.

WINE BARS

In these elegantly decorated rooms and Gothic cellars with vaulted ceilings, eating and drinking are not just a matter of taste, but a question of style as well. Wine bars are relatively expensive, and the price of a main dish here generally starts at around £3. It is recommended that you phone beforehand to reserve a table.

Most of the wine served in Prague's wine bars is of Czech or Slovak origin. At one time there used to be vineyards even in Prague; a fact recalled by the name of the district Vinohrady above Wenceslas Square. The best wine comes from Žernoseky in the Elbe Valley; including the wines from Melník. Good wines are also produced in Southern Moravia, in places like Nikolsburg, Göding, Znjomo or Valtice or from Slovakia. Some wine bars serve wine from "their own" cooperatives.

Foreign wines from Yugoslavia or Bulgaria are served in their respective speciality restaurants. Chianti Ruffino, for example, is served in the Trattoria Viola.

Snacks are also served in the wine bars. In recent years many wine bars have fallen into private hands and become expensive restaurants; some have thus lost a lot of their original charm. This is especially true in the Lesser Quarter.

Opening times vary, but most places stay open at least until midnight, some until 3am. Wine bars are thus often the last refuge of night owls in Prague.

Blatnice, Prague 1, Michalská 8. Tel: 224 751. Moravian wines from the area around Blatnice. Open: 11am–11pm. Closed: Saturday.
Klašterní vinárna (Monastery Wine Bar), Prague 1, Národní 8. Tel: 290 596. This large wine bar is built in the walls of the former Ursuline Convent, and serves wines from Moravia and Nitra. Open: daily 11am–1am.
Lobkovická vinárna, Prague 1, Vlašská 17. Tel: 530 185. A historic wine bar in the Lesser Quarter, dating from the 19th century; wines from Melník are served here.
Makarská, Prague 1, Malostranské nám. 2. Tel: 531 573. Balkan specialities and wines. Open: daily 11.30am–10.30pm.
Nebozízek, Prague 5, Petřínské sady. Tel: 537 905. Reached by funicular from the Lesser Quarter; with an impressive view of Prague and Hradčany. Open: daily 11am–6pm, 7pm–midnight.
Parnas, Prague 1, Smetanovo nábřeží 2. Tel: 265 017. International cuisine with an unforgettable view of the Hradčany. Open: daily 7pm–1am. Closed: Sunday.
Svatá Klara (St Clare), Prague 7, U trojského zámku 9. Tel: 841 213. Exclusive cellar wine bar at the entrance to Prague Zoo. Open: 6pm–1am. Closed: Sunday.
U labutí (The Swans), Prague 1, Hradčanské nám. 11. Tel: 539 476. Exclusive wine bar near the castle serving South Moravian wines. Open: 7pm–1am.
U malířů (The Painters), Prague 1, Maltezské nám 11. Tel: 531 883. A typical Old Prague wine bar dating back to 1583. Open: 11am–3pm, 6–11pm. Closed: Sunday.
U mecenáše (The Sponsor), Prague 1, Malostranské nám. 10. Tel: 533 881. There was an inn in the house "at the sign of the Golden Lion" as long ago as 1604; today this wine bar is among the nicest in the city. Open: 5pm–1am. Closed: Saturday.
U patrona (The Patron), Prague 1, Dražického nám. 4. Tel: 531 661. Cosy atmosphere, South Moravian wine. Open: Monday–Friday 4pm–midnight.
U pavouka (The Spider), Prag1, Celetná 17. Tel: 231 8714. This historic wine bar with its Gothic and Renaissance halls serves wines from Southern Moravia. Open: 11.30am–3pm, 6–11.30pm. Closed: Sunday.
U plebána, Prague 1, Betlémské nám. 10. Tel: 265 223. First-class cuisine with excellent wine from Znjomo. Open: 7am–11pm. Closed: Sunday.
U zelené žáby (The Green Frog), Prague 1, U radnice 8. Tel: 262 815. This venerable institution has poured wine from Velké Žernoseky in Bohemia since the 15th century.
U zlaté hrušky (The Golden Pear), Prague 1, Novy svět 3. Tel: 531 133. A stylish bar in the Romantic atmosphere of the Castle. Open: daily 6.30pm–12.30am.

U zlaté konvice (The Golden Pot), Prague 1, Melantrichova 20. Tel: 262 128. Wine bar in cellars dating from the 14th century; wines from Valtice.
U zlatého jelena (The Golden Stag), Prague 1, Celetná 11. Tel: 268 595. Cellar wine bar with wines from Southern Moravia. Open: Monday–Friday noon–midnight, Saturday–Sunday 6pm–midnight.

COFFEE HOUSES

Particularly in Prague there are a number of coffee houses rich in tradition, for example the Slavia, Arco and Evropa. These establishments serve a variety of lighter dishes and snacks, as well as anything you might care to drink (with the exception of beer). Read, smoke, discuss, let the day go by; that's what the coffee houses are all about. They have little in common with their cousins in Germany or Austria, which are more meeting places for ladies of advancing years. The Prague coffee house remains an important element in the daily life of the city. The coffee on offer, however, often prepared in 10 or more variations, is not always the strongest.

Arco, Prague 1, Hybernská 16.
Columbia, Prague 1, Staroměstské nám. 15.
Evropa, Prague 1, Václavské nám. 29.
Kajetánka, Prague 1, Hradčany, Kajetánska zahrada.
Malostranská kavárna, Prague 1, Malostranské nám. 28.
Mysák, Prague 1, Vodičkova 31.
Obecní dům, Prague 1, Náměstí Republiky.
Praha, Prague 1, Václavské nám. 10.
Savarin, Prague 1, Na příkopě 10.
Slavia, Prague 1, Národní 1.
U zlatého hada, Prague 1, Karlova 18.

BRATISLAVA

The local cuisine has been refined by a host of influences from other cultural regions. While farming provides a variety of meat, vegetables and fruit, the forests and the lakes provide copious quantities of game and fish. Typical Slovakian dishes include more down-to-earth dishes such as the butcher's platter, roast goose with *Lokše* (unleavened bread), the cabbage soup (*Kapustnica*), potato dumplings with sheep' cheese (*Bryndzové halušky*) and salted mashed potato with marjoram. Hungarian dishes can also be found: goulash in a variety of guises, seasoned with plenty of paprika, garlic and onions. *Lečo*, a vegetable and egg dish, was a great favourite with the Turks. The proximity of Vienna makes itself apparent through flour-based dishes: noodles, dumplings and pancakes, followed up by cake and espresso (known in Bratislava as "presso") or Turkish coffee.

RESTAURANTS

Restaurants are usually – but not always – closed on Sundays and rarely serve meals after 9pm. Booking a table is recommended. Some establishments might have a band playing; make sure that the amplifier isn't turned up so loud that you can't hear yourself speak.

Arkády, Zámocké schody. Tel: 335 650. Cosy, at the foot of the castle.
Azia, Riecna 4. Tel: 330 851. Fine Asian cuisine in Hotel Devín.
Maď'árská reštaurácia, Hviezdoslavovo nám. 20. Tel: 334 883. High-quality Hungarian cuisine.
Rybárský cech, (Fishermen's Guild), Žižkova 1. Tel: 313 048.
Slovenská reštaurácia Luxor, Štúrova 15. Tel: 52 881, Slovakian cuisine.
Stará sladovná, (Old Brewery), Cintorínska 32. Tel: 56 371. The largest and loudest restaurant in the city with a extensive varity of pulled beer.
Zelený dom, Zelená 5. Tel: 331 555. Very traditional establishment on the former market place.

WINE BARS

In this city of wine, the fruit of the vine and not beer is the most popular drink. Viticulture here has a long tradition stretching back to the Middle Ages, and even connoisseurs will find something to delight their palette. Most of the wine sold in Bratislava is dry white; it can be found in the traditional streetside pubs, the so-called *Viechas*, which are not only found in the small wine villages in the country, but also in the centre of Bratislava itself, for example on the Vysoká and the Obchodná ul. In October, after the harvest, there are large quantities of new wine to be found everywhere. The wine bars (*vináreň*) also have extensive menus. Wine bars are open until 11 pm, though some stay open longer. They are always closed on Sunday.

Bulharská, Zámočnicka 3. Tel: 333 828.
Kláštorná (monastery cellar), near the Franciscan Church, Pugacovova 1. Tel: 330 430.
Pod Baštou (under the Bastion), Baštová 3. Tel: 371 781.
Pri obuvníckej bašte, Hviezdoslavovo nám. 11. Tel: 330 596.
Puszta, Hviezdoslavovo nám. 20. Tel: 334 883.
Veľki Františkáni, Dibrovo nám. 10. Tel: 333 073.
U mýtnika, Mytná 26. Tel: 47 776.
U zbrojnoša, directly at St Michael's Gate, Zámocnícka 1. Tel: 333 828.
Vysoká 44, Vysoká ul.16. Tel: 57 67.
Vysoká 69, Vysoká ul. 39. Tel: 53 008.

SHOPPING

PRAGUE

Prague falls sadly short of other European metropolises when it comes to shopping. Despite this, the Czech capital is considered to be the absolute shopping paradise of what used to be known as the Eastern Bloc. Citizens from Poland and former East Germany used to come here for the weekend, shop like mad during the day and amuse themselves in the evening at nightclubs and pubs.

On the whole, Western European visitors seem most interested in the porcelain and crystal shops. Bohemian glass and china is held in high esteem throughout the world on account of its exceptional quality and extraordinarily low price. Due to this, tourists frequently spend hours queuing in front of the national retail outlets. Because the china and glass companies can scarcely keep up with the demand, they have taken to selling old stock to tourists and the majority of their new products is reserved for export.

It's almost impossible to find a good deal in the antique shops. Antique dealers have become wise to the Western predilection for their wares and have altered their prices accordingly. As a compensation, gallery sales are booming. Works by artists who until 1989 were excluded from the circle of artists' associations are now being exhibited and sold.

Private, more amateur arts and crafts items are also finding a ready market. Plain and carved wooden objects produced throughout the country are for sale at authorised Czech retail outlets. "Wandering street vendors" – usually young people on the Charles Bridge and in the street Na příkopě – sell handmade goods, for instance marionettes and costume jewellery. Quite recently open-air markets have sprung up in the pedestrian zones between Náměští Republik and Wenceslas Square. Clothes, household articles, souvenirs and odds and ends of every description eventually find buyers amongst the people strolling by.

Buying books written in both English and German is another popular pastime. But since the printing of books is no longer subsidised by the government, Czech publishing houses are on the verge of financial ruin and are looking for help from foreign investors. For the people of Prague this means books are getting to the point where practically no one can afford them; for foreign visitors, however, buying a book remains a relatively inexpensive pleasure.

Classical music buffs can look forward to acquiring quality and fairly inexpensive records in Prague. (CDs and cassettes are much harder to find.)

If you're looking for something typically Bohemian to take home with you as a gift, and don't mind a bit of searching, how about a Prague ham? Less troublesome to procure is a bottle of the herb liqueur Becherovka or Slivovitz. Fruity wines from Bohemia and Moravia are also gifts sure to be appreciated.

Visitors preparing to head out for an extensive round of shopping should bear in mind that such an excursion can turn out to be fairly time-consuming. Shopping can really turn into a test of patience, especially on the weekends when both tourists and Prague natives hit the streets. Taking this into account it's a good idea to get your errands and shopping accomplished during the week and to reserve the weekend for visiting the interesting sights that the city has to offer. As a rule most shops are open 10am–6pm Monday–Friday, and 10am–2pm Saturday. (Stores are closed on Sunday.) Department stores remain open somewhat later. The following list of some of the special retail shops located in the centre should be of help to you in finding what you're looking for.

INTERNATIONAL BOOKSHOPS
Kniha, Štěpánská 12 (in the courtyard), Prague 1. Open: 9am–6pm, Saturday 9am–1pm. Closed: Sunday. **Zahraniční Literatura**, Vodičkova 41 (in the Alfa Arcade, Wenceslas Square entrance), Prague 1. Open: 9am–6pm, Saturday 9am–1pm. Closed: Sunday. **Kniha**, Na příkopě 27, Prague 1.

SECONDHAND BOOKSHOPS
AD plus, Prague 1, Václavské nám. 18. Also in Prague 1: Dlážděná 5; Mostecka 22; Karlova 2; Ul. 28. října 13. Prague 2: Ječná 26.

HAT SHOPS
Tonak, Celetná 30, Prague 1. Open: 9am–6pm, Saturday 9am–1pm. Closed: Sunday.

ANTIQUES
Antikvita, Prague 1, Panská 1. Also in Prague 1: Mikulandská 7; Václavské nám. 60; Uhelny trh 6; Můstek 3. Prague 2: Vinohradská 45. Prague 7: Šimáčková 17.

JEWELLERY
Bijoux de Boheme, Prague 1, Dlouhá. Also in Prague 1: 28. října 15; Národní třída 25; Na příkopě 15; Václavské nám. 53. **Galerie Vlasta Wasserbauerova**, Staroměstské náměstí 5, Prague 1. Handmade individual pieces.

FASHION JEWELLERY
Na příkopě 12, Prague 1; Staroměstské náměstí 6, Prague 1. Beads, stones.

GARNET JEWELLERY
Granat, Prague 1, Václavské nám. 28 (Alfa Arcade).

GLASS AND PORCELAIN
Bohemia Moser, Na příkopě 12, Prague 1. **Bohemia**, Pařižská 1, Prague 1.

CRYSTAL, LAMPS, CROCKERY
Krystal, Václavské nám. 30, Prague 1.

CHANDELIERS
Superlux, Prague 1, Hybernská 32. **Lux**, Prague 1, Na příkopě 16.

OBJETS D'ART
Dilo, Vodičkova 32, Prague 1.

ARTS AND CRAFTS
Česká jizba, Karlova 12, Prague 1. **Krásná jizba**, Národní 36, Prague 1. **Slovenská jizba**, Prague 1, Václavské nám. 40. Open: daily 9am–12 noon, 2pm–7pm; Saturday 9am–1pm. **UVA**, Na příkopě 25, Prague 1. **A+G Flora**, Přemyslova 29, Prague 3. Tel: 27 17 16. No regular opening times; ring beforehand.

MUSIC AND INSTRUMENTS
Prague 1: Jungmannovo nam. 17 and 30; Na příkopě 24.

RECORDS
Prague 1: Jungmannova 20; Celetná 8; Václavské náměstí 17 and 51; Vodičkova 20.

SPORTS ARTICLES
Dům sportu, Jungmannova 28, Prague 1. **Sportovní potřeby**, Vodičkova 30, Prague 1.

WEAPONS AND HUNTING
Lověna, Prague 1, Hybernská 3. **Lověna**, Prague 1, Národní třída 38.

The department stores with the largest selection of goods (including gift articles, fabric, clothes, dishes, shoes, perfume, toiletries, groceries, travel accessories, writing materials, electrical goods, books, etc.) are: **Bílá labut'**, Prague 1, Na Porící; **Detský dům** (House of Children), Prague 1, Na příkopě 15; **Družba**, Prague 1, Václavské nám. 21; **Dům elegance** (House of Elegance), Prague 1, Na příkopě 4; **Dům kožešin** (House of Furs), Prague 1, Železná 14; **Dům módy** (House of Fashion), Prague 1, Václavské nám. 58; **Dům obuví** (House of Shoes), Prague 1, Václavské nám.; **Kotva**, Prague 1, Náměstí Republiky 8; **Máj**, Prague 1, Národní třída 26. Most large department stores have a supermarket in the basement. A delicatessen shop to be particularly recommended is: **Dům potravin**, Václavské náměstí 59, Prague 1.

BRATISLAVA

Because of its proximity to Vienna, Bratislava can hardly be called a paradise for cheap shopping. On the other hand, there is a good choice of quality consumer goods, and from the vast hinterland comes beautiful furniture, fashion goods and antiquarian books. Modern galleries also sometimes sell fine pieces of art, together with the tasteless kitsch that has invaded the city since the collapse of the old regime.

SECONDHAND BOOKSHOPS
Mickiewiczova ul.6, Dunajská ul. 5.

ANTIQUES
Leningradská ul. 7, Klobúčnická ul. 7.
International books
Rybárska brána 1.

CROCKERY AND CRYSTAL
Bohemia, Poštová 3; **Krištál**, Nálepkova 18.

GALLERIES
Dielo, Nám. SNP 12; **Dilo**, Nedbalova 4.

RECORDS
Supraphon, Nálepkova 27; **Opus**, Leningradská 11.

DEPARTMENT STORES
Prior, Kamenné nám. 1; **Veľkopredajná potravín** (food), Dunajská 2.

CULTURE PLUS

The cultural centre of the Czech Republic is undoubtedly Prague. Artists from other towns and cities wanting to establish themselves generally head for the capital, although a lively small theatre scene has developed over the last few years in Brno. Bratislava is the cultural centre of Slovakia; excellent opera and ballet is performed at the Slovakian National Theatre.

The exact times of concert, opera and theatre performances can be found in the local calendar of events available from the tourist board. They are also advertised on billboards. Tickets for concerts and operas in the main internationally-acclaimed venues can be booked in licensed travel agencies abroad.

Tickets for other events can be bought at advance booking offices, agencies, hotels and information offices.

PRAGUE

Prague has a very rich and varied cultural palette. More difficult than the choice is the problem of obtaining tickets. Sometimes you can book through Čedok, but this usually has to be done days in advance. Even then, it isn't guaranteed that you'll get tickets.

Often the only alternative is to go directly to the box office, where you might read *vyprodáno* – sold out. But don't let that put you off. If you are polite and point out that you came all the way just to see it then there's a good chance that you'll be successful. Some performances are reserved for companies and cooperatives. But it is still worth going along and looking around on the off chance.

Tickets for concerts and other public events can be obtained from the following booking offices:
Sluna: Panská 4, Passage Černá růže. Tel: 265 121, 221 206. Open: Monday–Friday 10am–6pm. Concerts and theatre: Václavské náměstí 28, Alfa Arcade. Tel: 260 693. Open: Monday–Friday 10am–6pm.
PIS – Prazská informacní sluzba (Prague Information Service): Staroměstské nám. (Old Town Square) 28. Tel: 224 453. Open: Monday–Friday 8am–6pm, Saturday 9am–6pm. Mainly concerts.
BTI – Bohemia Ticket International: Na příkopě 16. Tel: 227 838; Václavske nám. 25. Tel: 260 333; Karlova 8; Salvátorská 6. Tel: 231 2030. Open:

Monday–Friday 9am–noon, 1–6pm; Saturday and Sunday 9am–5pm.
Czech Philharmonic: Prague 1, Masná 21. Tel: 231 9164. Open: Monday–Friday 1.30–6pm.
Symphony Orchestra FOK: Prague 1, U obecního domu 2. Tel: 232 5858. Open: Monday–Friday 9am–noon, 1.30–4.30pm (Friday 3pm).
The box office for the **National Theatre** and the **New Theatre** is situated in the glass building of the New Theatre, Národní třída 4 (Monday–Friday 10am–6pm, Saturday and Sunday 10am–noon).

THEATRE & OPERA

National Theatre (Národní divadlo), Prague 1, Národní třída 2. Tel: 205 364. Opera, ballet, theatre.
Nová Scéna, Prague 1, Národní třída 4. Tel: 206 260. Theatre, opera, Laterna Magika.
Smetana Theatre (Smetanovo divadlo) Prague 1, Wilsonova 8. Tel: 269 746. Opera, ballet.
Laterna Magika, Prague 1, Národní třída 4. Tel: 206 260. A mixture of music, dance and theatre.
Estates Theatre (Stavovské divadlo), Prague 1, Ovocný trh 6. Tel: 227 281. Opera, theatre.
Theatre on the Balcony (Divadlo na Zábradlí), Prague 1, Anenské nám. 5. Tel: 236 0449. Theatre, mime.
Mime Theatre (Branické divadlo pantomimy), Prague 4, Branická 63. Tel: 460 307. Mime.
Spejbl and Hurvinek Theatre (Divadlo Spejbla a Hurvínka), Prague 2, Římská 45. Tel: 251 666. Puppet theatre.
Studio Gag Boris Hybner, Prague 1, Národní třída 25. Tel: 265 436. Mime.
Italian Theatre (Divadlo u Italů), Prague l, Šporkova 13. Tel: 535 181. Cabaret.
Prague Intimate Opera (Komorní Opera Praha), Opera Mozart "A" scéna, Prague 1, Novotného lávka 1. Tel: 265 371. Modern opera.
Supraclub, Prague 1, Opletalova 5. Tel: 224 537.
Music Theatre in Karlín, (Hudební divadlo v Karlíně), Prague 8, Křížíkova 10. Tel: 220 895.

Since July 1992, Čedok has been presenting a variation of "Laterna Magika" with the programme "Laterna Animata". This Audio-Video Show, combined with theatre and mime, is based on themes from "Faust and Margaret". Performances are held in the Spirala Theatre in the Prague exhibition centre.

CONCERT HALLS

House of Artists (Dům umělců), Prague 1, Nám. Jana Palacha. Tel: 231 9164.
Municipal House, Smetana Hall (Obecní dům, Smetanova síň), Prague 1, Nám. Republiky 5. Tel: 232 5858.
Atrium, Prague 3, Čajkovského 12. Tel: 274 080.
Palace of Culture (Palác kultury), Prague 4, 5. května 65. Tel: 417 2741.

Janáček Hall (Janáčkova síň), Prague 1, Besední 3. Tel: 530 546.
Mánes Hall in St Agnes Monastery (Mánesova síň kl. sv. Anežky České), Prague 1, U milosrdných 17. Tel: 231 4251.
Supraclub, Prague 1, Opletalova 5. Tel: 224 537.
Music Hall (Hudební síň Klárov), Prague 1, Klárov 3.
House of the Stone Bell (Dům U kamenného zvonu), Prague 1, Staroměstské nám. 13. Tel: 231 0272.
Foerstrova Hall, Prague 1, Pštrossova 17.
Hall of Mirrors (Zrcadlová síň Klementina), Prague 1, Klementinum 190. Tel: 266 541.
Strahov Monastery (Strahovsky Kláster), Prague 1, Strahovské nádvoří 1. Tel: 538 841.
Emmaus Monastery (Opatství Emauzy), Prague 2, Vyšehradská 49.
New Provost's House (Nové proboštství), Prague 2, K rotundě 10.
House of the Lords of Kunštát and Poděbrady (Dům pánu z Kunštátu a Poděbrad), Prague 1, Řetězová 3.
Schwarzenberg Palais (Schwarzenberský palác), Prague 1, Hradcanské nám. 2.
Lobkovic Palais (Lobkovický palác), Prague 1, Pražský hrad. Tel: 537 306.
Dvořák Museum (Muzeum A. Dvořáka), Prague 2, Ke Karlovu 20. Tel: 298 214.
Villa Bertramka, Prague 5, Mozartova 169. Tel: 543 893.
Martinic Palais (Martinický palác), Prague 1, Hradčanské nám. 8.
Knights Hall in the Waldstein Palace (Rytířský sál Valdštejnského paláce), Prague 1, Valdštejnské nám.
Troja Castle (Trojský zámek), Prague 7. Tel: 845 133.
Kaunitz Palais (Kaunicův palác), Prague 1, Panská 7.
Spanish Hall (Spanělsky sál), Prague 1, Pražský hrad (Prague Castle).

MUSIC FESTIVALS

In May/June there is the International Prague Spring Festival. Concerts are given in historical rooms and churches, for example: St Vitus' Cathedral, Hradčany; St James' Church, Jakubská ul.; Church of St Nicholas, Malostranské nám.

In cultural centres such as the Malostranská beseda there are daily musical and artistic performances, ranging from concerts of chamber music to jazz and rock.

CINEMA

While during the last decades Czech film achieved world renown and the Prague public poured into every première, since the collapse of Communism the cinemas have been invaded by Hollywood productions, often in English. Dubbed films are marked with a white square on the posters. The brochure "cinema" put out by PIS every week contains the cinema programme.

A visit to the **Barandov Studios** is a must for all film buffs. They became world famous especially for their children's and youth productions such as *Pan Tau*. Today primarily Western sponsored films are made here.

Also interesting are the British Cultural Section (Jungmannova 30), which shows only English-language films, and the Ponrepo (Veletržní 61, tel: 37 92 78), which shows black-and-white films in the original languages.

ART GALLERIES

Prague's museums contain an extraordinary wealth of art treasures. Note that most museums and galleries are closed on Monday.

NATIONAL GALLERY

The pride of Prague's museums is the **Národní galerie** (National Gallery). It contains seven collections housed in different buildings.

The Sternberg-Palais, Prague 1, Hradčanské nám. (open: 10am–6pm) houses the collections of **Classical European Art and French 19th- and 20th-Century Art**. The rooms of the former palace contain such incomparable masterpieces as the *Rosenkranzfeier* by Albrecht Dürer, fragments of an altarpiece by Lucas Cranach, and the *Martyrdom of St Florian* by Albrecht Altdorfer.

Among the works by Italian artists, we find *David with the Head of Goliath* and the *St Hieronymus* by Tintoretto, the *Portrait of a Patrician* by Tiepolo or the *View of London* by Canaletto.

The Dutch Collection includes the *Hay Harvest* by Pieter Brueghel the Elder, the *Winter Landscape* by Pieter Brueghel the Younger, the *Martyrdom of St Thomas* by Peter Paul Rubens and the *Rabbi* by Rembrandt.

Amongst the French 19th- and 20th-century contingent are Delacroix, Renoir, *The Green Cornfield* by van Gogh as well as works by Rousseau, Cézanne and Paul Gauguin. The collections with works by Chagall and Picasso are also very popular.

The third collection is found in St George's Monastery in Hradčany; Jiřský klášter, Prague 1, Hradčany. Open: Tuesday–Sunday 10am–6pm. It contains **Old Czechoslovakian Art**, including works by the artists Karel Škréta and Jan Kupecký.

The **Modern Art Collection** is to be found in the Městská knihovna (City Library) in Prague 1, Staré Město, nám. primátora dr. V. Vacka 1. Open: Tuesday–Sunday 10am–6pm.

The **Prints and Drawings Collection** in the Palais Kinsky displays Czech, Slovakian and foreign graphics from the last five centuries: Palác Kinských, Prague 1, Staroměstské nám. 12 .

The collection **Czech 19th-and 20th-century Sculpture** is housed outside Prague in Zbraslav

Castle. Open: Tuesday–Sunday 10am–6pm (April–November).

The restored St Agnes Monastery houses the collection **Czech 19th-Century Art**, including works by the brothers Quido and Josef Mánes, Karel Purkyně and Mikoláš Aleš: Anežsky klášter, Prague 1, U milosrdných 17.

EXHIBITION HALLS

Royal Palace Belvedere, Prague 1, Chotkovy sady. Open: Tuesday–Sunday 10am–6pm.
Waldstein Palace Riding School, Prague 1, Valdštejnská 2. Open: Tuesday–Sunday 10am–6pm.
Prague Castle Riding School, Prague 1, Hradčany.
Gallery of the Capital Prague: Old Town Hall Cloister, Prague 1, Staroměstské nám., open: daily 9am–5pm; Old Town Hall, 2. floor exhibition hall, open: Tuesday–Sunday 10am–5pm.

THE RUDOLFINIAN COLLECTION

In the 16th century, the collection of Rudolf II was one of the most important in Europe. Through looting after the Battle of the White Mountain, the annexation by the Habsburgs and Swedes in the Thirty Years' War and subsequent auctioning off, the collection dwindled drastically. Paintings by Rubens and Tintoretto were found when the rooms of the castle were thoroughly searched in the 1960s. Today, the collection has been partially restored and can be seen in the castle gallery. It contains pictures such as the *Scourging of Christ* by Tintoretto and the *Meeting of the Olympic Gods* by Peter Paul Rubens: Rudolfinian Collection, Prague 1, Hradčany (II. courtyard). Open: Tuesday–Sunday 10am–6pm.

FURTHER EXHIBITION HALLS

Mánes House of Fine Arts, Prague 1, Masarykovo nabř. 250; New Hall, Prague 1, Voršilská 3; Václav Spála Gallery, Prague 1, Národní třída 30; U Řečických Gallery, Prague 1, Vodičkova 10; Jaroslav Frágner Gallery, Prague 1, Betlémské nám. 5; Brothers Čapek Gallery, Prague 2, Jugoslávská 20; Gallery D, Prague 5, Matoušova 9; Vincenc Kramář Gallery, Prague 6, Čs. armady 24; ÚLUV Gallery, Prague 1, Národní třída 38; Clementinum Mirrored Hall, Prague 1, Clementinum 190; Melantrich Little Gallery, Prague 1, Jilská 14; Atrium, Prague 3, Čajkovského 1; Palais of the Golden Melon, Prague 1, Michalská 12; Odeon Exhibition Hall, Prague 1, Celetná 11; Clam-Gallas Palais, Prague 1, Husova 20; UBOK, Prague 1, Na příkopě 25–27.

GALLERIES

Hollar Gallery, Prague 1, Smetanovo nábř. 8; Pi-Pi Art Gallery, Prague 1, Národní třída 9–11; GGG Gallery, Prague 1, Husova 10; Klubu pratel Gallery, vytvarného umění U sv. Martina, Prague 1, Uhelný trh; A + G FLORA, Prague 3, Přemyslovská 29; Athena Gallery, Prague 1, U starého hřbitova 46; Forum, Prague 1, Ul. 28. října 12; C-ART Gallery, Prague 1, Loretánské nám. 2; České grafiky Centre, Prague 1, Husova 12; CRUX, Prague 1, Kostel Panny Marie Sněžné, Jungmannovo nám.; Golden Cup Gallery, Prague 1, Nerudova ul.; Carolinum, Prague 1, Ovocný trh 10–18; Letna Gallery, Prague 7, M. Horakové 22; Spektrum, Prague 1, Karlova 4; Gallery 33 Bergman, Prague 2, Vinohradská 79; U Hybernů, Prague 1, Nám. Republiky 4; U sv. Jindřicha Gallery, Prague 1, Jindřišská ul.; Vyšehrad Gallery, Prague 2, K rotundě 10; Chodovská vodní tvrz, Prague 4, Ledvinova 9; VIA ART Gallery, Prague 2, Resslova ul.; Alexy Gallery (Dům slovenské kultury), Prague 1, Purkyňova 4; ART Gallery, Prague 1, Haštalská 10; Gallery of the Association of Czech Photographers, Prague 1, Kamzíkova 8.

Dilo Galleries (selling galleries): Na Újezdě, Újezd 19; Můstek, 28. října 16; Centrum, 28. října 6; Karolina, Železná 6; Platýz, Národní 37; Zlatá lilie, Prague 1, Malé nam. 12; Zlatá ulička, Prague Castle.

MUSEUMS

Apart from the large and small galleries where art treasures from many centuries are on view, Prague has a number of other interesting museums to offer, ranging from natural science to technical and historical. Here is a selection:

National Museum
Národní Muzeum, Prague 1, Václavské nám. The Národní museum on Wenceslas Square is predominantly a natural science museum and contains an extensive mineral collection. In the foyer there are also statues from the Libuše legend by Ludwig Schwanthaler. The Museum Library is also extensive: it contains over a million books. Open: Monday and Friday 9am–4pm; Wednesday, Thursday and Saturday 9am–5pm. Closed: Tuesday.

National Technical Museum
Národní technické muzeum, Prague 7, Kostelní 42. For those interested in technical equipment, measuring equipment, and the first Czech car, the Koprivnitz "President" from 1897, the Národni technické muzeum is an absolute must. There are automobile and locomotive exhibits as well as a photographic exhibition; the Astronomy Department contains sextants from the 16th century, with which Kepler once worked. Open: Tuesday–Sunday 9am–5pm; Museum Archives Wednesday and Thursday 9am–5pm; Museum Library Monday–Friday 9am–4pm.

Historical Military Museum
Vojenské historické muzeum, Schwarzenberský palác, Prague 1, Hradčanské nám. Weapons of all kinds are to be found in the two military museums. In the Historical Military Museum in the Schwarzenberg Palais, many unusual weapons, uniforms and other

military hardware are displayed. The collection is one of the largest of its kind in Europe. Open: May–October, Monday–Friday 9am–3.30pm, Saturday and Sunday 9am–5pm.

Military Museum
Vojenské muzeum, Prague 3, U Památníku 2. The history of the Czechoslovakian army, and the battles of World War I and II as well as the resistance of the partisans are displayed. Open: Tuesday–Sunday 9.30am–4.30pm.

Náprstek Museum
Náprstkovo muzeum, Prague 1, Betlémské nám. 1. Ethnographic exhibits as well as technical gadgets from the respective countries are displayed in the Museum of Asiatic, African and American Cultures which dates back to the private ethnology museum established by Vojta Náprstek in 1862. Open: Tuesday–Sunday 9am–5pm (6pm Thursday).

Folklore Museum
Národopisné muzeum, Prague 5, Petrínské sady 98. On the lower section of the Petřín Hill is the former palace of the noble Kinsky family, which today contains the Folklore Museum. The collections include beautiful pottery, glass and toys as well as costumes and furniture from old farmhouses. Especially fine is the belfry from Wallachia which stands next to the museum, as well as the little Orthodox wooden church dating from the 18th century, brought here from the West Ukrainian village of Mukacevo in 1929. Open: Tuesday–Sunday 9am–6pm.

Arts and Crafts Museum
Uměleckoprůmyslové muzeum, Prague 1, Ulice 17. listopadu 2 (opposite the former Rudolfinum, today's "Artists' House"). Bohemian glass of various periods is displayed in the Arts and Crafts Museum. The glass collection is probably the largest in the world and the library with 100,000 specialist volumes is open to the public. Open: Tuesday–Sunday 10am–5pm.

Post Museum
Poštovní muzeum, Prague 5, Holečkova 10. Everything to do with postal history and large collection of European stamps. Open: Monday–Friday 8am–2pm, Saturday and Sunday only by appointment.

Museum of the City of Prague
Muzeum hlavního města Prahy, Prague 8, Nové sady J. Švermy. The Museum of the City of Prague is located at the Sokolovská Metro station. Apart from the countless exhibits describing the history of the city there is also a rare collection dealing with the guilds. But the main attraction remains the famous model of the city constructed between 1826 and 1834. Accurate to the last detail, it enables a good comparison to be made between the Prague of 160 years ago and the Prague of today. Open: Tuesday–Sunday 10am–5pm.

National Literature Museum
amátník národního písemnictví, Prague 1, Strahovské nadvoří 132. The Strahov Gospels from the 9th century consist of 218 handwritten manuscripts

which appear to have come from the monastery workshop in Trier. These gospels and a host of other interesting exhibits can be viewed in the Theologians' and Philosophers' Halls of the Monastery Library. The adjacent rooms of the monastery contain the Museum of Czech Literature, with a collection of around 50,000 objects including a letter from the hand of Jan Hus. Also worth seeing is the reconstruction of a 17th-century press. Open: Tuesday–Sunday 9am–5pm.

Museum of Musical Instruments

Muzeum hudebních nástrojů, Prague 1, Lázeňská 2. Prague is not only a city of architecture and literature, but also of music. This fact is mirrored in the museums. The music lover has a total of four important places to go in Prague, and he should really try to see all of them. The Collection of Old Musical Instruments is the second largest of its kind in the world. Apart from old musical instruments, there is also a large collection of musical scores from various archives. Open: Saturday and Sunday 10am–noon, 2–5pm; weekday visits subject to arrangement.

Antonín Dvořák Museum

Muzeum Antonína Dvořáka, Prague 2, Ke Karlovu 20. This beautiful little building known as "Villa Amerika", designed by Kilian Ignaz Dientzenhofer and built between 1717–1720 for Count Michna, today contains the Antonín Dvořák Museum. Exhibits include manuscripts, documents, photographs and letters to such important personalities as Johannes Brahms or the conductor Bülow. Open: Tuesday–Sunday 10am–5pm.

Bedřich Smetana Museum

Muzeum Bedřicha Smetany, Prague 1, Novotného lávka 1. The Smetana Museum is housed in the former waterworks on the banks of the Vltava. Manuscipts, notes and other documents illuminate the life and work of this great Czech composer. Open: Monday–Sunday 10am–5pm. Closed: Tuesday.

Museum of Czech Music

Muzeum české hudby, expozice W. A. Mozarta, Prague 5, Mozartova 15. Music lovers know that Prague is also linked with Wolfgang Amadeus Mozart – catchword *Prague Symphony* or *Don Giovanni*. Mozart lived in Prague in the Villa Bertramka, which today houses the Mozart Museum. The harpsichord and piano are the very instruments that Mozart composed his music on. Most of the furniture also dates from the time of his stay. Open: Monday–Friday 1–3pm, Saturday and Sunday 10am–noon and 1–4pm.

Judaic Museum

Different departments of the National Judaic Museum can be found in the synagogues of the old Prague Ghetto. It is a tragic irony that the Nazis, to whom 90 percent of Prague's Jews fell victim, laid the foundations for this museum with their plans for a "Museum of the Extinct Jewish Race". They collected cultural and artistic objects from all over the country. The present museum was founded by the Czech government in 1950. Due to restoration work it will not be possible to see the exhibits in the Pinkas Synagogue for some time.

BRATISLAVA

The monthy magazine *Kam v Bratislave* outlines cultural events in the city. The most important perennial events are the Spring Music Festival, the International Art Festival in September and the Jazz Festival in October. Performances of opera and ballet take place in the National Theatre, orchestral concerts in the Redoute building of the Slovakian Philharmonic.

THEATRES & CONCERT HALLS

Slovakian National Theatre

Opera and ballet stage: Hviezdoslavovo nám.; advance booking office at Komenského nám.. Tel: 55 228. Theatre stage: Divadlo Pavla Országa Hiezdoslava, Leningradská 20; advance booking office at Obchodná 30. Tel: 335 512.

In addition: Malá scéna (Little Stage), Dostojevského rad 7; **Nova scéna** (New Stage), Kollárovo nám.; **Štúdio Novej scény** (Studio of the New Stage), Suché Myto 17; **Štúdio S**, Nám. 1 mája 5. Tel: 52 552; **Reduta**, Palackého 2; **Dom odborov**, (Trades Union building), Nám. F. Zupku 1.

MUSEUMS

Slovakian National Museum, Vajanského nábr. 2
Municipal Museum: Old Town Hall, Primaciálne nám. 2; Apponyipalais, Radničná 1; St Michael's Gate, Michalská.
Johann Nepomuk Museum, Klobúčnická 2.
Treasury of the Franciscan Church, Dibrovo nám..

GALLERIES

Slovakian National Gallery, Rázusovo nábr. 2.
Galleries of the City of Bratislava: Archbishop's Palace, Primiciálne nám. 1; Mirbach Palais, Dibrovo nám. 11; Pálffy Palais, Nálepkova 19.
Art Gallery of the Fine Arts Foundation: Michalská 7; Art Gallery, Nám. SNP.

WHERE TO STAY

Booking a hotel room in Prague, particularly during the peak tourist season, can prove to be a hopeless task. In other parts of the Czech Republic and Slovakia it is not such a problem and generally a lot cheaper. Outside cities, you'll find a number of travellers' inns along the national thoroughfares. These offer relatively inexpensive accommodation.

PRAGUE

Due to the fact that hotel managements often have fixed contracts with foreign tour agencies, rooms can be reserved for travel groups for up to 14 days prior to the beginning of the intended trip. Because of this, independent travellers are frequently able to book a room only at the last minute, and even then, especially in the city, the number of beds available is quickly exhausted. A possible alternative to this often frustrating and sometimes fruitless searching is to reserve a room through a travel agency or the Čedok agencies, which have recourse to a certain number of rooms in various hotels. However, you cannot bank on finding cheap accommodation through this channel.

Private rooms can be booked through the following agencies:
Čedok, Panská 5, Prague 1. Tel: 24 70 04, 22 56 57. Open from April to September on weekdays from 9 am–9.45 p.m., Saturdays from 9 am– 6 pm and Sundays from 9 am– 4.30 pm. From October to March the office is open on weekdays until 8 pm and until 2 pm at weekends.
Pragotour, U Prašné brány (near the Powder Tower), Prague 1. Tel: 23 17 281 or 23 19 245.
Rekrea, Pařižská 28, Prague 1. Tel: 23 22 751.
CKM, Žitná 10, Prague 2.
Hello, Gorkeho-Senovázné náměstí 3, Prague 1. Tel: 22 24 283.

HOTELS

The choice of hotels in Prague ranges from expensive and luxurious to cheap and simple. The expensive hotels are a category unto themselves; decor and service conform to international standards. As a rule the bill must be paid in Western currency. Credit cards are accepted.

Our list covers only some of the hotels typical for each category. Because of the high demand, it can be assumed that the choice will increase dramatically in the near future. We recommend the following:

DE LUXE ☆☆☆☆☆

Alcron, Prague 1, Štěpánská 40. Tel: 235 9296.
Esplanade, Prague 1, Washingtonova 19. Tel: 222 552.
Inter-Continental, Prague 1, Náměstí Curieových. Tel: 2899.
Jalta, Prague 1, Václavské nám. 45. Tel: 265 541-9.
Palace, Prague 1, Panská 12. Tel: 236 0008.
Prague, Prague 6, Sušická 20. Tel: 333 8111.

☆☆☆☆

Ambassador, Václavské náměstí 5. Tel: 221351-6.
Atlantik, Prague 1, Na poříčí 9. Tel: 231 8512.
Atrium, Prague 8, Pobřežní ul. Tel: 284 1111.
Diplomat, Prague 6, Evropská 15. Tel: 331 4111.
Forum, Prague 4, Kongresová ul. Tel: 410 111; Fax: 442/420684; Telex: 122 100.
International, Prague 6, Námfstí Družby 1. Tel: 321 051.
Olympic, Prague 8, Invalidovna, U Sluncove. Tel: 828 541.
Panorama, Prague 4, Milevská 7. Tel: 416 111.
Parkhotel, Prague 7, Veletržní. Tel: 20 380 7111.

☆☆☆

Axa, Prague 1, Na poříčí 40. Tel: 232 7234.
Belvedere, Prague 7, Obránců míru. Tel: 374 741.
Beránek, Prague 2, Bělehradská 110. Tel: 258 251.
Budovatel, Prague 1, Nám. Curieových 100. Tel: 231 4812.
Centrum, Prague 1, Na poříčí 31. Tel: 231 0135.
Družba, Prague 1, Václavská nám. 16. Tel: 235 1232.
Evropa, Prague 1, Václavské náměstí 25. Tel: 236 5274.
Flora, Prague 3, Vinohradská 121. Tel: 274 250.
Golf, Prague 5, Plzeňská 215a. Tel: 521 098.
Karl-Inn, Prague 8, Šaldova 54. Tel: 232 2551; Fax: 232 8030.
Koruna, Prague 1, Opatovická 16. Tel: 204 368.
Olympik II-Garni, Prague 8, Invalidnova, U Sluncové. Tel: 830 274.
Pařiž, Prague 1, U Obecního domu 1. Tel: 231 2051.
Splendid, Prague 7, Ovenecká 33. Tel: 373 351-9.
Tatran, Prague 1, Václavské nám. 22. Tel: 235 2885.
U tří pstrosů, Prague 1, Dražického nám. Tel: 536 151.
Zlatá husa, Prague 1, Václavské nám. Tel: 214 3111

Adria, Prague 1, Václavské nám. 26. Tel: 263 415.
Ametyst, Prague 2, Makarenkova 11.
Tel: 259 256-9.
Balkan, Prague 5, Svornosti 28. Tel: 540 777.
Bohemia, Prague 1, Královdorská 4.
Tel: 231 3795-6.
Central, Prague 1, Rybná 8. Tel: 232 4351.
Erko, Prague 9, Kbely 723. Tel: 850 1138.
Hvězda, Prague 6, Na rovni 34. Tel: 368 965.
Hybernia, Prague 1, Hybernská 24.
Tel: 220 431-2.
Juniorhotel, Prague 2, Žitná 12. Tel: 292 984.
Juventus, Prague 2, Blanická 10. Tel: 255 151.
Kriváň, Prague 2, I. P. Pavlova 5. Tel: 293 341-4.
Merkur, Prague 1, Těšnov 9. Tel: 231 6840.
Meteor, Prague 1, Hybernská 6. Tel: 235 8517.
Michle, Prague 4, Nuselská 124. Tel: 426 024.
Modrá hvězda, Prague 9, Jandova 3. Tel: 830 291.
Moráň, Prague 2, Na Moráni 15. Tel: 294 251-3.
Opera, Prague 1, Těšnov 13. Tel: 231 5609.
Ostaš, Prague 3, Orebitská 8. Tel: 272 860.
Praga, Prague 5, Plzeňská 29. Tel: 548 741-3.
Savoy, Prague 1, Keplerova 6. Tel: 537 450.
Transit, Prague 6, Ruzyňská 197. Tel: 367 108.
U blaženky, Prague 5, U blaženky 1. Tel: 538 286.
Union, Prague 2, Jaromírova 1. Tel: 437 858.

BOTELS

Staying at one of the floating hotels along the Vltava in Prague can be an experience you won't soon forget. However, they tend to be booked out by the coach tour operators:
Admiral, Hořejší nábřeží, Prague 5. Tel: 547 4.
Albatros, Nábřeží L. Svobody, Prague 1.
Tel: 231 3634.
Racek, U Dvořecké louky, Prague 4. Tel: 425 793.

MOTELS

Club Motel Průhonice ☆☆☆☆, Tel: 723 241-9.
In Průhonice southeast of Prague (15 minutes from the centre) on the motorway E 14 towards Brno; adjacent to the Botanical Gardens and the castle grounds of Průhonice. This motel opened in 1991, with two sports halls, tennis and squash courts, bowling alleys, swimming pools, fitness centre etc.
Hotel Golf, Plzeňská 215a, Prague 5. Tel: 523 252-9. On the E 15 in Motol.

CAMPING

Information regarding camping is available through automobile associations or the headquarters of the Czech Automobile Association: **Autoturist**, Prague 1, Opletalova 29. Tel: 223 544-9. Open: Monday–Friday 9am–noon and 1pm–4pm.

As a rule, campsites are divided into three categories; all have cold running water and lavatory facilities. Those falling into the third and simplest category "C" do not have access to electricity. In addition to plots reserved for caravans and tents, some campgrounds of the first category "A" also have holiday houses for rent. Generally speaking, don't expect anything luxurious with this kind of accommodation. It does, however, present a clean and inexpensive alternative to staying in a hotel:

Caravan, Prague 9, Kbely, Mladoboleslavská 27.
Tel: 892 532. May–October.
Caravancamp, Prague 5, Plzeňská. Tel: 524 714.
March–October.
Dolní Chabry, Prague 8 – Dolní Chabry, Ústecká ul. June–September.
Kotva, Prague 4, U ledáren 55. Tel: 461 712. May–September.
Mejto, Prague 10 – Nedvězí, Rokytná 84. Tel: 750 312-5. Open all year round.
Sportcamp, Prague 5, V podhájí. Tel: 521 802.
March–October.
TJ Aritma, Prague 6, Nad lávkou 3. Tel: 368 351.
April–October.
Xavercamp (bungalows), Prague 9, Božanovská 2098. Tel: 867 348. May–October.

YOUTH HOSTELS

Information pertaining to both youth hostels and student housing, both of which are available to young people during the summer months for about £2 per day, is furnished by: **CKM**, Žitná 12, Prague 2. Tel: 23 66 640 or 29 99 49. (There are CKM Agencies – or at least relatively cheap "junior hotels" – in the cities of Plzeň, Brno, and Bratislava.)

KARLOVY VARY

(*Dialling code 017*)
Booking a room in Carlsbad (Karlovy Vary) in the high summer or at Christmas is almost as difficult as in Prague. The only good chance of obtaining reasonable accommodation is in the off-season and the wintertime. The Čedok Agency located in the Hotel Atlantik (Tel: 24 378) is a good place to begin if you're in need of aid.

HOTELS

Atlantik, Tržiště 23. Tel: 24 715. Top-class hotel.
Grandhotel Pupp, Mirové náměstí 2. Tel: 22 121-5. The elegance of the 19th century.
Hotel Národní dum, Masarykova 24. Simple and reasonably-priced.
Juniorhotel Alice, Pětiletky 147. Tel: 24 848-9. Cheap accommodation south of the city. There is a youth hostel next door.
Slavia, Lidická 12. Tel: 27 271-3.
Turist, C. Dimitrova 18. Tel: 26 837. Cheap.

GUESTHOUSES

Ubytovna TJ Slavia, Lidická 12. Tel: 25 235.
Ubytovna TJ Slovoj, Skolní 21. Tel: 25 235.

CAMPING

Camping Brezová. Tel: 25 221, some miles from the town.

PLZEŇ

(Dialling code: 019)
Both national travel agencies are located in the town centre, very close to the market place: Čedok, Prešovská 10. Tel: 36 243; **CKM**, Dominikánská 1. Tel: 37 585.

HOTELS

Continental, Zbrojnická 8. Tel: 33 060.
Plzeň, Žižkova 66. Tel: 27 26 56.
Škoda, Náměstí Českých bratrí 10. Tel: 30 531.
Slovan, Smetanovy sady 1. Tel: 33 551.
Ural, Náměstí Republiky. Tel: 22 67 57.

GUESTHOUSE

Ubytovna TJ Lokomotiva, Úslavská 75. Tel: 48 041.

CAMPING

Intercamp Bílá Hora, Ul. 28. října. Tel: 35 611.

BRNO

(Dialling code: 05)
Brno is a city of trade fairs, and so the hotels are often booked out. If this should be the case when you arrive, then either the room agency (Tel: 23 166, 23 178-9) or the national travel agencies should be able to help: Čedok, Divadelní 3; **CKM**, Česká 11, Tel: 23 64 13; **Rekrea**, Radnická 11.

HOTELS

Avion, Česká 20. Tel: 26 675, 27 606, 27 797. Middle of the range.
Continental ☆☆☆☆, Kounicova. Tel: 75 05 01. Impersonal and overpriced.
Evropa, Náměstí Svobody 13. Tel: 26 611, 27 851. Reasonably-priced.
Grandhotel ☆☆☆☆, Třída 1. máje 18–20. Tel: 26 421. Opposite the station, expensive.
International ☆☆☆☆, Husova 16. Tel: 21 34 111. In the city centre; modern and too expensive.
Slavia ☆☆☆☆, Solniční 15/17. Tel: 237 11. Recently renovated Art Nouveau hotel in the centre, beneath the castle.
Slovan ☆☆☆, Lidická 23. Tel: 74 55 05. City.

Voroněž, Křížkovského 47. Tel: 33 31 35, 33 63 43.

CAMPING

Camping Bobrava, Modrice. Tel: 32 01 10. Situated some distance south of the city.
Obora, Brnenská přehrada. Tel: 49 42 84.

BRATISLAVA

(Dialling code: 07)
In the Slovakian capital, five large travel agencies are at your service: Čedok, Stúrova 13. Tel: 52 081, 55 280; **CKM**, Hviezdoslavovo námestie 16. Tel: 33 16 07; **Tatratour**, Dibrovovo námestie 7. Tel: 33 58 52; **Autoturist**, Stúrovo námestie 1. Tel: 33 73 81-4; **Slovakturist**, Nálepkova 13. Tel: 33 34 66.

HOTELS

Bratislava ☆☆☆, Urxova 9. Tel: 51 278. Modern hotel at the edge of the city, near the airport.
Carlton ☆☆☆, Hviezdoslavovo námestie 7. Tel: 58 209. Centrally located and relatively cheap.
Clubhotel ☆☆☆, Odbojárov 3. Tel: 65 47 32. Small hotel near the sportsground.
Děvín ☆☆☆☆, Riecna 4. Tel: 33 08 51-4. Classic luxury hotel, right on the Danube.
Flora ☆☆☆, Zlaté piesky, Senecká cesta 10. Tel: 67 28 41. Outside the city on a campground with artificial lake; cheap.
Forum ☆☆☆☆, Mierové námestie 2. Tel: 34 81 11, Fax: 31 46 45. Top-class hotel (opened 1989), on the motorway.
Kyjev ☆☆☆☆, Rajská ulica. Tel: 56 341. Centrally situated.
Sputnik, Drieňová 14. Tel: 23 43 40, 23 80 84. Hotel for young people, outside the city.

CAMPING

Autocamping Zlaté Piesky, Senecká cesta 10. Tel: 60 578.

NIGHTLIFE

The kind of lively, varied nightlife indigenous to many Western European cities doesn't yet exist in either the Czech Republic or Slovakia. Up till now Czechoslovakian natives have preferred to meet each other after dark within their own four walls, at a favourite restaurant or perhaps during a visit to the theatre or concert hall. Because of this predilection, entertainment options for tourists after 11 pm are mainly confined to gambling casinos, nightclubs and discos. These places, however, tend to cater to generous travelling businessmen who have nothing at all against sharing a bottle of champagne with an anonymous female companion. So far the women encouraging get-togethers of this nature are not subject to any kind of medical supervision, so potential customers should be aware of the dangers of venereal diseases and AIDS.

The young and young-at-heart with other interests may want to pay a visit to one of a number of jazz clubs. The Reduta Jazz Club and the Rock Café (both located in Prague) are international meeting places for music enthusiasts.

Since 1991 the previously nationally-operated young people's clubs have been taken over and are now run by young people themselves. If you're curious as to what's happening in Czechoslovakia on this front, be sure to stop in at one of these clubs.

One more tip: if you get hungry in the middle of the night, make a bee-line for a nightclub in one of the bigger cities. You'll be able to order something to eat here until at least 3 am.

PRAGUE

During the socialist era there was no nightlife to speak of in Prague (the pubs all closed at 10pm), but the metropolis on the Vltava is now doing its best to be like any other international city. If you're not keen on plunging in on your own, then put your trust in Čedok which runs the "O.K. Revue in Prague" in the Alhambra Club. Another option is the programme "Dinner and Show". For those in search of "good old Bohemia", the official travel agency offers two entertaining evening events:
Prague Festival/Country Fair is held from May to October in the Hotel International. It is one big party with typical Bohemian fare and as much beer as you like; a colourful folklore programme, brass band, dance and lots of fun.

"Bohemian Fantasies" A musical odyssey through the history of the country held from April to October in the hall of the Lucerna Palace which was built by Václav Havel's grandfather. There is a varied programme, with classical music, folklore and other entertainment.

NIGHT CLUBS

The night clubs offer variety programmes, revues or cabarets and live music to dance to. They are smart places and the cost is correspondingly high. There are an increasing number of striptease shows. A popular address is the Alhambra with its "Nightshow" of music, black theatre and the usual variety numbers: Alhambra Nightshow, Prague 1, Václavské nám. 5. Tel: 220 467. Open: 8.30pm–3am.

The Est-Bar in the Hotel Esplanade is a very elegant place indeed. The reputation of the hotel extends to the night club with its varying programme. Est-Bar, Prague 1, Washingtonova 19. Tel: 222 552. Open: 9pm–3am.

The two nightspots Jalta Club and Jalta Bar are to be found in the venerable hotel of the same name. There is an orchestra, variety and disco: Jalta Club, Jalta Bar, Prague 1, Václavské nám. 45. Tel: 265 541-9. Open: 9pm–3am.

One of the best programmes in Prague's nighlife scene is offered by the Interconti Club in the Inter-Continental Hotel: Interconti Club, Prague 1, Náměstí Curieových. Tel: 28 9. Open: 9pm–4am.

The Lucerna Palace also offers variety entertainment. The Lucerna Bar is one of the largest of Prague's bars and dance floors; it is also a venue for concerts: Lucerna Bar, Prague 1, Štěpánská 61. Tel: 235 0888. Open: 8.30pm–3am.
Monica, Prague 1, Charvátova 11. Open: all night. Often live jazz and striptease.
Narcis, Prague 1, Melantrichova 5. The usual bar atmosphere.
The Park Club in the Park Hotel is a popular haunt of business people: Park Club, Prague 7, Veletrzní 20. Open: 8.30pm–3am, Friday and Saturdays until 4am.
The Tatran Bar offers an exciting programme and has a coffeehouse with dancing on a glass floor: Tatran Bar, Prague 1, Václavské nám. 22. Open: 8.30pm–4am, dance-café 5pm–midnight.
Varieté, Prague 1, Vodičkova 30. The famous revue theatre has now become a strip joint.

Here are a few of the coffeehouses with dancing and bars:
Alfa, Prague 1, Václavské nám. 28. Open: 6pm–1am; Astra, Prague 1, Václavské nám. 4. Open: 10am–midnight; Barbara, Prague 1, Jungmannovo nám. 14. Open: 8.30pm–4am; T-Club, Prague 1, Jungmannovo nám. 14. Open: 8.30pm–4am.

DISCOTHEQUES

Most discotheques are located in the Wenceslas Square area. They attract a very mixed clientele, and most locals avoid them. They are frequented by prostitutes and female tourists who enter such establishments unaccompanied should expect constant advances.

There is usually a bouncer at the door and admission prices vary from between 50–100 crowns. Jeans and trainers are not accepted as suitable attire. The botels on the Vltava (*see Accommodation*) offer an attractive alternative.

Classic Club, Pařížska 4 (1. floor). Meeting place for artists. Open: until 3am.

A Scéna (in the Smetana Museum on the Vltava), Novotného lávka 1. Prague Scene, usually bursting at the seams later on.

Starlight Discoteka, Palác Kultury, Vyšehrad. Nice view of Prague, but the usual disco sound. Open: until 6am at weekends.

New D Club, Vinohradská 38. Mostly locals, few tourists.

Peklo (Hell). The latest rage. Gothic catacomb disco in the Strahov Monastery. Admission for members only.

Adria, Národni třída 40. Open: daily from 8.30pm.

Astra, Václavské náměstí 28. Open: daily 7pm–2am.

Habana, V jámě 8. Open: daily 9.30pm–4.30am.

Rostov, Václavské náměstí 21. Open: daily 8pm–3am.

Video-Disco, in the Hotel Zlatá Husa, Václavské nám. 7. Open: daily 7.30pm–2am.

Botel Admirál, Horejší nábřezí.
Botel Albatros, Nábřezí L. Svobody.
Botel Racek, Dvořecká louka.

JAZZ, ROCK & POP

Prague is not only a city of classical music. There is a rich calendar of rock and pop events, and since the fall of the iron curtain, the city has hosted many an international star band. For friends of jazz, Prague was always an important venue, especially for traditional jazz:

Agharta Jazz centre, Krakovská 5. Swing and new rhythms.

Club 007, Kolej Strahov (student residence), Prague 1, Spartakiadní 7. Tel: 354 441. Student club with ever-changing bands. Open: Saturday from 8pm–midnight.

Lidový dům, Prague 9, Emanuela Klímy 3. Tel: 823 434. Heavy metal and hard rock scene. Open: until 1am.

Malostranská Beseda, Prague 1, Malostranské náměstí 21. Variable programme, partly jazz.

Metro, Prague 1, Národní třída 20. Tel: 262 085. Jazz club, bands representing all styles. Open: Tuesday–Friday until 2am.

Na Chmelnici, Prague 8, Koněvová 219. Tel: 828 598. First address for local talent.

Palác kultury (Palace of Culture), Prague 4, Ulice 5. května 65. Tel: 417 2741. A multi-purpose six-floor centre with a variety of concert halls and stages.

Reduta, Prague 1, Národní třída 20. Tel: 203 825. The best known jazz club in the city. All styles, always full. Open: Monday–Friday until 2am.

Jazz Art Club, Prague 2, Vinohradská 40. Tel: 757 654. Modern jazz, Prague bands. Open: daily 9pm–2am, except Monday.

Rock Café, Prague 1, Národní třída 20. Meeting place of the Underground scene.

Sněhobílá kočka, Prague 9. Českomoravská 15. Rock and beer until 4am.

Újezd, Prague 1, Újezd 18, New Wave und Underground. Open: until 6am.

Press Jazz Club, Prague 1, Pařížská 9. New club with a varying programme. Open: Monday–Saturday 9pm–2am.

Viola Wine Bar, Prague 1, Národní třída 7. Tel: 235 87 79. Intimate stage for the literary scene with a programme of jazz on Saturdays. Open: 8pm–midnight.

CASINOS

Casinos seem to be shooting up like mushrooms in Prague. There are now about a dozen clubs where you can gamble your money in the company of a special breed of *nouveau riche* locals, many of whom have earned their money on the black market and need to launder it. They take the matter very seriously indeed. Only foreigners give tips to the croupiers.

There are four hotels that run casinos: Forum, Ambassador, Palace and the Diplomat Club. Bets are placed in US-Dollars. The casinos are open from 9pm–4am.

BRATISLAVA

There is not as much nightlife in the Slovakian capital as there is in the Bohemian metropolis. More so than in Prague, during the Communist era nightime venues were forced to keep a low profile and the scene is only just beginning to emerge from its underground refuge. What is important here, however, is good food and wine, and as a result the wine cellars with their gypsy musicians are always pretty full in the evening.

Those who prefer beer should head for an establishment such as the Stará sladovná, the city's former brewery with its 1,600 places (and very loud live music). Bear in mind that food is not available after 9pm.

The cafés in the city centre are another alternative. They have a truly cosmopolitan atmosphere and some have summer terraces good for wiling away the afternoon.

BARS

The Hotels Bratislava Devín, Carlton und Forum have their own night clubs. In addition, the following addresses are worth seeking out:
Jalta, Gorkého ul 15. Tel: 51 552.
Krištáľ, Ul. Čs. armády 37. Tel: 33 55 48.
Park, Hviezdoslavovo nám. 21. Tel: 53 008.

Once upon a time discos only existed in the various student clubs. With the privatisation of the entertainments industry, other places to dance are now emerging, such as the **Espresso-Diskotéka** on Michalská 13.

SPORTS

Emil Zátopek, the triple olympic winner at Helsinki in 1952, Vfra Cáslavská, the queen of the Mexico Olympics in 1968, Martina Navrátilova, Ivan Lendl – they are just some of the sportsmen and women who made Czechoslovakia an internationally respected sporting nation. Today, both the Czech and Slovak republics offer the tourist not only a host of spectator sports, but also a diverse choice for active participation.

FOOTBALL

The number one spectator sport is football. The national team has reached the World Cup finals two times, and after the last World Cup in 1990 many top players such as goalkeeper Tomáš Skuhravý left for top international clubs.

The best known clubs are in the large cities: in Prague (Sparta, Slavia, Dukla and Bohemians), in Bratislava (Slovan and Inter) and in Brno (Zbrojovka). The First Division plays all year, with two breaks (June–August and December–February). The country's most successful club is Sparta Prague; it provided most of the players for the last World Cup. At the time of going to press it was not clear how the division of Czechoslovakia would effect the composition of the football league. Compared to England, tickets are still relatively cheap, despite the fact that capitalist values have now invaded the pitch.

ICE HOCKEY

While in terms of crowd sizes the world's quickest team sport comes second in the popularity stakes, during the winter it has no serious competition. There are strong teams naturally from Prague (Sparta), Bratislava (Slovan) and Brno (Zetor), but high-quality ice-hockey is also played in the smaller towns such as Pardubice (Tesla), České Budějovice (Motor), Košice (VSŽ), Litvínov (CHZ), Plseň (Škoda) and Trenčín (Dukla). The army team from Jihlava (Dukla Jihlava) once held a regular position right at the top of the league. In general games are played on Tuesdays and Fridays after 6pm.

TENNIS

For years now, Czechoslovakian tennis players, both men and women, have found themselves right at the top of the world rankings. The Czechoslovakian Tennis School has an international reputation, and Steffi Graf certainly wouldn't have got where she is were it not for her trainer Pavel Složil.

The Prague Tennis Arena on the island of Štvanice in the Vltava, the venue for Davis Cup and Grand Prix tournaments, is considered to be one of the most beautiful tennis complexes in Europe. But tourists can also play tennis in Prague. Between June and September Čedok organises courses for both beginners and advanced under the instruction of top trainers.

The best known tennis courts are at:
Štvanice Stadium Prague 7. Tel: 2316323. About £7 per hour.

Indoor courts can be found at Štvanice, as well as at Prague 7, Kostelní (Tel: 37 36 83) and Prague 7, Stromovka (Tel: 325479, 324850). An all-year-round tennis school is offered by the **Club Hotel** Praha Průhonice, Průhonice near Prague. Tel: 00422-723241-9.

WINTER SPORTS

World-class Czech or Slovak wintersportsmen can be counted on the fingers of one hand. The most successful internationally are the ski-jumpers with the Olympic winner Jiří Raška and the world champion Jiří Parma. Nevertheless, wintersports are still extremely popular, with no less than 3.5 million active participants. In the wintertime, large areas of the countryside lie under a thick blanket of snow and the children learn how to ski as soon as they go to school.

Skiing in the Krkonoše (Giant Mountains) started over 100 years ago: it was in the 1880s that Count Harrach first introduced skis to Bohemia. The Czech winter sports centres are often the venues for world cup cross country events, ski-jumping and occasionally alpine disciplines as well.

In 1970 the Slovakian ski centre Štrbské pleso in

the High Tatra was the venue for the world championships in the Nordic competitions, in 1983 the ski-jump world championships were decided at Harrachov in the Krkonoše.

Today, the best conditions for alpine skiing are provided by the Low Tatra in Slovakia; fans of cross-country skiing find ideal conditions in the Iser Mountains, the Krkonoše, the Beskids and the Bohemian Forest.

In comparison to the Alps, the prices for ski-lifts are very low indeed, although one's expectations should not be too high. Queueing is the rule, especially during the holidays and at weekends. You should preferably bring all your own gear as rented skis and boots don't generally meet the standards to which westerners are accustomed.

Further information can be obtained from Čedok and other travel agencies.

MOTOR SPORTS

Speedway and Motocross have been popular for years in the Czech Republic. New tracks in Most and Brno (Grand Prix circuits) have recently extended the range still further – particularly for motorbike racing. Important dirt-track events are held in Prague, Slany, Žarnovica, Mariánské Lázně and Pardubice.

GOLF

Situated in beautiful settings, the golf courses at Mariánské Lázně and Karlovy Vary are of international standard. They are open all the year round with winter greens from November to April.

Prague also has an 18-hole golf course, adjacent to the Hotel Golf Praha in the district of Motol in the west of the city:

Hotel Golf, Prague 5 (Motol), Plzeňská. Tel: 59 66 93. Open: daily 8am–8pm (1 April–30 October) and from 9am to dusk in the low season.

There is also a golf course at Poděbrady, although its course is shorter.

MOUNTAINEERING

The ranges of the Czech and Slovak republics offer climbing to all degrees of difficulty. The hardest routes are to be found in the High Tatra and in the Lesser Fatra (Malá Fatra). Excellent training for rock can be found on the sandstone crags of the "Bohemian Switzerland" (Ceské Svycarsko) around the Labe (Elbe) Valley in Northern Bohemia. Again, you are advised to bring along all your own gear as quality equipment is difficult to get hold of.

HIKING

For both Czechs and Slovaks, hiking has been a popular activity for generations. Both republics together have a total 50,000 kilometres (30,000

miles) of marked trails, from the gentle hills of the Bohemian Forest to the alpine summits of the High Tatra.

All paths are marked with colours (red, blue, green and yellow) and often with information about how long a certain stretch is expected to take. The majority of routes are tailored to the average walker, so that normal equipment is sufficient. However, mountain equipment is necessary in the high mountains, especially as one has to expect rapid changes in the weather. If it gets cloudy in the mountains you should not continue as snow storms are possible even in summer.

The hiking maps (*turistická mapa*) are very detailed and there are two different sets for winter and summer. The winter maps (*zimní mapa*) show the the pistes and ski-lifts and the summer maps (*letní mapa*) show the campsites.

CAVING

The Karst regions of the Czech and Slovak republics contain vast cave systems, which are partly open to the public. The most famous ones are the Koněprusy Caves between Karlstejn and Beroun in Central Bohemia, the cave complex of Demänovské jaskyňe in Central Slovakia and the Dobšinská ľadová jaskyňa ice caves, also in Slovakia. The focal point of the Moravian Karst (Moravsky kras) is the Punkva Cave, which is accessible by boat.

WATERSPORTS

The country possesses thousands of ponds which were used as long ago as the Middle Ages for the breeding of fish. In addition there are extensive river and stream sytems as well as countless lakes and barrages, most of which have been constructed in the last 40 years for energy purposes. Most of the artificial lakes have now blended in with the natural environment and they have become a paradise for water leisure activities for both Czechs and Slovaks.

Slovakia has the best stretches for canoeists. In the spring, when the snow has melted, streams and rivers offer fantasic possibilities for white water canoeing. Things are more leisurely on the dam lakes or on the Danube, whose islands and meadows supporting unique flora and fauna make it an important European biotope.

The most popular stretches for boating in the Bohemian part of the country are the upper reaches of the Vltava and its tributaries the Sázava, Otava and Luznice. The lower reaches of the Vltava and Labe are less suitable on account of pollution.

FISHING

Fishing is a widespread hobby. The local fishing clubs make sure that the stocks are constantly replenished from the national breeding stations. The most common species are eel, barbel, perch, brace, trout, pike, carp, tench, silurid and zander. Foreign tourists require a general fishing permit as well as permission for specific areas and species. These can be obtained from Čedok representatives.

HUNTING

Hunting trips are possible all the year round. Game allowed to be shot includes: small game, stags and deer, fallow deer and wild boar as well as bears. One can also shoot pheasant and hare. Hunting permits can again be obtained from Čedok or on the border. Shooting fees must be paid in Western currencies. On top of these come fees for guides or interpreters as well as organisation and insurance. Nights are normally spent in the accommodation of the state forestry commission.

RIDING

There are many opportunities for riding, particularly around the spa towns. For spectators the most exciting event is undoubtedly the Pardubice Steeplechase with the famous Taxis Ditch (*see feature page 236*). Further racecourses are in Prague-Chuchle and in Slušovice.

PHOTOGRAPHY

Photography materials are available in speciality shops, souvenir and department stores. In addition to an assortment of indigenous products, various internationally known brand-name items can also be purchased. Minilab studios offer quick-developing services. The quality of developed prints and slides tends to be just about as good – or bad – as it would be in any other country. Because it is rather difficult to obtain video and movie camera film in Czechoslovakia, it's a good idea to bring everything you think you may need with you from home.

LANGUAGE

As Western Slavic languages, Czech and Slovakian have a common linguistic background and are closely related. Czechs and Slovaks have no trouble at all communicating with one another.

PRONUNCIATION

Vowels:
Accents above the letters indicate long vowels: á, é ,í, ó, ú, ů.

ý	long "e".
ou	pronounced "show"
ě	pronounced ye

Consonants:

č	pronounced "church"
ř	pronounced with a silibant
š	pronounced sh
ž	pronounced with a "j" as in "journey"

The Czech letters ě, ř and ů do not exist in Slovakian; Slovakian also contains its own letters such as ľ (soft l) and ä (pronounced ey).

CZECH WORDS & PHRASES

ano/ne	yes/no
děkuji/prosím	thank you/please
dobré ráno	good morning
dobrý den	hello
dobrý vecer	good evening
na shledanou	good bye
promiňte	sorry
co to stojí?	How much is that?
dejte mi	Could you give me
chtěl bych	I would like to
jak dlouho/daleko?	how far/long?
dobrý/spatný	good/bad
levný/drahý	cheap/expensive
horky/studený	hot/cold
volný/obsazený	vasant/occupied
otevřeno/zavřeno	open/closed
nerozumím	I don't understand
vinárna	wine bar
pivnice	pub
oběd	lunch
večere	supper
budu platit	I would like to pay

NUMBERS

jeden	one
dva	two
tri	three
čtyři	four
pft	five
šest	six
sedm	seven
osm	eight
devět	nine
deset	ten
jedenáct	eleven
dvanáct	twelve
dvacet	twenty
sto	one hundred
dvěstě	two hundred
třista	three hundred
čtyřista	four hundred
pětset	five hundred
tisíc	one thousand

TIME OF THE DAY

ráno	morning
poledne	noon
odpoledne	afternoon
večer	evening
hodina	hour
den	day
noc	night

DAYS OF THE WEEK

pondělí	Monday
útery	Tuesday
středa	Wednesday
čtvrtek	Thursday
pátek	Friday
sobota	Saturday
neděle	Sunday

DRINKS

Becherovka	bitter cordial
čaj	tea
černy čaj	black tea
káva	coffee
černá káva	Turkish coffee
káva s mlékem	milk coffee
videnská káva	coffee with whipped cream
limonáda	lemonade
pivo	beer
malé pivo	small beer
černé pivo	dark beer
svetlé pivo	lager
točené pivo	draught beer
slivovice	slivovitz
bilé víno	white wine
červené víno	red wine
voda	water

FOOD

bažant	pheasant
biftek	steak
bramborák	potato fritter
brambory	potatoes
buchty	Bohemian sweet dumplings
chléb	bread
bílý chléb	white bread
černy chléb	brown bread
cukr	sugar
drůbež	poultry
fazole	beans
guláš	goulash
houby	mushrooms
hovězí	beef
hovězí pečené	roast beef
hovězí vařené	boiled beef
hruška	pear
husa	goose
houska	roll
jablka	apple
kachna	duck
kančí	wild boar
kapr pecený	fried carp
kapr smažený	garnished carp
kapr varený	boiled carp
kapusta	savoy cabbage
kaše bramborová	mashed potatoes
knedlíky bramborové	potato dumpling
knedlíky houskové	white bread dumpling
knedlíky ovocné	fruit dumpling
králík	rabbit
krocan	turkey
kuře	chicken
kuře smažené	roast chicken
kyselé zelí	sauerkraut
ledvinky	kidneys
máslo	butter
meruňky	apricots
mrkev	carrots
ořechy	nuts
ovoce	fruit
palačinky	thin pancakes
párky	sausages
pečené	roast meat
pečivo	biscuits
polévka	soup
polévka dršťková	tripe soup
pstruh	trout
rajčata	tomato
rostěnka	roast meat
ryba	fish
rýže	rice
salám	sausage, salami
salát	salad
sardinký	sardines
sekaná	meat loaf
sladký	sweet
slaný	salty
srncí	roast venison

štika	pike
šunka	ham
telecí	veal
topinky	toast
třešně	cherries
uzenina	smoked meat
vejce do skla	egg in a glass
vejce na měkko	soft boiled egg
vejce na tvrdo	hard boiled egg
vepřová	roast pork
zajíc	hare
zelenina	vegetables
zmrzlina	icecream
zvěřina	game

OTHER USEFUL WORDS

avárna	coffee house
restaurace	restaurant
hostinec	pub
vinárna	wine bar
snídaně	breakfast
oběd	lunch
večeře	supper
volno	free
obsazeno	occupied
stůl	table
židle	chair
nůž	knife
vidlička	fork
lžice	spoon
talíř	plate
sklenice	glass
číšník	waiter
vrchní	head waiter
sevírka	waitress
ubrousek	serviette
jídelní lístek	menu
specialita	speciality
párátko	toothpick

SPECIAL INFORMATION

TRANSLATION SERVICES

Artlingua, Prague 2, Myslíkova 6. Tel: 29 51 69/ 29 55 97/29 37 41/29 41 98. Interpreting and translation services offered in 30 languages; organisation of congresses and press conferences.
KAHLEN Service, Prague 4, Strakonicka 510. Tel: 34 53 46.
BABEL SERVICE, Prague 4, Palác Kultury (Palace of Culture). Tel: 692 67 41.
TAP, Prague 1, Helichova 1. Tel: 54 78 44.

AUTOMOBILE SERVICES

PRAGUE
CAR REPAIRS

W, Ford, Nissan: Severní XI, Prague 4. Tel: 766 752–4. Open: Monday–Friday 7am–3.45pm.
Fiat: Na strži 35, Prague 4. Tel: 692 2434. Open: Monday–Friday 6.30am–3.45pm.
Simca, Peugeot, Vauxhall Opel, Oltcit: Dáblická 2, Prague 8. Tel: 887 803, 888 257. Open: Monday–Friday 7am–3.45pm.
Vaz: Podbabská 3, Prague 6. Tel: 32 43 16, 32 40 78. Open: Monday–Friday 7am–3.45pm.
Daewoo, Renault, Dacia: Novostrašnická 46, Prague 10. Tel: 78215 01. Open: Mon–Fri 7am–3.45pm.
Škoda: Černokostelecká 114, Prague 10. Tel: 704 650. Open: Monday–Friday 6.30am–3pm.
BMW: Průbfěžná 76, Prague 10. Tel: 781 11 09. Open: Monday–Friday 8am–4.30pm.
Mercedes: Jeremiášova 11, Prague 5. Tel: 526 311, 523 229. Open: Monday–Friday 7.30am–5pm.

TYRE & BATTERY SERVICE

Vinohradská, Prague 2. Tel: 272 419. Open: Monday–Friday 6am–8pm.

PETROL STATIONS

4-hour service: Prague 3: Olšanská (special, super), Kališnická (special, diesel); Prague 4, Újezd u Pruhonic. Prague 5: Motol, Plzenská (special, super, diesel, unleaded). Prague 7: Argentinská (special, super, diesel, unleaded). Prague 8: Prosek (special, super, diesel); Českobrodská (special, super, diesel, unleaded).

Stations with **unleaded petrol**: Prague 3: Olšanská, Kališnická. Prague 4: Újezd u Průhonice, Podolská, U Pragocaru. Prague 6: Mackova, Ve struhách, Ruzyně (Dedina), Evropská, Bělohorská. Prague 7: Argentínská. Prague 8: Liberecká. Prague 9: Liberecká. Prague 10: Limuzská.

BRATISLAVA
CAR REPAIRS

Drutechna, Drienova ul. 33. Tel: 23 51 42; Mlynské Nivy 34. Tel: 62 703; Žabotova 16. Tel: 42 420/ 47 183; Školská. Tel: 43 136, 43 279.
Mototechna, Stará Vajnorká cesta 11. Tel: 21 40 67.

TYRE SERVICE

Vkus, Ul. Račianska 30. Tel: 60 135; Vajnorská cesta 95. Tel: 69 178.

PETROL

Petrol (24 hours), Bajkalská, Ul. Račianska 103, Lamačská cesta. Vainorská cesta.

USEFUL ADDRESSES

TRAVEL AGENCIES

PRAGUE

Autoturist, Prague 2, Na rybníčku 16. Tel: 203 35 58; Prague 10, Limuzská 12. Tel: 77 34 55.
AveUd., Prague 2, Sokolská 56. Tel: 20 52 29; Prague 2, Main Station, Wilsonova 8. Tel: 236 25 60/236 30 75.
Balnea, Prague 1, Pařížská 1. Tel: 232 37 67/29 28 68. Specialises in the spa resorts.
Bohemia Tour, Prague 1, Zlatnická 7.
CKM, Prague 2, Žitná 12. Tel: 29 99 49. For young people.
ČSD, Prague 1, Na příkopě 31. Tel: 236 32 38; Prague 2, Wilson Station (main station). Tel: 235 28 84; Prague 7, Holesovice Station.
Pragotur, Prague 1, U Obecního domu. Tel: 23172 8.
Rekrea, Prague 1, Revoluční 13. Tel: 231 06 33. Room reservations.
Sport-Turist, Prague 1, Národní třída 33. Tel: 26 38 86. Air and train tickets.

BRATISLAVA

Slovakoturist, Volgogradská 1, Bratislava. Tel: 55 827/52 313, Fax: 55 882.
Javorina, Sedlárska 6, Bratislava. Tel: 33 15 79/33 07 64.
Tatratour, Bajkalská 25, Bratislava. Tel: 68 877, Fax: 65 530.
CKM, Hviezdoslavovo nám, Bratislava. Tel: 23 80 84.

ČEDOK OFFICES ABROAD

Austria: Parkring 12, 1010 Wien. Tel: 43/222 512 1374, Fax: 43/222 512 591 685.
France: Čedok France S.a.r.l., Avenue de L'Opera 32, 75002 Paris. Tel: 33/1 4742 7487, Fax: 33/1 4924 9946.
Germany: Čedok Reisen GmbH, Kaiserstrasse 54, 6000 Frankfurt 1. Tel: 49/69 274 017, Fax: 0049/ 69 235 890.
Italy: Čedok Italia S.R.L., Via Piemonte 32, 00 187 Roma. Tel: 39/6 483 406, Fax: 39/6 482 8397.
Sweden: Nordisk – Čedok, Sveavaegen 9–11, 111 57 Stockholm. Tel: 46/8 207 250, Fax: 46/8 200 090.
Switzerland: Čedok – Tschechoslowakisches Reisebüro GmbH, Uraniastrasse 34/2, 8025 Zürich. Tel: 41/ 1 211 4245, Fax: 41/1 211 4246.
United Kingdom: Čedok London Limited, Czechoslovak Travel Bureau, 17–18 Old Bond Street, London W1X 4RB. Tel: 44/71 629 6058, Fax: 44/ 71 493 7841.
United States: Cědok, Czechoslovak Travel Bureau Inc., 10 East 40th Street, New York N.Y. 10016, 1/212 609 9720, Fax 1/212 418 0597.

ČSA OFFICES IN PRAGUE

Tickets and reservations: Revoluční 1 (*Kotva*) Prague 1. Tel: 2146 (reservations); tel: 232 2006 (domestic tickets). Flight information: Revoluční 25 (*Vltava*) Prague 1. Tel: 231 7395, 2146. Both offices are located near the Metro station *Náměstí Republiky*. Central information service, Ruzyně Airport, Prague 6. Tel: 367 760, 367 814, 334 1111.

OTHER AIRLINES IN PRAGUE

Aeoroflot, Na příkopě 20, Prague 1. Tel: 232 4707, 260 862. Airport: Tel: 367 815.
Air Algerie, Žitná 23, Prague 1. Tel: 265 483, 275 770. Airport: Tel: 225 770.
Air France, Václavské náměstí 10, Prague 1. Tel: 260 155. Airport: Tel: 367 819.
Air India, Václavské náměstí 15, Prague 1. Tel: 223 854.
Alitalia, Revoluční 5, Prague 1. Tel: 231 0535.
Austrian Airlines, Prague 1, Tel: 231 2795. Airport: Tel: 231 6469, 367 818.
British Airways, Stěpánská 63, Prague 1. Tel: 236 0353.

Delta, Pařížska 11. Tel: 232 4772.
KLM, Václavské náměstí 39, Prague 1. Tel: 264 362/264 369. Airport: Tel: 367 822.
Lufthansa, Pařížska 28, Prague 1. Tel: 231 7440, 231 7551. Airport: Tel: 367 827.
SAS, Stěpánská 61, Prague 1. Tel: 228 141. Airport: Tel: 367 817.
Swissair, Pařížska 11, Prague 1. Tel: 232 4707. Airport: Tel: 367 809.

ČSA OFFICES ABROAD

Austria: Parkring 12, 1010 Vienna. Tel: 01-523 805 or 512 9886.
Canada: 2020 rue Universite, Montreal, Quebec H3A 2A5. Tel: 514-844 4200 or 844 6376; 401 Bay Street, Suite 1510, Toronto, Ontario M5H2Y4. Tel: 416-363 3174 or 363 3516.
Germany: Baselerstrasse 46-48, 6000 Frankfurt/ Main. Tel: 069-253 559.
Switzerland: Sumatrastrasse 25,8006 Zurich. Tel: 01-363 8000 to 363 8009; ČSA Office 334, Postfach 219, 1215; Geneva Airport: Tel: 022-798 3330.
United Kingdom: 12a Margaret Street, London W1N 7 LF. Tel: 071-255 1898 or 255 1366.
United States: 545 Fifth Avenue, New York, New York 10017. Tel: 212-682 7541 or 682 5833.

EMBASSIES IN PRAGUE

Algeria: Prague 6, Korejská 16. Tel: 312 0758.
Argentina: Prague 1, Washingtonova 25. Tel: 22 854.
Austria: Prague 5, Victora Huga 10. Tel: 546 557.
Belgium: Prague 1, Valdštejnská 6. Tel: 534 051.
Brazil: Prague 1, Bolzanova 5. Tel: 229 254.
Canada: Prague 6, Mickiewiczova 6. Tel: 312 0251.
CIS: Prague 6, Pod kaštany 16. Tel: 381 940.
Denmark: Prague 2, U Havlíčkových sadů 1. Tel: 254 715.
Finland: Prague 2, Dřevná 2. Tel: 205 541.
France: Prague 1, Velkopřevorské nám. 2. Tel: 533 041.
Germany: Prague 1, Vlašská 19. Tel: 532 351.
Greece: Prague 6, Na Ořechovce 19. Tel: 354 279, 356 723.
Hungary: Prague 6, Mičurinova 1. Tel. 365 041.
India: Prague 1, Valdštejnská 6. Tel: 532 642.
Italy: Prague 1, Nerudova 20. Tel: 530 666.
Japan: Prague 1, Maltézské nám. 6. Tel: 535 751.
Mexico: Prague 7, Nad Kazankou 8. Tel: 855 1539.
Morocco: Prague 6, K Starému Bubenči 4. Tel: 329 4404.
Netherlands: Prague 1, Maltézské nám. 1. Tel: 531 378.
Norway: Prague 6, Na Ořechovce 69. Tel: 354 56.
Poland: Prague 1, Valdštejnska 8. Tel: 536 951.
Portugal: Prague 7, Bubenská 3. Tel: 878 472.
Romania: Prague 1, Nerudova 5. Tel: 533 059.
Spain: Prague 6, Pevnostní 9. Tel: 327 124.
Sweden: Prague l, Úvoz 13. Tel: 533 344, 533 865.

Switzerland: Prague 6, Pevnostní 7. Tel: 328 319.
United Kingdom: Prague 1, Thunovská 14. Tel: 533 347/533 370.
United States: Prague 1, Trziste 15. Tel: 53 66 41.

EMBASSIES ABROAD

Because of the division of property, the premises of the embassies of the former Czech and Slovak Federal Republic are now occupied by either the Embassy of the Czech Republic or the Embassy of Slovakia, but not both. At the time of going to press, a complete list of new addresses and telephone numbers was not available. Visitors are advised to contact the embassies at their old addresses:

Argentina: Embajada de la Republica Federativa Checa y Eslovaca, Av. Figueroa Alcorta 3240, Buenos Aires.
Austria: Botschaft der Tschechischen und Slowakischen Föderativen Republik, Penzinger Strasse 11-13, 1140 Wien.
Australia: Embassy of the Czech and Slovak Federal Republic, 47 Culgoa Circuit, O'Malley, Canberra ACT 2606.
Belgium: Ambassade de la Republique Federative Tcheque et Slovaque, 152 Avenue A. Buyl, 1050 Bruxelles.
Brazil: Embaixada da Republica Federativa Tcheca y Eslovaca, Avenida das Nacoes, lote 21, Caixa Postal 07-0970, Brasilia DF.
Bulgaria: Embassy of the Czech and Slovak Federal Republic, Bulvar Janko Sakazov 9, Sophia.
Canada: Embassy of the Czech and Slovak Federal Republic, 50 Rideau Terrace, Ottawa, Ontario, K1M 2A1.
Cyprus: Embassy of the Czech and Slovak Federal Republic, 7, Kastorias Street, PO Box 1165, Nicosia.
Denmark: Embassy of the Czech and Slovak Federal Republic, Ryvangs Alle 14-16, 2100 Kobenhavn O.
Finland: Embassy of the Czech and Slovak Federal Republic, Armfeltintie 14, 00150 Helsinki 15.
France: Ambassade de la Republique Federative Tcheque et Slovaque, 15, Avenue Charles Floquet 75 007 Paris.
Germany: Botschaft der Tschechischen und Slowakischen Föderativen Republik, 5300 Bonn, Ferdinandstrasse 27.
Greece: Ambassade de la Republique Federative Tcheque et Slovaque, 6, Rue Seferis, Palaio Psychico, 15452 Athenes.
Iceland: Embassy of the Czech and Slovak Federal Republic, Smargata 16, 101 Reykjavik.
India: Embassy of the Czech and Slovak Federal Republic, 50/M Niti Marg, Chanakyapuri, New Delhi – 110021.
Ireland: Trade Mission of the Czech and Slovak Federal Republic, Confederation House of Irish Industry, Kildare Street, Dublin 2.

Israel: Embassy of the Czech and Slovak Federal Republic, Zaitlin Str. 23, PO Box 16361, 61664 Tel Aviv.

Italy: Ambasciata della Repubblica Federativa Ceca e Slovacca, Pontificio Collegio, Nepomuceno, Via Monte Santo 25, 00195 Roma.

Japan: Embassy of the Czech and Slovak Federal Republic, 16-14, Hiroo 2-chome, Shibuya-ku, Tokyo 150.

Malaysia: Embassy of the Czech and Slovak Federal Republic, 32 Jalan Mesra (off Jalan Damai), PO Box 12496, 50780 Kuala Lumpur.

Mexico: Embajada de la Republica Federativa Checa y Eslovaca, Cuvier, No. 22, Colonia Nuevo Anzures, Mexico 5 DF.

Netherlands: Ambassade de la Republique Federative Tcheque et Slovaque, Parkweg 1, 2585 JG Den Haag.

Norway: Embassy of the Czech and Slovak Federal Republic, Thomas Heftyes gate 32, 0264 Oslo 2.

New Zealand: Embassy of the Czech and Slovak Federal Republic, 12 Anne Street, Wadestown, PO Box 2843, Wellington.

Poland: Ambassada Czeskiej i Slowackiej Republiki Federacyjnej, Koszykowa 18, Warszawa, Skr. poczt. 00-555.

Portugal: Embaixada da Republica Federativa Checa e Eslovaca, Rua Pinheiro Chagas No. 6, Lisboa.

Romania: Ambassade de la Republique Federative Tcheque et Slovaque, Strada Ion Ghica 11, Sector 4, Bucuresti.

Russia: Embassy of the Czech and Slovak Federal Republic, Moscow D-47, ul. J. Fucika 12/14.

South Africa: Consulate General of the Czech and Slovak Federal Republic, LO 3, Matroosberg Road, Waterkloof Park, Pretoria, PO Box 3326.

Spain: Embajada de la Republica Federativa Checa y Eslovaca, Pinar 20, 28006, Madrid 6.

Sweden: Embassy of the Czech and Slovak Federal Republic, Floragatan 13, 11431 Stockholm.

Switzerland: Ambassade de la Republique Federative Tcheque et Slovaque, Muristrasse 53, 3000 Bern 16.

United Arab Emirates: Embassy of the Czech and Slovak Federal Republic, PO Box 27009, Abu Dhabi.

United Kingdom: Embassy of the Czech and Slovak Federal Republic, 25 Kensington Palace Gardens, London W8 4QY.

United States: Embassy of the Czech and Slovak Federal Republic, 3900 Linnean Avenue NW, Washington DC, 20008.

FURTHER READING

Kafka, Franz, *America/ The Trail/ The Castle*. Translated by W. and E. Muir, Penguin Modern Classics.

Kafka, Franz, *Description of a Struggle and other stories*. Translated by W. and E. Muir, Penguin Modern Classics.

Kafka, Franz, *Diaries*. Translated by W. and E. Muir, Penguin Modern Classics.

Hašek, Jaroslav, *The Good Soldier Schweik*. Translated by Sir C. Parrot, Heinemann.

Vaculík, Ludvík, *A cup of Coffee with my Interrogator*. Translated by G. Theiner, Readers International.

Vaculík, Ludvík, *Prague Chronicles*. Translated by G. Theiner, Readers International.

Seifert, Jaroslav, *Selected Poetry*. Translated by E. Osers, Andre Deuts.

Neruda, Jan, *Tales of the Little Quarter*. Translated by E. Pargetwr, Greenwood Press London.

OTHER INSIGHT GUIDES

From the *Insight Guide* collection comes a range of travel guides, specially designed to help make your visit an unforgettable one.

A practical and inspiring guide to the "Golden City" on the Vltava.

Insight Guides unveil a whole new world recently opened up to travellers.

ART/PHOTO CREDITS

INDEX

D

E

F

I

J

K

Krakova hoľa 307
Kralice nad Oslavou 255
Kremnica 305
Křížový pramen 216
Krkonoše Mountains 68, 81, 118, 227–228, 230
Krkonoše National Park 119
Kroměříž 268
Kronika Trojanska 195
Kuks 230
kulaks 75
Kůlna cavern 248
Kundera, Milan – *The Joke, The Unbearable Lightness of Being* 60, 62, 99–100
Kutná Hora 234
Kuttenberg Decree 234
Květná zahrada 269
Kyselí Canyon 310

L

Labyrinth of Mirrors 161
lace making 230
land reform 47, 75
Laterna Magika 166, 171, 173
Latran 188
Lázeňske oplatky (wafers) 209
Lázně Kynžvart 217
Lázně Poděbrady 237
Le Corbusier 267
lead crystal 237
Ledeč 239
Lednice 253
Lehmann, Caspar 226
Lehár, Franz 299
Leopold II 40
Lesser Fatra 266, 307
Lesser Fatra National Park 120
Lesser Quarter 93, 151–154
Lesser Quarter Bridge Towers 152
Lesser Quarter Square 152
Letter of Majesty 38, 86
Levetzov, Baroness Ulrike 215–216, 217
Levoča 83, 311
Liberec 68, 225, 228
Libosad 227
Libuše legend 25, 167
Lidice, massacre at 49, 178
lignite 80, 81
Limbach 288
Lipnice nad Sázavou 239
Lipník nad Bečvou 262
Lipno Dam 64
Lipno Reservoir 189, 189
Liptovský Mikuláš 120, 307
Liszt, Franz 263, 282
literature 97–101
Litice 230
Litoměříce 222, 224
Litomyšl 239
Litovel 261
Little Carpathian Mountains 288, 289
Little Entente 48, 49
Little Square (Prague) 141
Lomnický štít 118, 318
Loos, Adolf 243
Loreto of Prague 153–54
Lower City (Brno) 246
Lower Gate (Domažlice) 201

Lower Tatra 120, 303, 307
Lower Tatra National Park 120
Lucerna Palace of Culture (Prague) 113
Ludwig, King 32, 37
Lützen 39
Luhačovice 267
Luisin pramen (Františkovy Lázně) 214
Lurago, Anselmo 140, 155
Lusatia 28, 86
Lustig, Arnošt 99–100
Luther, Martin 86
Lutherans 86
Lužnice River 63
lynxes 120
Lysá hora 266

M

Mácha, Karel Hynek 97, 167
Machek, Antonín 67
Máchovo Lake 224
Macocha Abyss 248
Madonna of Košice 309
Magistrale 318
Magyarisation 41
Magyars 26
Mahler, Gustav 256
Main Railway Station (Prague) 113
Main Square (Bratislava) 286
Maj department store (Prague) 165
Malá Fatra *see* Lesser Fatra
Malá Strana *see* Lesser Quarter
Malé Karpaty *see* Little Carpathian Mountains
Malostranská beseda 153
Malovaný dům 255
Maltese Grand Prior's Palace 152
Maltese Square 152
Mánes, Josef 141
Manés House of Fine Art 166
Manětín 197
Mariánské Lázně 91, 212, 214–215
Maria Theresa, Empress 40, 70, 222, 279
Marienbad *see* Mariánské Lázně
Mariin pramen (Mariánské Lázně) 216
marionette festival (Chrudim) 239
Marionette Theatre (Plzeň) 195
marmots 119
Martinů, Bohuslav 94
Marx, Karl 207
Masaryk Square 264
Masaryk, Tomáš Garrigue 42, 47, 49, 60, 69, 83, 85, 99, 255, 269
Masaryk, Jan 52
Masné krámy 185
Matthew of Arras 155, 156
Matthias Corvinus 283, 303, 304
Matthias Gate 155
Matuš Tower 295
Maulbertsch, Anton 161
Maximilian II, Emperor 37, 238
Meciar, Vladimír 56, 57
Mělník 178
Mělník Castle 178–179
Mendel, Gregor Johann 247
Mengusovská dolina valley 318
Methodius (Slavic apostle) 27, 83, 87, 97, 151
Metternich, Prince von 208, 217
Miča, František Václav 254

N

O

P

Q – R

S

Strela river 197
Stříbro 201–202
Studenovodská dolina valley 318
Studenovodské vodpády waterfall 315, 319
Studený pramen 214
Štúr, Ľudovit 100, 281, 282, 287
Štúrovo 299
Sucharda, Stanislav 113
Sudeten German Gau 48
Sudeten German Home Front 48
Sudeten German Welfare and Cultural Association 68
Sudeten Germans 49, 52, 67, 68
Suk, Josef 227
Šumava National Park 117
Šumperk 262
Svatopluk Čech Bridge 113
Švabinský, Max 146
Svatý Vavřinček mountain 200
Svět Lake 186
Světlá 239
Švihov 199
Svišťová valley 319
Svitavy 239
Svoboda, Milan 171
Swedish Army 207, 243, 261, 269
Sychrov Castle 225

T

Tábor 32, 93, 180, 181
Taborites 85
Tachov 201
Tále 307
Tatra automobile plant 265
Tatra Mountains 77
Tatra National Park 315
Tatranská Kotlina 317
Tatranská Lomnica 317, 318, 319
Tatranská Polianka 319
Tatrzanski Narododowy National Park (Poland) 118
taverns
  U Fleků 169
  U Kalicha (The Chalice) 101, 169
  U Pinkasů 169
  U svatého Tomáše 169
  Zelený dom (Bratislava) 286
Taxis Ditch 236
Technical University (Brno) 247
Technical University of Košice 309
Telč 253, 255
Teplá 215
Teplice nad Metují 228
Teplice 64, 69, 222
Terezín 50–51, 70, 144, 222
Téryo chata 319
Testament of Bratislava 32
textiles 40, 225, 228, 230, 243, 256, 297
Thám, Václav 107
theatre
  ABC Theatre 105
  Andrej Bagar (Nitra) 298
  Braník Theatre 171
  Castle Theatre (Česky Krumlov) 189
  Cinoherni klub (The Actors' Club) 104
  Czech National Theatre (Vienna) 92
  Czech Theatre of the Absurd 105
  Divadlo Na zábradlí (Theatre by the Railings)
    104–105

Divadlo za branou (Theatre behind the Gate) 104
Empire Theatre 199
Estates Theatre 105, 106–7, 139, 141
Gag Theatre 171
German National Theatre 107
Ha Theatre (Ha Divadlo) 107
Janáček Opera House and Ballet 246
Jaroměřice Castle 254
Krušnohorské divadlo 222
Liberated Theatre 104
Mahen Theatre 246
Municipal (Trnava) 293
Municipal (Karlovy Vary) 209
Municipal (Mariánské Lázně) 217
National Theatre (Bratislava) 60, 287
National Theatre (Prague) 165–6, 171
Nová Scéna 171
Reduta Theatre 245
Rokoko Theatre 104
Semafor Theatre 104
Smetana Theatre 107
Spejbel and Hurvínek (puppet theatre) 107
Studio Ypsilon 107
Theologians' Room (Strahov) 161
Theresienstadt see Terezín
Thermal Baths of Trenčianske Teplice 297
thermal springs 207, 210, 211, 294, 299
Thirty Years' War 38, 159, 180, 207, 243, 246, 261,
  262, 269
Three Golden Lions guest house 139
Thurzo House 303–304
Tichá Orlice river 230
Tiské skály (sandstone cliffs) 223
Tiso, Josef 50, 61, 70
Tomášek, Cardinal 83, 85
Torture Chamber (Bratislava) 285
tourism 75, 81, 106, 117, 119, 120, 190, 256, 306,
  315, 316
town halls
  Bardéjov 309
  Bratislava 286
  Brno 245
  České Budějovice 185
  Český Krumlov 188
  Cheb 203
  Jihlava 256
  Karlovy Vary 211
  Kutná Hora 234
  Liberec 225
  Litoměřice 222
  Mělník 180
  Olomouc 261
  Plzeň 196
  Trnava 293
Townson, Robert – Journeys through Hungary
  in 1793 118
trade 29, 39
Trades Fair Complex, International (Brno) 243, 248
trading routes 267–268, 279, 293, 306
Treaty of Bratislava 286
Treaty of St Germain 47
Treaty of Trianon 47
Treaty of Versailles 47, 67
Treaty of Westphalia 39
Třebíč 254
Třeboň 186
Trenčín 295, 298
Trenčín Gallery 295

INSIGHT GUIDES

COLORSET NUMBERS

You'll find the colorset number on the spine of each Insight Guide.

EXISTING & FORTHCOMING TITLES:

Aegean Islands	Ireland	Phuket
Algarve	Istanbul	Prague
Alsace	**J**akarta	Provence
Athens	**K**athmandu	**R**hodes
Bali	*Bikes & Hikes*	Rome
Bali Bird Walks	Kenya	**S**abah
Bangkok	Kuala Lumpur	San Francisco
Barcelona	**L**isbon	Sardinia
Bavaria	Loire Valley	Scotland
Berlin	London	Seville/Grenada
Bhutan	**M**acau	Seychelles
Boston	Madrid	Sikkim
Brittany	Malacca	Singapore
Brussels	Mallorca	South California
Budapest &	Malta	Southeast England
Surroundings	Marbella/	Sri Lanka
Canton	*Costa del Sol*	St Petersburg
Chiang Mai	Miami	Sydney
Costa Blanca	Milan	**T**enerife
Costa Brava	Morocco	Thailand
Cote d'Azur	Moscow	Tibet
Crete	Munich	Turkish Coast
Denmark	**N**epal	Tuscany
Florence	New Delhi	**V**enice
Florida	New York City	Vienna
Gran Canaria	North California	**Y**ogyakarta
Hawaii	**O**slo/Bergen	Yugoslavia's
Hong Kong	**P**aris	*Adriatic Coast*
Ibiza	Penang	

United States: Houghton Mifflin Company, Boston MA 02108
Tel: (800) 2253362 Fax: (800) 4589501

Canada: Thomas Allen & Son, 390 Steelcase Road East
Markham, Ontario L3R 1G2
Tel: (416) 4759126 Fax: (416) 4756747

Great Britain: GeoCenter UK, Hampshire RG22 4BJ
Tel: (256) 817987 Fax: (256) 817988

Worldwide: Höfer Communications Singapore 2262
Tel: (65) 8612755 Fax: (65) 8616438

" I was first drawn to the Insight Guides by the excellent "Nepal" volume. I can think of no book which so effectively captures the essence of a country. Out of these pages leaped the Nepal I know – the captivating charm of a people and their culture. I've since discovered and enjoyed the entire Insight Guide Series. Each volume deals with a country or city in the same sensitive depth, which is nowhere more evident than in the superb photography. **"**

Sir Edmund Hillary